THE FUTURE OF THE MUSIC BUSINESS

FOURTH EDITION

HOW TO SUCCEED WITH THE NEW DIGITAL TECHNOLOGIES

A Guide for Artists and Entrepreneurs

STEVE GORDON

HAL LEONARD BOOKS
An Imprint of Hal Leonard Corporation

Hal Leonard Books
An Imprint of Hal Leonard Corporation
7777 West Bluemound Road
Milwaukee, WI 53213

Trade Book Division Editorial Offices
33 Plymouth St., Montclair, NJ 07042

Fourth edition published in 2015 by Hal Leonard Books

Third edition published in 2011 by Hal Leonard Books; second edition published in 2008 by Hal Leonard Books; first edition published in 2005 by Backbeat Books

Cover design: Patrick Devine
Front cover photos: Powell Burns (top), Comstock Images © Getty Images (bottom)

Book Design by John Flannery

Printed in the United States of America

The Library of Congress has cataloged the Backbeat Books edition as follows:

Gordon, Steve.
The future of the music business : how to succeed with the new digital technologies / by Steve Gordon
p. cm.
Includes index.
1. Music trade—Vocational guidance. 2. Sound—Recording and reproducing—Digital techniques. I. Title.
ML3790.G67 2005
780'.68—dc22 2005007155

ISBN 978-1-4803-6065-5

www.halleonardbooks.com

THE FUTURE [illegible] THE MUSIC BUSINESS

FOURTH EDITION

To access video visit
www.halleonard.com/mylibrary
Enter Code

7459-5257-6211-6926

music PRO

For Amy

CONTENTS

FOREWORD *to the Fourth Edition*

When I was a boy, and I would see scary things in the news, my mother would say to me, "Look for the helpers. You will always find people who are helping."
—Mister Rogers

If you're reading this, you're already not normal—normal people generally don't want to legitimately "work" in the music business. If you're reading this, you're either an artist, in which case you've taken a decidedly difficult path in life (why not go into insurance sales?), or you're somehow affiliated with the giant variety of jobs that are supposed to help the connection between the artist and the rest of the world: a club booker, a music lawyer, a producer, a sync agent.

I say "supposed to help" because this basic truth can get lost when people head into the noisy, confusing marketplace of sharing, selling, and commodifying music—especially as things are changing at the speed of the Internet.

The music business I experienced as a kid was the golden cage/age of the 1980s and '90s, in which the goal was to get signed, and in which the middlemen (the managers, agents, promoters, and mainstream media) provided the conduit from the artist to the wide world. The artist's job was to make music and tour, and it was the music business's job to carry the heavy load of records out the door, make people listen, make people come, make people care.

That era is over.

We now live in a world where artists, if they want to, can skip most of the old-school steps and make their own material (recorded on the relative cheap), release it (uploaded to the net at no cost to the artist), promote their own music and book their own tours (via web tools and e-mail lists); and, if their music is any good, they can make a living wage. If they have a strong work ethic and good enough material, and a few thousand fans, they can earn enough to survive without ever being "successful" in the eyes of the mainstream media. You'll never hear about these people. They are out there, working, and they probably have a small handful of people helping them.

A lot of the jobs that used to be executed by a manager, agent, or producer-engineer are now doable by the small-to-mid-level artist, or the artist's girlfriend or boyfriend (if the artist's girlfriend or boyfriend knows basic GarageBand and/or Facebook techniques). Google and e-mail have unlocked of lot of the doors to which only the experts in the music business once had the keys.

It used to be that if you needed to rent gear, only the local promoters knew how to come to your aid. Now, you can google, make a cell phone call from the back of the van, or, if you're well-loved, tweet to fans to please loan you an bass amp because yours got blown out last night in Chicago.

It used to be that if you had a handful of fans in St. Louis, you had to rely on the middlemen to get the word out to those people if you were going to return to town. You needed radio. You needed a label with a street team. Now you can post a pdf to your website and e-mail it to your fans in St. Louis, asking them to please hit the coffee shops and college bulletin boards on your behalf.

This may all seem to spell the beginning of a giant DIY culture—and in a way, it does—but in a way, it's the opposite: no artist can do absolutely everything himself.

Here's the thing everyone has to bear in mind as we transition from a stiff hierarchy in music to more of a level playing field, with room for a bigger middle class:

Working artists still need HELP.

Someone has to design that pdf. Someone has to make sure it gets to the fans. Someone has to organize and maintain the e-mail list once the artist gets too big to keep track of everything.

People are constantly wondering what's going to "become" of the labels of yore. They've already collapsed. The old majors are shadows of themselves, or they've merged into super-structures.

The ones that are succeeding, and the ones that will survive, have to somehow managed, in the thick of things, to find a way to do one fundamental thing, to fulfill a need that will never vanish. The artists need help.

The companies and individuals who are evolving in the new landscape are able to see that fundamental truth as a ground zero and work upwards from there.

Whether an artist is trying to make a living via Bandcamp and Kickstarter or signing their entire future and firstborn child to Giant-Major-Label-Promoter-Conglomerate (and both of these things are totally legitimate, depending on the artist), they are still the same: they are working artists.

If they're going to *actually* work on art:

They need help getting from place to place.
They need help answering calls.
They need help getting the word out.
They need help collecting their paychecks.
They need help sending and delivering goods and services to their fans.

The women and men I know working on the support side of the new-model music industry who are blazing new trails (and blowing by all the people who are bemoaning the past and clinging to the old rules) all have this one thing in common: they *want to help.* (Or, to be honest, they're really good at faking it—whatever, it works most of the time.)

Those winning in the music business today adopt an attitude of *service*. They look at the world and locate who wants the music. They assess the crazed artists who want to make a go of it, and they don't ask:

What's in it for me?

They ask:

How can I help?

And they project this attitude toward those they court and work with.

In 2010, I broke very loudly and openly from my label, Roadrunner Records. I decided not to sign with another label, and instead, I worked with a small team and we sold things directly to my fans. We used Kickstarter. We used Twitter. We blogged and e-mailed up a storm. We went direct, we mailed records to tens of thousands of homes. It was a shit-ton of work. I needed a lot of help. I was on tour. From the ground control of Amanda Central, people had to man the phones, filter the help lines, provide customer service, and arrange ALL sorts of inexplicable things. By the time my Kickstarter was over, at least a couple hundred of my fans were on a friendly first-name basis with eric@amandapalmer.net, the guy on my team who helped everyone, tirelessly, with their nitty-gritty order questions. We didn't know what kind of help he was going to have to provide for me until the crises happened, but when help was necessary, he helped.

I've been through a mill of managers, assistants, agents, and publicists. Some of them wanted to make money more than they wanted to help. Some of the members of my extended team have been with me for 12 years, and some have only lasted six weeks.

What's the general pattern? The ones who wanted to *help* more than they wanted to make money have stayed with me.

My booking agents used to just call up halls and book gigs for me. Things were simple. Then Twitter and Facebook came along and made flash gigs possible. (I call them "ninja gigs," and I recommend them to any artist with an acoustic instrument.)

After endless phone calls, explanations, and arguments, some of my agents began to understand that my desire to show up and play a Twittered flash-event in a public park on the day before a gig in Detroit is a feature, not a bug. People would come to the free gigs, connect, and then I'd take polls at the ticketed, money-making show the next night. A lot of people came because they were turned on to the information, one way or another, through the existence of the free flash gig the day before. Promoters used to call my agents, screaming that I was sucking away ticket sales. But the numbers would eventually speak for themselves. Now they listen. They even *help.*

The agents who didn't listen to me, who didn't try to help, who fought me . . . they didn't last.

Managers used to roll their eyes when I asked them to please, please, *please* read my blog comments and my Twitter feed, so they could understand the day-to-day vibe of the community, so they could listen, and therefore know how to help me and the fans to connect in the best ways possible.

The ones who never got it didn't last.

Publicists used to agonize, telling me to please shut up and lie low whenever I traipsed into a controversial situation. I ignored them, kept talking, arguing and engaging people, and all of that work eventually landed me a TED talk that's been viewed almost 10 million times, my own book deal, and a gig writing this foreword. You can't force people to want to help you, but you can walk away and gravitate toward those who really do want to help.

And how do you help someone with a big mouth? Or how do you help an artist who barely wants to talk?

It's HARD to help an artist. This will also never change.

Artists are inherently weird. Music is intangible. Music isn't concrete, even though it can sometimes seem to be. You're dealing in the business of feelings, and a strange kind of exchange that extends far beyond the eye-for-an-eye exchange of most businesses. The gray area between *help* and *coercion* is wide, and many artists don't even *know* what kind of help they need. Worse, many artists have an allergy to certain varieties of help. Letting the artist take the lead is essential if you're going to be seriously helpful. You can't assume that all artists want the same things. Ask first, then attack.

To put it crassly, but it's a fine analogy . . . you can't insist that someone have an orgasm by simply pounding away at them. Asking how they need it may be hard, or awkward, but it's essential if you're going to be a good lover.

All of the tools that Steve is laying out and explaining in the pages to come are for your arsenal of tools, artist and helper alike. Keep everything handy, and know that using the right tool in the right moment is what makes you truly helpful (and, if you're an artist, able to help yourself and those around you who need a lift up).

The roles that exist in "music business land" (manager, publicist, lawyer, promoter, etc.) originally developed to serve the artist and the audience. To act as a bridge. A connector. A *helper*. Through the years, that concept has been obscured in a jangle of label expense accounts, self-aggrandizing gatekeepers, and gold chains.

So, as the whole system goes up in beautiful new flames, ask yourself: where are you? In the burning building?

Or are you looking for a way to act as a bridge somewhere on the long, craggy trek a soulful song takes from a Finnish musician's heart to the heart of a 16-year-old kid in rural Wisconsin, who's listening with headphones in a crowded cafeteria or standing in the back of a shitty local bar, having snuck in with her fake ID, crying her eyes out?

Can you imagine yourself thinking—assessing what you're doing with your time, your energy, your talents, your *life*—not about your own success, but something even more divine:

I helped make that moment happen.

And if you can't imagine that moment being the most satisfying moment of your life, more satisfying than making all the money, more satisfying than climbing up the corporate ladder, you probably shouldn't go into the music business.

Choose something more concrete.

Go into insurance sales.

Amanda Palmer
February 28, 2014

PREFACE

People often ask how I got my start in entertainment law. I got my foot in the door by helping my entertainment law professor at NYU, Mel Simensky, research and write a casebook he co-authored.[1] Mel was also a litigator at a small firm and eventually hired me as an associate. But I've continued researching and writing legal articles ever since, and have been writing and revising this book in new editions since 2005. Much of my knowledge of the law and the entertainment business comes from my experience as a litigation associate and then as a lawyer for entertainment companies including SESAC (one of the three US performing-rights organizations), De Laurentiis Entertainment Group (a Hollywood movie studio), Atlantic Records, and then Sony Music. But since leaving Sony in 2002 and starting my own firm, I've gained knowledge and experience that would be impossible to acquire by only working in the legal or business affairs departments of an entertainment company. At Sony, I worked on matters involving stars like Michael Jackson and Bruce Springsteen. In private practice, my client list includes indie artists and labels, songwriters and publishers, music producers, and music business entrepreneurs. I work with a wide variety of people, companies, and cultural organizations on indie films, reality TV shows, musical theater, and stand-alone digital projects as well as the production and distribution of recorded music. Compared with this diversity of projects, my experience with each of my old employers seems incredibly narrow. Of course, working with those companies was great in a number of ways, including a steady pay check, vacation pay, health insurance, and I could go on. But the knowledge I gained there can't compare to the experience of the last 12 years. And in this edition of the book I've striven to make the reader the beneficiary of that experience. For instance, in Part I of the book, I give practical advice on the questions that are most asked of me by clients. In Part II, I provide actual numbers that a producer can use to determine his music budget for projects ranging from indie movies, to musical theater, to apps involving music.

The purpose of the book has always been, and continues to be, to provide a road map for success for both creators of music and music business professionals and entrepreneurs. The recording industry and the music publishing business have been profoundly impacted by new technologies: entirely new rules, business practices and business models have emerged. This book explains them and their application to songwriters, recording artists, music business executives, and entrepreneurs.

The introduction analyzes the music business as it exists today by focusing on its three main components: recording, publishing, and live performance. We use documented facts and figures demonstrating that the recording industry has declined drastically to only 35 percent of what it was at its highpoint in 1999, although in the last several years it has been stabilizing. Since 1999 the publishing business has also suffered a decline, although not as severely as the record business. Paradoxically, only live performance has grown in the digital era.

Part I provides an overview of the basic rules and business practices that apply to the record and music publishing businesses, including the most recent developments spurred by new technologies. Chapter 1 summarizes the copyright law as it pertains to the recording and music publishing industries. Chapter 2 discusses the most often asked questions in my practice concerning copyright infringement trademark and whether to use a lawyer to shop. We transition to digital music in Chapter 3 by setting forth the principal statutes concerning the digital distribution of music and explaining how they apply to downloading and streaming. In Chapters 4–6 we provide overviews of the business of (i) downloading, including iTunes; (ii) interactive streaming, including ad-supported services, such as YouTube and free Spotify, and subscription services, such as Spotify's premium service, Beats Music, Rhapsody, and YouTube's new subscription service, Music Key; and (iii) noninteractive streaming, including Pandora, the Internet radio service, and Sirius XM, the satellite service. In each of these chapters, we explain

1. How much the services pay for copyrighted music
2. How the money flows from the services to the labels, artists, publishers and songwriters

With regard to each of these three digital music businesses, we present a chart from the Recording Industry Association of America (RIAA) showing exactly how much money each of these sectors generates, followed by a chart developed by the Future of Music Coalition (FMC) illustrating exactly how that money flows to labels, artists, publishers and songwriters. We also address current controversies about how labels, particularly the majors, pay their artists (or don't).

Chapter 8 explains one of the hottest issues in the music business today: how major publishers are breaking away from ASCAP and BMI to make deals directly with digital music services.

Chapter 9 discusses the global digital music business and the intricacies of international digital music licensing.

Part II is intended both for producers of audiovisual works such as films, documentaries, and television, and for record producers who often need to license music to use in their projects. We also discuss how to clear music for stand-alone digital projects as well as special projects such as musical theater and fashion shows. Each chapter in this section focuses on practical issues that arise in clearing music and how producers can save money.

Part III offers a history of the recording industry's struggle to come to grips with the digital era, explores current issues and controversies, and provides some hope for the recovery of the record business.

Part IV provides a "how to" guide to the business of music in the digital age, ranging from how to write hit songs in the digital era, to how to market a record now, to how to raise money for a project, to how to use a music education to succeed.

Online Files and Free CLE Credits for Attorneys

Attorneys can obtain two free CLE credits by using the DVD included with this book. The DVD contains two programs, including a conversation between myself and Bob Clarida, a leading copyright lawyer and adjunct professor at Columbia University Law School, in which we discuss Robin Thicke's legal battle with Marvin Gaye's estate, and whether Thicke's "Blurred Lines" infringed the copyright of Gaye's song "Got to Give It Up." The other program is a lecture on the fundamentals of the music business and law. Lawyers can obtain the CLE credits by watching the videos and registering at the following web pages:

Thicke v. Gaye: Musical Copyright Infringement (http://bit.ly/17vdMBZ)
Legal Fundamentals of the Music Business (http://bit.ly/14F1xzw)

Updates

This book was submitted in January 2015. To keep it current after it goes to print, I created www.futureofthemusicbusiness.com. Through this site I will continually update the book, particularly the Introduction and Parts I and III. This site also provides author news, speaking engagements, podcast interviews with music industry leaders and experts, and links to other music business resources.

Disclaimer

This book has been created for informational purposes only and does not constitute legal advice. The book should be used as a guide to understanding the law, not as a substitute for the advice of qualified counsel. You should consult an attorney before making any significant legal decisions.

INTRODUCTION
The Current State of the Music Business

It is a mistake to equate the recording industry with the entire music business. There are two other major components: music publishing (which is the business of generating money from songs rather than records), and live performance and touring. The recording industry has experienced a cataclysmic decline during the digital era, beginning in 1999 with the emergence of the original Napster, but the music publishing business, which has always been much smaller than the recording industry, has also declined, although not as much. On the other hand, the live performance and touring business is thriving and in better shape than it was at the dawn of the digital era. Spending to see iconic artists such as Paul McCartney, Bon Jovi, and U2, as well as younger superstars like Taylor Swift, Beyoncé, and Justin Timberlake, has increased threefold. In addition, for these famous artists, there is additional money to be made from "branding," that is, partnering with corporations to use their celebrity status to create even more money than they make from selling records. But most people who pursue careers as artists or songwriters continue to struggle financially just as they did before the digital era.

The irony is that technology created and nourished the recording and contemporary music publishing businesses—from the invention of the record player and the radio to the introduction of new distribution formats, such as the CD. But in the last 15 years, newer technologies, specifically the Internet and high-speed digital networks, have taken back much of that financial success by creating a panoply of ways—some illegal and some legal—to consume recorded music without paying for it. And now, the only sector of the business that is growing, live performance, is the part that existed before any of those technologies.

I. Current State of the Recording Industry: Cataclysmic Decline from Approximately 14.5 Billion in 1999 to Less than 7 Billion Although Revenues Have Not Decreased as Much in the Last Several Years

Cataclysmic Decline in Revenue

The following graph, which was generated by data from the Recording Industry Association of America (RIAA),[2] shows the crisis that has beset the recording industry:

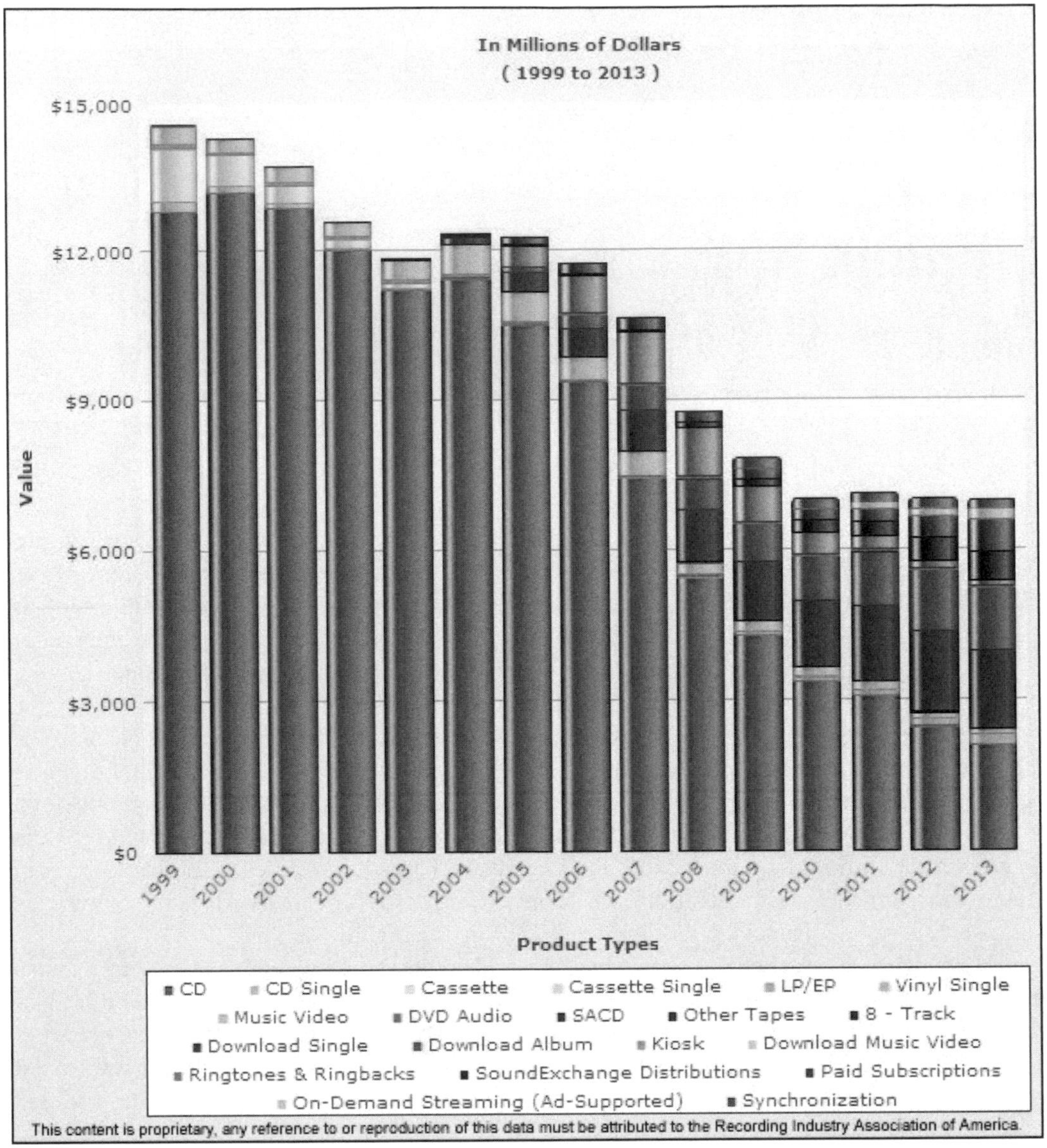

The graph shows that in 1999, income from sales and licenses of recorded music in the United States was approximately 14.5 billion dollars.[3] Since that year revenues have dropped to less than $7 billion—a decline of more than 50 percent. Worse, this graphic shows that, when accounting for inflation, the record business is only about one-third of what it used to be in terms of income; revenues have declined by more than 65 percent.[4]

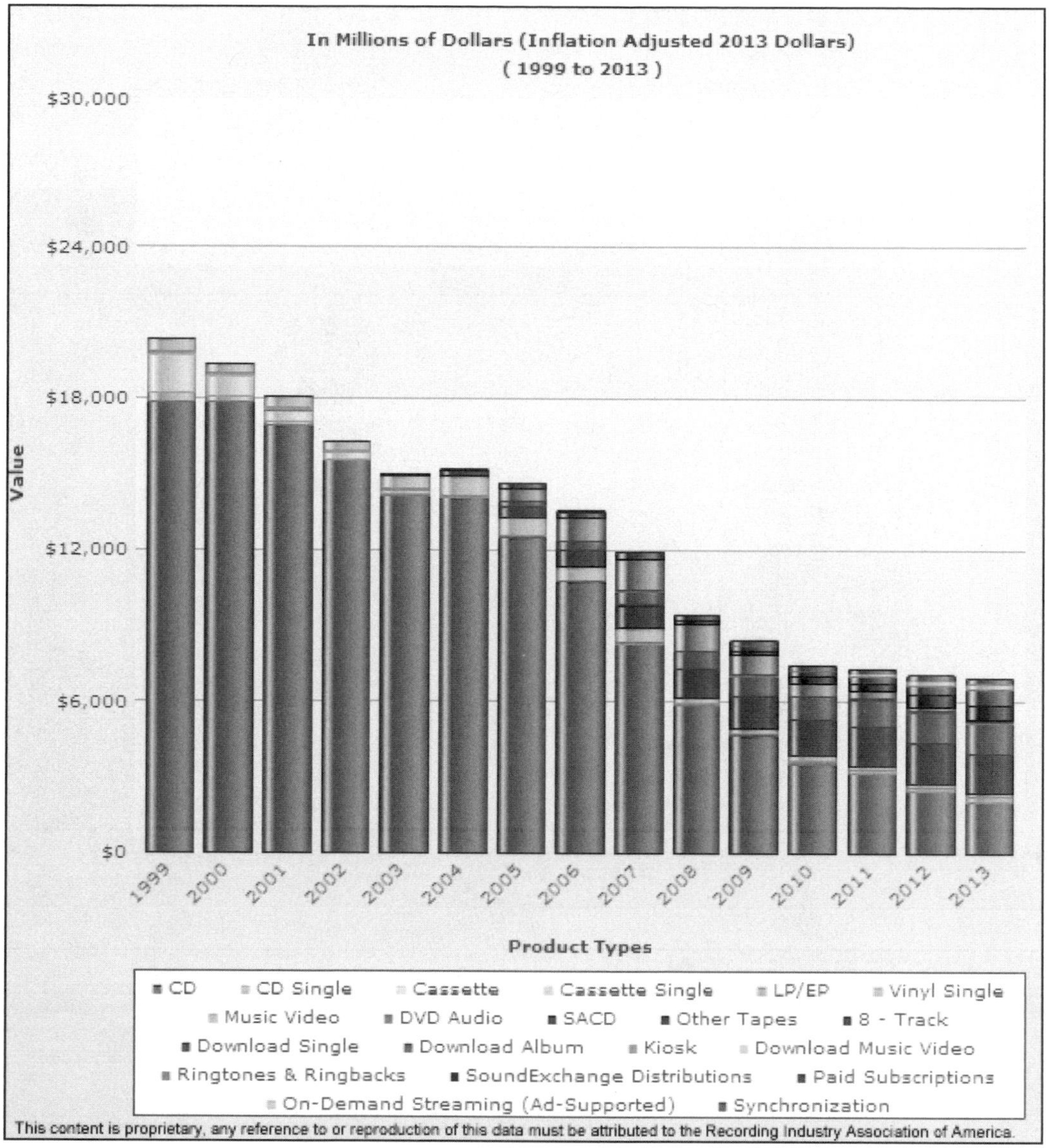

In fact, accounting for inflation, the recording industry is at its lowest level since the RIAA began keeping tabs on industry-wide income in 1973.

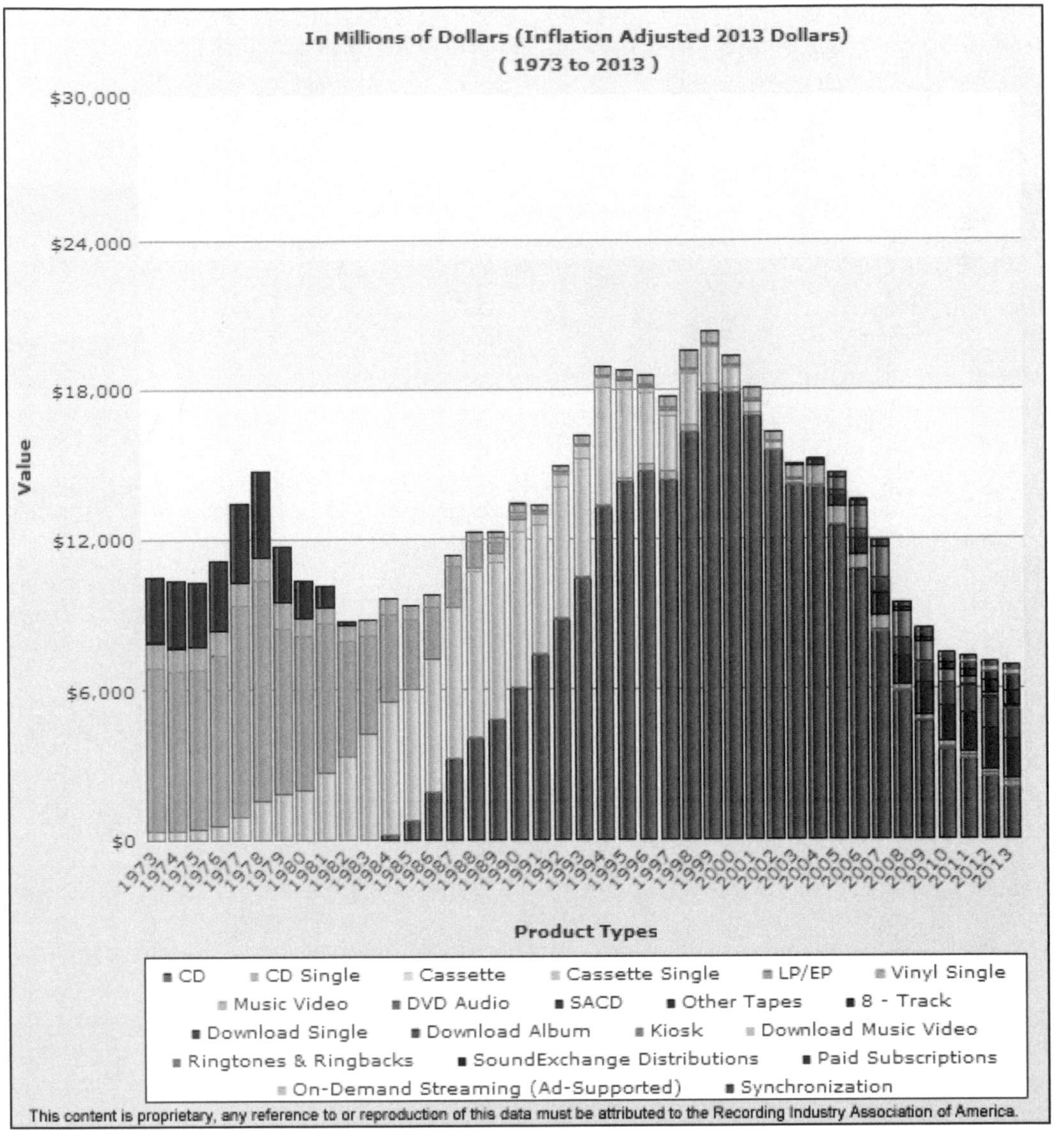

The numbers above indicate that the record business has declined horribly. However, these numbers also indicate that since the publication of the last edition of this book, things have *not* gotten significantly worse. By 2010, gross revenues had declined to approximately 7.01 billion dollars. Although by 2013 revenues had dropped to $6.99 billion, the decrease over those three years (less than 1 percent)[5] was less severe than in any years since 1999. This is not exactly good news, but it's the best news that can be reported. On the other hand, the RIAA's *2014 Mid-Year Industry Shipment and Revenue Statistics* indicated that for the first half of 2014 overall revenues were down 4.9 percent compared to the first half of 2013.[6]

Worldwide, the figures are even bleaker. According to a report from the International Federation of the Phonographic Industry (IFPI) issued in early 2014,[7] global revenues from recorded music fell 3.9 percent to approximately $15 billion in 2013. In 1999, those revenues exceeded $38 billion, according to IFPI's report in 2000.[8] That's a steeper decline than in the US.

Reasons for Decline

Many have speculated on the causes for the decline of the recording business. The two main theories are (1) the Internet has made it easy to provide and share unauthorized music, and (2) the major record companies did not respond quickly enough to the digital revolution. These critics maintain that the labels did not act early enough to create or support alternatives to free music, and that by the time they backed the launch of iTunes in 2003, it was already too late to cure the fans of their habit of getting music for free from unauthorized services such as the original Napster, Kazaa, Limewire, and now BitTorrent sites. I think both theories are true, but I also contend that the emergence of iTunes itself was incredibly harmful to the business. iTunes turned what had been an album business into a singles business. Steve Jobs' insistence on offering to sell individual tracks encouraged those people who continued to actually buy records to "cherry pick" their favorite songs rather than pay for an entire album. The labels, desperate to compete with free and monetized digital music, probably thought they had no choice but to cooperate. I discuss these theories, corresponding events, and the recording business's continuing efforts to battle piracy in Part III of this book.

The Majors: Further Consolidation but Continuing Relevance

As income went down, consolidation of the "majors," which still distribute over 80 percent of recorded music, continued. Instead of the five majors that dominated in the '90s, when I was at Sony (specifically, Sony, BMG, EMI, Warner, and Universal), there are now only three (Sony, Universal, and Warner). However, they are still relevant because, unlike most indies, (1) they still provide (although not as often) significant advances that support new and emerging artists who are working to establish themselves, and (2) more importantly, they are still the only players that can provide the worldwide marketing, promotion money, manpower, and expertise to raise an unknown English art school student such as Adele (Sony) or an obscure New Zealand schoolgirl (Lorde) to superstar status. Even Prince, who famously declared war on his label, Warner, many years ago, has rejoined the fold. He decided to re-sign with Warner in 2014, probably because of a massive cash offer and because of the worldwide marketing machine at the label's disposal. See Chapter 1 for my interview with David Massey, president of Island Records.

The Emergence of Streaming as the Revenue Model of the Future— Revenues from CDs, as the following chart indicates, continue to fall:

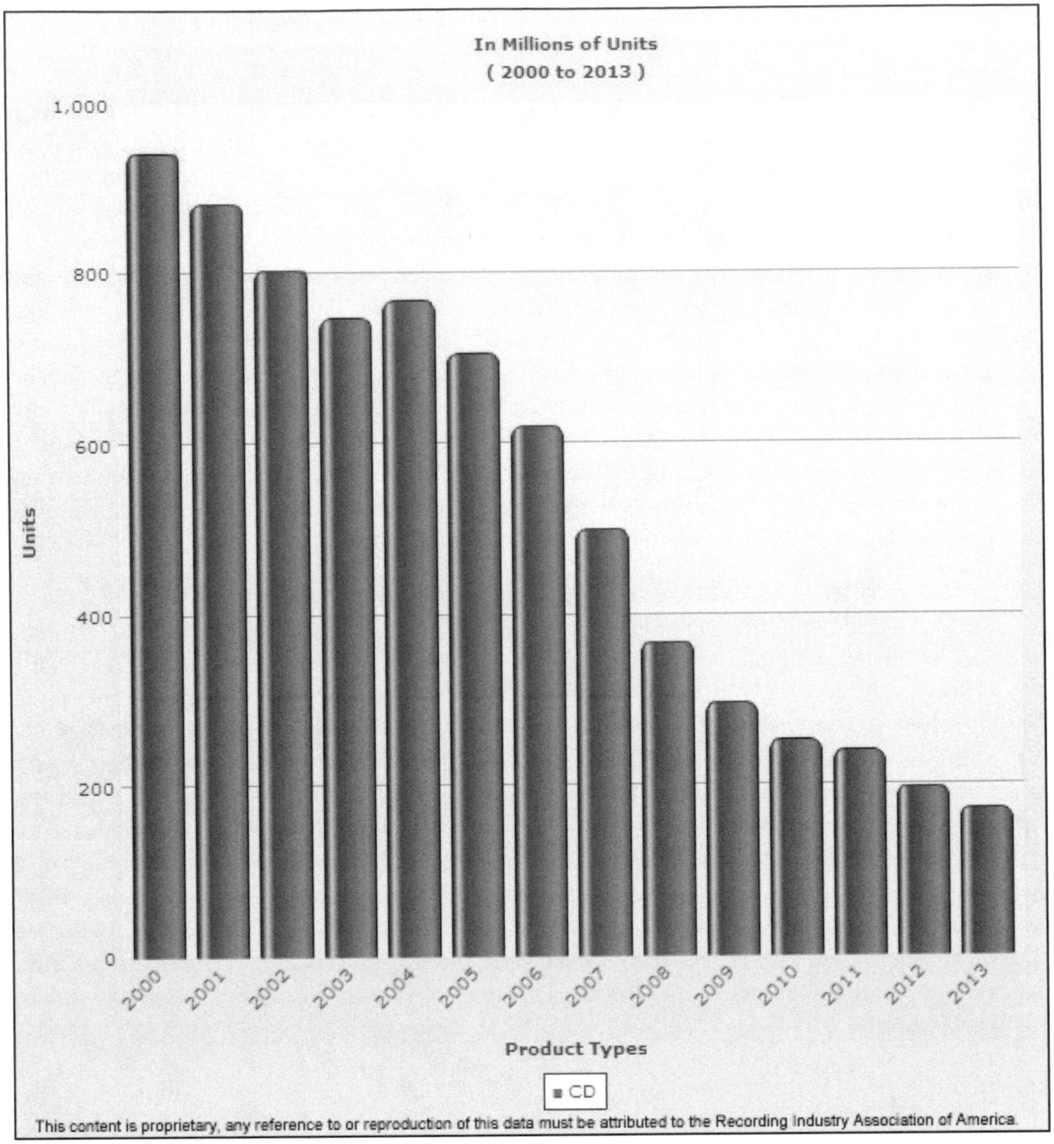

However, for the first time since the introduction of iTunes, income from downloading has declined as well:

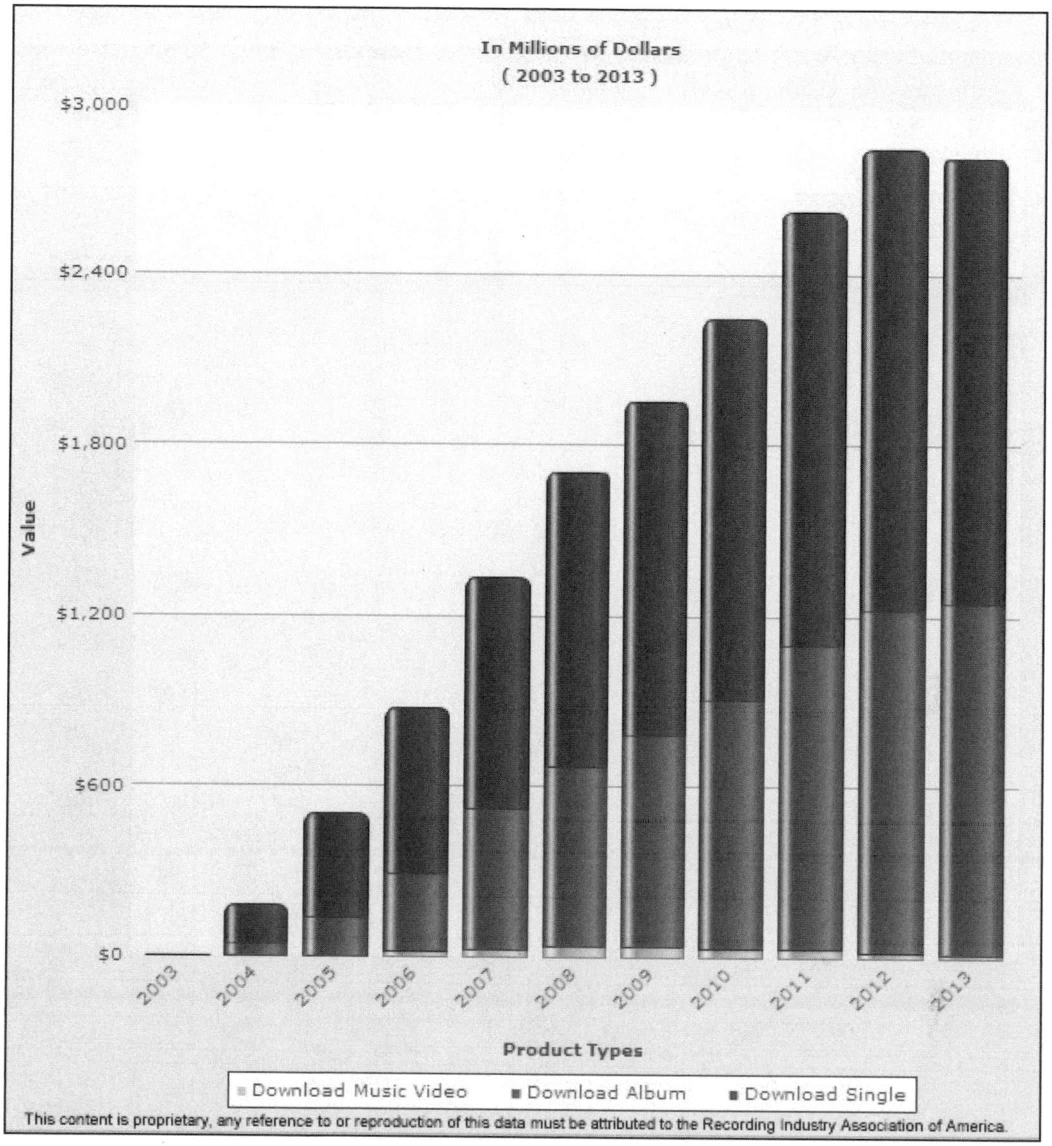

The current hope of the recording business is the possibility that streaming can save the day. There are three types of streaming, as we discuss in much more detail in Part I of this book. They are:

1. Noninteractive "Internet radio" services such as Pandora and iHeart Radio, and Sirius XM's noninteractive satellite radio service
2. Advertising-based interactive streaming, such as the free version of Spotify
3. Subscription services, such as premium Spotify, Rhapsody, and Google Play Music

Pandora claims that it pays approximately 50 percent of its income in royalties to the recording industry (via SoundExchange, as we discuss in more detail in Part 1). Spotify claims it is paying an even greater percentage of its income to the labels (although those deals are confidential). It is true that these three sources of new income have been growing, as the following chart indicates:

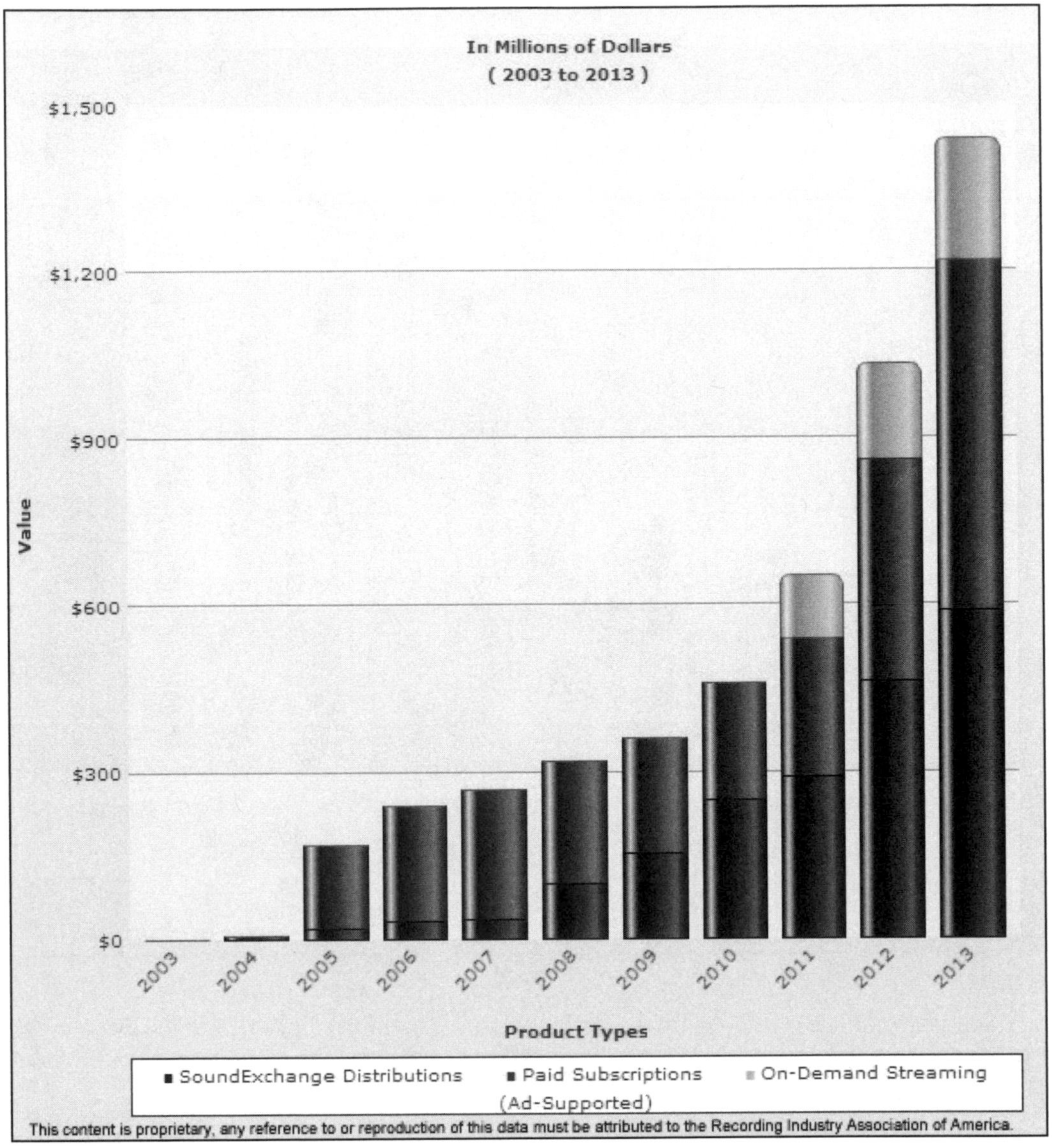

However, if you compare downloading with streaming, the majority of money still comes from downloading:

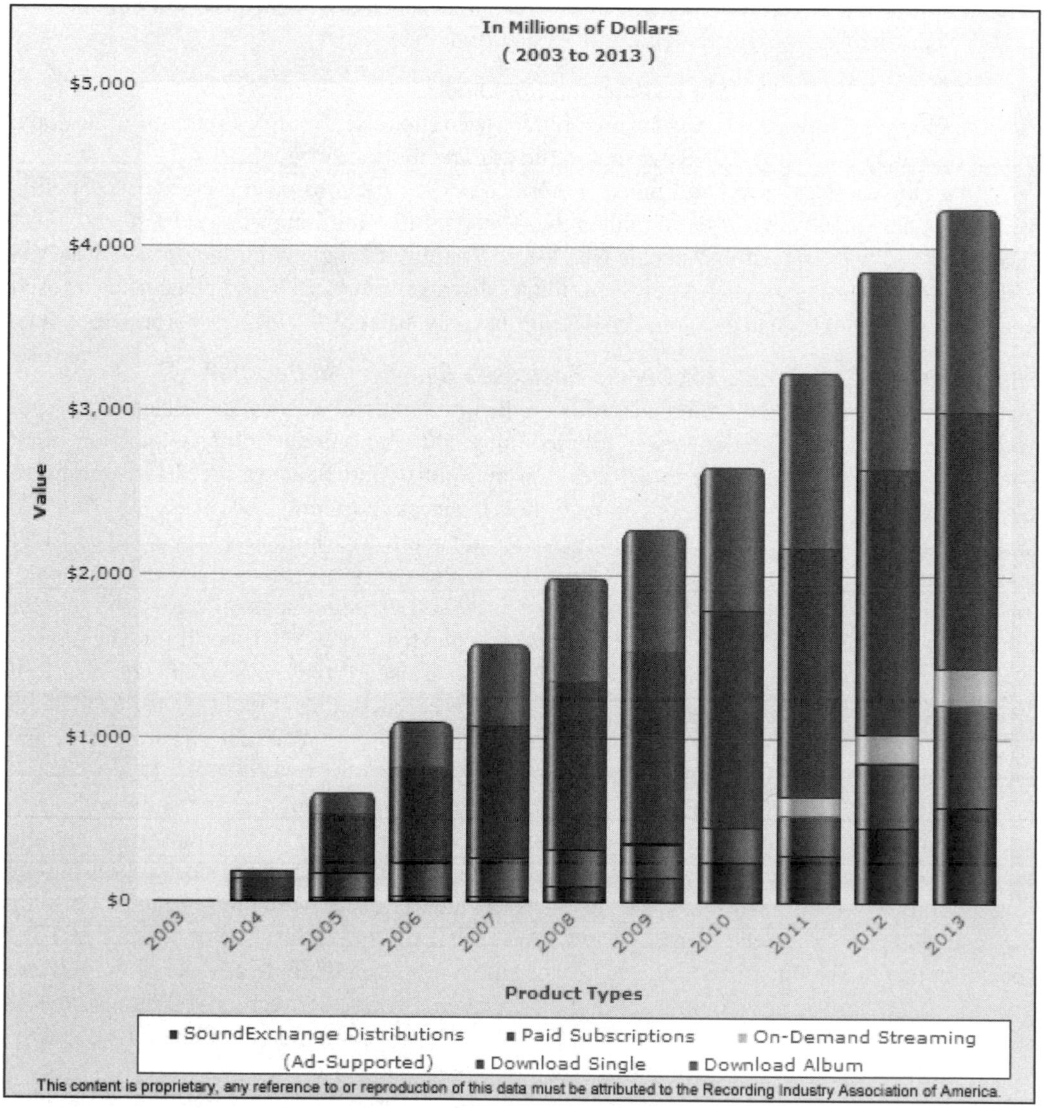

Paid Subscription vs. Ad-Supported, On-Demand Streaming

Which generates more money? Subscription, hands down. The goal of many of the services has been to convert "free," ad-supported listeners to premium subscribers. As the chart immediately above indicates, most of the money from interactive streaming comes from subscriptions ("Paid Subscriptions" as opposed to "On-Demand Streaming Ad-Supported"). This is also the case for Pandora. Pandora has 76 million active users and only 2.5 million paid subscribers. That's 3.3 percent. However, the subscribers account for over 18 percent of Pandora's income.[9]

The money that music streaming services such as Spotify and Pandora earn from advertising is limited because money from advertisers will always be at the mercy of marketing budgets, which have been slow to adopt streaming audio as a place to buy. Neither Pandora nor Spotify is profitable; in 2013, Pandora lost $38 million.[10]

Lack of Success in Converting Listeners to Customers

Pandora charges $4.99 per month for premium service (no ads); Spotify Premium, Rhapsody, and Google Play all charge $9.99 per month (no ads and mobile service).

Streaming services have had limited success converting users to paying customers. Spotify, which launched in 2008, has over 50 million users but only 12.5 million paying subscribers.[11] That means that less than one out four people who listen to Spotify are paying for the service. Pandora, as discussed previously, streams to only 2.5 million subscribers out of 76 million total listeners. And Rhapsody, which has been in the game for 13 years, has only just recently hit 1.7 million subscribers.

Will Streaming Turn Around the Record Business's Cataclysmic Decline?

Although the success of streaming has softened the losses that the recording industry has experienced year after year, the industry is still declining, although not as rapidly as in prior years. The conversion rates from free to subscription by Spotify and Pandora are disappointing to anyone hoping for the recovery of the recording business. Expecting people to pay $10 per month, or any amount of money per month, seems almost overly optimistic when you consider how easily available music is for free, sometimes by the same services that are asking money for premium listening, and more often by quasi-legal software and apps such as programs for converting YouTube to MP3s or apps that make free playlists from YouTube. It may be unrealistic to expect young people to pay subscription fees, because (a) they may not be able to afford them; (b) they are not used to paying anything for prerecorded music; and (c) they have many alternative ways of listening to music for free—both legal (e.g., YouTube) as well as illegal (pirate sites, and online and off-line sharing).

Free streaming has also undercut efforts to bring in revenue through partnerships with wireless service providers. By including a music service in the cost of a basic phone plan, mobile carriers could raise their rates and share the surplus with the music service—yet customers would perceive the bundled music service as "free." These deals would also benefit artists by increasing streaming services' royalty payments to the recording industry. But the carriers have been reluctant to take this step precisely because users can already get free music from Pandora and in many other ways, including sharing on private networks, converting YouTube videos to MP3s, using a variety of apps to make playlists of any songs contained in online music videos, or using BitTorrent sites.[12] Customers are used to free music, period.

With the exception of a deal between a small carrier, Cricket Wireless, which was recently purchased by AT&T, and a music service called Muve Music, carriers have not elected to include a music service in the cost of a basic phone plan. They are making a lot of money already without bundling music services, so they lack the incentive to develop these bundling partnerships with the streaming services. Instead they may offer customers a "special deal" on a premium music service. For instance, when Beats Music rolled out in January 2014, AT&T offered an exclusive $14.99 family plan to let five users stream to 10 devices total. Despite a Superbowl ad featuring Ellen DeGeneres, this strategy was a disappointment, and in October 2014 AT&T announced that was no longer offering Beats Music subscriptions.

Apple's Purchase of Beats Music

On May 29, 2014, Apple announced that it would purchase Beats Music for 3 billion dollars. In so doing, they acquired both the financially successful Beats headphones business and the far-from-successful Beats Music streaming subscription service—yet Apple may have wanted the streaming service even more than the revenue from the headphones business. Downloading is going down, and streaming is going up. Apple already has an Internet radio service, iRadio, but Beats puts Apple in the interactive streaming business. And considering their revenue reserve of over 150 billion dollars, the 3 billion that they paid for Beats was a drop in the bucket. Apple could also decide to charge less for subscriptions to Beats Music than Spotify or the other streaming services charge, or give Beats away for free for a limited period of time to purchasers of new iPhones or even bundle the service with the price of an iPhone, that is, give it away free. Even if Apple had to pay major record labels minimum guarantees or advances and lose money on Beats Music, offering the service could presumably increase sales of their gadgets. This was exactly Steve Jobs' strategy for initiating iTunes. Although the iTunes store has sold over 25 billion songs worldwide[13], no one can be sure how much Apple has profited from iTunes. That's because iTunes generally pays 70 percent of the retail price of each download to copyright owners of the recordings and songs (see Chapter 3 for a breakdown of how much they pay for each), plus the expense of bandwidth, marketing, transaction costs, staff, overhead, etc. But it is beyond dispute that, after the introduction of iTunes in 2003, Apple's sales of iPods, introduced in 2001, skyrocketed.

In January 2007, Apple reported record quarterly revenue of $7.1 billion, of which 48 percent was made from iPod sales.[14] Apple has made even more money from iPhones than from iPods. In fact, iPhones are the most profitable product on earth.[15] In the first quarter of 2014, which runs from the beginning of October to the end of December, the company earned a record $57.6 billion in revenue;[16] 56 percent of that income came from iPhones and only 7.6 percent came from iTunes (and some of that revenue was from movies, videos, and other content besides songs).[17] But, as with iPods, the success of iPhones is largely based on the device's ability to play recorded music, including free services such as YouTube and Pandora, and apps such as InstaTube that allow you to listen to free music without advertising. The point is that Apple has used music to sell technology more than it has used technology to sell music.[18] And if Apple bundles or discounts Beats Music with purchases of new iPhones, Apple will sell even more iPhones.

In Chapter 6 we'll talk about how streaming services pay artists and labels, and how (or whether) those labels pay their artists in turn.

Licensing Recordings for Movies, TV, Games and Ad Campaigns

Besides record sales, downloads, and streaming, the recording industry makes money from licensing recorded music for use in movies, TV, video games, and ad campaigns. In Part II we discuss in detail how much producers can expect to pay the record companies and artists. But it is worth noting here that despite the hype to the contrary, licensing recordings for movies, commercials, games, and television has not grown in the last several years. The RIAA, which has only kept track of these numbers in the last several years, has this data on income from "master-use" licenses:

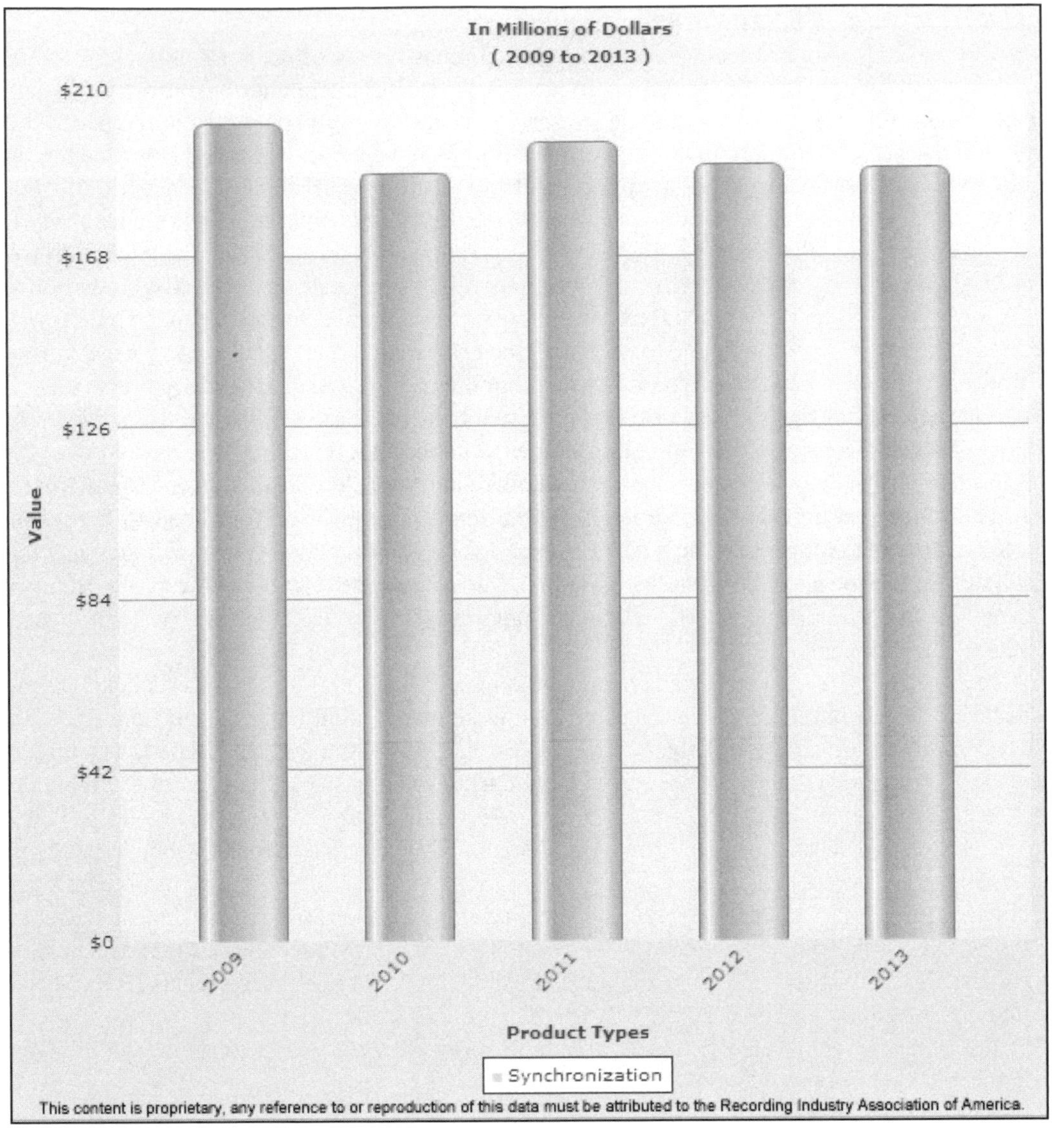

II. Music Publishing Business: Performance Income Up, Mechanical Income Down, Total Income Stagnant

The good news about music publishing is that it has not suffered the dizzying bloodletting that the recording industry has endured. Accounting for inflation, revenues from music publishing worldwide are about the same as they were in 1999, that is, approximately $6 billion worldwide and $2 billion in the US alone. The bad news is that this measurement indicates stagnation rather than growth. And at its height, music publishing's income of $6 billion was only a fraction of the income flowing from record sales at $38 billion (and now $15 billion) globally.

What Are Publishing Revenues?

- Public performance royalties: These are monies from the public performance of songs on radio; on TV; at venues, including nightclubs,and restaurants; and on streaming services.
- Mechanical royalties: These are monies from the inclusion of songs in records sold in any format, including downloads, CDs, cassettes, and vinyl.
- Sync fees: These are fees from the "fixation" of music in an audiovisual work such as a movie, TV show, TV ad campaign webisode, concert video, or video game.
- Other: Songwriters and music publishers also receive income for the use of their content in other categories, such as sheet music and lyric websites.

Over the years since 1999, mechanical income has plummeted as income from sales of records has declined, but the steady increase in performance income has enabled publishers to compensate somewhat for the loss.

Global Publishing Revenues

The National Music Publishers Association (NMPA) issued reports on total publishing revenue from 1995 until 2001. These are the total global figures for each year:

Global Music Publishing Revenues[20]
1995–2001 ($Millions)
1995 6,208.7
1996 6,224.5
1997 6,157.1
1998 6,440.3
1999 6,429.4
2000 6,877.3
2001 6,626.8

The following data was published in 2011 by Enders Analysis, which shows global publishing income from 2005 and estimates revenues after 2010:[21]

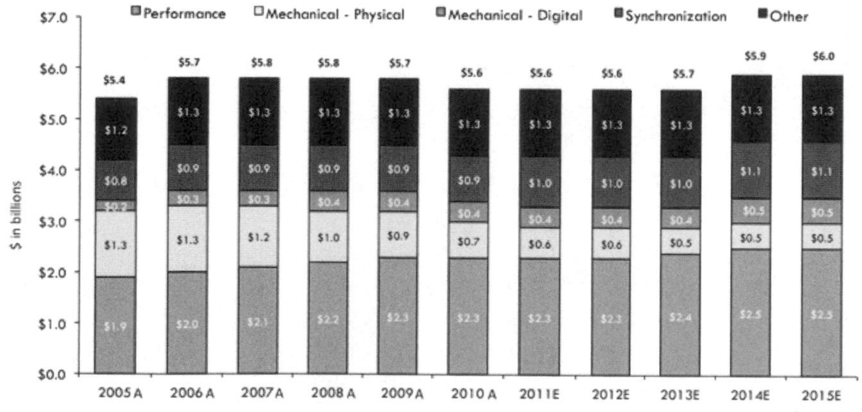

Source: Enders Analysis on Music Publishing, July 2011

These data show that during the period from 1999 to 2013, while the recording business declined from $38 billion down to $15 billion, the publishing business declined from approximately $6.5 billion to approximately $5.5 billion.

The Ender chart also shows that, although mechanical income from downloading has increased, total mechanical income has shrunk dramatically, because income from digital mechanicals is not making up for losses from declining CD sales. It is the steady increase in performance income, as shown on the chart, that has kept the music publishing business from imploding to the extent that the record business has.

US Publishing Revenues

According to the NMPA's reports, publishing income in the US from 1995 to 2001 was as follows in billions of dollars:

1995	1996	1997	1998	1999	2000	2001
1.1	1.2	Webpage unavailable	Webpage unavailable	1.49	1.66	1.56

In June 2014, the NMPA announced publishing income figures for the first time since 2001. By their account, revenue across all income sources totaled 2.2 billion dollars in 2013.[22] This is a moderate increase since 1999, when the business generated 1.49 billion dollars, but accounting for inflation income the value of that amount in 2014 dollars is 2.13 billion. So real growth from 1999 to 2014 has been stagnant.

The 2014 announcement detailed the industry value in the following breakdown of publishing revenue in the US:

- Performance License: 52 percent ($1.14 billion)
- Mechanical License: 23 percent ($506 million)
- Sync License: 20 percent ($440 million)
- Other: 5 percent

Compare these numbers with the figures from the last NMPA report in 2001:

- Performance License: 48 percent ($752.29 million)
- Mechanical License: 37 percent ($584.24 million)
- Sync License: 10 percent ($157.92 million)
- Other: 5 percent[23]

Obviously, performance and sync income have increased, but mechanical income decreased from 37 percent of total publishing revenue to 23 percent.

It makes sense that publishing has not suffered as much as the recording business. According to RIAA stats, in its peak year in 1999, when the recording industry made over $14.5 billion in the US alone, almost all of the income was generated from sales of CDs. The largest segment of music publishing revenues, on the other hand, has always been public performance. As we will discuss in Part I, the recording industry is not entitled to this kind of revenue except for digital transmission. For this reason, a boom in the live performance sector has helped sustain music publishing's overall numbers even as record sales have tanked.

III. Current State of the Touring and Live Performance Business: The Only Sector of the Music Business That Is Making More Money than before 1999

Touring and live performance make up the third leg of the stool of the music business and have fared much better in the digital era than either the recording industry or the music publishing business.

According to Pollstar, the concert industry's leading trade publication, in 2013 the North American concert business brought in a record high of $5.1 billion. "That's a particularly surprising number in light of the fact that in 2000, the total was only $1.7 billion.[24]" Live performance revenue increased more than threefold over the same period of time that the recording industry lost three-quarters of its value in the US and around the world, while the music publishing business remained stagnant. So if there is hope for the music business, it's with this third leg of the stool—the one that existed before the recording or music publishing business even began.

Mozart and Beethoven were playing to packed houses before Edison invented the first record player, back when music publishing was indeed nothing but selling handmade transcriptions. In the last century, the record player, radio, and other technological advances created new music industries and sent profits soaring. Yet, paradoxically, over the last 15 years we've seen the march of technology reduce that formidable business to near rubble. The music business that's thriving now is, in essence, the one that existed prior to the modern era.

In fact, the same recent technology that is hurting the recording and publishing businesses so badly is actually helping the live performance business. According to *Billboard*, concert attendance has thrived during the digital era "because of the extremely targeted and efficient marketing opportunities afforded by new media and strategic use of mobile, social, e-mail, channel marketing, and digital sales channels."

Given the importance of the live music business, let's explore the economics of the touring business and the people who profit from its surge. Also according to Pollstar, "The Top 100 Tours of North America hit a new record high at $2.79 billion. That represents a 10.3 percent increase over 2012."

However, the money from live performance and touring is not democratically distributed. It is largely reserved for the most celebrated artists. The chart below shows gross revenues from the top 145 North American tours and is based on data from Pollstar.[25] For iconic artists and superstars, there is more money in touring now than ever before:

GROSS MILLIONS	ARTIST	AVERAGE TICKET PRICE	GROSS MILLIONS	ARTIST	AVERAGE TICKET PRICE	GROSS MILLIONS	ARTIST	AVERAGE TICKET PRICE
$112.7	Taylor Swift	$84	$47.9	Trans-Siberian Orchestra	$54	$33.7	Michael Bublé	$84
$107.3	Bon Jovi	$96	$44.4	Luke Bryan	$39	$31.9	Rihanna	$78
$90.9	Kenny Chesney	$76	$43.3	One Direction	$62	$31.4	New Kids On The Block	$62
$87.7	The Rolling Stones	$228	$43.1	Zac Brown Band	$50	$31.2	Muse	$55
$76.4	Beyoncé	$119	$43.0	Bruno Mars	$69	$30.4	Maroon 5	$68
$69.0	Jay Z/Justin Timberlake	$110	$41.0	Elton John	$112	$30.3	Maroon 5/Kelly Clarkson	$49
$66.7	Fleetwood Mac	$110	$40.9	George Strait	$89	$29.8	Rascal Flatts	$41
$62.9	Pink	$82	$40.2	Dave Matthews Band	$56	$29.7	Drake	$75
$59.7	Eagles	$126	$38.8	Celine Dion	$145	$28.0	Justin Timberlake	$116
$55.9	Justin Bieber	$77	$37.5	John Mayer	$52	$27.4	Kanye West	$87
$51.0	Jason Aldean	$47	$34.6	Phish	$54	$27.2	Tim McGraw	$39
$49.6	Paul McCartney	$128	$34.2	Miranda Lambert	$44	$26.3	Carrie Underwood	$60

GROSS MILLIONS	ARTIST	AVERAGE TICKET PRICE
$25.3	Brad Paisley	$43
$24.6	Kid Rock	$30
$24.3	Bob Seger & The Silver Bullet Band	$84
$24.1	Pearl Jam	$69
$24.0	Andrea Bocelli	$162
$23.0	Jeff Dunham	$47
$22.5	Lady Gaga	$112
$21.4	Shania Twain	$129
$21.3	Rod Stewart	$129
$21.2	Mumford & Sons	$44
$20.4	Keith Urban	$45
$20.3	Luis Miguel	$82
$19.8	Marc Anthony	$87
$19.7	Swedish House Mafia	$68
$19.7	Black Sabbath	$67
$19.5	Blake Shelton	$36
$17.8	Depeche Mode	$64
$17.7	The Killers	$55
$17.1	Steely Dan	$77
$16.9	Selena Gomez & The Scene	$50
$16.6	Jimmy Buffett	$79
$15.5	Goo Goo Dolls/ Matchbox Twenty	$37
$14.9	Rush	$74
$14.7	Vans Warped Tour	$30
$14.5	Alicia Keys	$79
$14.4	Theresa Caputo	$65
$14.4	Nine Inch Nails	$73
$14.2	Willie Nelson	$53
$14.1	Gentlemen Of The Road Stopovers/Mumford & Sons	$101
$13.6	Chicago	$53
$13.5	The Who	$95
$13.3	Journey	$69
$13.1	Eric Clapton	$81
$12.9	Toby Keith	$36
$12.7	Heart	$47
$12.3	Motley Crue	$82
$12.2	Furthur	$61
$12.2	KISS	$85
$11.9	Jay Z	$87
$11.7	Vicente Fernandez/ Vicente Fernandez Jr.	$116
$11.6	Romeo Santos	$65
$11.5	Sarah Brightman	$81
$11.2	Emmanuel/Manuel Mijares	$67
$11.2	fun.	$37
$11.1	Widespread Panic	$41
$10.6	Macklemore & Ryan Lewis	$38
$10.5	Americanarama Festival Of Music/Bob Dylan	$57
$10.4	Backstreet Boys	$43
$10.3	Leonard Cohen	$109
$10.3	Barry Manilow	$74
$10.0	The Lumineers	$35
$9.9	Train	$32
$9.8	Ron White	$51
$9.6	The Avett Brothers	$40
$9.3	Earth, Wind & Fire	$52
$9.3	Ricardo Arjona	$84
$9.3	Alejandro Fernandez	$91
$9.0	Pitbull	$59
$8.9	Black Crowes	$50
$8.8	Imagine Dragons	$32
$8.8	Josh Groban	$63
$8.6	Prince	$168
$8.5	Mary J. Blige	$61
$8.4	B. B. King	$58
$8.3	Florida Georgia Line	$28
$8.2	Marco Antonio Solis	$72
$8.1	Chris Tomlin	$28
$8.1	Buddy Guy	$51
$8.1	Alejandro Sanz	$65
$8.1	Diana Krall	$81
$7.8	Mannheim Streamroller	$56
$7.8	The Tragically Hip	$65
$7.7	Matchbox Twenty	$60
$7.7	Jim Gaffigan	$45
$7.7	ZZ Top	$55
$7.6	Big Time Rush / Victoria Justice	$31
$7.6	Celtic Woman	$57
$7.4	The Allman Brothers Band	$88
$7.2	Lionel Richie	$77
$7.1	Dixie Chicks	$75
$7.0	The Postal Service	$41
$6.9	Fall Out Boy	$35
$6.9	Wiz Khalifa / A$AP Rocky	$26
$6.9	Tony Bennett	$79
$6.9	Hillsong United	$36
$6.8	Winter Jam / Tobymac	$12
$6.8	Bad Company	$32
$6.6	Lewis Black	$51
$6.6	Jonas Brothers	$52
$6.6	Paramore	$36
$6.5	Andre Rieu	$73
$6.5	Alabama	$63
$6.5	Lil Wayne	$51
$6.4	Green Day	$50
$6.4	Bassnectar	$36
$6.4	Mike Epps	$54
$6.3	Pretty Lights	$37
$6.3	Straight No Chaser	$42
$6.1	Eric Church	$48
$6.0	Shinedown/ Three Days Grace	$39
$6.0	Iron Maiden	$51
$6.0	Steve Miller Band	$62
$5.9	Barenaked Ladies	$42
$5.8	Charlie Wilson	$60
$5.7	Styx / REO Speedwagon	$38
$5.7	Tiesto	$32
$5.7	A Day To Remember	$33
$5.7	Tom Petty & The Heartbreakers	$80

Gross Income vs. Guarantees and Net Profits

When looking at the numbers, it is important to note that not all the money flows to the artists. The touring business for top stars generally works as follows:

The promoter (the two largest in the US are Live Nation and AEG) pays a guarantee to the artist up front for each show. The promoter also covers the artist's travel expenses, sound and lighting, the cost of the venue (e.g., a stadium or amphitheater renting for six figures) and other costs associated with the show. Generally, after deducting all these costs from income from ticket sales, the promoter pays the artist 85 percent to 90 percent of net income, keeping the balance for its services. Therefore, the artists' share of the Pollstar numbers is a great deal less than the overall money generated by touring. However, top artists can still demand enormous guarantees. The following information is from a database reporting the minimum guarantees of major artists:

- Bruce Springsteen: $200,000–$1,000,000
- Taylor Swift: $1,000,000–$4,000,000
- The Rolling Stones: $1,500,000–$3,000,000
- U2: $1,500,000–$4,000,000
- Bon Jovi: $1,000,000–$5,000,000

Anecdote from My Own Practice

I was authorized by a successful promoter to offer a $2.7 million guarantee to an iconic artist for two concerts in two cities in Japan during a one-week period. In addition, the artist received 90 percent of ticket sales after expenses—which came to more than 3 million dollars. Not bad for a week's pay.

Top DJs Also Get PAID

In the last 10 years or so electronic dance music, or EDM, has emerged as one of the leading genres of music for live performance. Festivals such as Electric Daisy Carnival, Ultra Music Festival, and Electic Zoo in the US; Tomorrowland and Ultra Europe in Europe; and Mysteryland in both attract tens of thousands of fans who pay good money to writhe to the beats of their favorite DJs. And the top DJs can make from $300,000 to $1 million or more for a headlining gig at major festivals. *Billboard* recently names about two dozen DJs in this category.[26]

Stars vs. Indie Artists and Baby Bands: A True Case of "Income Inequality"

The economics of touring and live performance for a baby band or even an established indie band with a following are radically different from those we've seen for A-list performers and top DJ's. A band at a small venue can expect to receive a portion of ticket sales for their show. If tickets sell for $15, and the band of four musicians sells 50 tickets, they might expect to make 50 x $15 = $750, minus 20 percent to the club to cover light and sound and 15 percent payable to a promoter who helped book the club and promote the show. That would leave approximately $400 for the band, or $100 for each member.

Established indie bands or emerging artists with a "buzz" who can book medium-sized venues such as Irving Plaza or the main room at Webster Hall in New York, and who can sell 500 tickets at $25 to $50, can expect to come away with several thousand dollars, even over $10,000 for a show. Although this is respectable, it's an incredibly low fraction of the $1 million to $4 million guarantee that Taylor Swift can demand. The problem is that there are only so many artists with the fame and the fans to fill arenas or stadiums.

Jazz musicians may make $50 to $150 a night for playing at a club. The leader usually receives all the money and pays the sideman what he deems fair. The leader can make up to $500 at a small club and has to share that money with the band. A jazz artist who was headlining at a small club in Manhattan told me she didn't even know what the club would pay her—she was only sure that whatever she got would be negligible.

On the other hand, if a jazz artist is one of a select group who can pull in paying crowds to upscale clubs, he or she can demand $1,000 a night or more, and some can even make six figures for a weeklong engagement. But according to research of the Future of Music Coalition (FMC), a nonprofit organization specializing in education, research, and advocacy for musicians, only two to three percent of full-time jazz musicians make more than $100,000 per year—and that includes all sources of revenue, such as record sales, as well as live performances.[27]

IV. Branding

For the same top artists who are making millions from touring and live performance there are additional millions to be made from "branding." According to the Future of Music Coalition, branding includes traditional forms of revenue such as merchandise sales, endorsements, and corporate support for tours. Stars can make millions in royalties (usually 30 to 40 percent of the retail selling price) from sales of mugs, T-shirts, and other "merch" sold at arena and stadium concerts. Artist endorsement of products stretches back for generations; for instance, Nat King Cole, the great singer and pianist, was a pitchman for Camel cigarettes in the '50s. Regarding corporate tour support, over a decade ago I drafted documents on behalf of Dodge Viper, who paid millions to Aerosmith in connection with a tour. Dodge received benefits such as having their name appear on stage, Aerosmith meet-and-greets with Viper dealers, and a national commercial using an Aerosmith song. Also, each member of the band had to promise to use "reasonable efforts" to drive a Viper which Dodge provided gratis.

In the last several years, "branding" has really taken on new meaning as the deals have become far less obvious than the old income streams just described. For instance, branding can include judging positions on reality TV shows. Last season, Jennifer Lopez was paid an astounding $17.5 million to return to her post as judge on *American Idol*, and Britney Spears was paid $15 million to do *The X Factor*.[28]

Today, according to certain industry experts, the primary way to maximize money in the music business is to turn the artist herself into a brand—then do everything in one's power to maximize that brand's value. For instance, Taylor Swift, for her last album, *Red*, had a list of marketing partners who left virtually no category unturned, including a branded store in Walgreens that sold Swift-themed merchandise incorporating artwork from *Red*: T-shirts, bracelets, backpacks, tour books, posters, journals, notebooks, calendars, iPhone and iPad accessories, and other items. Swift also launched her own line of sneakers for Keds. In addition, she inked a deal for a new fragrance with Elizabeth Arden, Enchanted, that followed up the hugely successful Wonderstruck, the No. 2 women's scent launch in 2011. The list embraces only a fraction of Swift's branding deals.[29]

The best deals, in addition to being lucrative, also make an artist's brand more appealing for future endeavors. Steven Tyler was cast as a judge on *American Idol* and earned a fat check—around $10 million.[30] But the show also introduced Tyler to a new generation and became a showcase for Tyler's personal style, which helped him land deals with fashion companies. According to Tyler's attorney: "We did a deal with Tommy Hilfiger's rock-and-roll line, Andrew Charles, last year. And that was successful because we had a debut of his own menswear and womenswear. Now we're putting together a deal with a very prominent fashion executive and business owner, and Tyler is doing his own line."[31]

In the current market, there are good reasons for artists to pursue such opportunities. As we noted earlier, income from recorded music is down more than 65 percent from its peak in 1999. And, while touring can be very lucrative, tours are also expensive to produce and aren't necessarily as profitable for the artist as they initially appear. For this reason, major artists and their "teams" (manager, lawyer, business manager, etc.) have gotten increasingly creative with their business ventures.

Tyler's attorney told the *Huffington Post*, "Ten years ago, if you had a hit song on the radio, and you had a great tour, then you'd sell a million records, 2 million records. That's not necessarily the case anymore. But today, if you have a hit song and you have a sold-out tour, then other ancillary opportunities are available to you: sponsorships, endorsements, TV, movie, animated features . . . all different types of things. Recording an album really has become like a promotional tool."[32]

Beyoncé is another great example of an artist who makes a great deal of money from branding as well as live performance. *Forbes* noted, in the year leading up to June 2014,

> Queen B played 95 shows, bringing in an average $2.4 million per stop, according to Pollstar. . . .
>
> But Beyoncé doesn't stop with music—she's built a small business empire. She earns millions endorsing companies like H&M and Pepsi. She has a line of fragrances with names like Heat, Rise, and Pulse, and then there's her clothing company House of Dereon, which features jeans, shoes, and accessories. All together we estimate that Beyoncé earned $115 million between June 1, 2013 and June 1, 2014.[33]

V. Current Conditions for Most Full-Time Musicians: Overall the Same as In Prior Years; Digital Has Not Lived Up to the Promise of Leveling the Playing Field

Jean Cook, the program director at the Future of Music Coalition, told the *Huffington Post* that just 2 percent of musicians' total income in America comes from "brand-related revenue." "Anybody who's able to leverage their brand and get income from it is probably doing fairly well," she said. "But most people are not in a position to leverage their brand."

In fact, the Future of Music Coalition found that musicians made an average of about $34,000 off their music in America, before deducting expenses from touring and recording.

Most musicians don't have the brand recognition of Steven Tyler, so they couldn't land his branding deals even with the best attorneys and managers in the industry. According to Cook's data, though, side jobs end up boosting the average total income for a musician to $49,000, pre-expenses—still less than a tenth of a percent of what Taylor Swift generates.

"Musicians are poor," Cook said, "There's no getting around that. Freelance musicians have to tie together a lot of different things to make a living, and don't have a lot of support from their teams. There are successful musicians—but the vast majority of people aren't that."

Perhaps the digital era has made things even worse for most artists. Rock musician and blogger David Lowery has developed a theory he calls "the new boss, even worse than the old boss."[34] Lowery points out that under the old label system, when the labels were healthy enough to sign a lot of artists, they financed production and provided advances. The artists may never have seen recording royalties (see why in the "Record Business" section of Chapter 1), but at least they did not have to pay to produce and market their records, and the labels provided additional money to live on—sometimes enough to buy a new car or a house. If an artist caught on, he or she could become very rich. Now, most "successful" indie recording artists have to pay for their own records, receive very modest payments from downloading or streaming, and tour almost constantly to make a living.

According to FMC research, it is impossible to tell whether musicians' incomes have gone up or down in recent years.[35] There are just too many variables, including whether a person is performing music for a living on a full-time basis, how much he or she must pay for recording and touring, and whether income from teaching is included or not. One thing is for sure: the promise that the Internet would create a worldwide market for record sales without the help of labels, and that many artists would be able to sustain themselves by recording and uploading their own tracks to their websites or to iTunes and other stores through aggregators such as TuneCore or CD Baby, has been profoundly disappointing. In 2008, it was estimated that there were 10 million tracks on iTunes that were never downloaded—not even once.[36] That number is probably even greater now because the number of tracks being produced and uploaded to the Web has increased. Despite the hype put out by some of these companies, musicians often spend more money using their services to upload songs to iTunes or Amazon than they make from sales.

But if you are an indie artist, Part IV of this book contains some smart tips and some real success stories of how artists can use digital tools, such as YouTube, to succeed without wasting time and money.

PART I
MUSIC LAW AND BUSINESS PRACTICES

Part I provides an overview of the record and music publishing businesses, including the rules and business practices that apply to the digital distribution of music. After giving an overview of how copyright law applies to the record and publishing industries and the basic statutes applicable to digital music distribution, we identify and describe the three principal digital distribution formats: downloading, interactive streaming, and Internet and satellite radio. Then we focus on artists, record companies, songwriters, and music publishers, analyzing how much money each format generates, what statutes or licenses apply to how the way stakeholders get paid, and most importantly, how much each group actually receives.

The balance of Part I addressees the very hot issue of "direct" licensing. Currently, only ASCAP and BMI can license public performance rights on behalf of the music publishers they represent. We consider whether changing the law to allow these music publishers to make deals directly with digital services, such as Pandora, could hurt songwriters even though the publishers state that they have their writers' best interests at heart. Finally, we discuss the global digital music business and the intricacies of international digital music licensing.

Chapter 1

MUSIC LAW AND BUSINESS PRIMER

This chapter is intended to provide an overview of the rules and business practices pertaining to the music publishing and recording businesses.

What's important to understand is the connection between copyright and these industries. They are both based on copyright, and without copyright, they couldn't exist. By protecting the exclusive rights of authors, the copyright law allows creators and their representatives to monetize their musical compositions (the music publishing business) and sound recordings (the record business).

We will start by defining what copyright is, the rights it protects, the kinds of works to which it applies, and how to get it back. Then we will be ready to discuss how the music publishing and recording businesses work.

Copyright Law: The Foundation of the Music Publishing and Recording Businesses

What Is Copyright?

Copyright is a form of protection provided by the laws of the United States, that is, the Copyright Act (Title 17 of the US Code), to the authors of "original works of authorship," including literary, dramatic, musical, artistic, and certain other intellectual works.

The "Works" that Copyright Protects, Including Musical Compositions and Sound Recordings

Copyright protects original works of authorship fixed in any tangible medium of expression, rather than mere ideas. Works of authorship include the following categories (emphasis added):

(1) Literary works
(2) **Musical works, including any accompanying words**
(3) Dramatic works, including any accompanying music
(4) Pantomimes and choreographic works
(5) Pictorial, graphic, and sculptural works
(6) Motion pictures and other audiovisual works
(7) **Sound recordings**
(8) Architectural works[37]

Musical works are musical compositions, including songs as well as longer works such as a symphony or a movie score. *Sound recordings* are defined in the Copyright Act as "works that result from the fixation of a series of musical, spoken, or other sounds . . . regardless of the nature of the material objects, such as disks, tapes, or other phonorecords, in which they are embodied." The Act further defines *phonorecords* as "material objects in which sounds, other than those accompanying a motion picture or other audiovisual work, are fixed by any method now known or later developed." The difference is that *sound recordings* refers to works that are subject to copyright, and *phonorecords* are physical embodiments of such works. In music-business parlance, though, the word *master* is used to refer to the copyright in a sound recording.

The Exclusive Rights That Copyright Affords

Section 106 of the 1976 Copyright Act generally gives the owner of copyright the exclusive right to do, and to authorize others to do, any of the following:

(1) To reproduce the copyrighted work in copies or phonorecords
(2) To prepare derivative works based upon the copyrighted work
(3) To distribute copies or phonorecords of the copyrighted work to the public by sale or other transfer of ownership, or by rental, lease, or lending
(4) In the case of literary, musical, dramatic, and choreographic works; pantomimes; and motion pictures and other audiovisual works, to perform the copyrighted work publicly
(5) In the case of literary, musical, dramatic, and choreographic works; pantomimes; and pictorial, graphic, or sculptural works, including the individual images of a motion picture or other audiovisual work, to display the copyrighted work publicly
(6) In the case of sound recordings, to perform the copyrighted work publicly by means of a digital audio transmission

The origins of copyright law go back to the protection of books by the Statute of Queen Anne adopted by the British Parliament in 1710. The law provided protection for publishers against those who would make physical copies and sell them without permission. The United States continued this tradition by including a provision in our constitution that specifically protects "works of authorship." The federal copyright law was implemented in 1790 and initially protected only books, maps, and charts but was eventually expanded to protect other works, including songs in 1831.[38] Long after the invention of the phonograph player, federal copyright law was extended to sound recordings. Until the Sound Recording Act of 1971 made sound recordings subject to the protection of the federal copyright law,[39] sound recordings came under the protection of the laws of individual states. Although the Sound Recordings Act extended federal copyright protection to sound recordings fixed on or after February 15, 1972, it declared that sound recordings fixed before that date would remain subject to state or common law copyright (see "Duration of Copyright" later in this chapter).

The Copyright Act specifically protects songs (musical works) and masters (sound recordings) by spelling out the precise rights reserved to the copyright owner. For example, without item 3 on the previous list, anyone could record your song and sell copies without paying you. Without item 1, anyone could take your record and make copies without your permission and without paying you. Without item 4, anyone could publicly perform your song, on the radio, for instance, and not pay you. Copyright is the house in which the music business lives, and without it the business would be homeless and broke.

Note that the public-performance right in item 6 applies to sound recordings, but only by means of digital distribution, not traditional "analog" methods of performance such as radio. We will discuss this critical distinction later in this chapter (see "The Record Business") and in Chapters 3 and 6).

Copyright Registration: Why Do It, and How

Why Register?

Registration is not a prerequisite for copyright protection. Under the Copyright Act of 1976, a copyright comes into existence as soon as a work is fixed in a tangible medium of expression, and registration is not a condition of copyright protection. However, registration provides crucial benefits to copyright owners. Those benefits are set forth in the US Copyright Office's website at www.copyright.gov/circs/circ01.pdf:

1. Registration establishes a public record of the copyright claim.
2. Before an infringement suit may be filed in court, registration is necessary for works of US origin.[40]
3. If made before or within five years of publication, registration will establish prima facie evidence in court of the validity of the copyright and of the facts stated in the certificate.
4. If registration is made within three months after publication of the work or prior to an infringement of the work, statutory damages and attorney's fees will be available to the copyright owner in court actions. Otherwise, only an award of actual damages and profits is available to the copyright owner.
5. Registration allows the owner of the copyright to record the registration with the US Customs Service for protection against the importation of infringing copies.

Of the reasons to register set forth above, the most important are that, without registering, a copyright owner cannot start a lawsuit for copyright infringement and cannot secure statutory damages or attorneys' fees. For published works (that is, works released for sale) that are registered prior to the infringement, the Copyright Act provides for statutory damages of up to $150,000 per infringement and attorneys' fees. If the published work was not registered prior to an infringement, the plaintiff must prove actual damages, which can be difficult to quantify, or may equal a negligible amount unless the defendant earned a significant amount of money from the infringing work. And, because a lawsuit for copyright infringement can take a great deal of work and time on the part of the attorney, it would be difficult to retain the services of an experienced copyright litigator without the potential for recovering attorney's fees.

Note that the only way to secure the benefits of copyright registration is to register with the US Copyright Office. These benefits cannot be obtained any other way, including by sending a copy of your song or master to yourself (even by certified or registered mail).

How to Register

To register a work, including a song or a master, you need to submit a completed application form, a nonrefundable filing fee, and a nonreturnable copy of the work. More details are provided below—but you can get all the details from the website of the US Copyright Office (www.copyright.gov). Here are answers to some of the most important questions:

Where to apply? You can find and complete the copyright registration application online at http://www.copyright.gov/eco (eCO is an acronym for Electronic Copyright Office).

How much will it cost? Online registration through the electronic Copyright Office (eCO) is the preferred way to register basic claims for musical works, including songs and sound recordings, as well as literary, visual arts, and audiovisual works. The filing fee is $35 if you register one work by a single author who is also the claimant and the work is not made for hire. Otherwise, the fee for online registration is $55.

What else needs to be done? It is also necessary to provide a "deposit" of the work. This can be done online by uploading an MP3, or one can print out a "shipping slip" to be enclosed with a CD and mailed to the Copyright Office within 30 days of applying for the registration.

Is it possible to register a sound recording and a song in one application? Yes. To register a master and a song in one application, click on "Sound Recording" in the drop-down menu in the part of the application asking for the type of work to be registered. Later in the application you will be able to claim copyright of your music and lyrics as well as the sound recording.[41]

The US Copyright Office's website (www.copyright.gov) is an invaluable source of information not only on registration, but also on how copyright law protects songs and masters.

Duration of Copyright[42]

The term *public domain* refers to the status of a work having no copyright protection and therefore belonging to the "public." When a work is in or has "fallen" into the public domain, it is available for unrestricted use by anyone. Permission and/or payment are not required for use. Once a work falls into the public domain (has become "PD"), it cannot be recaptured by the owner (except for certain foreign-originated works eligible for restoration of copyright under section 104A of the Copyright Act). But copyright protection does not last forever. Many musical compositions, such as most of the great classic repertoire, are now PD. Generally, a work goes into the public domain after a specific period of time. Over the years, Congress has extended the duration of copyright. The original Copyright Act of 1790 officially established US copyright as a term of 14 years with the right to renew for an additional 14 years if the copyright holder was still alive. The Copyright Act of 1831 extended the term to 28 years with the option to renew for 14 years, and the Copyright Act of 1909 extended the term of the renewal to 28 years.

Works Originally Created on or After January 1, 1978

Under the Copyright Act of 1976, a work created (fixed in tangible form for the first time) on or after January 1, 1978, is automatically protected from the moment of its creation and is ordinarily given a term enduring for the author's life plus an additional 70 years after the author's death.[43] In the case of a "joint work prepared by two or more authors," the term lasts for 70 years after the last surviving author's death. For works "made for hire," also sometimes referred to as a "corporate copyright," the duration of copyright will be 95 years from *publication* or 120 years from creation, whichever is shorter. A *work made for hire* generally refers to a work made by an employee of a corporation, such as a staff writer at a company that creates commercial jingles. A work for hire may also refer to a person who is commissioned to do a job under certain circumstances. For whether masters are works for hire under standard recording agreements, see the section on termination rights below. "Publication" is defined in Section 101 of the Act as "the distribution of copies or phonorecords of a work to the public by sale or other transfer of ownership, or by rental, lease, or lending. The offering to distribute copies or phonorecords to a group of persons for the purposes of further distribution, public performance, or public display, constitutes publication."

The term of copyright used to be life plus 50, and for a corporate copyright the term was 75 years from publication or 100 years from creation, whichever was shorter. The duration of copyright was extended under the Sonny Bono Term Extension Act, signed into law on October 27, 1998. The act is named after its sponsor, the pop star and former husband of Cher who became a Republican congressman before his untimely demise in a skiing accident. The act is also sometimes referred to as the Mickey Mouse Protection Act, as it was heavily supported by Disney and other corporations that make a great deal of money by licensing their copyrights.

Many have criticized the extension. Professor Lawrence Lessig, the principal attorney representing a party challenging the constitutionality of the law, has argued that the law was designed to protect big corporations who use the copyright law to control culture and extract profits at the expense of those who would use previous works to contribute to society.

Pre-'78 Works

Under the old 1909 Act, works were entitled to two consecutive 28-year terms of protection provided they were published[44] with notice and properly registered and renewed. The 1976 Act, which went into effect on January 1, 1978, provided that in regard to those works that were still protected by copyright on January 1, 1978,[45] the renewal term would be extended from 28 to 47 years, making these works eligible for a total term of protection of 75 years. The Sonny Bono Term Extension Act further extended the renewal term for an additional 20 years, for a total period of protection of 95 years from the initial date of registration. As a result, any song published with notice on or after 1923, and properly registered and renewed, is still protected by copyright for a period of 95 years from publication. For instance, a work published with notice in 1945, if properly registered and renewed, would be protected by copyright until 2040.

Special Rules for Sound Recordings

Though before 1972 sound recordings were not subject to federal copyright, copying was nonetheless regulated under various state statutes, some of which had no duration limit. The Sound Recording Act of 1971 extended federal copyright to recordings fixed on or after February 15, 1972 (the effective date of the act), and declared that recordings fixed before that date would remain subject to state or common law protection.[46] The Copyright Act of 1976 maintained this protection until February 15, 2047, and this period was subsequently extended by the Sonny Bono Copyright Term Extension Act to 2067. As a result, no sound recording can reliably be considered in the public domain in the United States before that date, even if the recording was in existence before 1923 and even if it originated in another country where it has entered the public domain.[47]

Termination Rights (How to Get Your Copyrights Back)

The contracts that both music publishers and record companies offer songwriters and artists usually require them to transfer their ownership in their copyrights (i.e., songs and recordings) to the publisher or label (see "Music Publishing Agreements" and "Recording Agreements" later in this chapter). The 1976 Copyright Act, however, contains a "termination right," which cannot be contractually given up and which allows the original content creator to "reclaim" the copyright in his or her works and terminate any other rights granted in those copyrights.

The House Report accompanying the 1976 Act explained that the right to terminate was "needed because of the unequal bargaining position of authors, resulting in part from the impossibility of determining a work's value until it has been exploited."[48] The termination right acknowledges that creators, including artists and songwriters, generally have less bargaining power than the companies that represent them, particularly at the beginning of their careers, when they are more likely to enter into bad contracts because their work is not yet highly valued. The law's intent was to allow them to withdraw from these deals and reclaim their copyrights.

Sections 203 and 304(c)

There are two distinct termination clauses in the 1976 Copyright Act: Sections 203 and 304(c). Section 203 permits authors (or, if the authors are not alive, their surviving spouses, children or grandchildren, executors, administrators, personal representatives, or trustees) to terminate grants of copyright assignments and licenses for any works other than "works for hire" (see the previous discussion of this term in "Duration of Copyrights" and in more detail below) that were executed by the author on or after January 1, 1978. For these grants, termination is available 35 years from the date of execution of the grant, or, if the grant is for a continuing series of works (such as songs or records), then 35 years from publication[49] (i.e., distribution for sale or license) of the work or 40 years from the date of execution of the grant, whichever date is earlier. Section 203 also applies to works, other than works for hire, made under contracts that predate 1978 if the works themselves were created on or after January 1, 1978.[50] Therefore, works created in 1978 were subject to termination in 2013 (1978 + 35) and those created in 1979 are subject to termination in 2014.

Section 304(c) applies to pre-'78 works that were still protected by copyright in 1978, except works for hire, and provides for termination 56 years from the creation of those copyrights. So, for instance, a song written in 1950 would have been subject to termination in 2006, and song written in 1960 would be subject to termination in 2016.

Special Issues Regarding Termination of Post-'78 Sound Recordings

A great deal of controversy has surrounded Section 203's application to sound recordings. The principal issue is whether Section 203 would apply to standard record contracts, including those offered by all three major record companies (Sony, Universal, and Warner), their affiliates, and their predecessors (including BMG and EMI, which were acquired by the other three), which state that any recordings made under the contract are works for hire.[51] Standard music publishing agreements, on the other hand, do not use work-for-hire language and rather make the writer "assign" the copyrights in his or her songs to the publisher. An additional complication comes into play when the artist is not the only "author" of his or her recordings but shares joint authorship with a producer or other contributor.

Whether artists can terminate their recording agreements and reclaim their copyrights is important, because if they can it would have an extremely adverse economic impact on the record companies, particularly the majors. "Legacy" recordings, or reissues, particularly from Sony, Warner, Universal, and their associated labels, are a huge part of all record sales. In fact, in 2013 sales of catalogue albums accounted for well over 47 percent of all album sales.[52] If artists could reclaim rights in their recordings, they could use the Internet to distribute them without the record companies and pocket all the money instead of the label's retaining the lion's share of income (the normal artist's royalty is around 15 percent after recoupment of production and marketing costs and a myriad of deductions (see "The Record Business" later in this chapter). Some of the most famous 1978 recordings include: Bruce Springsteen's "Darkness on the Edge of Town," Billy Joel's "52nd Street," the Doobie Brothers' "Minute by Minute," Kenny Rogers's "Gambler" and Funkadelic's "One Nation Under a Groove." These albums have generated tens of millions of dollars for the major record companies. But thanks to Section 203, those artists—and thousands more—now have a legal basis for reclaiming ownership of their recordings, potentially leaving the labels out in the cold. However, as we discuss below, the RIAA, which represents the majors and many of the leading indies, has taken the position that the work-for-hire provision in standard recording agreements are valid and that therefore these agreements and the works created under them cannot be terminated.

The Work-for-Hire Issue

Section 101 of the Copyright Act defines a "work made for hire" as follows:

> (1) a work prepared by an employee within the scope of his or her employment; or (2) a work specially ordered or commissioned for use as a contribution to a collective work, as a part of a motion picture or other audiovisual work, as a translation, as a supplementary work, as a compilation, as an instructional text, as a test, as answer material for a test, or as an atlas, if the parties expressly agree in a written instrument signed by them that the work shall be considered a work made for hire.

In a court battle between a recording artist trying to terminate and a label, which is not unlikely to happen, the label may argue that (a) the artist was an "employee" and therefore any works (i.e., recordings) made under the agreement were works for hire; and, even if the artist was not an employee, (b) the sound recordings produced under the agreement were works for hire under subsection (2) of the above quoted definition.

The argument that a recording artist is an employee is weak. Whether an individual is an employee for the purposes of the "work made for hire" doctrine is determined under the common law of agency, in which a court looks to a multitude of factors to determine whether an employer-employee relationship exists. In *Community for Creative Non-Violence v. Reid*,[53] the US Supreme Court listed those factors:

> In determining whether a hired party is an employee under the general common law of agency, we consider the hiring party's right to control the manner and means by which the product is accomplished. Among the other factors relevant to this inquiry are the skill required; the source of the instrumentalities and tools; the location of the work; the duration of the relationship between the parties; whether

> the hiring party has the right to assign additional projects to the hired party; the extent of the hired party's discretion over when and how long to work; the method of payment; the hired party's role in hiring and paying assistants; whether the hiring party is in business; the provision of employee benefits; and the tax treatment of the hired party.[54]

Under these criteria, most recording artists would not qualify as "employees" because most record companies generally do not "control the manner" in which artists make their records. In addition, artists almost never receive "employee benefits," and record companies generally do not withhold payroll taxes from any advances or royalties or pay any payroll taxes based on advances or royalties.

Nevertheless, a record company could argue that an artist had been an employee because the label usually has the right to approve the songs artists record, it pays for the studio time for the recording, and it has approval rights over what is recorded. But the labels may be reluctant to make the employee argument, because if artists were found to be employees, the labels might be responsible for paying back taxes. Indeed, most recording agreements specifically state that the artists are not employees for this very reason.

In a court battle the labels would certainly argue that any sound recordings made under a standard record agreement are covered by subsection (2) of the definition of work for hire because (a) the agreements specifically state that any recordings made during the term of the agreement are works for hire for the label; and (b) each recording an artist makes can be considered to be a "contribution to a collective work" or "compilation" (that is, an album) and therefore fits into one of the categories of commissioned works for hire. In fact, many recording agreements include language describing an artist's performance as a contribution to a collective work. The argument is that each individual sound recording of a musical composition is a contribution to the collective work or compilation, that is, the finished album, and thus a work made for hire. But the artist may contend that each individual sound recording stands by itself and is only incidentally compiled into a collective work as one of its uses.

The Artist May Not Be the Only Author

Even if a recording produced under a standard recording agreement is not a work for hire, there is another important issue that must be considered. Producers may be considered as authors, too. This is because they don't necessarily act at the direction of the label or the artist. In fact, producers are often an integral part of the creative process, and may be deemed to be "joint authors." Therefore, artists who notify their record company that they are terminating the transfer of rights in any recording may have to sort out a new deal with the producer of that recording prior to exploiting the recaptured recordings or risk a lawsuit by the producer. It is also possible that audio engineers and session musicians may have a claim of authorship, although these people generally do work at the direction of others and taxes are usually withheld, so they may well be considered employees.

What Happens Now?

In accordance with Section 203, artists first gained the ability to terminate recording agreements in 2013. While there have been no court decisions as yet, the RIAA, which represents the majors as well as many important indies, has publicly taken the position that the work-for-hire provisions in the standard recording agreements are enforceable.[55] So far there have been multiple settlements between recording companies and artists, whereby the artists secure additional advances for legacy recordings by waiving their rights to terminate, and the record companies try to avoid court battles that could backfire if they lose. According to a 2011 *New York Times* article, "Given the potentially huge amounts of money at stake and the delicacy of the issues, both record companies, and recording artists and their managers have been reticent in talking about termination rights."[56] As of the submission of this book in January 2015 this remains true. The reason for this may be that there are significant differences of opinion among the record companies, which has prevented them from taking a unified position. The *New York Times* article quoted a record company executive as stating, "Some of the major labels favor a court battle, no matter how long or costly it might be, while others worry that taking an unyielding position could backfire if the case is lost, since musicians . . . would be so deeply alienated that they would refuse to negotiate new deals and insist on total control of all their recordings."

The Steps Artists Need to Take to Terminate Grants

Whatever the ultimate result, here are the actual steps that artists, their successors, or their estates need to take to initiate termination of transfer of rights in their recordings under Section 203:

Who Can Terminate?

If the artist is deceased, his or her "statutory successor" can terminate. The statutory successor is the surviving spouse, or surviving children or grandchildren. If none of them are alive, the author's executor, administrator, personal representative, or trustee can terminate. If the artist is a band or group, termination requires a majority vote of the band members or their successors.

When Must Notice Be Served?

The artist or statutory successor may give notice of termination no less than 2 years and no more than 10 years before the date that the transfer will terminate.

Content of Notice

The notice must be in writing, signed by artists or by their duly authorized representatives, and must state the effective date of the termination. The notice must also comply in form, content, and manner of service with the requirements of the Register of Copyrights.

To Whom Should Notice Be Sent?

The notice must be served upon the grantee (i.e., the label with whom the artist contracted) or the grantee's successor in title. A copy of the notice must also be recorded in the Copyright Office before the effective date of termination, as a condition to its taking effect.

How the Fair-Use Doctrine Applies to the Music Business

Fair use is a complete defense to copyright infringement. Under Section 107 of the Copyright Act, the defense applies where a work is used "for purposes such as criticism, comment, news reporting, teaching . . . scholarship or research." In evaluating whether the fair-use defense is available, courts must evaluate (1) the purpose and character of the use, including whether such use is of a commercial nature or is for nonprofit educational purposes; (2) the nature of the work; (3) the amount and substantiality of the portion used in relation to the copyrighted work as a whole; and (4) the effect of the use upon the potential market for or value of the copyrighted work.

In the context of the music business, fair use arises frequently in the context of parody. In order to constitute fair use, a parody of a song must be targeted at the original work and not merely borrow its style. In the *2 Live Crew* case,[57] the Supreme Court of the United States determined that that the band's parody of "Pretty Woman" was a fair use because it poked fun at the original even though they used some of the lyrics and melody of the original song. (See "Are Parodies a Fair Use?" in Chapter 11 for a detailed conversation about this case.) Outside of the parody, however, the following cases show that deciding what is or is not fair use depends on the particular facts of each case.

Performing a 30-Second Excerpt to Sell Ringtones Is Not Fair Use

Ringtones became a fashion statement in the 1990s, as consumers wanted to have the latest hits play when their phone rang. Later, consumers also bought ringback tones to play for people who called them. (See Chapter 13 for the business history and current licensing structure applicable to ringtones and ringbacks.)

In 2009 the rate court (a special court set up in the Southern District of New York to decide disputes between PROs and their licensees) determined that playing excerpts of music to promote sales of the recordings from which the excerpts were taken was not a fair use.[58] AT&T had set up online and mobile stores to sell ringtones and ringbacks. For the purpose of attracting customers, they allowed people to listen to 30-second previews of songs but failed to seek the permission from the copyright owners. ASCAP challenged this practice in a rate proceeding before the federal court in New York delegated to handle such controversies. ASCAP argued that AT&T's usage was completely commercial in nature, intended to increase sales, and therefore should have been licensed. ASCAP also pointed out that in its online storefront, AT&T promoted other products alongside music, and that playing excerpts of music helped sell these products as well as ringtones. Finally, they argued that dozens of other organizations already licensed the same previews and that AT&T simply did not want to compensate songwriters in ways that everyone else already did. AT&T pointed out that they were using only 30-second excerpts, not full songs, and claimed their use of these excerpts would not affect the potential market for sale of full songs.

The court ruled in favor of ASCAP, holding that:

> AT&T erred in assuming that the performance of previews of music compositions on its Internet website would be ruled a fair use of the copyrighted material and, therefore, did not include such previews in its license fee proposal. Although AT&T does not charge for previews, they clearly increase the revenue from sales of Ringtones and Answer Tones, which are made after an average of between three and four previews for each sale. Thus, a fee should be paid for these performances of music to generate revenue.[59]

The court went on to emphasize that AT&T was using the music to facilitate sales of AT&T's products as well as ringtones, that it was customary in the music business to pay for use of excerpts, and that AT&T's usage exploited the melody or chorus, which is often the most interesting and entertaining portion of a song.

Using 15-Second Excerpts in a Documentary Is Fair Use Since the Use Was "Transformative"

Expelled was a 2008 documentary directed and narrated by the political pundit and satirist Ben Stein. The movie addressed the "intelligent design" movement, which some educators espouse as an alternative to Darwin's theory of evolution, and the ongoing difficulty that various scientists have when attempting to practice their faith alongside their field of study. At one point in the movie, several speakers expressed negative views of religion and advocate for religion's diminished role in society. The producers of the documentary criticized this view as "merely lifting a page out of John Lennon's songbook" and then followed up with 15 seconds of the song "Imagine," written by John Lennon. While the song was played, subtitles displayed the lyrics "Nothing to kill or die for / And no religion too." Behind the subtitles are images of black-and-white footage, ranging from children frolicking to a military parade, and then a close-up of former Soviet ruler Joseph Stalin. No license was obtained for the commercial use of this excerpt, but licenses were secured for all the other music used in the movie.

Yoko Ono Lennon started a lawsuit in the federal court in the Southern District of New York to force the removal of the excerpt of "Imagine" from the film.[60] The court, however, ruled that the defendants were likely to prevail on their affirmative defense of fair use. The court took into account that the original song was three minutes long but the excerpt was only 15 seconds long. The plaintiffs rightly pointed out that that the excerpt was the hook of the original song and therefore had greater value and impact. The court, however, found that the use was a form of criticism of the song itself and that the movie directly commented upon the music. Rather than using the music as entertainment, the movie was "transformative," in that it was using the music to make the point that, stretched to the furthest degree, the concepts celebrated in "Imagine" were compatible with totalitarianism. The court also emphasized that this transformative use would not usurp the market for licensing the original song.

The foregoing cases demonstrate that fair use is fact-specific. There are no bold lines separating what is fair use and what is not. Each case may depend on the temperament and philosophy of the court before which the case is tried.

Minimum Use and Sampling

In addition to fair use, the doctrine of "de minimis" use has provided wiggle room to many creators, especially in the area of digital sampling of music. Courts have dismissed copyright-infringement cases on the grounds that the alleged infringer's use of the copyrighted work was so insignificant as to be de minimis. However, in 2004 in *Bridgeport Music, Inc. v. Dimension Films*, the US Court of Appeals for the Sixth Circuit, which includes Nashville, explicitly declined to recognize a de minimis standard for sampling musical recordings. See Sample Clearances in Chapter 11 for a detailed discussion of this case.

Creative Commons: An Alternative to Copyright

Creative Commons, founded by Harvard professor Lawrence Lessig and two other technology and intellectual-property experts, offers musicians, songwriters, and other creators an alternative to copyright law. The idea underlying Creative Commons is that some people may not want to exercise all of the intellectual-property rights the law affords them. According to the Creative Commons website,

> We believe there is an unmet demand for an easy yet reliable way to tell the world "Some rights reserved" or even "No rights reserved." Many people have long since concluded that all-out copyright doesn't help them gain the exposure and widespread distribution they want. Many entrepreneurs and artists have come to prefer

> relying on innovative business models rather than full-fledged copyright to secure a return on their creative investment. Still others get fulfillment from contributing to and participating in an intellectual commons. For whatever reasons, it is clear that many citizens of the Internet want to share their work—and the power to reuse, modify, and distribute their work—with others on generous terms. Creative Commons intends to help people express this preference for sharing by offering the world a set of licenses on our website, at no charge.[61]

Creative Commons provides creators with a choice of licenses that they can append to their works. Under a Creative Commons (CC) license, a composer, for example, can choose to allow others to use her compositions in new songs, such as a remix, in exchange for credit and/or compensation if the remix is released commercially. Under another type of CC license, a songwriter could waive the right to compensation, including public-performance fees, entirely.

Under traditional copyright law, if a creator makes his work, such as song, available to the public, it comes with many strings attached. Specifically, as we discussed earlier in this chapter, the copyright law reserves to the creator the exclusive rights to distribute, copy, or publicly perform the work, and to create derivative works. That means that even if I buy a song from iTunes, I have no right to redistribute it, publicly perform it, or make derivative works from it. A derivative work is one that is based on another work but is not an exact, verbatim copy. Mash-ups and remixes are examples of derivative works; another example is a movie based on a novel. Although the fair-use doctrine may protect some forms of derivative use, as we discussed earlier in this chapter, each court must decide what use is "fair," and an artist can never be certain her use will be judged to be a fair use. However, a creator can use a Creative Commons license to make it absolutely clear that someone else may reuse his or her work with impunity. Such a license offers an alternative to the restrictive nature of copyright.

To take advantage of Creative Commons, creators go to the Creative Commons website (wiki.creativecommons.org), choose a license that works best for them, and then follow instructions to include certain HTML code in the work. This code will automatically generate a license button and a statement that the work is licensed under a Creative Commons license. The HTML code will also include the metadata that enables the work to be found via Creative Commons–enabled search engines.

The following are descriptions of various types of Creative Commons licenses, starting with the most restrictive and ending with the most accommodating type of license you can choose.

Attribution Noncommercial No Dirivitives (BY-NC-ND)

This license is often called the "free advertising" license, because it allows others to download your works and share them with others as long as they mention you and link back to you, but they can't change them in any way or use them commercially.

Attribution Noncommercial Share Alike (BY-NC-SA)

This license lets others remix, tweak, and build upon your work noncommercially, as long as they credit you and license their new creations under the identical terms. Any derivative work has to be made available under this same license.

Attribution Noncommercial (BY-NC)

This license lets others remix, tweak, and build upon your work noncommercially, and although their new works must also acknowledge you and be noncommercial, they don't have to license their derivative works on the same terms.

Attribution No Dirivitives (BY-ND)

This license allows for redistribution, both commercial and noncommercial, as long as it is passed along unchanged and in whole, with credit to you.

Attribution Share Alike (BY-SA)

This license lets others remix, tweak, and build upon your work even for commercial purposes, as long as they credit you and license the new creations under identical terms. This license is often compared to open-source-software licenses. All new works based on yours will carry the same license, so any derivatives will also allow commercial use.

To find out more about Creative Commons, go to www.creativecommons.org.

Music Publishing Business

Principal Sources of Income

As we discussed in the introduction, the three basic sources of revenue from songs are public-performance royalties, mechanicals, and synchronization. There are other sources of income, including sheet music in physical and digital formats. All income from the commercial exploitation of musical compositions, no matter what the source, is referred to as "publishing income."

The music publishing business generates approximately $5.5 billion worldwide, approximately $2.2 billion from the United States alone. According to the National Music Publishers Association (NMPA), a trade group representing both major publishers and many of the leading independents, the breakdown of that income in the United States is as follows:[62]

- Performance License: 52 percent ($1.14 billion)
- Mechanical License: 23 percent ($506 million)
- Sync License: 20 percent ($440 million)
- Other: 5 percent

The worldwide breakdown follows a similar pattern.[63]

In this section we discuss each of these sources of income in more detail, along with the business practices that have developed around them. At the outset, it's important to understand that if a songwriter becomes commercially successful, he or she will usually enter into an agreement with a music publisher. Most music publishers, including the majors (Sony/ATV Music Publishing, Universal Music Publishing, Warner/Chappell Music, and BMG Rights Management),[64] will usually offer an advance against royalties as an incentive to sign, as well as an organized machine to collect monies from the multiple sources of revenues we are about to discuss and the ability to generate additional revenues from the writer's songs by shopping them to other artists to record and trying to place them in TV shows, movies, and commercials. We will discuss the role of music publishers and their various deals with songwriters in detail next, but for now it's important to note that they are an integral part of the food chain in the music publishing business.

Public Performance Rights and Royalties

Section 106(4) of the Copyright Act gives the copyright owners of musical compositions, including songs as well as orchestral works, the exclusive right to "perform the copyrighted work publicly." The US federal copyright law first recognized the right of public performance in musical compositions in 1897.[65] Today, public performance is the most lucrative source of income for many songwriters. What does "perform publicly" mean?

The Copyright Act states that to perform or display a work "publicly" means:

(1) to perform or display it at a place open to the public or at any place where a substantial number of persons outside of a normal circle of a family and its social acquaintances is gathered; or

(2) to transmit or otherwise communicate a performance or display of the work to a place specified by clause (1) or to the public, by means of any device or process, whether the members of the public capable of receiving the performance or display receive it in the same place or in separate places and at the same time or at different times.

In the case of musical compositions, public performances includes concerts and live performances (e.g., Bruce Springsteen performing at the Meadowlands or your gig at a local club); a jukebox playing in a bar; background music at a restaurant, bar, bowling alley, amusement park, or mall; or music playing at any other public venue, whether by a live artist or a recording. But public performances go well beyond performances at physical venues. Playing music on the radio and television also constitutes public performance, because these are "transmissions" to the public under subparagraph (2). Also, as we discuss in Chapter 3 and in more detail in Chapters 5 and 6, transmitting music on an interactive streaming service or on an Internet radio service or Sirius XM qualifies as public performance, even if the music is heard in a private place such as at home or in your car. All of these public performances require licenses from the copyright owners–and those copyright owners receive money based on all of these licenses.

The PROs: ASCAP, BMI, and SESAC

Since copyright owners of songs and other musical compositions enjoy exclusive public-performance rights, others who wish to perform their works publicly need permission need to do so. Performing-rights organizations (PROs) facilitate the process of obtaining that permission by offering blanket licenses to users of music, including physical venues[66] (such as concert halls, bars, clubs, restaurants, shopping malls, and amusement parks) as well as users who transmit music to the public via radio, television (network, cable, and pay TV), background music services, websites, and online music radio and interactive streaming services. These blanket licenses authorize the user to use any song they wish in return for payment of a license fees. The PROs then turn around and pay their members, the songwriters and music publishers.

Origins and the Direct-Payment-to-Writers Business Model

In 1914, a group of songwriters, composers, and publishers formed ASCAP (American Society of Composers, Authors and Publishers) to enforce their performance rights, and to create a joint pool of musical compositions that could be licensed in bulk to music users. Their aim was to be compensated by clubs, bars, and restaurants where live musicians played their songs. Perhaps because of the strong presence of songwriters, ASCAP deployed a business model that is one of the fairest business structures in the music industry for creators: from the beginning ASCAP paid 50 percent of the money it collected directly to the songwriter, and the other 50 percent went to the songwriter's publisher. Beyond any advances from a publisher—which the songwriter is expected to pay back over time through "recoupment" of income generated from their songs, including mechanical royalties and sync fees—performance income from ASCAP or the other PROs may be a composer's only source of earnings. Sometimes this money is referred to as the "ASCAP check," even if the songwriter belongs to one of the other PROs.

After the advent of radio, in 1939, the broadcast community, which complained that ASCAP's rate were too high, formed a competitor called BMI (Broadcast Music, Inc.). A third, much smaller PRO, SESAC (which used to stand for "Society of European Stage Authors and Composers"), subsequently emerged. As its name suggests, SESAC originally represented contemporary classical music. It now represents and licenses all kinds of music. Like BMI, it has adopted ASCAP's original business model of paying the songwriter 50 percent directly.

Who They Represent and the Purpose They Serve

ASCAP represents 500,000 US composers, songwriters, lyricists, and music publishers; BMI represents 600,000. SESAC represents far fewer songwriter and publishers but has a diverse repertory, including gospel, jazz, Latin, and such songwriters as Bob Dylan and Neil Diamond. Each of them also has reciprocal deals with every other PRO in the world,[67] which means that together they represent virtually any song that a music user would wish to play. Without the PROs it would be virtually impossible for most small venues, broadcasters, or webcasters to identify and license all the music they might wish to use. Even large TV or radio networks might find it impossible to make deals with all the songwriters and publishers they would need to contact. Thus the PROs provide an invaluable service for both creators and users.

How They Operate and the Direct-Licensing Controversy

ASCAP and BMI both operate under government consent decrees that allow them to bargain on behalf of their members, even though they don't qualify as unions, as their songwriters and publishers are not employees. SESAC is a private organization that does not operate under a consent decree and whose legal authority to negotiate licenses on behalf of its members has been called into question from time to time.[68] The consent decrees are important because they place certain constraints on the PROs' ability to bargain with users (for instance, they cannot withhold a license and are subject to the determination of a fair rate by a federal rate court in cases where they cannot conclude a deal). Moreover, recent rate court decisions have held that no publisher can negotiate direct deals with any service while still being a member of ASCAP or BMI. Major publishers (particularly Sony ATV and Universal) are currently trying to amend these consent decrees so they can negotiate directly with digital music services in order to extract higher fees than what ASCAP and BMI have been able to accomplish. We discuss this issue in Chapter 7 ("The Direct-Licensing Controversy"), but for now it's worth noting that what may be at stake is the business model of paying writers directly.

Whereas ASCAP and BMI operate on a not-for-profit basis, SESAC retains some income as profit. While ASCAP and BMI distribute all income from performance royalties to their composer and publisher affiliates (less administrative fees of approximately 10 percent), SESAC retains an undisclosed amount of performance royalty income. SESAC is also unique among the US performing-rights organizations in that it does not offer open membership—one must be approved to join. It is important to note that none of the PROs requires writers to have a third-party publisher. Writers can be their own publishers until they enter into an agreement with a major or indie music publisher.

Important and Growing Source of Income

PROs represent a very important source of income for writers and publishers. We've established that public-performance royalties account for more than half of the 2.2 billion dollars generated by the music publishing business in the United States.[69] In fact, even as income from mechanicals has fallen through the years (see the introduction and "How Much Various Users Pay the PROs" below), ASCP and BMI report that they are making more money than ever. BMI reported record-setting revenues and royalty distributions for the fiscal year ending June 30, 2013. Revenues increased by $45 million, a 5 percent gain over the prior fiscal year, exceeding $944 million.[70] According to BMI's website:

> This resulted in a historic high royalty distribution of $814 million to BMI-affiliated songwriters, composers, and music publishers. Royalty distributions increased by $64 million or 9 percent compared to the previous year. This represents the largest fiscal year revenue posted and royalties distributed in the Company's 74 years of operation and tops a five-year period in which BMI generated more than $4.5 billion in revenues and paid out royalties of $4 billion.[71]

ASCAP also announced record earnings in 2013 and that it had paid out more than $851.2 million in royalties to its songwriter, composer, and publisher members in the calendar year ending 2013, an increase of nearly $24 million over 2012.[72]

How Much Various Users Pay the PROs

The fees charged by the PROs to those users who transmit music to the public, such as radio, television, Internet radio, and interactive streaming, are usually based on a percentage of income, including advertising revenue and subscription income if any. The aggregate amount payable to all three PROs generally falls between three and six percent, depending on the type of service, with interactive music services at the high end of the scale. We will discuss specific numbers in the Chapters 5 and 6. As we will explain in Chapter 4, permanent downloading does not trigger a public-performance royalty so long as the user does not hear the song as its being downloaded.

Physical venues will generally pay the PROs a fee calculated on a number of different factors, such as whether admission is charged, the seating capacity and size of the venue, and whether live music (as opposed to recorded music) is presented. All three PROs provide many of the basic licenses for all kinds of services and venues on their websites.

How They Pay Their Members

As we discussed at beginning of this section, all three PROs pay writers and publishers equally (50/50) and pay the writers directly (so publishers cannot recoup any unpaid advances from the writer's share). But when it comes to calculating what a given song earns, each PRO uses its own algorithms to credit each song in its repertoire with a share of the money it collects. ASCAP's website explains:

> The value of each performance is determined by several factors, including the amount of license fees collected in a medium (television, cable, radio, etc.), how much we receive in fees from the licensee that hosted the performance, and the type of performance (feature performance, background music, theme song, etc.).

The formulas used for actually computing royalties are extremely complicated because of the many different types of users of music—for instance, bars, restaurants, concert halls, radio (including local stations, networks, small towns, and major markets), television (including public access, basic and premium cable, local broadcast and network), Internet, satellite, mobile, etc.—and the many different ways music can be used, especially on radio and television—for instance, full songs vs. excerpts, featured vs. non-featured use, theme music as opposed to music used in a program, the time of day a program is broadcast, etc.[73] There has never been a consensus on whether one PRO pays more for any particular performance than the others. If there were, no one would join the other two. But over the years there has been general criticism that songs that do not play on commercial radio or TV in major markets will not receive their fair share of earnings.

How You Can Get Paid

Perhaps in reaction to this criticism, all three PROs now have a special program that differs from the others in its details but is the same in purpose: They all pay songwriters who play their own songs at venues of any size. This means that songwriters can now receive royalties when they perform their own songs in venues of all sizes throughout the country by just providing the basic details of the performance (usually a set list) and which of their songs were performed. The amount you receive may depend on the size of the venue or the license fee paid by the venue to the PRO. As venues with larger capacities pay a larger license fee to the PROs, the royalty generated by these venues will be larger than venues with smaller capacities. None of the PROs provide actual numbers, but one of my clients faithfully reported each of her gigs (about one a week) at small clubs that did not charge admission, and she made $1,200 (which represented about $3 per song) over a three-month period. Twelve hundred dollars is not a lot of money, but it was $1;200 more than she received from any of the clubs and much more than the she got from passing the hat. If you are a young or new singer, songwriter, or jazz musician, you should definitely take advantage of these programs. Here are the relevant webpages for each PRO:

http://www.ascap.com/onstage/
http://www.bmi.com/special/bmi_live
http://www.sesac.com/WritersPublishers/HowWePay/LivePerformances.aspx

Dramatic Works

PROs do not grant public-performance licenses for dramatic works. The term "*dramatic works*" refers to productions that use music to directly advance the plot, such as opera, musical theater, or ballet. Public-performance rights for music in dramatic works are called "grand rights." The producer of a dramatic work must negotiate such rights directly with the publisher or composer.

We discuss the definition of dramatic works in more detail, as well as the standard business terms that apply to licensing songs for dramatic works, in Part II (see Chapter 12).

Mechanical Rights and Royalties

"Mechanical rights" refers to the right to reproduce and distribute to the public a copyrighted musical composition or song in audio recordings referred to in the Copyright Act as "phonorecords," including CDs, tapes, vinyl, or in any digital format such as MP3 or WAV. Under Section 106 of the Copyright Act, owners of song copyrights have the exclusive right to make copies of and distribute phonorecords containing their song.[74] The use of the word "mechanical" to describe this right dates back to the days of the player piano, when a mechanical object—a cylinder wrapped with perforated paper—was inserted into a piano, and the music was literally "mechanically" reproduced.

Section 115 Compulsory License

Licenses to exploit mechanical rights are called *mechanical licenses.* The Copyright Act contains "compulsory" licensing provisions governing the making and distribution of phonorecords containing musical compositions, although "dramatic works" such as operas are excluded from the compulsory license (see Chapter 12). Section 115 of the Act provides that once phonorecords of a nondramatic musical work have been publicly distributed in the United States with the copyright owner's consent, anyone else may obtain a compulsory license to make and distribute phonorecords of the work without securing the owner's consent. For instance, once the Beatles recorded and released the record containing the song "Yesterday" by Lennon and McCartney, anyone else could rerecord "Yesterday" without having to obtain consent so long as they paid the compulsory mechanical license fee.

Anyone may use the compulsory licensing provisions of the Copyright Act to rerecord a previously released song by following the procedures established by the Act. Those procedures require giving notice to the owner and paying a statutory royalty for each phonorecord manufactured and distributed. This is called a "statutory" or "compulsory" license because the copyright owner cannot deny permission. On the other hand, it ensures that copyright owners will be paid for the use of their work. For the period from January 1, 2004, to December 31, 2005, the statutory mechanical royalty rate was 8.5 cents for songs of five minutes or less. As of January 1, 2006, and to the current day, the statutory mechanical rate is 9.10 cents for songs of five minutes or less, or 1.75 cents per minute or fraction thereof over five minutes. For example:

E 5:01 to 6:00 = $.105 (6 x $.0175 = $.105)
E 6:01 to 7:00 = $.1225 (7 x $.0175 = $.1225)
E 7:01 to 8:00 = $.14 (8 x $.0175 = $.14)

As we discuss in Chapter 3, these rates apply to permanent digital downloads of songs as well as CDs and other physical formats.

Now that we know what the compulsory license for mechanicals is, how to secure such a license, and how much it costs, let's be clear about what it does not cover. The compulsory license is available only for musical works that have been previously authorized for release to the public. It does not extend to recordings of songs that have never been released to the public. Those would require a special license sometimes referred to as a "first-use mechanical," and the copyright owner can deny permission or ask for more money. Also, you cannot secure a compulsory mechanical license for the use of music in audiovisual works such as music videos, television programs, or motion pictures (see the discussion of synchronization rights in the next section and in Chapter 10). The technical reason for this is that the compulsory mechanical license only gives you the right to make and distribute "phonorecords" of a previously recorded song, and "phonorecords" do not include audiovisual works such as music videos, TV programs, and movies. It also makes sense that the law limits the compulsory license to "phonorecords," because it would be unfair to the copyright owner of a song to be paid the same amount for different uses that may be radically unlike in terms of their financial character. For instance, think of the use of "New York, New York" by Fred Ebb and John Kander over the credits in the next Steven Spielberg blockbuster, compared to the use of the same song in an indie documentary film about New York City. As we discuss in depth in Part II, although use of music in audiovisual works is subject to negotiation, the "standard" fees paid for use of songs, even famous ones, in documentaries is radically different (that is, much less expensive) than for major motion pictures (that is, extremely expensive). It would be unreasonable to make the owner of a song accept the same compensation for these very different uses.

The compulsory mechanical license was primarily intended to permit "covers," that is, new recordings of songs by different performers that are faithful to the original music. Although the compulsory license includes the privilege of making a musical arrangement of the work "to the extent necessary to conform it to the style or manner of interpretation of the performance involved," Section 115 specifically provides that the arrangement "shall not change the basic melody or fundamental character of the work, and shall not be subject to protection as a derivative work . . . except with the express consent of the copyright owner." For instance, you cannot change the lyrics. If you do, you will need the consent of the copyright owner.

The Harry Fox Agency

The Harry Fox Agency, organized by the NMPA in 1927, handles Section 115 compulsory mechanical licenses for the major publishers, most indies, and many songwriters who are self-published. Like the PROs, HFA is basically set up to license and collect monies for one kind of right; whereas that right is public performance for the PROs, it's mechanicals for HFA. The Fox Agency acts as licensing agent for more than 27,000 music publishers, who in turn represent the interests of more than 160,000 songwriters. Although the rate is the same whether the licensee obtains a license from the owner or from the Fox Agency, or if the licensee goes through the procedures set up by the Copyright Act, the license issued by the Fox Agency is far simpler to obtain and comply with. For example, HFA makes it very easy to secure a license through its website, www.harryfox.com. It also only requires quarterly accounting instead of the monthly accounting required under the Copyright Act. Also, the Copyright Act requires filing with the copyright owner a detailed annual statement of account certified by a public accountant. So if you are planning to release your own original recording of someone else's song and your arrangement of the song hasn't substantially altered it, the quickest and most efficient path is to license the mechanical right through Harry Fox. We talk about this process in more detail in Chapter 11, particularly "Covers and Parodies."

Sync Rights and Licenses

The right to record a musical composition in synchronization with an audiovisual work such as a motion picture, television program, television commercial, music video production, or website is called the synchronization (or "sync") right. Similar to the mechanical right, it is based on the exclusive right of copyright owners to make and distribute copies in Section 106 of the Copyright Act. That's because to "synchronize a song to a visual image involves making a copy of that song. To sell or license the resulting product would be to distribute it."[75]

There is no compulsory license for sync rights. Each sync license must be negotiated with the owner of the copyright of the song or his or her representative. The Harry Fox Agency used to handle sync licenses for some of its publisher members but discontinued this service in June 2002. As a rule, one must secure synchronization rights by contacting the songwriter or his or her representative, usually a music publisher (see the the upcoming section "Role of the Music Publisher"). You can search for publisher information using the database of the Fox Agency, www.songfile.com, as well as the websites of the PROs (see Chapter 9 for research techniques).

We discuss sync licensing for all kinds of projects in depth in Chapter 10 of this book—but it's worth noting here that the fees for sync licenses will vary dramatically depending on the nature of the project and the identity of the song. For instance, it will cost a great deal more to use a song by the Beatles in a major motion picture than a song by an obscure garage band in a low-budget indie feature. It's also important to point out that producers of movies, TV shows, and ad campaigns are usually expected to obtain sync rights to use songs in their projects, but television networks and stations, cable networks, and websites like Hulu or Netflix are usually responsible for obtaining blanket licenses for the public performance of songs from ASCAP, BMI, and SESAC.

Over the years the sync business has grown in income as TV shows and Hollywood movies adopted the habit of using popular music in their projects and the advertising business largely switched from playing jingles to using well-known songs to sell goods and services. (See "A Brief History of Music in Advertising" in Chapter 10.)

Sheet Music and Other Sources of Income

Sheet Music

After performance, mechanical, and sync, the other single biggest way songs may generate income is sheet music, whether on their own or as one song in a "folio" (for instance, *The Best of the Beatles* or *Movie Songs of the '60s*) containing a number of songs, and whether on paper or in digital form. Successful songs may also be distributed in a multitude of arrangements for different instruments. Orchestral sheet music is usually sold as a set containing sheet music specifically for the conductor and different arrangements for various players. Of course, after Gutenberg introduced the modern printing press in the 15th century, and before the inventions of the phonograph and the radio in the late 19th century, music publishing and the sheet music business were basically synonymous. Now, however, sheet music only accounts for a fraction of the 5 percent that the NMPA refers to as "other" income.

Most music publishers enter into agreements with print publishers such as Hal Leonard or Alfred, who specialize in publishing sheet music. These print publishers pay a royalty of between 40 and 50 cents per single sheet of music and approximately 10 to 12 percent of the retail price of the folio prorated by the number of the publisher's songs in the collection. In turn, the publishers pay their writers from 6 cents to 10 cents per song and 10 to 12 percent of the *wholesale* price of the folio prorated by the number of that writer's songs in the folio.[76]

Other Income

Other possible sources of income for a song are myriad. Here are some examples: karaoke (both DVD and online), greeting cards that play music from a mini-chip when they open, dolls or toys that perform songs, reprints of lyrics in books and games, and on T-shirts and other merchandise,[77] doorbells that play music instead of ring, and even "singing fish"—recall the gift that Meadow gives her father, Tony Soprano, of a largemouth bass mounted on a plaque that sings "Take Me to the River" by Al Green and Mabon "Teenie" Hodges. Hodges said he received more royalties from the fish than he did from the record.[78]

Role of the Music Publishers

Who They Are

Music publishers are companies that first and foremost ensure that songwriters and composers receive payment when their compositions are used commercially. They also perform many other functions, we will soon discuss. Through an agreement called a publishing contract, a songwriter or composer transfers the right to collect these monies to the publisher (except for the writer's share of public performance monies—see "Public-Performance Rights and Royalties" presented earlier in this chapter) and usually, but not always, "assigns" the copyright of his or her composition to a publishing company. Often, but not always, publishers pay writers up-front cash advances to induce them to sign these agreements.

The largest music publisher is Sony ATV, which recently took over the administration of the EMI catalogue. Sony ATV currently has a market share of approximately one-third of the global music publishing business. The next three biggest are Universal Music Publishing, Warner/Chappell, and BMG Rights Management.[79] Each of these publishers, except for BMG, is associated with the three major labels, i.e., Sony, Universal and Warner. However, there are tens of thousands of other publishers throughout the world, ranging in size from big companies to one-person operations.

What They Do

The relationships between songwriters and music publishers vary according to the deals that we describe below, but historically songwriters granted publishers the exclusive right to exploit songs written during the term of the agreement, and the writer and publisher shared fees that were received from most uses on a 50/50 basis.[80] The publisher's 50 percent was generally referred to as the "publisher's share," and the other 50 percent was known as the "writer's share." While this standard deal has widely been replaced by what is known as a co-pub deal (see "Music Publishing Contracts" below), the essence of all publishing deals is the same: The publisher gains the exclusive right to collect monies earned from the commercial exploitation of the songs subject to the agreement. As discussed in "Other Income" previously, a popular song can earn money in a remarkable number of ways in addition to the biggest money makers, public performance, mechanicals, sync, and sheet music. The publisher's primary responsibility is to assure that all these uses are properly licensed and paid for.

But the publisher also undertakes other essential functions, including negotiating and issuing licenses for use of the songs; registering copyrights in songs with governmental bodies,

PROs, and mechanical collections collection societies (see the discussion on registration at the beginning of this chapter); and other administrative chores. Here is a list of additional services that publishers provide to their writers:

- Produce demos
- Secure record deals for writers who are also performers
- Secure covers by third-party artists
- Secure placements in advertising campaigns
- Register songs with collections agents, including PROs and mechanical societies
- Monitor payments and make sure royalties (from record companies, video distributors, ringtone companies, television and film producers, etc.) are paid on time
- Check royalty statements for accuracy and audit licensees in case of possible underpayment
- Litigate against licensees who fail to pay or against users who do not acquire licenses
- Promote interest in songs to representatives in foreign countries
- Lobby for legislation helpful to writers
- Negotiate blanket deals with services such as interactive streaming

Since publishers generally negotiate rights on behalf of the writer, if, for example, you were to seek a license to use "Wild Horses" by Mick Jagger and Keith Richards in your movie, you would approach the song's publisher, ABKCO, not Mick and Keith. If a song has more than one writer, or if it contains a sample, it may be represented by more than one publisher. But even a song by a single writer can have more than one publisher due to special agreements or catalogue acquisitions.

Music Publishing Contracts: Single-Song, Traditional-Term, Co-Pub, and Admin Deals

The following are thumbnail descriptions of the four basic agreements between music publishers and writers:

> *Single-song agreements:* This agreement is designed to apply to one song or a group of songs that the writer and publisher have mutually decided on. Additional songs may be added with the mutual approval of the parties. Under this arrangement the writer will usually assign the copyright in the subject songs and 50 percent of income. The publisher may or may not pay an advance. This type of deal provides the writer the benefit of reserving rights in songs that he or she writes that are not named in the agreement.
>
> *Traditional-term contracts:* Under this agreement the writer assigns the copyright in any song written during the tenure of the agreement. The term for this type of deal is usually one year to two years, with several more options of one year to two years each that the publisher can elect to exercise at its discretion. The publisher will usually pay the writer an advance against future royalties, and it is not unusual for major publishers to pay commercially successful writers advances of six figures. But this type of deal is also risky for writers, as the songs could potentially end up "on the shelf" if the publisher loses interest in the work, and the writer cannot get the copyrights back until 35 years after the transfer (see "Termination Rights (How to Get Your Copyrights Back)" earlier in this chapter).
>
> *Co-publishing deals:* As writers gained bargaining power starting in the '60s with artists who performed their own songs, such as Bob Dylan, the Beatles, the Stones, Bruce

Springsteen, Michael Jackson, and many others, co-pub deals started to replace the traditional exclusive-term deals. Basically, the difference is that the writer only assigns 50 percent of the copyright in his or songs and retains 50 percent of the copyright. The publisher only receives half of the publisher's share, so the writer ends up with 75 percent of the income from his or her songs instead of just 50 percent.

Admin deals: Hugely successful writers can get a publisher to perform all the functions named above without giving up their copyrights. Instead, the publisher merely earns from 10 percent to 20 percent of the income from each song. Moderately successful writers may get an admin deal, but the advances they receive will be more modest than if they entered into a co-pub or traditional-term deal.

Other Players: Sync Reps and Music Libraries

Sync reps, also known as licensing agents or simply as reps, will represent songwriters for the sole purpose of generating sync income. One major corporate player in this area is Pump Audio, now owned by Getty Images. Pump Audio represents independent music from around the world, for licensing to advertising, television, film, and web clients. There are legions of other firms and individuals in the business of trying to get songs placed in these "windows." Some offer exclusive deals, others non-exclusive, but usually there is no advance payment. The commission varies but is usually 50 percent. For a songwriter, the major advantage of a non-exclusive deal is that more than one person or firm is shopping your music, and you can do direct deals without paying any commission. The advantages of an exclusive deal are that some good firms will not do a non-exclusive, and there is less likelihood that a particular user will be annoyed that the same song is being shopped by multiple operators. At the end of the day, the best rep for you is the one that will make the most (and most lucrative) placements for your music.

Music libraries perform basically the same function as reps, except that they will often create their own music for clients by using in-house staff for particular jobs so they can offer both the publishing and the master rights. They are also set up to do bulk deals and provide cut rates. For instance, a Hollywood studio or TV network will rely on libraries to provide generic music that they can use in diverse projects without spending a lot of money. See later in this chapter for an interview with Adam Taylor, the president of APM, one of the largest music libraries.

Interview with Jake Wisely, Cofounder of Bicycle Music

Jake Wisely is a partner and copresident of the Bicycle Music Company, an independent music publisher and rights holder based in Beverly Hills and New York City. Wisely was instrumental in the 2005 acquisition and funding of Bicycle, a family business established in 1974. Since then, he has helped to usher the company into a new age, overseeing the business affairs and administration of an ever-expanding catalogue of evergreen songs spanning genres and eras. Since Wisely and his partners took the helm at Bicycle, it has amassed standards and hits as well as song catalogs by such legendary recording artists as Dwight Yoakam, Cyndi Lauper, Roy Ayers, Nine Inch Nails, Jefferson Starship, Pete Seeger, and Tammy Wynette. In 2013 Bicycle Music was named independent Music Publisher of the Year by the AIMP (Association of Independent Music Publishers). In this interview, Jake Wisely and I discuss how songwriters and composers make a living in the music business and how music publishers assist them in doing so.

SG: In the early part of your career you worked at ASCAP in the membership department. What was that like?

JW: It was a real eye opener to start as a membership representative of ASCAP in Chicago, where my main goal was to basically sign up new songwriters, those writers who had potential to go on and receive broadcast performances of their works from live performance through to radio, TV, and any other place that publicly performs music. At the time there was no such thing really as Internet or satellite radio, and the Internet, in terms of music, was in its infancy. We supported the membership in any way we could, which was through hosting showcases and events; sponsoring opportunities for these acts to perform at South by Southwest, CMJ, or other music conferences; and linking them up with record labels and other people, producers, booking agents, managers . . . anything that assisted the songwriter or the songwriter and the working band with their career growth. Our only competition was BMI and, to a certain extent, SESAC. It was a very eclectic job. Sometimes it was just feeding touring musicians as they came through Chicago; taking them out to dinner. Other times it was helping to sort through legalese in contracts and things they may have been contending with as songwriters.

SG: Your comments are important because, although ASCAP, BMI, and SESAC are all primarily collection societies, a lot of people who sign up with these organizations don't know all the resources that they have and their ability to help them as songwriters.

JW: That's true. And it's all about having a relationship with individuals there. Obviously, ASCAP's membership is huge, and the membership department is relatively small. But all of the PROs make a great effort to support their membership in more ways than just licensing and paying royalties.

SG: You moved to the West Coast and held jobs at both EMI and Universal Music Publishing. Tell us, first of all, how these publishing companies were different from ASCAP, and describe your role at these organizations.

JW: As you know, the PROs' principal function is to collect public-performance royalties on behalf of songwriters and publishers. Publishers, on the other hand, collect monies on behalf of their writers from all the other sources of income, such as synchronization of music in movies, TV shows, video games, mechanical income from sales of records containing their songs, use of music in merchandise such as toys or greeting cards, sheet music both physical and digital—the list is almost endless. Plus, publishers try to generate more income from individual songs by pitching them to music supervisors, producers, artists, advertisers, and on and on. My jobs at EMI and Universal were not totally dissimilar to my work at ASCAP in that I was assisting songwriters, but my principal role at these publishing houses was to find the next big thing, to identify the songwriter who was going to go on to earn a lot of money. Of course at ASCAP we also wanted hit songwriters to maintain ASCAP's effective market share, so that its weight in negotiations with broadcasters was substantial enough to keep the numbers going up. In any event, at EMI and Universal my experiences were incredible with respect to learning the publishing business, learning the pitfalls as well as the upsides and nuances, where the money comes from, how various types of deals can be or are made. But my experience there also led me to understand that I was probably more suited for the independent music publishing world.

SG: What were biggest source of revenues for the publishers?

JW: Mechanical royalties in the form of compositions that are sold on compact disc used to be much larger in the heyday of the record business and the publishing business. Mechanical royalties from record sales still constitute the largest part of earnings. But mechanical revenues from interactive streaming are on the rise and hopefully will compensate for decreased CD sales and downloads. Otherwise, synchronization income has become a much larger portion of the pie. Publishers put great effort into securing uses in film, TV, video games, commercials, advertising, trailers for film—all different types of new media. Then there's a whole host of other income, as I mentioned, from print sheet music and online sheet music, and music lyrics online becoming a growing market.

SG: I know from personal experience that there can be a great deal of money to be made from sync alone. I recently licensed a hit song from the 60's for several hundred thousand dollars for a national TV campaign.

You said you felt more comfortable in an indie environment, then you went on to help acquire Bicycle, and now you are a leading indie publisher. What made you decide to leave the majors and cofound an indie publishing company?

JW: I have a very entrepreneurial spirit, and may not be the most corporate animal. At EMI and Universal there was just a more limited scope of what I was expected to do within the context of doing A&R at a major music publisher. As an indie I can sign a songwriter or a catalogue that isn't necessarily going to be successful on the charts, but might be more important for synchronization. Or I could sign a composer who earns more from performance of his movie scores. Whereas at the majors, in the A&R departments where I worked, there was more of the notion of chasing the charts. The next huge hit was the holy grail. In the independent world you can wear a lot of hats. At a major you might step on a lot of people's toes in the process. Ultimately, in the indie world you can bring more opportunities to the table that majors may not necessarily be interested in. They already have large, diverse catalogues. To be able to build a large and diverse catalogue ultimately from scratch is quite an opportunity and very exciting.

SG: I know what you're saying, from having been with Sony for many years. People were pigeonholed into their roles, and at the end of the day it was just about the stars. But, talking about stars, from looking at your website, you do seem to have a lot of them, such as Dwight Yoakam, Cyndi Lauper, Roy Ayers, and Nine Inch Nails. How did you get to work with these big names?

JW: All of the songwriters and artists that you mentioned were actually brought to us through purchases of catalogues and acquisitions. That is one type of deal that we make. Buying copyrights, in certain instances you have heirs or estates that are looking to sell through all the rights associated with songwriters. That's how we acquired Tammy Wynette's songs, for instance.

That said, we absolutely are active in signing new songwriters and signing legacy songwriters to new deals as well.

SG: Tell us about some of the deals you make with new songwriters and catalogues.

JW: Deals take many shapes. First and foremost, for a lot of the legacy artists who are more interested in retaining their rights for the long haul, it could be a very simple administration deal where we will go out and handle all of the title registrations at societies throughout the world and basically collect the money. Ultimately we then account that income to those writers. Those tend to be percentage-based deals; the terms often vary based on whether or not that songwriter or catalogue owner is seeking an advance royalty payment. The more they get up front, the less favorable the back end.

The rates are anywhere from 90/10, where we would just retain 10 percent of gross receipts, all the way up to 25 percent, depending upon how aggressive we are with the advance.

Twenty-five percent typically ends up being the share that publishers retain under a "co-publishing" agreement, which traditionally splits that copyright 50/50 between the songwriter and the publisher, often coming with perpetual, at least for the life of copyright, worldwide administration. Certain territories can be excluded, but that 75/25 split is really based on the notion that 50 percent is the songwriter share and the other 50 percent is the publisher share split 50/50, hence on gross receipts 75/25.

Then of course there's the outright publishing deal, which was more traditional in the earlier days of rock 'n' roll and country music. In these deals writers don't retain any share of copyright. These are usually work-for-hire agreements. The benefit to songwriters under these deals is that the publisher has more incentive to exploit those songs and generate more income from them because the publisher is receiving the full 50 percent. And of course, for a publisher, having 100 percent of the control can be a great benefit.

SG: The co-pub deal, the 25 percent deal, seems to be the most popular. Does that mean songwriters have gotten more powerful? That they've been able to avoid the full publishing agreement, which is a 50/50 split, and now they're taking 75 percent?

JW: I think the evolution of the industry has certainly developed different standards. Competition is really what that's all about. When it comes time to bid on the next big thing, certainly one way to improve your deal is to make sure that that songwriter actually retains some portion of the copyright. There are many terms that obviously have come to benefit the songwriters over time. The pendulum swings a little bit. Back in the '90s there was a lot of competition, and there were a lot of publishers doing co-publishing deals that actually included reversion rights—that is, contractual reversions where rights in songs would come back to the songwriter after a certain period of time. To me, that's basically a glorified administration deal. So, there really is a movement in a different direction now for life of copyright, but co-publishing remains a very strong standard, particularly in rock and pop music.

SG: I think we should point out that this is a lot like professional sports. We're not talking about amateurs. We're talking about songwriters who have an established record of success and who are making real money. The major publishers are not going to sign you unless you already have a strong income flow or a star just recorded one of your songs. People should know that they can't just walk off the street into some publishing company and expect a big advance and a co-pub deal.

Is there more room for emerging songwriters at Bicycle than, say, at Sony ATV or Warner/Chappell, who focus on the biggest players?

JW: There are major music publishers who are willing to take a risk on a developing writer. There are a lot of executives who have different styles as well. But I think independents are generally more willing to take a flyer on something that, again, doesn't have a huge price tag attached to it, but that they can get their hands dirty with and be involved.

SG: You said that in the '90s there was increasing competition among publishers for successful catalogues or successful writers. But now we have seen a lot of consolidation. Recently Sony/ATV, which was one of the biggest, acquired EMI, which I think was the biggest.

What is your opinion of the increasing consolidation in the music publishing business? Do you think it's a good thing for the music business and songwriters?

JW: I actually think that it can create opportunity for independent publishers like Bicycle. There comes a time when songwriters feel like they're getting lost in the shuffle at companies that large, with catalogues of a couple million songs, as you refer to Sony/ATV and EMI combined. And sometimes these writers become free because of contractual reversions, and there are also termination rights in accordance with the copyright act that can allow certain writers to reclaim their rights at certain times.

By the same token, we work with those companies all the time and facilitate opportunities for songs we co-publish with them. In certain instances these companies actually administer rights that we own. There is a spirit of cooperation among publishers.

SG: Has the dramatic decline in record sales that has devastated the recording industry affected the music publishing business as much in terms of lost income?

JW: The publishing business was always a little more diverse than the record business. For instance, in terms of broadcast revenues, radio pays music publishers and songwriters through ASCAP, BMI, and SESAC, but there's still no performance royalty right for record companies with respect to normal broadcast.

SG: Tell us about the culture of Bicycle. You've acquired catalogues, but you also deal with songwriters. Can you give us a feel for how much of your business is from catalogue and how much is from emerging songwriters, or new songwriters, or established songwriters you've done deals with directly?

JW: I don't know the exact ratio of that; I think it's not really an analytic that we look at, but I can say that a good portion of our catalogue, probably upwards of 90 percent of it, really is legacy works. When I say 90 percent I mean in terms of just song count. In terms of earnings, a new artist can burn very hot, very quickly. So in one year we may have a top songwriter that's somebody that's brand new, and when you put them up against guys who have written songs like "Slow Ride," "Sister Christian," or "Eye of the Tiger," or Cyndi Lauper's "Time After Time," or Glen Ballard's "Man in the Mirror," you look at those earnings, you go, "That's staggering." And then you realize that one quick burn from a new artist can outpace even those great classics.

SG: Well, for emerging songwriters out there, what are you looking for? What would qualify someone to be seriously considered for a deal with Bicycle?

JW: It's always nice when somebody is going to meet us halfway. They've already demonstrated their ability to network and find opportunity for themselves. If somebody's relying solely on their publisher—or, for that matter, their manager or record label or booking agent—to make or break their career, I think that that's somebody who is going to be sorely disappointed and probably pointing the finger very quickly at somebody other than themselves for why they're not the next big thing. We are always looking for self-starters, people who have made their presence felt, either through the A&R world, or through the film and TV world, or through their social media and through their ability to build a fan base.

Obviously character and personality and being somebody who we could really feel good about working for is paramount. We want to make sure we're working with people with whom we can have a basis of mutual respect and whom we can meet halfway.

SG: Do you listen to unsolicited material?

JW: There can be liabilities associated with receiving unsolicited materials, same in the book-publishing world. There is always a chance that that person will claim that you stole his work. Usually the best way to submit material, for both the writer and the publisher, is through a trusted source, a lawyer or a manager.

SG: So many people are complaining about Spotify not paying enough money or Pandora trying to get ASCAP's rates down. There's constant harping about songwriters or artists who have tens of thousands of hits on one of these services and are making very little money from it. What's your point of view on that controversy?

JW: It's definitely all about scale at this point. I think the record business and, to a large degree, the publishing business are relying on the fact that streaming will become more ubiquitous. Until such time as you're paying for not just music, but movies, TV, perhaps even other intellectual property through maybe your ISP or through your cell phone provider, that's a tenuous bet, because right now we haven't seen the earnings. Certainly they're not making up for the lost mechanical revenues from declining CD sales. But, by the same token, you have the biggest players in the digital domain entering the market now. Only recently iTunes Radio launched, joining other major players including Google Play and Amazon. This could be the beginning of the real tipping point. It's yet to be seen.

SG: What's next for Bicycle?

JW: We've recently acquired a number of independent record label catalogues, including Delicious Vinyls, Tone Lōc, Young M.C., the Pharcyde, Born Jamericans, the Brand New Heavies, incredible stuff there. Also we acquired the Wind-Up records catalogue, including all the records by Evanescence, Creed, Caesar, and Finger Eleven. We think diversification really is the key and that a rights company, not just a publishing company or a record company, represents principles that are key to the future of any music company. Diversification in investing is kind of a standard of investing, and what we are, to our investors, is a diverse investment. That's what we try to achieve. Ultimately I think continuing to grow through acquisition, but also through new songwriter and new artist signing, is where we're headed.

Interview with Adam Taylor, President of Leading Music Library APM Music

APM Music, a joint venture between Universal Music Publishing and Sony ATV, is one of the largest and most successful music libraries in the world. As its president, Adam Taylor continues to grow one of the largest and most diverse collections of original production music available, including every conceivable genre of music. Before coming to lead APM, he was founding partner of Goldman/Taylor Entertainment, where he developed numerous properties, including the television series *Confessions of Crime*, for Lifetime Network, and the PBS series *Joseph Campbell: Mythos*, hosted by Academy Award winner Susan Sarandon in partnership with the Joseph Campbell Foundation. In this interview we discuss the role of the music library and how it differs from that of the music publisher.

SG: What is a music library, and how does it differ from being a music publisher?

AT: We are publishers, but a music library is a specific kind of publisher and has a specific kind of structure. Libraries were organized to make the licensing of music for various programs easy and seamless. Consequently, we control rights in master recordings as well as the musical compositions, and we can grant rights in both. Most music publishers only control compositions, not recordings. So libraries are a one-stop shop for everything that you need as a producer of a movie, TV show, soap opera, commercial, or any other project. Another unique feature of a music library is that the music is pre-cleared. If you are willing to pay our rate card, or if you have a pre-negotiated agreement with us for some kind of discount or blanket agreement, you can use the music for your production. You don't even need to check with us before you use the music. There is a rate card, which specifies the rate, and every track in the library is the same price. It's just the prices vary depending upon what you want to use the track for. So it would be relatively inexpensive if you wanted to use it for a local radio spot, but would be considerably more expensive if you wanted to use it for a national film trailer campaign, for example. Those are the essential elements that distinguish a music library from just a publishing company.

SG: If I am a songwriter, why would I need a publisher or a library, or would I want to represented by both?

AT: If you are a songwriter or composer, or you're just producing tracks, you can have certain songs with publishers and you can have other tracks with libraries. It's a matter of trying to develop a variety of different income streams for yourself. If you look at the number of writers and composers in the world, there are many, and only a very small percentage of them can really make a living from the commercial release of records. Especially with the demise of the record company model, for many people that isn't an avenue anymore.

Of course, the advent of all the digital technology has made it less expensive to produce music and gives an artist more control over distribution. So people are looking at a variety of different sources of revenue—putting things up on iTunes and on YouTube, and streaming revenue from Pandora and Spotify and other sources. And then, of course, sync; the synchronization of music into programming has become a very viable income stream for songwriters and composers. So we have all kinds of people coming to us, many of whom have some kind of commercial releases, but also would like to do library.

SG: How big is APM? How many songs do you currently represent, and how many songwriters?

AT: APM is a joint venture between Universal Music and Sony ATV. We have approximately 400,000 recordings and songs by about 4,500 different composers. The music started being produced for the library in the early 1950s—for example, the original Superman series with George Reeves is mostly our music. And there are archival recordings that have been acquired that go back to the early 1900s. Between us and the catalogues that we represent we release probably 2,000 or 3,000 new recordings every month.

SG: Can you give us an idea of how much money is involved in placing syncs?

AT: In terms of the pricing, a variety of different things come into play. Our business can generally be divided into two halves in terms of the type of sync revenue that exists: needle drop and what we call term contracts. A needle drop is a track at a time: some clients have not made an up-front commitment for a certain amount of money; they just have a willingness to pay our rate card, or we have a pre-negotiated discounted rate card with them, like we have with most motion picture studios, for example. So they might come to us and say, "I'm looking for a track for this project, what do you have?" Or they go to our search engine, which is what most people do, and they look through and find tracks. If they find one they want to use, they put it into the program, they let us know, and we invoice them. So that's the needle drop side of the business. The rates can vary from $50 to $75 for a local TV spot, or even less for a web ad. Or it can go all the way up to $7500 or more for a film trailer campaign. In the advertising world, depending upon how the music is being used, and other factors, a national campaign can cost $7,500 or more. It really depends on a variety of factors, but that's the range.

SG: Of course, we are not talking about a well-known hit song. I guess that's why they call it library music. Now, I licensed "Born to Be Wild" by Steppenwolf for a national TV commercial. It was $375,000 for the song and $375,000 for the master!

So, if you're an advertiser or movie studio, you can spend a lot less money by using a library, correct?

AT: For sure. You're not going to necessarily get a popular song that people know, and so if that's important to you you're going to have to pay the extra dollars. But for us—I don't think I know the rate card by heart, but a national campaign can be as little as a couple of thousand dollars. So, obviously, from a price perspective it's completely different. It's just a matter of creatively what the producers are looking for, and financially what they're able to afford.

I want to go back to answer the second part of your question. The other part of our business is what we call term contracts. And that's where clients commit up front to a payment for the use of a certain amount of money, or music for a certain number of productions. They could say, we want a blanket agreement for an episode or a blanket agreement for a series. For example, we do *The Daily Show*. So we have a blanket agreement with *The Daily Show* where they can use our music on all of their episodes, as much music as they want. We also do blanket agreements with networks, where they can use our music on all of their programs and all of their promos. We also have a lot of just promo-only deals, where music in the program itself is based on needle drop licensing, but music in the promos is covered by blanket agreements.

SG: Is the Jon Stewart theme from your library?

AT: No, that's not. Most shows like to develop their own themes and they like to own the themes because there's a lot of money in owning themes from the performance revenue perspective.

[Author's note: Adam is referring to monies collected by PROs such as ASCAP and BMI.] We generally don't own themes. We did the *Oprah Winfrey Show* for about 15 years or so; we did probably 90 percent of the music on the show, but she owned the theme. Our biggest theme is the *Monday Night Football* theme, which was a library track. We also own the two themes from *This Week in Baseball*; we own the *People's Court* theme, the US Open, Wimbledon, and a few other ones.

SG: So every time it plays you get the ASCAP, BMI, or SESAC performing-rights royalties?

AT: Correct.

SG: How does APM find new music to sign? Are you looking to add more music to your library now, and if so, what kind of music are you looking for?

AT: Well, we're always looking for new writers, new music. Clients always want something new. The traditional way of bringing artists' music into the library is to commission it, so when composers approach us to see if we're interested in working with them, we commission a song or a CD and it goes into the library. That's one whole approach, and that is still most of our music; we continue to get music that way.

I should add that we produce music ourselves, but the preponderance of our music is actually produced by other libraries that we represent. We work very closely with them. Many of them are abroad, some of them are in the United States, and we refer artists to them. Those libraries not only have that music represented through us in the United States and Canada, which are the two regions we primarily handle, but they license their music in other territories around the world. So the music gets distributed all over the world.

The second thing that has developed over the last number of years, with the advent of the indie artist as a dominant component of the music industry, and with a lot of indie music being made available to programming, and music supervisors really liking that music, is that we look for artists who have songs. We already have a lot of songs with vocals in them, but we want to get a lot more. Of course, trends change all the time; the music that is popular today isn't going to be that important for sync two years from now, so we're not necessarily looking for thousands and thousands of songs to put into the library. We're looking more for music that will be popular for a period of time.

SG: Let's talk about the basic contract between you and the creators.

AT: A general library deal for APM, and the songwriters and other libraries, is generally 50/50. The artist/songwriter would get 50 percent of whatever the library gets. So, for example, if we represent a UK library and we get a license from a client for $1,000, we send $500 to the library in the UK, and the library in turn sends 50 percent of that, or $250, to the artist/songwriter. If the UK library does the license for $1,000, they send $500 to the artist/songwriter. So it's a 50/50 deal based on receipts. There are a lot of other libraries, particularly in the United States. Some of our competitors do buyouts of the composers, where they'll pay a small creative fee, cover the production costs, and all the writer gets after that is a 50 percent share of the performance income, that is, the "writer's share." In 99 percent of cases, we don't do that. We like the artist/songwriter to continue to get a share of the sync, because that's actually where the bulk of the money is. It makes it a bit harder for us to make as much money as others, but it does give us the best music.

SG: So, if you make a deal directly with a songwriter, and I do have a client who has a deal with you, they'll receive their 50 percent of sync fees directly from you, and they'll collect the performance income—the writer's share—directly from ASCAP, BMI, or SESAC, correct?

AT: That's correct. I also just want to clarify that not every deal is 50/50. The indie artist deals can be anywhere from 25 to 50 percent; it really depends upon a variety of factors. By way of example, we have an agreement with ReverbNation, the great music site, where artists who are on ReverbNation who feel they are good have the opportunity to submit music to the ReverbNation/APM library that we've built together. If we like the music, we accept it into the library. In this case there are three parties, so the rates vary a bit, but we try to be very fair. Again, we don't do buyouts of the sync rights and payments, and so artists do very well with us.

SG: If I submit a song to you as a songwriter, would I get the rights in the song back at some point, or is your deal for the duration of the copyright like a standard music publishing contracts?

AT: If it is going into the traditional library, then it goes in for perpetuity. However, composers continue to get their share of the sync revenue in perpetuity. The copyright is owned by the library. If it is one of our newer indie artist's deals, the term may be as brief as one or two years. It goes in there exclusively for sync for that period, not for iTunes or anything else, just for sync. So it's a shorter window—we're not looking to tie up a track forever—and we never own the copyright in that case.

SG: Now we want to talk about exclusivity. This is a hot issue in music licensing circles.

Your deals are exclusive, but I know that some people argue that non-exclusive deals are better because it's better to have multiple reps working your song, especially, for example, if the A&R person who signed you leaves the company. There's a fear that the music may be shelved.

How would you justify the exclusivity part of your deal with the songwriters and the other libraries?

AT: In regard to exclusivity, our view is that we can do a better job representing a track by having it exclusively and not worrying about if clients are going to be receiving the same track from other libraries or licensing reps and having price negotiations against it, one against the other. If you had everybody out there in the world representing it, we would have no control over pricing. Also from a client perspective there's been a great deal of negative feedback and pushback. We've gotten letters from TV networks and movie studios stating that they will not license from non-exclusive sources. With a non-exclusive track, a client may not even know who they got it from or to pay. So it causes a lot of complications. For instance, if there's any type of copyright infringement issue, who do you hold responsible? With our tracks you know who to pay and who is responsible for clearing the rights. Therefore clients feel more secure.

One of the biggest issues coming up with exclusivity—which is a major issue, and I think it will probably be the death knell of non-exclusives—is the fact that the performing-rights societies are now starting to use digital detection in order to pay performance revenues. So, when you have multiple instances of a track with different publishers, all of whom are registering those songs, the society isn't going to know which rep made the deal or who to pay. They're not going to know who the source is. Then the money goes into a black box and they don't pay anybody.

SG: So even if you rename the song for another rep, the PROs are confused because the system picks that up as both the original named song and the newly named song. Then they put the money in a black box instead of paying the money to the publisher or writer?

AT: Right, exactly. And it doesn't matter if it's re-titled or not. Even if it has a different title, it's just going to not be paid. And performance revenue is sometimes the only revenue a composer or writer is getting. ASCAP is using Soundmouse now for digital detection. BMI has their Landmark system, which is the Shazam technology. SESAC has been using TuneSat and is talking to some of the other companies. And when you go international, the performance revenue is a much higher percentage of the income than it is here in the United States, so it has even more impact. Many foreign territories are now using digital identification. So, this is happening.

SG: If I enter into a deal with you as a songwriter I suppose you expect me to either deliver a fully commercially acceptable master, or perhaps you help me by allowing me to go into your studio to record the songs?

AT: Yes, we, or the libraries we represent, work very, very closely with the songwriters and composers. It's not that often that somebody just delivers a finished master and we don't have anything to do with that. In fact, most of the libraries that we represent do the mastering themselves. They like consistency of sound and want a certain level of quality on the mastering. Often there's a lot of back and forth between the artist/songwriter and the library in order to get to a finished track or a finished CD.

SG: Okay, let's close this interview with the impact of digital, what the future looks like for your business and the future of the music business in general. Has digital opened up new opportunities for library music?

AT: Absolutely, from every angle you can think of, I think. Certainly from production and distribution income streams. There are so many things that are going on, so many different ways to use music. On the web there are so many more advertisements now than have ever been done before. All previous ads were on TV or radio, and now they're on the web as well. So the sheer quantity is staggering. Lots of opportunities there. Obviously YouTube has also made an enormous impact, and we have over 1 million videos on YouTube that have our music in them that we have discovered so far, and we monetize the videos containing our music and we share that revenue with the libraries that we represent and the composers. And it's significant revenue.

SG: How do you make money from YouTube?

AT: If we've given a client the right to use our music in videos on YouTube, then we don't put advertising over those videos. We just receive income from the client. However, a very high percentage of the usages are just posted by individuals, without our permission. So, where they've grabbed stuff from TV, or radio, or wherever, and they've put up stuff on the web that includes our music, then we will monetize those videos by attaching ads to the video. I mentioned before that our music was used in the original *Superman* series. Well, there are thousands of *Superman* postings up on YouTube, and none of them done with permission. The same thing with our music in the *Spider-Man* cartoon series in 1970, and the *Oprah* episodes. So, whenever that music plays, if it's an unauthorized posting, we have an opportunity to monetize that. YouTube has an auto-detection system [Author's note: This is known as "Content ID."] that identifies it as our music. So they share advertising revenue with us, and in this way the videos get monetized. This is another argument against non-exclusivity: When YouTube recognizes the track, if there is only one rep, they pay a share of ad revenues. If there are multiple claims, they hold the money.

We also have the right to block our content, and if you set it that way, when YouTube finds a track that contains our music it will block the video and tell the user to replace the audio track.

SG: Are you optimistic about the future for your business? And how do you feel about the music business in general?

AT: Every change in technology changes the power structure. An example I give often is, a few hundred years ago Gutenberg reinvented the printing press, and that really weakened the power of the church, which controlled the distribution of information prior to the printing press. With music, digital technology has changed everything, and it's moved the power a bit away from the producers of music to the distributors of music. Yes, it has had a severe negative effect on the overall dollars out there for content owners. On the other hand, digital technologies have allowed composers and songwriters to write and produce at a level they were never able to do before, and to experiment with sounds and share sounds and ideas in a way that was never possible before in human history. Digital has, from a creative perspective, opened up incredible doors for songwriters and composers and for the world at large to be able to hear these things. So I think that the music business, from a creative perspective, is incredibly vibrant. People are finding ways of making money. Not everyone's going to become a superstar because of the Internet, but there are ways of controlling your destiny and making a certain amount of money. Of course we still have superstars, but, at the same time, there are tens or hundreds of thousands of artists who are making a living from music from the variety of things that they do.

From the library perspective, we're doing quite well. Our business continues to grow. I think the library business on the whole is growing. There are threats; there are people who are willing to give their music away for free. There are libraries that are sync free. There are libraries that are performance free. Artists are willing to give their tracks away so that they get placed on TV, which I really don't think that they should do. They get promised a lot of credit, but I don't really think it ends up amounting to very much in value to their career. But I think that in spite of all that the library business is doing well. I think there are a couple of reasons for that. One is that the need to have sync revenue for an artist has become extremely important, and a lot of really great creative music is coming into libraries. In many ways, libraries are at the forefront of music creativity, because they're much more nimble. They can react more quickly. They don't have the same constrictions that the publishing industry has. We can offer a lot of different varieties and styles of music; because we're a multi-transactional business and do millions of transactions per year, we get a really good sense about what the trends are. We can use that to really push creativity.

At the same time, there are many more productions being done today than there ever were before, because of amateur productions. Ten years ago, 99 percent of all video production was done by professionals; today, 99.9 percent are done by amateurs. There are so many different types of productions and channels and cable channels and digital channels and other things that are cropping up, and I think it's going to continue. Video has become one of the major forces for expression today, and you see that in so many different areas. Not only on YouTube videos, but in the resurgence of documentaries. We're probably in the golden era of documentaries right now. So, there's no shortage of productions, and they need library music good quality music at reasonable rates.

We're doing well, we continue to make a creative contribution to the world, and it's great to get this music out into programming. It's a wonderful thing for composers and songwriters to be able to write something and actually get it placed in not maybe one thing because they went through a commercial publisher, but in hundreds of things.

SG: I always encourage songwriters and producers to think in terms of the fact that the song can generate income for your lifetime, and if you've got just one or two that are great, it really could be the difference between having a financially rewarding life or not.

AT: Well, it's true. Libraries are a mass business, a volume business. It's the Rolls-Royce product at a Chevy price. And you want to have your music used in a lot of different productions because not only do you get the sync income for that up front, but you get the performance revenue on an ongoing basis. If you ultimately end up in hundreds or thousands of programs that are broadcast all over the world, you make money. The great thing about library is, you never know when you're going to get something. I was lucky enough to do a number of CDs with the great lyricist Hal David, who passed away last year, unfortunately. We did five CDs together, and we became friends. He had told me at one point that there was a track he had done for us, a number of years before, that was used in some program and aired in Belgium and apparently the show aired over and over and over again. The performance payment for that show for that track, which had been recorded years ago and hadn't really made a lot of money, was out of the blue $15,000. And that's just for him—he just wrote the lyrics, his half. The composer got the other $15,000. It's an interesting opportunity for composers. We have composers who earn a living just from us. That's what they do.

The Record Business

As we discussed at the beginning of this chapter, copyright law forms the foundation of the record business by giving owners of sound recordings the exclusive right to copy and distribute their records. The Copyright Act of 1976 protects sound recordings produced on and after February 15, 1972. Recordings produced prior to that date are protected under the common-law or antipiracy statutes of the various states.[81]

Why Radio Does Not Pay for Broadcasting Sound Recording

Under the Copyright Act, the owners of sound recording copyrights enjoy all the same exclusive rights (including copying, distribution, and making derivative works) as other copyright owners do (including owners of copyrights in musical compositions), *except*, as was just mentioned, public-performance rights. As we discuss in more detail in Chapters 3 and 6, there is generally no right of public performance for sound recordings except on digital platforms such as Internet radio and satellite services. The recording industry has tried for decades to change the federal copyright law so that terrestrial radio stations would have to pay them. Their efforts became more intense after 1999 as revenues from record sales started to dramatically decline. But the radio stations, led by their powerful lobbying group, the National Association of Broadcasters, have blocked their efforts by advancing the same argument that they used to persuade Congress to deny public-performance rights to owners of sound recordings in 1976. That is, the radio stations' performance of the labels' records help sell those recordings, resulting in revenue for the labels—in fact, teams of in-house or freelance radio promoters employed by the labels are constantly beseeching stations to play their records—therefore it is unfair to make radio stations pay the labels. Whatever the merits of this argument, the NAB has over the years had much more clout with lawmakers than the labels. Congresspeople, after all, need the good will of their local broadcasters because they rely on the news media to cover their re-election campaigns. So far the labels have failed in all their many efforts to change the law. Their latest bid to do so was the introduction in September 2013 of the Free Market Royalty Act (HR 3219). Like previous attempts to change the law, such as the Performance Rights Act introduced in 2009, and the bill of the same name introduced in 2007, this bill would require AM/FM broadcasters to pay performers and copyright owners. If this bill or any other does get any traction after this book is published, it will be reported in the update of this section of the book in www.futureofthemusicbusiness.com.

The US is one of a very few countries in the world that does not provide public performance rights for sound recordings. Not only do labels and artists suffer from not getting royalties from US radio stations as music publishers and songwriters do, they are also denied another stream of revenue. Foreign societies do collect monies from radio for the performance of sound recording and distribute those royalties to labels and artists. However, they withhold royalties to US labels and artists, since the US does not pay for performance of their recordings.

Another controversy surrounding performance rights in sound recordings is presented by two current lawsuits by the recording industry against Sirius XM and Pandora. Although the federal copyright law provides that owners of records should be compensated for digital transmissions, including those by Sirius XM and Pandora, federal copyright law only applies to records fixed after February 15, 1972. These lawsuits raise the issue of the scope of protection that state law affords to pre-'72 sound recordings.[82] We discuss these cases at the end of Chapter 6.

Record Companies vs. DIY

Record companies, especially the majors and their affiliates, have been reviled for years for a number of "standard" practices, such as:

- Stripping artists of their copyrights in their recordings (see "Transfers of Copyright" later in this chapter)
- Paying artists as little as possible by including all kinds of reductions in calculating their recording royalty, such as deducting 20 to 25 percent for CD packaging, which doesn't actually cost the labels nearly that much (see "Standard Deductions to the Artist Royalty" later in this chapter)
- Paying a reduced mechanical royalty to artists who write and record their own songs (see "Controlled Composition Clause" later in this chapter)
- Using "360" deals to tap into all of the artist's revenue streams, including concerts; publishing, endorsements, and branding; and appearances on television and film—even if the label does nothing to deserve any of this income (see "The 360 Deal and How to Avoid Getting Completely Screwed" later in this chapter)

And this is just a partial list.

However, for all their sins, the major labels and their affiliates have helped make household names of many artists that you would otherwise never have heard of by paying for their recording costs and videos, getting them on radio and TV, paying their expenses during tours before they are well known, and arranging for them to open for already established artists. They also play a vital part in launching the careers of new artists by paying the artist advances that allow them to quit their day gigs and apply themselves full-time to music. They have done all these things for decades, made thousands of artists quite wealthy, and provided a source of income to untold numbers of producers, studio managers, lawyers, accountants, and middle managers.

Moreover, there are very few sources of funding for new artists trying to "get to the next level." Although an artist can use the Internet and digital services such as Facebook, iTunes, Twitter, and YouTube to reach a mass audience, none of them provides advances, pays for recording costs, or offers tour support. In his diatribe "Meet the New Boss, Worse than the Old Boss?" musician David Lowery complained:

> I was like all of you. I believed in the promise of the Internet to liberate, empower, and even enrich artists. I still do, but I'm less sure of it than I once was. I feel that what we artists were promised has not really panned out. Yes, in many ways we have more freedom. Artistically this is certainly true. But the music business never transformed into the vibrant marketplace where small stakeholders could compete with multinational conglomerates on an even playing field.In the last few years it's become apparent [that] the music business, which was once dominated by six large and powerful music conglomerates, MTV, Clear Channel, and a handful of other companies, is now dominated by a smaller set of larger, even more powerful tech conglomerates. And their hold on the business seems to be getting stronger.[83]

The promise of the Internet to level the playing field for new artists has come true with a bitter twist. Because you can potentially reach a worldwide audience by getting on iTunes or Spotify through an aggregator for little or no money up front, the field *has* become level. But the sad reality is that aside from the aggregators and the platforms themselves, which make money from advertising and/or taking a piece of every transaction, very few unsigned artists are making a living from these services. Those who hoped "the cream" would rise to the top on its own have been sadly disappointed.[84]

The DIY Model

We pre-published Amanda Palmer's foreword to this book in *Digital Music News* and it garnered over a hundred comments within a few hours. They were almost all passionate, and very divided. Some people responded positively to her philosophy that artists should ask those who enjoy their music for help. Others were tremendously negative. But, for better or for worse, a new artist *does* need help in many ways. For instance,

Building her website
Keeping up with social media
Finding musicians who will play at her gigs for little or no money;
Publicizing her events
Producing her videos
Introducing her to producers and writers

Booking her in clubs and festivals
Remixing and mastering her records
Arranging for photo shoots
Getting her on radio and television
Buying her a new guitar
Fixing her computer

And, not least importantly, giving her enough money to quit her day job and to pay her rent.

These are all things labels used to do (if not buying the guitar, at least giving her advance money so she could purchase it herself.) But the labels don't sign as many artists as before and advances are ever harder to come by. So if you are like Amanda, you ask for help—and stand the consequences.[85]Although DIY has always been a very tough row to hoe, these days you may not have much of a choice. So here are some tips:

Be very suspicious of "indie labels" that offer you 360 deals for no money up front (see again "The 360 Deal and How to Avoid Getting Completely Screwed" later in this chapter);
Be wary of websites that want to "help" you but ask you to pay them first; and
If you can't afford a lawyer to evaluate opportunities or deals that you are offered, call Volunteer Lawyers for the Arts (http://www.vlany.org/). They may be able to give you some free or at least low-cost advice.

And *never* sign any contract without having a trusted and competent adviser review it first. There are, regrettably, many music business hustlers who will promise you the world and may even give you a few dollars or a studio to record in, and then do nothing to help again. But if you reread the contract they gave you (and that you signed because they "loved" your music) carefully, you may very well see that they made themselves entitled to your next album and the next five after that, plus 50 percent of your publishing and a healthy slice of any income you may make anywhere in the entertainment business, including everything from live gigs, to T-shirts, to writing a cookbook. And *if* you should somehow make it, they will approach you or your future real label with that old contract in one hand, and the other hand out for cash. I'm presently in the process of extricating a young artist from a particularly nasty example of this kind of "deal." It's so bad that the label winds up with 80 percent of any income she makes from any song she writes in the indefinite future as well as 30 percent of her income from anything she does in the entertainment business. The latter clause was buried in two pages of fine print, titled "rights." And here's the kicker: The label is owned by a lawyer. It's enough to make you cringe.

At the beginning of the digital era the dream developed that a new artist could create great tracks on a laptop and use the Internet for worldwide distribution for almost no cost. That dream is true, except that without marketing, promotion, and all the other jobs a label used to do, your record may well end up as another grain of sand in the vast digital beach. On the other hand, if you are brilliantly talented and/or amazing to look at, and/or really good at getting people who can help you to actually help, there is always hope! On that note, here are your choices for distributing your record without a record company, courtesy of the Future of Music Coalition:

HOW TO GET **YOUR MUSIC** INTO DIGITAL STORES AND STREAMING PLATFORMS

Most digital music stores don't have the capacity to deal with individual artists directly.

But that doesn't mean you can't participate. If you're an artist who is self-releasing your music, you can use aggregator services like CD Baby, TuneCore, or DistroKid to get your music into a vast array of digital music stores/services. Here's a snapshot of what they offer:

DIGITAL DISTRIBUTION FOR SELF-RELEASED ARTISTS

CD Baby

For a small fee per album, CD Baby offers an impressive array of sales and distribution options.

YOUR MUSIC	SERVICES OFFERED	MUSICIANS' SHARE OF REVENUE *
CD Baby Pay one-time fee of $59 fee per album or $14.95 per single song.	**Mailorder:** sends CDs to mailorder customers.	Artist sets price. CD Baby gets $4 of every album sale. Artist gets the rest.
	Digital sales: offers MP3s to website customers.	Artist gets 91% of any MP3 sales off CD Baby website.
	Digital distribution: encodes and delivers your music to services including iTunes Music Store, Amazon, Spotify, Rhapsody, Google Play, eMusic, etc.	Of what the services send to CD Baby, artist gets 91% of revenue, whether it's download sales on iTunes or streams on Spotify.
CD Baby PRO Pay one-time fee of $89 fee per album or $34.95 per single song. Get all the services offered above, plus publishing administration.	**Publishing administration:** if you are a self-published songwriter, CD Baby Pro can help you retrieve some publishing royalties that are otherwise difficult to collect.	Of the publishing royalties CD Baby Pro is able to collect, songwriter gets 85% of royalties.

For more information about pricing and additional services offered: members.cdbaby.com

TuneCore

TuneCore provides digital distribution for music, video and films, publishing administration for songwriters, and a full interactive administrative accounting solution.

YOUR MUSIC	SERVICES OFFERED	MUSICIANS' SHARE OF REVENUE *
TuneCore Pay $49.99 annually for each album distributed, or $9.99 annually for single distribution.	**Digital distribution:** encodes and delivers your music to services including iTunes Music Store, Amazon, Spotify, Rhapsody, Google Play, eMusic, etc.	Of what the services send to TuneCore, artist gets 100% of revenue, whether it's download sales on iTunes or streams on Rhapsody.
TuneCore Music Publishing Admin Pay a one-time fee of $75 for TuneCore's Music Publishing Administration services.	**Publishing administration:** if you are a self-published songwriter, TuneCore can help you retrieve some publishing royalties that are otherwise difficult to collect.	Of the publishing royalties TuneCore is able to collect, songwriter gets 90% of royalties.

For more information about pricing and additional services offered: tunecore.com. Note that TuneCore is not well suited to ingest music from classical performers that are playing repertoire pieces from other composers.

* *With these digital aggregator options, it is the artist's responsibility to pay the songwriter and publisher any mechanical royalties due.*

Revenue comparison	CD Baby	TuneCore
Distribution costs for 3 years	$59 + $0 + $0 = $59	$30 + $50 + $50 = $130
Selling 100 digital albums on iTunes at $9.99	$630	$700
Selling 100 digital singles on iTunes at 99¢	$63	$70
Digital sales revenue	$693	$770
Distribution costs	-$59	-$130
Net revenue	$634	$640

More digital aggregators for self-released artists

There are additional companies that each provide an array of services for musicians and filmmakers, from digital distribution/aggregation, to promotion, ringtones, apps, download cards, physical manufacturing/distribution, synch placements, charting and more. Check each site out to compare prices and services.

DistroKid distrokid.com
Ditto Music dittomusic.com
Loudr loudr.com
ReverbNation reverbnation.com

DIGITAL DISTRIBUTION FOR INDIE LABELS

If you are working with an independent record label, the label will submit your albums to various services and platforms via label aggregators like The Orchard or INgrooves.

YOUR MUSIC

MUSICIANS' SHARE OF REVENUE

→ **Your indie label** → **Orchard/INgrooves** →

Your indie label submits your album to its aggregator for digital distribution. Orchard/INgrooves encodes and delivers the music and data to all the stores and streaming services.

Both Orchard and INgrooves offer many other services including promotional networks, publishing royalty collection and licensing assistance.

Digital distribution: encodes and delivers your music and data to services including iTunes Music Store, Amazon, Spotify, Rhapsody, Google Play, eMusic, etc.

↓

Of the collected revenue that the services send to Orchard/INgrooves, they keep a small % and send the rest to your indie label. → Indie label then splits revenue with its artist based on the agreement between label and artist.

Future of Music Coalition
Education, Research and Advocacy for Musicians

Information compiled by the nonprofit Future of Music Coalition,
www.futureofmusic.org | money.futureofmusic.org

Artist Revenue Streams
money.futureofmusic.org

Recording Agreements

A detailed analysis of recording agreements is beyond the scope of this book. However, we can outline the basic terms of the standard deal. These terms have been offered by the major labels, their affiliates, and most independent labels for decades, and they have served as the foundation on which the recording industry has done business.

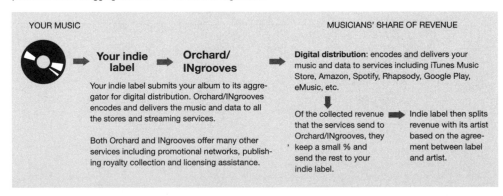

Exclusivity

A standard record contract requires the artist to record music exclusively for the record company. This means that only the record company has the right to distribute records and music videos containing the artist's performances created during the term of the agreement. The artist may perform live concerts without permission. Generally, the exclusivity clause, no matter how broadly drafted, will not be enforced in such a manner as to prevent the artist from performing on a television program, although technically a TV show usually entails a recording. For instance, while I was at Sony, our in-house video production company, Automatic, produced a TV series featuring performances of new and some established recording artists. The show was called *Sessions at West 54th* and aired initially on PBS. Many artists who performed on the show were not signed to Sony. Those artists did not secure the consent of their record companies to perform on *Sessions*. But when Sony wanted to include their performances in a "best of" CD, it needed to secure the permission of the record companies for each artist who was not signed to Sony.[86]

Transfers of Copyright

Record companies make and sell records. But first they must acquire the rights in the performances on a recording. Unlike a song, which is often created by just one person or two people (e.g., Lennon–McCartney), a major label recording is usually a highly collaborative enterprise involving the artist, one or more producers, engineers, background vocalists and side musicians, A&R staffers who work for the label, and the record company, which is paying for everything. Therefore, the performances preserved on a master are a result of various creative contributions. Yet the record company will usually be the only copyright owner of the master. This ownership is generally accomplished as follows: In regard to the artist, the standard recording agreement will contain a "work for hire" clause that states that any recording that the artist makes during the term of the agreement shall be a work for hire for the label. Under federal copyright law, the author of a work for hire is the person or company that commissions that work—that is, the label, not the artist. Therefore the label becomes the sole owner of the recording.[87] This same clause is usually contained in the producer's contract, as well any contract with the studio with regard to the use of its facilities or the services of its studio engineers. For those "non-royalty" who do not have a direct deal with the label, including backup musicians, who are members of the AFM (American Federation of Musicians), and the backup vocalists, who are members of AFTRA (American Federation of Television and Radio Artists), a work-for-hire transfer of rights is included in the standard union contract to which the record companies are signatories.

Although the record company usually owns copyright in the master, this does not mean that it has absolutely unfettered rights to use the masters for any purpose. The label's rights may be limited by the negotiated provisions in the recording agreement. For example, the label usually needs the consent of the artist to license the masters in a commercial for alcohol, tobacco, or feminine hygiene products. And as artists become more successful, or are already successful and enter into new deals with other labels, they may win more concessions such as approval over licensing any of their masters for any ad, TV show or movie. Or the label may seek artist approval even if it's not technically required by the contract in order to maintain good relations with a powerful artist.

Duration and Options

Perhaps the most important provision in the record contract is its duration. Customarily, the record companies require the artist to deliver one or two albums followed by a series of "options" under which the record company can require the artist to deliver additional albums. A typical record deal may have five option periods or more and may require two albums during each option period. The record company can terminate the contract at any time. The artist cannot. The result of this structure is that the record company can drop the artist even before the first album is released, or it can require an artist to record multiple albums over a number of years that may encompass an artist's entire career. In the 1990s, George Michael wanted to terminate his relationship with Columbia Records. But his recording contract required him to record more albums at Columbia's option. Michael brought a lawsuit in England to get out of his contract, alleging, among other things, that Columbia's option for additional albums should be unenforceable because it made him a virtual slave of the record company. He contended that the eight-album contract he had signed in 1988 was unfair under British and European Union law because it bound him to the company for up to 15 years. He also argued that, since every major record company has these options for additional records, he had no real choice and no real bargaining power. Sony's lawyers tried throughout the trial to establish that Mr. Michael had been well aware of the terms of the contract he signed in 1988, and that the deal was a considerable improvement over his earlier contracts with CBS Records, which Sony had acquired a short time before entering into a new agreement with Michael.[88] He lost the case. In the High Court in London, Justice Jonathan Parker largely accepted Sony's view of the matter, saying that the contract was "reasonable and fair" and that Mr. Michael had understood the deal.[89] The English court found that he had entered the contract voluntarily and that he could not prove collusion between the major labels. From the record companies' point of view, the rationale for options is that the label makes a very substantial financial investment in an artist's career, and it wants to be around to share in the artist's success—both to realize a return on that investment and to help offset investments in new artists that don't pay off.

Advances and Recording Royalties

The record company may provide a "budget" from which the artist pays for the production of an album and retains any money not used during the course of production. Alternatively, the record company may pay for the costs of production directly and pay an "advance" to the artist on top of production expenses. As we discuss in the next section, in either scenario, all of these payments are recoupable from the artist's royalties.

The normal recording royalty for new artists and artists with niche audiences, like jazz musicians, ranges from 10 to 15 percent of the suggested retail price of a record. Ten percent of a $15 album (whether a CD or an album download) is $1.50, and 10 percent of a 99-cent download is approximately 10 pennies, but there are all sorts of deductions, as we will see later, that severely reduce the amount of that royalty. In Chapter 4 we will discuss in detail how and how much artists, whether signed to a major, to an indie, or to no label, are paid from permanent downloads. In Chapter 5 we will discuss how and how much artists earn from on-demand services like Spotify, and in Chapter 6 we will discuss how artists are paid for the performance of their record on Internet radio services such as Pandora and satellite services, i.e., Sirius XM.

Standard Deductions to the Artist's Royalty

One of the biggest deductions that labels subtract from the artist's recording royalty is "packaging," that is, album art and the CD jewel case, album jacket, or any other physical container.

Mercifully, most labels don't charge packaging fees for online downloads or streams, although in the early days of iTunes they all did.

Another huge bite out of an artist's royalties are producer fees. Typically producers will be paid a royalty from three percent to five percent per track. These "points" are deductable from the artist's royalty. (Plus, if the producer receives any advance or fees, these amounts are recoupable from the artists royalties.)

Net receipts or net sales of 10 percent is a particularly interesting deduction, based on the historical fact that, until the early 1940s, records used to be made out of shellac and would occasionally break before they could be purchased. Records don't break any more, and have not for a long, long time. Yet the net receipts deduction clause is still common in many standard agreements.

Foreign sales: Even though the foreign affiliates of major record companies receive 100 percent of income from sales of records abroad, the US component that signed the artist will deduct 10 percent to 15 percent from the artist.

The "new technology deduction" appeared in the '90s, when CDs came on the scene and the record companies needed to build factories to make them. They kept the deduction as other "new technologies" rolled out.

At the end of the day after all these deductions, some of which make no sense, an artist's lawyer just has to add up the pennies and calculate how much the label is really offering.

Recoupment at Artist's Royalty Rate

All the money that a label spends to produce an album, EP, or single recording, whether it pays the artist to make the record or pays for costs directly, is treated as "recoupable advances." In addition, at least 50 percent of the cost of producing videos is also deemed to be an advance, as well as any money that the label pays directly to the artist. Under the standard record contract, the artist is supposed to repay all these advances to the label. This repayment happens through "recoupment." Suppose that recording costs and the artist's share of promotion and video expenses add up to a million dollars. In record-company parlance, the artist recoups at his royalty rate. If the artist's royalty is $1, the album must sell 1 million units as a download or a CD before the artist has repaid the record company. Some artists' advocates claim this is unfair, because if the record company has sold a million units at a wholesale price of, for instance, $7 a unit, the record company has pocketed $7 million. In other words, the record company has already made enough money to pay itself back for all its costs and make a profit. But the record companies argue that very few albums ever sell a million units, and they usually barely break even or lose money on most releases. In other words, they need the surpluses from the hits to subsidize all the losers.

In any event, this is the way the game has been played. The result is that very successful artists who sell millions of units recoup and make substantial royalties. The record companies also reward such artists with huge advances. However, relatively few artists ever reach this level of success.

Controlled-Composition Clauses

"Controlled compositions" are songs written or cowritten by the artist or the producer of the track in which the song is embodied. Typically, the recording company will pay 75 percent of the minimum statutory rate (see "Section 115 Compulsory License" earlier in this chapter for the current "stat" rate) for these compositions. Also, they usually impose a "cap" of 10 songs per album. So if the artist writes 12 songs, he will be paid for only 10 at 75 percent of stat rate. Or, if the artist wrote only 2 songs, if the company has to pay another writer or writers for 10 songs, the artist gets zilch. Many in the songwriting community have complained about this practice for years, claiming there is no justification for it except that all the major labels do it and so artists have little choice other than to accept it. It is true that if an artist becomes a huge success, he or she may be able to negotiate the controlled-composition clause out of the contract, as well as increase the recording royalty. Generally all artists, even stars, grant the label a free promotional sync license for use of controlled compositions in music videos.

The 360 Deal and How to Avoid Getting Completely Screwed

In the past, record companies focused on making money from selling records. It was a very profitable business. Income rose from hundreds of millions in the early 1960s to billions in the 1990s. This spurt in income was fueled by a new format—the CD—that allowed the labels to sell all the old records that they had already sold on vinyl and cassette in a shiny new format. But the artists got to keep money earned from live performances, endorsements, and music publishing. In fact, all of these sources of income were vital, because the overwhelming majority of artists never recouped advances and recording costs, and therefore never received recording royalties, or if they did recoup, they still did not see much money from recording royalties..

The "old" days are now long over. The landscape has dramatically changed for labels, especially the majors. As we discussed in the introduction, income from recorded music is only 35 percent of what it was in 1999. Although income is not declining as steeply as it was from 1999 to 2010 (thanks largely to the increasing popularity of interactive subscription services, and Internet and satellite radio) the labels are still not making what they used to from records. Not long after the start of the decline of income started in 2000, the majors and many other labels resorted to "360 deals," which entitle them to "share" artists' income from other sources than just record sales and licensing. They revised their standard recording agreement to get 20 percent or more in the following areas:

- Touring and live performances.
- Merchandise—and that doesn't just mean T-shirt sales. The labels are seeking income from corporate sponsorships, endorsements, and any goods or services carrying the artists' names or likenesses.
- Publishing—under a 360 deal, the labels take a cut of the artists' income from songs that they write.
- Any other income that an artist may earn in the entertainment business, including acting in movies, television, or live theater; modeling; writing books, etc.

These agreements are called 360-degree deals, or 360 deals, because they permit the record company to participate in income generated from all aspects of an artist's career. For a major artist like Coldplay, if the label succeeds in negotiating a piece of live performance, it may cost them a huge advance, or serious money for tour support and promotion revenue. The same will happen if it wants a percentage of a major artist's merchandise, promotion, or publishing. Since new artists don't wield the same bargaining power, the labels make no additional advance payments and do no additional work for the privilege of taking a piece of performance income. So for new artists, a 360 deal can be a terrible bargain and may provide additional incentive for artists to do it on their own!

According to leading entertainment lawyer Elliot Groffman, "Too many people are falling for the cry that [the labels] can't sell CDs so they need more rights. My concern is that we are going to allow [labels] to eat part of the artist's lunch while [labels] are starting to figure out the new distribution models, then in 5 to 10 years they're going to control distribution again and control a good portion of the artist's income."[90] The following article, which I originally published in *Digital Music News*, provides guidance:

How to Avoid Getting Completely Screwed by a 360 Degree Deal

360-degree deals present major disadvantages for artists; still faced with a choice of the 360 versus no deal, the 360 may be worth accepting—but only if properly negotiated and only if the major pitfalls touched upon in this article are avoided.

First, let me give every artist and manager a quick primer on what a 360-degree deal is. Basically, the 360 is an exclusive recording contract between a record company and an artist in which, in addition to monies from sales of the artist's recorded music, the label shares in other income streams, such as touring and live performance, merchandise, endorsements, appearances on television and film, and, if the artist also writes songs, publishing.

In fact, most 360 deals have catch-all phases giving the label a financial interest in everything else that the artist does in the entertainment business.

A traditional recording agreement only provides an income stream for the label from record sales. The label acquires the copyrights in the artist's recordings and options for multiple albums. It also deducts from the artist's royalties for expenses such as producer royalties, packaging, "net sales," foreign sales, midprice and budget records, and even "new technology" (originally applied to CD royalties and now to digital sales).

The traditional recording agreement had a lot of bad stuff in it for the artist. The 360 deal usually has all of that, and a lot more.

ORIGINS OF THE 360 DEAL

The 360 deal is not new. The first reported one was English recording star Robbie Williams' deal with EMI in 2002. But in the last few years 360 deals have become commonplace. New artists signing with a major label or their affiliates can expect it as a matter of course. The reason for the prevalence of the 360 deal is the dramatic decline in income from sales of recorded music.

Income from sales of pre-recorded music reached its peak in 1999 at approximately 14.5 billion dollars. By 2012 that amount had shrunk to only approximately $7 billion—a decline of more than 50 percent not accounting for inflation.

This is the reason that labels began to pursue income from sources that would have once been sacrosanct to the artist.

Under the traditional paradigm, the label would pay the artist a small royalty, made even smaller by the various deductions. The artist could expect to receive no recording royalty at all unless his album was a major commercial success. But he got to keep everything else: publishing, merch, touring, endorsements, etc.

However, these days artists often generate more money from other activities than record sales. For instance, Lady Gaga's Monster Ball Tour grossed over $227 million dollars, and 50 Cent's deal with Vitamin Water turned golden when he accepted shares in the company in exchange for authorizing the use of his professional name in "Formula 50." It is reported that his shares were worth over $100 million after Coca-Cola purchased Vitamin Water's parent, Glacéau, for $4.1 billion.

These developments have spurred the labels to seek to participate in all the possible revenue streams generated by an artist. In my own practice, I have seen small labels, also known as production companies, get in on the act and insist that new artists sign 360 deals with them, even if they put little or no money into recording and make no promises in regard to marketing or promotion. These companies expect the artist to provide fully mastered recordings for little or no money up front, and they demand income from all sources of revenue. Bottom line: These are horrible deals.

THE LABELS' JUSTIFICATION

Record labels argue (and majors that pay big advances have more credibility in making these arguments) that they make significant investments in an artist's career by, among other things, putting up considerable sums for recording (including paying advances to A-level producers), getting the artist's music on commercial radio, securing invitations for the artists to perform on popular television shows, paying for one or more top quality videos for YouTube and other outlets, and providing tour support before the artist is popular enough to demand significant sums for live performances.

For emerging artists, a major label deal may be the path to becoming famous and rich. For instance, Lady Gaga was a virtual unknown before Interscope spent a vast sum putting her on tour as an opening act for the New Kids on the Block, paying for marketing (particularly to the gay community), hiring wardrobe and makeup, and paying all her other expenses for over a year, not to mention using their clout to get her invited as a guest on almost every important radio station in the country.

The labels argue that 360 deals are fair because monies generated from touring, merch, endorsements, and other streams would not exist at all without their efforts.

Many artists and their representatives would contend that it isn't their fault that the labels are making less money from their records, and that 360 deals are just a cynical money grab by record companies who have failed to react appropriately to the changing industry. Asking artists to foot the bill hardly seems fair. But the reality is that since all the major labels and affiliates usually demand 360 terms, the artist may not have much choice. Given that reality, let's discuss how the artist's attorney can improve the deal.

HOW TO IMPROVE THE DEAL

The ability of the artist's attorney to improve a 360 depends on the artist's leverage as much as the lawyer's knowledge and negotiating skills. For instance, if there is a bidding war among multiple labels, the lawyer's ability to improve the deal increases immensely. If the artist is already making significant income from live shows, if not from record sales, this can also aid the lawyer in negotiating better terms or at least carving out those areas where the artist is already earning money from the 360 deal.

Carve Out Income Streams

If an artist is already earning revenues from a particular source, the lawyer should try to carve that stream out of the 360 deal. For instance, certain EDM artists are earning tens to hundreds of thousands of dollars playing large venues and festivals. If a label wants this kind of artist, it should be prepared to forgo tapping into live performance income, as they had nothing to do with creating it.

Get the Label to Work for the Money or at Least Pay Advances for Each Stream

The following percentages of income payable to the label were contained in an actual major record company recording agreement:

- 50 percent merch
- 25 percent touring and live performance
- 25 percent of "digital products" such as ringtones and sales from the artist's fan site
- 25 percent publishing
- 25 percent of endorsements
- 25 percent of any other income from the entertainment business, including appearances on TV and movies, theater, book publishing, etc.

Although the above percentages are typical, the actual amounts vary from deal to deal. Whatever the splits are, the artist's attorney should try to get the label to commit to doing something to deserve a share of each income stream. For instance, in return for its 25 percent the label should commit to manufacture merch, sell it at retail via the Internet, and supply the artist with merch for sales on tour.

Protect Your Publishing

In regard to publishing, a 360 deal may include a "co-publishing" agreement in which the label has exclusive control of any songs that the artist writes during the term, and the label retains 25 percent of any monies generated from the songs. Or the label may demand 100 percent of the "publisher's share" or 50 percent of all income generated by the artist's songs. In exchange for either of these arrangements, which are major gives, the label should have a dedicated staff committed to collecting monies generated by the artist's songs, and that can pitch the songs to other artists for covers and to music supervisors for placements in movies, television, video games, etc.

Negotiate Advances

If the label is not equipped to provide support in respect to any income stream, or even if it is, the lawyer should try to exact advances for each stream. In addition, he or she should try to negotiate that as soon as the label recoups each advance for each income stream, the label's right to commission that income stream terminates. For instance, if the label advances $25,000 against a 25 percent commission for branding and endorsements and the artist gets an endorsement deal for $100,000, the artist would pay $25,000 to the label (25 percent of $100,000), but thereafter the label would not be entitled to any more money from that income stream.

Avoid Cross-Collateralization

Just as important as negotiating for the label's commitment to earn its keep for each stream and to pay advances for each stream, the lawyer should make sure that the label cannot cross-collateralize each stream. This means that the label should not be able to take money from one stream to pay for unrecouped balances for another. For instance, if the label pays $100,000 for recording costs and the artist's royalty after deductions is 50 cents for an album that sells at $12.00, the artist must sell 200,000 albums to break even.

Now, suppose the artist only sells 100,000 (still a considerable feat in today's market), and his income from touring is $50,000. If the contract allows the label to cross-collateralize the various streams, the $50,000 will be applied to the "red balance" in his recording royalty account. This means the artist would receive nothing from touring—the monies would be applied to the unrecouped recording costs.

Net versus Gross

If the artist must shell out a percentage of her touring or merch or other income to the labels, her lawyer has to insure that the percentage is based on net, not gross. For instance, if a tour earns the artist $25,000 but her expenses added up to $20,000 (for hotels, transportation, booking agent fees, sound and lighting, etc.), the label should only commission the $5,000 in profits, not the entire $25,000. Indeed, if the label's commission was 25 percent and that was based on gross, the amount due to the label would actually exceed the artist's profit.

SUMMARY

A 360 deal is generally unfavorable to an artist, compared to the old standard deal under which the labels only made money from selling records and the artist retained all other forms of income. Nonetheless, a 360 deal can work for both parties *if* the artist has sufficient leverage plus a good lawyer who can secure non-crossable advances for different income streams and/or make the label actually do something to earn a commission for other forms of income besides record sales.

Master-Use Licenses

A master-use license grants permission to use a preexisting recording of music for various projects. For instance, a movie producer who wishes to use a recording of music in his or her film will need to negotiate a master-use license with the copyright owner of the master—usually a record company. Similar to sync licenses for use of songs, there is no compulsory rate for master-use licenses. We discuss master-use licenses and their costs for all kinds of projects, including movies, TV programs, documentaries, ad campaigns, audio compilations, and digital stand-alone projects such as music apps and web series, in detail in Part II of this book. As we mentioned in the introduction, master-use licenses account for relatively little money in the entire recording business. On the other hand, income from master-use licenses has been relatively stable at 200 million dollars in the US since RIAA began tracking income from this sector in 2009, while income from sales of recorded music, accounting for inflation, has experienced year-to-year declines in every year but one from 1999 forward. (See the introduction for graphs on overall record industry income as well as income from master-use licenses.)0

Role of Major Labels: Interview with David Massey, President of Island Records

In the digital age, do the major labels continue to serve a useful purpose? Will they survive? In spring 2014 I talked with David Massey, president of the legendary music label Island Records, founded by the legendary Chris Blackwell and the original musical home of Bob Marley. Before taking over at Island, Massey was executive vice president of A&R for Sony music. During his time at Sony, he worked with such artists as Shakira, Des'ree, Franz Ferdinand, and Oasis.

SG: Can you tell us a little bit about the artists that you're currently working with at Island and Mercury?

DM: We have quite a wide variety of artists, ranging from people who've been with us for over 30 years, like Bon Jovi and Melissa Etheridge, to artists such as Mariah Carey and young superstars such as Justin Bieber. We have some fantastic established bands, like the Killers and Fall Out Boy—who've had a particularly good year—and artists who are breaking now, like Avicii and the boy band the Wanted, and our new band, American Authors, who are sort of set to be one of the major hits of the first part of this next year.

SG: As president of these labels, let's talk about your role. I imagine it includes overseeing everything, including signing new artists, production, marketing, publicity . . . but where do you put your focus? What do you spend most of your time on?

DM: My focus is on . . . I mean, I'm an artist-based person. I was an artist manager for nine years. My responsibilities at Sony were generally A&R led. I tend to focus on the artists. I still do some A&R, but I am very close with the artists, with their signings, with the business side of that, and I would say with the marketing . . . We have a great promotion team here who do a fantastic job. I would say it's A&R and marketing that I'm most focused on, and very much the business side, as well.

SG: Can you give us a brief description of a typical day? For instance, today what are you doing the rest of the day?

DM: Today's a good example. Well, of course I'm talking . . . I've been in meetings for the last couple of hours. I tend to start fairly early by business standards, maybe about nine, because that's before it gets crazy. I tend to regroup with my A&R team pretty well every day on an informal basis, but with a very detailed A&R meeting every Monday for about two and a half hours. I've already this morning had meetings with the marketing staff and after this call there'll be an in-depth meeting with marketing and digital marketing and the creative team about this new band, American Authors. So I tend to have at least one meeting a day that's focused on an artist that we want to break. Because one of my big priorities, always has been, is artist development, which is very much taking an artist from zero to the top. Honestly, I think that's what excites me the most. We're always focused on the artist that we're going to break.

Today though, there are an unusual number of meetings. We have our new artist, Jake Bugg, in town, who's doing Channel 5 tonight. So he'll be in the building and see the staff this afternoon. I have meetings with lawyers for an hour this afternoon. I have various managers coming; my meetings don't end actually until 9:00 tonight. Then I go jump over for Jake's performance at 10:00 tonight, at 10:05. So, the days are long, I have to say. They start around 9, 9:30, and there are a lot of meetings, but there's always time to have a good conversation with any artist that wants to talk. I always really like to keep a direct line to the artists. That's a focus of mine, and I think it really helps a lot to stay on the cutting edge of that.

SG: How did you break into the business? Also, tell us a couple of your proudest accomplishments.

DM: I had read law at Cambridge, which in the UK is an undergraduate degree. I was intending to be a barrister, but met a young band called Wang Chung coming out of college back in the early '80s. Just fell in love with their music, and I had a background in the music business. My mother was the first female manager in the music business in England. She managed a pop star called Lulu, who had a hit in America with "To Sir, With Love" many, many years ago. I had watched her build a career, so I was pretty attuned to the management world.

I started managing Wang Chung out of enthusiasm and a desire to create my own business. I signed them to David Geffen in the early years of Geffen, in 1983. That was quite an accomplishment because we were the first new band that he signed. There were some big acts on Geffen already. There was John Lennon, who unfortunately passed away. There was Elton John, and Donna Summer, and Neil Young, and Asia. He had some quality stars, but no young artists, so we were pretty well the first to do a new deal with him, which was excellent and worked out so well. I think that was a great introduction to management, and most of all, also, an amazing introduction into the American business.

From then on I was immersed on the American side, because my career developed in LA with David Geffen and Eddie Rosenblum and that whole team. They were incredible mentors, because it was a small label and they were fantastic. They had great values and they were artist driven, and they took the long-term view on things. I think it was unbelievably fortuitous that I fell into those hands in my early years. That was how I started. From there I managed many other artists, and also writers and producers, and became a music publisher, and also had an independent label. Basically, I was an independent for the first nine years.

Then Tommy Mottola and Michelle Anthony called me at a certain point after Wang Chung had split up. I was around 30 and I was starting a family, and they were like, "Come and join us in New York. Join the Sony family and help us build the company." They imported me and my wife and my two young babies into New York. I thought it would be maybe for a couple of years, but 22 years later I'm still here. It happened in an incredibly organic way; it was so natural. We've ended up remaining here very happily, and certainly forever at this point.

So, in terms of accomplishments, I think a very meaningful thing for me was certainly Oasis, because a guy called Alan McGee discovered the band in England. I was lucky enough that he brought me their very first demos on a day that I was relaxed and really had time to focus. I recognized their brilliance immediately. It was a real blessing. I was able to be involved for the world outside of England from the very beginning and stayed with them through their entire Sony contract. Worked with them for certainly at least 12 to about 14 years; now I still work with Noel Gallagher. That I think's a real accomplishment. *Morning Glory* especially, the second album, which ended up selling a total of 17 million albums, was definitely a highlight for me.

SG: Let's switch gears and discuss the business. According to the Recording Industry Association of America, gross revenues from the sale and licensing of recorded music have declined dramatically from their high point in '99 (when I was still at Sony) of approximately $14.5 billion to a little over $7 billion in 2012. That's a loss of more than 50 percent without accounting for inflation and a loss of more than 70 percent accounting for inflation; international revenues are down a comparable amount.

What do you think is the reason for this dramatic loss? Is it piracy, file sharing, sales of singles rather than albums on iTunes, or something else?

DM: I think it's a perfect storm of all of those things, and more. There was some analysis done around that time, '99/2000, of the business. I got a forewarning that if the business slipped slightly in volume the profitability of the majors would suffer very quickly. I think, obviously, it started with piracy. I think the technological side of things definitely started the ball rolling in terms of piracy, especially in certain generation groups that were vital to the business. For example, at the college level, almost everyone until recently did not acquire music legally. There's certainly been bandwidth increase. Broadband became the norm; I definitely think that contributed significantly to the impact on sales. I think the advent of iTunes, which obviously I see as a positive thing—genuinely—led us toward becoming a singles-driven business. We all know that in '99, or around that time, if an artist like Chumbawamba had a hit single, everyone bought the album, because there were no singles to buy. So they would sell millions of albums. Today, an artist like that would most likely sell 2 to 4 million singles and that would sort of be it; maybe 100,000 albums. Obviously the change to singles has dramatically increased sales of singles and the diminishing of the album. We know that is a factor.

At this point I feel like 2014 is the year that we will really start to feel the impact of streaming. In fact, I think that some of the early decline that we're seeing in '13 at iTunes, which was the first time that there had been a decline in volume at iTunes, is definitely connected to streaming, on some level. Because if you look at the growth of streaming, in certain sectors, it's really quite significant, and I think it's going to become more significant this year. Some of the more important providers—Spotify, the new Beats Music, and others—have made deals with the telecom companies such as AT&T to make sure that the subscribers' bill goes directly onto their phone bill. It all is going to strengthen the streaming and subscription side of the business.

SG: You just referred to Beats Music and its deal with AT&T. Did Dr. Dre and Jimmy Iovine finalize their deal with AT&T?

DM: I don't know if it's finalized, but I think that's likely to happen if it hasn't already. I know that some of the other companies have already done so. [91]

SG: Do you think streaming can revive the record business?

DM: I think it's going to make a big difference. I think those scenarios are likely to happen. Obviously you've looked at the Swedish model, which is very different, but it is absolutely remarkable, the hold that Spotify has on the Swedish market and how it's affected the overall marketplace. [Author's note: Spotify was launched in Sweden in 2008 and launched its US service in 2011 after protracted negotiations with the major record companies.]

I believe that music has never been more powerful. One thing that we see in our business is, for example, the incredible result with music sync. It just grows and grows and grows. Music is everywhere. Take an example like our young band American Authors, who're only just about to have their first hit. The amount of placements for this song already is absolutely astounding. I just believe entirely in the business and I believe that the sources of income are simply changing.

There's the opportunity for the business to truly start growing. It is starting to grow back. I think you'll see over the next few years that that's going to happen. It's just going to be completely different sources. It isn't going to be about just album sales, although obviously the album is surviving and there are going to be artists who are going to benefit from album sales. You're not seeing the 5 to 6 million albums, but you are still seeing people like Justin Timberlake and Bruno Mars selling 2.5 million albums and many millions of singles. So, obviously, in my company at Island we think in terms of the combination of singles and albums. The singles sales are so significant. So if you take someone like Avicii; in our first few months working with him, he's already, and this in his infancy, he's already sold in excess of 4 million singles and a couple hundred thousand albums. We're just starting a second single, and I anticipate that a second single will also sell millions. He's also one of the most Spotify-driven artists in the world.

I believe that subscription will get stronger in relation to free use of these services. That's obviously what's needed. If this relationship with the telecoms does grow, I think people will subscribe more, and that becomes a very important part of this, I think, moving forward.

SG: If music is built into the basic subscription and the mobile customer doesn't have to pay an additional fee to access Beats or Spotify or whatever service it may be, I think that's a winner, provided the telecoms share some of that money with the service, which in turn pays the labels and the artists. But on the flip side of the coin, there has been much criticism of how streaming services pay or don't pay the creators. For instance, in regard to Spotify, which I listen to all day long, a lot of indies—and there's a lot of press on this, as you know—complain that Spotify doesn't pay them enough. We don't hear much or see much press about how the major labels are doing with Spotify. Are you satisfied with your relationship with Spotify? Are they paying Island and Mercury enough?

DM: It's the early days. The problem is they only actually have a couple of million paid subscribers at this point. For me, Spotify and those services are more like mobile phones. It's only going to be truly impactful and valuable when you're talking tens of millions of people. The numbers are still relatively small. This needs to be almost universal in terms of its usage, which it is, for example, in Sweden. I see this as the very early days of Spotify. I'm a fan of the site; I want to see how it grows. I believe that the next year to two years are really going to tell the tale on how this goes. I do support the idea of it, and as long as more people pay for it, I think that it can be very valid. I'm excited about Beats as well. I think that's going to be a really good service that is going to make an impact.

SG: Let's talk about digital tools in the indie marketplace. There are dozens of digital tools now at the disposal of indie artists and indie labels that didn't exist before, including ways to promote and market their music, whether it's on YouTube, Facebook, or Twitter. And they can use services like TuneCore and CD Baby to distribute throughout the world without the help of a major. That raises the question, what is the role of the major labels? Are they still necessary, and what do you offer artists that they cannot do on their own?

DM: I'm a huge fan of independents. I come from the independent sector. But I also see at close quarters the immense value that a major can add, especially in certain kinds of artists. I think some of this is actually genre related as well. When you look at an artist such as Katy Perry or Rihanna or Gaga or Timberlake, those mainstream global superstars, it's remarkable how much a major does contribute. With some artists that I can name, even the creative process has been hugely helped by the majors. There are many artists who benefit directly from genuine A&R contributions from the major labels, and many executives that I can think of that have really made a difference in artists' careers, bringing great song ideas, producer ideas, that have literally changed the game for an artist. That's just at the very beginning of the artist's development.

Obviously, everyone knows that in terms of promotion, a good major label can do wonderful things to expedite exposure through radio and video outlets, and there is still a physical marketthat matters. The major label makes a big difference with that part of it. Also, even though there are those international platforms you mentioned, there's nothing like a coordinated effort by a major label to develop an international superstar.

Look at what we're doing with Avicii. Avicii could have, I suppose, gone an independent route. This is one of the biggest EDM artists in the world, who has millions of followers and obviously is an incredibly high earner in terms of his live performances. He is also one of the biggest stars, as I mentioned, on Spotify. But what we've been able to contribute globally to Avicii's career is remarkable. I think on his first single, globally we're probably sold over 8 million singles in just a few months. His album is prominent all over the world and it's a concerted global effort that is synchronized. You get a sense of him dominating the worldwide market right now, in terms of exposure, presence, and what that means to his stature as an EDM star and in a way as a pop star. I feel like we've made a huge difference, and it was definitely the right thing for him and for us. That's where you see that global teamwork, one company working on a major superstar—and, if you would, I'm sure you remember from your Sony days, the intensity of the communication between all the countries of the world and the presidents and the staff to make this happen on a global basis is very valuable, if that's your goal. That's one aspect where I think majors can really make a difference.

I also think majors have been maligned in terms of the incredible contribution they make to artist development. Certainly at Island we're very much involved; we don't wait till someone has a hit. We jump in when we believe artists. We nurture them. We help them make an amazing record. We help them with their designs and artwork. We get involved in every aspect of their career, as much as they want us to. Whether it's a rock band like Neon Trees or the Wanted, an English-Irish boy band, or people like Taio Cruz, there have been a lot of international artists that we've been involved with that have really benefited from our contribution.

SG: I used to work with Sony's studio at West 54th. It was one of the biggest studios in New York, but Sony sold it, and now it's a condo. Recording studios have not fared well in the digital era, because new technologies have made it possible for many artists to record on their own. Home recording studios and Pro Tools have replaced to some extent the big studios. Recording costs, according to many, have fallen a great deal.

Have recording costs decreased dramatically as many people think?

DM: The answer is it varies very much based on genre. In the mainstream, the pop and urban arenas, I don't feel the costs have come down that much. What happens is that when you're dealing with a very competitive producer they are still able to command significant fees for their work. Recording costs have come down, but not that significantly in rock music. I also believe that with young bands and with people who are creatively independent, the costs are able to come down considerably. I've seen that happen.

SG: Let's talk about music videos. I used to administer the contracts for the production of all the music videos produced at Sony in the '90s and early 2000,s when MTV played videos 24/7. We made videos from $100K to way on up, for Michael Jackson for instance, to over $1million. Are the majors still spending massive sums on music videos as they did in the '90 s and early 2000s?

DM: Rarely. You're right, MTV doesn't play them, but what I'm finding more and more is that the value of videos is definitely on the rise in terms of marketing. There was a period where videos maybe weren't making as much difference, but if you look at videos today like the Blurred Lines video, you're actually seeing videos making a difference.

But it isn't about cost. It's about ideas. Where you've got a really original idea, it doesn't have to cost a lot of money to produce, but if it connects . . . For example, Pharrell is about to have a huge record in America with a song called "Happy," which is a video that is so simple. It was actually filmed over a 24-hour period in real time. This is not my artist; I'm just a real fan. That video's going to be really impactful.

I think costs have gone down a lot in video. I've also noticed that some of my videos, which were made very inexpensively, have gone viral, and have had as much or more impact than the actual official video.

SG: American Authors are one example that comes to mind. They have a little viral video for their single, "Best Day of My Life," that involves a very cute little dog. It's a great viral video and it's so popular. Neon Trees is another example. Their viral videos are very popular. Definitely, our video costs have come down significantly. Compared to your expense, I would say there is very significant difference, and much more sensible. Because videos are now based much more on ideas and creative impact than makeup artists and the kind of things that money was wasted on 10 years ago. That tends to have gone away, except for the superstars.

Do you see any other differences between the way business was done when we were at Sony in the '90s and early 2000s and now?

DM: Overall, my sense is that the business is so much better run now. The people who work in record companies now are totally committed. They are there because they really want to be there. I find the young generation incredibly hardworking. They don't see much delineation between work and play. They're available and they want to work and give everything to it. I see a big difference in commitment. The business is working because the values have shifted, so that it isn't about spending huge sums of money on videos anymore or traveling in private planes. It's more efficient. The money is better spent than it was. Although revenues have dropped, also the overheads have dropped and the way that people spend money has changed in a more responsible way, in a way that makes much more business sense. If you combine that with the potential monetization of the 360 components, which does sometimes genuinely make a big difference and which is part of deals now, by and large, and the monetization of streaming and, obviously, the growth of those services, I feel that we are definitely in a real business.

SG: Well, you just referenced 360 deals as a significant part of the business now. As you know, under the old standard recording contract, the record companies used to make money only from selling records; now they're sharing in other monies, including publishing, live performance, touring, merch, even appearances on television and film. Do you see any benefits to the artist in 360 deals?

DM: Yeah, I do, actually. We have a department that involves branding and strategic marketing, and brings so many opportunities to artists; I think that there is actually a genuine potential partnership there. I think when it comes to touring revenue, where we sign artists at the very beginning of their careers and we pour all our energies into helping bring them fame by our press efforts, by our TV efforts, by our radio efforts, given the dominance of live in generating money, I think it's a sensible thing for us to have a small contribution from them from that given what we're contributing to get them there. Ancillary interest is valuable in this marketplace, and it's valuable for both sides.

SG: One last question. What's next for David Massey, Island Records? What next big thing should we be looking for in 2014?

DM: I think this young band, American Authors, will make a big impact. I'm excited about the next Gaslight Anthem album. I feel that Avicii is going to go from strength to strength, and there's a young British teen group called the Vamps who are now completely unknown, but I believe that they will have made an impact this year for sure. I'm very excited about them. There's numerous others. I'm also very excited about the third Neon Trees that comes out in April. I've never been more excited about what we have coming than I am this year. It's a bit of a big list this year.

SG: I appreciate your time. Good luck to you in 2014.

DM: Thank you for the great questions. I really appreciate being included. Thank you.

Role of an Indie Music Label: Interview with Jay Frank, President of DigSin Music (How to Run a Successful Record Label by Giving Away the Music for Free)

Jay Frank, a former VP at Country Music Television and Yahoo Music, recently launched his own record company, called DigSin. Based in Nashville, DigSin, which stands for digital single, has a very unique business model: It gives away all its music for free. (In Part IV we also interview Frank on his book *FutureHit.DNA*, where he addresses how to write hit songs in the digital age.)

SG: Tell us a little bit about your background and what inspired you to launch your own record label.

JF: A couple years ago I started having this idea for a record company with a completely new model. Every time I thought about the problems the labels were having making as much money as they used to, I would say to myself, "There is a problem with the old business model," and then I would think about a way to solve it. And I just kept doing that. And I realized DigSin is one of those things that just needed to be tried.

SG: I want to talk about your new business model, but first tell me a bit about the artists you have signed.

JF: The artists are varied. When I go out to find people, they say, "What genres are you looking for?" I say, "I look for one genre, and that is the genre of great music."

Right now our artists include NNXT, an electropop artist who is also a writer/producer. She's rare, because when you really get down to the electronic pop artists out there, there is no female who is actually writing, producing, and singing her own songs. We also have an alternative singer-songwriter from LA. Musically, she is somewhere between Imogen Heap and Regina Spektor. She regularly sells out Hotel Café in LA. Just absolutely fantastic voice.

Then we have a roots revival band called Bronze Radio Return that have built up an amazing following. With very little traditional exposure, they've gotten millions of Spotify and YouTube plays. The passion from their fans has led to great opportunities in the sync world, which just generates more sales and fans. Like Swimming is a Swedish trio that is well loved in the blog world, which has led to a lot of strong opportunities in Europe and the US Our newer signings Lauren Shera and Stargroves are also ones we're very excited about.

What I look for in an artist is that I can say, "The artist and the songs are fantastic." I've instilled in my staff that if they bring an artist and they say, "This act is really good," I'll tell them, "Let's not sign them." Really good is just not good enough. Nowadays, for whatever genre and niche you're in, you have to be great. There is no business around "really good" anymore.

SG: In regard to DigSin, you wrote in an e-mail blast, "Part of the hook is that everyone who is on our company's mailing list will get every single release for free for life." How do you make money if you give away all the music on your website?

JF: People underestimate the value of the free download. I am sure that your readers have downloaded plenty of songs for free that bands are giving away on their websites. People who are discovering new music in this way and download songs usually listen to those songs only once. Also, as you know, people are starting to actually move their discovery over to streaming on-demand services such as Spotify. That means that if they only listen to it once, the value of the song is actually not the 99 cents that one would get on iTunes. The value of the song is actually one listen, which means that is how much I would get paid on Spotify. On Spotify, we can have a whole other conversation on whether or not artists are getting paid fairly. Whether we like it or not, right now, the going rate is somewhere around 2/10 of a cent. That means that the value of the free download is not 99 cents, it's 2/10 of a cent.

When somebody comes to the DigSin site and downloads the song for free, we're serving advertising. That advertising money is part of the pool that's shared with the artists on the royalty side. So by serving advertising, once we get to scale, we're actually going to make more money than we would on Spotify.

So when I give away a free download, the funny part is I do not look at it as saying, "Geez, I am making less money." I am actually sitting there saying, "I am making more money," because I know that most people are going to listen to it once and I am going to make more money than that same one listen on Spotify. So my free download is actually more lucrative for me, not less.

On top of that, I get to have a relationship with the customer. When people hear my music on Spotify, I have to hope that they spend the extra time to find my website. I, on the other hand, am establishing a regular communication with people who like my label's music. I'm able to tell people who like my label, "Go check out this other music you haven't heard." In addition I get analytics. I am able to see who the people who sign up on the mailing list are. Not super in-depth, but I know enough. I know if they're male or female, I know how old they are, and I know the general area where they live. So through that I can see who responds to the free download and I can start to paint a picture of who that potential fan is. Then I can use that information to better target-market that artist to the next group of potential fans. All of a sudden the free download, which seems like it's a liability in terms of making the label money, becomes the asset I can use to actually grow the company, and simultaneously make money.

I should add that we will also be offering T-shirts and other merch for the artist. That's part of the revenue pool, so if you like an artist I want to be able to sell you a T-shirt.

SG: I understand that in addition to giving music away on your site you sell the same music on other sites. Doesn't your website cannibalize those sales?

JF: We are doing our releases all the same way. We are selling music on iTunes; we have the music up on Spotify; we have the music up on YouTube and generating revenue from there. Every digital retailer you can think of, our music will be available on. The important part for us is, we want to make sure that when people hear about our music they are able to experience it—and in a way that we can monetize, however small that monetization may be. And the reality is, we will sell downloads.

We launched our company on a Monday. We got a lot of press, and every single article that came out about us said the same thing: that we gave away our music for free. It mentioned the artists, but it wasn't about the artists. It was about the fact that this was something different, giving away music for free. That was Monday. Tuesday, our first single was available for sale on iTunes, and we sold copies. So the reality is that even though all the publicity was about giving it away for free, we still sold music immediately.

Now, did we sell thousands? No, we did not sell thousands. But this was a brand new artist, NNXT, who nobody had ever heard of before, who had very little fan base to speak of. So the reality is that we're able to actually sell a little bit off of virtually no publicity. When the song actually becomes popular, even though we are giving away the song for free, we will still sell plenty on iTunes.

I look at it this way. Let us say you and I are in New York and we say, "Hey, let's go for a beer." We say, "Where do you want to go?" "Oh, I know that there's a bar across the street, let's go." We walk across the street. We drink Bud Light for $5 a bottle. Now, two doors down there could be a bar that has a happy hour. We did not go. We could have gotten two for one. There could have been a party around the corner that some artist was throwing, and that same Bud Light could have been free. So why did we go and spend $5 when we could have gotten drinks for half price or for free somewhere else equally as convenient? And the answer can be a number of things. One, it may have been around the corner, but we may not have known about it. Maybe we preferred the atmosphere. Maybe the party around the corner, you and I said, "Oh, you know, we would like to go there, but we're going to get hit up by this guy and I just don't want to talk to him." Any number of reasons could cause you to not go to where something is free. Music consumers are much the same way. Just because I'm giving it away for free, doesn't mean everyone is going to experience it that way.

For me, it is really just one avenue. And again, going back to the main tenet, how are people consuming music? Many people are consuming music for free. I am providing them a viable legal option that I can monetize and monetize well. Plenty of other people are buying music, and we're going to take advantage of that as well.

SG: Well, the trick with iTunes and Spotify and the others is you're just one out of millions of artists and tracks. How do you get people to go to your artists in those outlets?

JF: Well, the way you do it is you make the song popular. Again, we're using analytics extremely heavily in order to be able to better target-market our artists and make sure that they're visible. I tell my artists all the time, "In our initial phase we're going to take 99.9 percent of the Internet and we're going to ignore them. We are going to focus just on 0.1 percent, but most importantly the 0.1 percent that would actually care about you."

If we do our job right, we can go and pinpoint to say . . . with the example of NNXT, our electropop artist, not just to say that she's an electronic artist and let us find electronic music fans. But to know, as we have seen in the early days as an example, that there is a UK artist named Neon Hitch. People who like her seem to like NNXT. That profile also seems to be 16- to 24-year-old girls. So we now can say, "All right, as part of our profile let us find 16- to 24-year-old girls who like Neon Hitch." If we can find them and communicate with them through social networks, we have a higher likelihood of them responding positively than if we just went to electronic music fans. The more we can find details like that, and the more we can pinpoint that information and use that through all of the available tools that are out there now—through Twitter, Facebook, YouTube, now Pinterest, any of those things—we can now actually go and find these people, communicate directly with them, provide them something that enriches their life because we did the research. And they then not only enjoy the song, but they have a high likelihood of telling their friends, and through that something spreads. Going back to the quality, if the quality of the music is good enough, when we make that introduction, that introduction won't stop with that person. That introduction will be the starting point for that person's group of friends.

SG: Do you do 360 deals with your artists?

JF: We focus on what I call the 360 of the song, versus the 360 of the artist. So you have the master and publishing. With regard to the song, we are in fact promoting the song very heavily and trying to make that song extremely active. So we do participate on the publishing side of things. All of our deals are the same, which is that all of the money comes in, expenses are taken off the top, and everything that remains is a 50/50 split.

Outside of the couple of T-shirts that we license, we do not have any additional 360. So, an artist's live touring, an artist's endorsements, and artist's future record deals are not on the table. The major label people have told me I'm absolutely crazy that with my deals I don't get any back end, other than the songs. They say, "Surely you must have something where if that artist gets signed you will get points on their first two records with the major." I said, "No." They said, "Why not?" I said, "Because I am not greedy." They said, "But you deserve it." I said, "Yeah, but if I am signing the right songs, I am going to do just fine. Why should I worry?"

The masters we own and the publishing, that's a healthy enough revenue stream. Why do I need to cut any further onto the artist's income? That is kind of just my attitude that I take toward the whole thing.

Others have said to me, "If you are making these songs popular you need to have a rerecord clause to make sure the artists can't just go and get a new master from a major label." I said, "Do not want it." "Well, why not?" The answer is if I have got publishing then there's my income. If the major label thinks that they can record it better, then it is in their better interest and bless them, sure. I will be able to participate on the publishing. Why do I need to be greedy about the whole thing?

SG: That's extremely unique. Usually small labels have a clause with their artist that if a major label wants to sign the artist, the label gets half of what the major label is willing to pay the artist. But you are saying that an artist is free to leave your label at any time and you won't share in that label income?

JF: I got one better. All of my deals that I have—I am never afraid to tell this—all of my deals are six-song deals, which are two songs firm and an option for four more songs. I actually have something written in my deal that says if before they have delivered their six songs a major label comes along and the artist wants to accept the deal that the major label has offered, at that moment my options accelerate and I either have to pick up those songs right then and there, or I lose them. So I actually have a clause that makes sure that I will not be in a position to prevent an artist from graduating to a major label. I'm in a position to make sure that just because I'm involved it will not muck up their major label deal, if that is what they choose to do.

SG: Okay, sounds like a very fair deal. So, even though you're a record company, you are not evil.

JF: I try not to be. Seriously, if you look at new businesses that have succeeded, for the most part they have succeeded by being open and they've succeeded by listening to their client base. I listened for years, as you have, to the complaints that artists have had around record companies.

SG: So how are you breaking artists?

JF: For me it is about spending my time on the Internet, building the audience, building it to a point where I'm doing okay with that song and know that I have enough ammunition that when I present it to radio I can present it to them in as close to a no-brainer position as I possibly can. If I am able to do that, then I think we can get radio traction. And, more importantly, when you have to spend the money in order to promote it on radio I am in a much better position to do so, because I've probably set it up where prior to that point I've probably broken even or created a modest profit for that particular song. Then I am going to radio, not hundreds of thousands of dollars in the hole, like a major label is. I am going to radio already in the black. So therefore radio to me just becomes an effective spin to keep the ball growing and growing bigger, as opposed to a desperate situation of trying to create something and hope that it works to make my money back. And I will not work every song that is on my label to radio. I will only work the songs where the Internet and the fans have told me it has a high likelihood of succeeding.

SG: Aside from the media buzz that you've already received, how are you doing? How are you doing artistically and financially?

JF: Artistically I think I am in a fantastic spot. I feel strongly about all of my artists. I feel that they represent close to the best of what a new artist in their particular genre has to offer. If I'm able to maintain that level of quality, you may not like the electronic song, for an example, but hopefully you will recognize that for electronic music it is better than your average song, or better than your average artist. That is what I'm hoping to achieve.

Commercially, we are off to a great start as well. We are garnering interest across the web. We are getting regular write-ups on blogs. Film and TV people are starting to sniff around to see what we're doing. And, more importantly, those iTunes sales are increasing every single week. They are not taking huge leapfrog jumps, but they are growing every single week. And the web traffic is growing every single week. So, from my perspective, the seeds are in the ground and you can see that they're going to sprout and become beautiful plants.

But the trick is, just because I have a new model, doesn't mean this is any different than any other record label. You have to pay attention. You have to care about the artists. You have to nurture them along. You have to continually promote them and not stop. And you have to just grow and just recognize that it will be worth it, and you need patience, time, and a lot of elbow grease.

Managers and Artists

The Manager's Role

Managers have never played a more important role in the music business than today. Good managers should be able to advance the careers of their clients. Among the things that managers traditionally do are providing advice on all aspects of an artist's professional life, using their relationships to generate opportunities, negotiating deals when those opportunities arise, and helping the artist select other members of his or her "team," such as accountants, lawyers, booking agents, and publicists. In a sense their job has always been and still is to hold the artist's hand through all the inevitable trials and tribulations of being an artist in the rough and tumble of the music business. Traditionally, though, the manager has been most responsible for "shopping" the artist to a record label to secure the holy grail of a recording agreement, particularly with a major label.

That was the "payday" for both the artist and the manager. Managers work on commission, so the goal used to be to sign with a major label and negotiate the largest "advance" possible. When I was a lawyer at Sony Music, advances for a new artist ranged from $250,000 to more than $500,000. And an artist who caught on—and consequently his or her manager—could become very wealthy, just from record sales. Those days are largely over.

In 2014, record labels, which have lost roughly 65 percent of their income accounting for inflation from 1999, are signing fewer and fewer artists, and for those they do sign, the advances are far less lush. In fact, the artist may never get a "deal," or may be dropped from the roster sooner than in the old days, when the labels had spare cash to support an artist through one or two not very successful albums. For instance, it is well known that Bruce Springsteen did not catch fire until he had already put out two albums on Columbia. But the company had faith and stood by him. That is less likely to happen now, when even the major labels are trying hard just to survive. They would rather put resources in already established acts, where a return on investment is more likely.

Due to the current financial chaos in the record business, the manager's role is more crucial than ever. In the old days, once the artist was signed to a big label, the manager served as a liaison between the record company and the artist, and sometimes as a shield against the record company. For instance, if the label pressured the artist to change his or her style or to record a particular song, the manager would intervene on the artist's behalf or try to arrive at a compromise with the label. The manager would also work in conjunction with and sometimes prod the marketing department at the label to spend more time and money on marketing and promoting his or her artist. But due to budget cuts and massive layoffs at the labels, the manager may be called upon to do some of that work personally. For example, the manager may take over social networking, try get his artist's music in movies or advertising campaigns, or find branding opportunities with sponsors. And if the artist can't find a deal or a deal good enough to accept, the manager may become the artist's de facto label. A manager in that situation may try to secure monies to produce records and videos from investors or crowdfunding, arrange for both physical and digital distribution, and do everything else that record companies traditionally have done.

Management Contracts

Most manager agreements have boilerplate wording stating that the manager's role is to counsel the artist and do everything possible to enhance the artist's career. The artist on the other hand is supposed to agree to pay a manager a "commission" in exchange for the manager's performance of these duties. The most important terms in a management agreement are

- The definition of the manager's "commission"
- The duration of the agreement
- The period of time during which the manager is entitled to a commission
- Who collects the money

Definition of the Commission

Managers work on spec. If an artist pays an hourly rate or salary, then the person or company who is performing the functions of a manager should instead be called a paid "consultant." Managers are, or are supposed to be, people who believe in the artist so much that they are willing to work for little or no money until the artist becomes successful, although some managers will not take on an artist who is not already earning at least a moderate income from which the manager can take a commission. In any event, the manager's income consists of a piece of the income that the artist earns in the entertainment business. That piece is referred to as a commission and is generally 15 percent to 20 percent. Usually, but not always, the commission is based on "gross receipts or earnings." Here is a typical clause:

> For the purposes of this Agreement, subject to the terms and provisions of this Agreement, the term "Gross Earnings" shall mean the total of all earnings and other consideration, whether in the form of salary, bonuses, royalties (or advances against royalties), settlements, payments, fees, interests, property, percentages, shares of profits, stock, merchandise or any other kind or type of income or remuneration, related to Artist's career in the entertainment industry in which Artist's artistic talents or services are exploited that is received at any time by Artist, or by any person or entity (including Manager) on Artist's behalf

This clause is from a standard "pro-management" deal. It's a kind of contract that almost every music lawyer has on the shelf (along with the "pro-artist" agreement). It is crucial for the artist that this definition be revised so that "Gross Earnings" excludes certain forms of income that the artist needs to spend in furthering his or her career.

For instance, if a recording agreement provides that a label will pay an advance of $50,000, most of that money may be used for recording costs, such as payments for studio time, producers, side musicians, and mixing. If the payout to those third parties amounts to $40,000, and manager's commission is 20 percent, the manager's take would be $8,000 and the artist would only receive $2,000. Moreover, the artist would still be responsible for paying taxes, and for all other expenses such as the accountant, attorney, vocal coach, etc.

Similarly, if the artist is unsigned and paying for the costs of touring, unless the management agreement is carefully negotiated, the artist could easily finish a tour with little or no profit, or even a debt to the manager. For instance, perhaps expenses—such as a tour bus, gas, hotel, etc.—come to $12,000 on a tour that's brought in $15,000 for playing live gigs. The manager's commission would be 20 percent of $15,000, or $3,000, leaving the artist with exactly nothing.

The bottom line is all reasonable expenses, such as production costs (including videos as well as records) and touring costs (including light and sound expenses as well as travel and accommodations) have to be spelled out in the agreement and deducted from "Gross Earnings." The quibbling comes in when the attorneys try to define reasonable expenses. For instance, if the artist has to fly to a gig, the manager's attorney may insist that he or she fly coach, spend less than $50 a day on food, rent an economy car, and stay at no better than a 3 star hotel. The artist's attorney will want to deduct car rental and any other costs that the venue does not cover.

Duration of the Agreement (the Term)

The duration of the agreement is just as important as the definition of the manager's commission. Management-artist relationships are like marriages: They can be great, or they can go bad. If things do not work out, it is very disadvantageous to the artist if the manager still has the right to a commission, because the artist may want to have nothing more to do with the manager. It's in the manager's interest for the term to be longer, because it gives him or her more time in which to help make the artist successful (which could be in the artist's interest if things work out) and over which to claim a commission (which is practically never in the artist's interest). A "pro-management" form of agreement, which most music attorneys have ready at a moment's notice, may be three years with options to extend the term of the agreement at the manager's election. A fairer deal would be 18 months with the option to extend being tied to certain performance goals. For example, the manager would have the right to extend the term for an additional year, but only if the artist makes over a certain amount of money, and an additional year after that if the artist makes more than he or she did in the first option year. The actual amounts are often spelled out—after protracted negotiations. Alternatively, performance goals can be tied to other goals, such as getting a deal with a label or publishers. Everything is subject to negotiation, although everything also depends on the bargaining power of the parties and the negotiating skills of their attorneys.

How Long the Manager Is Entitled to a Commission

An off-the-shelf pro-management agreement will have absolutely no time limits on the manager's right to receive a commission from agreements entered into during the term of the contract. It will state that any agreement entered into during that term, or any "renewal, extension, modification, or substitution" of such an agreement, will be subject to a manager's commission. This means that as long as the artist is with the same label or music publisher as the one the manager helps the artist get signed to, the artist will be obliged to continue to pay the manager. Many successful artists, such as Bruce Springsteen, Billy Joel, and Bob Dylan, have been with same the record company for decades. For example, Bob Dylan signed with Columbia Records in 1961 and is still with that label!

The artist will want to negotiate a "sunset clause." Sunset clauses specify that even if the artist is making money from a contract originally entered into during the term of the agreement, the manager will not receive a commission after the termination of the agreement or at least will receive less than the full commission. Here is a typical sunset clause:

> Following the commission term, Artist shall pay Manager's commission ("post term commission") with respect to Artist's gross earnings, as and when collected, derived from term products, term services, and pre-term products as follows:
> Post-Term Years Consultant's Commission
> 1 12.5 percent
> 2 7.5 percent
> 3–4 2.5 percent
> 5+ 0 percent

Sunset clauses reward managers for their work during the term of the agreement and at the same time afford the artist the ability to sign with another manager and avoid paying two full commissions.

Who Collects the Money

Many good managers do not want to collect the money and be required to prepare accounting statements to an artist, because that can be a big job in itself. These managers would prefer generating opportunities. The artist in turn may not feel completely comfortable relying on the manager to pay him or her. A good alternative, at least when the artist is making significant income, is for the parties to mutually approve a third-party "business manager" (usually a certified accountant) who can collect and accurately account to both the artist and the manager. The business manager can also be responsible for paying the artist's taxes, managing the artist's money (so it isn't spent too quickly), and advise the artist on investment opportunities. Business managers usually receive a 5 percent fee for these services. Again, just as in the deal between the artist and the manager, that fee should be a percentage of the artist's income, excluding income that the artist must spend for production costs, touring, and other reasonable expenses.

Other Important Terms and Issues

Power of attorney: Some managers will ask for the right to enter into agreements on behalf of an artist. The artist may wish to give the manager the right to sign agreements on their behalf but only after the manager consults with him and he is apprised of terms of any agreement and accepts the contract.

Audit and accounting: If the artist or the manager collects the money, there should be an accounting and audit provision applying to that party;

"Key man" or "key person" provision: If the manager is in an individual working at a management company, a "key man" provision states that that person will have day-to-day responsibility for managing the artist's career. Here is a typical "key man" provision:

> During the Term the "Key Person" shall be actively involved in rendering services hereunder. In the event both Key Persons are not actively involved in rendering services hereunder, Artist shall notify Manager of such default and Manager shall be allowed a period of thirty (30) days after receipt of such written notice, within which to cure such default. In the event that such default is not cured within said thirty (30) day period, Artist's sole remedy shall be to terminate the Term of this Agreement by written notice to Manager, effective upon Manager's receipt of such notice.

"Carve-out" clauses: These are clauses designed to exclude income that it may be unfair for a manager to commission. For instance, for a DJ at a radio station who makes a salary but wants to hire a manager to promote her career as a live performer and recording artist, it may be reasonable to "carve out" the salary from the radio station from the income the manager can commission.

Songs, masters, and other intellectual property: A truly pro-management form will include a clause allowing a manager to commission ". . . any product of Artist's services or talents or of any property, including musical compositions, created by Artist in whole or in part during the term hereof."

This is sometimes referred to as a manager's "pension" clause, since one great song can generate income for a lifetime or longer. Unless revised, this little sentence would allow the manager to commission income from a song that the artist happened to write during the term forever (or at least until the song fell into the public domain—life of the artist plus 70 years!). In any competently drafted management agreement there should also be a clause that states that the manager has no duty to find an artist "employment," but if he does, this will be "incidental" to his other duties. In most states, including New York and California, only licensed talents agents are authorized to find an artist employment, including live gigs.

Interview with Emily White, Cofounder of Whitesmith Entertainment

Although only 30 years old, Emily White is already a force in the entertainment business as the "White" in WhiteSmith Entertainment, a talent management company that represents both music artists and comedians. Current music clients include Brendan Benson and Urge Overkill. The firm's comedy division, headed by Keri Smith Esgula, has launched the careers of Kamau Bell (*Totally Busted* on Fox) and Kevin Avery (*Chappelle's Show*), among others. Emily also founded the company's sports management division following the 2012 Olympics, developing gold medalist swimmer Anthony Ervin's presence and brand with tactics rooted in modern music marketing. Emily also cofounded a record label with client Brendan Benson in 2012.

SG: Please give a thumbnail sketch of your career.

EW: I definitely set out to work in the music industry. I did about eight internships as an undergrad music industry major at Northeastern University. When I was still in school, I met the Dresden Dolls when they were a local band and became their tour manager, which took me all over the world. Upon graduating, I began working at their management company, Madison House, for Mike Luba. At Madison House, I worked with the Dolls, the Fiery Furnaces, Dinosaur Jr., Angelique Kidjo, Taj Mahal, and others, really learning the craft of management. Luba eventually left to work at Michael Cohl's Live Nation Artists. I went, too, accepting a position from Bob Ezrin in the recording division. Following that, I launched Whitesmith Entertainment in 2008 with Keri Smith Esquia, Readymade Records and Publishing with Brendan Benson in 2012, and recently cofounded Dreamfuel, which is crowdfunding for athletes.

SG: What is the role of a manager in a musical artist's career?

EW: The manager is the point person for all aspects of an artist's career. We set the short- and long-term plan with the artist; we assemble, inherit, and tweak the team around them to ensure everyone is constantly working hard towards those short- and long-term goals. We are the liaison between the artist and the rest of the world, working as partners with the artist and basically as CEO of their business.

SG: Tell us about some of your clients and what you do for them.

EW: I have been working with Brendan Benson of the Raconteurs for almost five years. Brendan is an interesting example because he's been on a slew of labels, is in a huge band, has a well-respected solo career, and, in addition to being an artist, is a producer, songwriter, multi-instrumentalist, and vocalist. We do everything for Brendan, and because he is so prolific as an artist and a producer, we helped him set up his own label and publishing company, Readymade Records, a few years ago. This gives Brendan a well-deserved platform to record and release music in a sustainable manner forever. Prior to that, he had released four albums on four labels. There had been no consistency in his career, and hopefully we have changed that for good. Beyond that, we always make sure Brendan is feeling good about what kind of work he is doing, as technically my title is Personal Manager. Our office handles all promo requests and there pretty much isn't anything he does that we aren't directly spearheading and/or involved in.

SG: Managers don't need a license, and there is no school for music management that I know of, so what qualifies a person to be a good manager?

EW: I have a lot of pride in the skills that it takes to be a manager and feel incredibly grateful to have been schooled under Mike Luba and Kevin Morris when they were at Madison House. They are music-loving people who work in the industry for the right reasons. Through their ways of doing things, I was taught to build businesses around the artist and always take care of the fans. That mentality has been the foundation of my career and I've never looked back. Beyond that, it's important to be honest, a good person, and do the things you say you're going to do, being accountable at all times; otherwise as a manager you're not going to get anywhere.

SG: If you are an emerging band or artist, how do you go about finding a good manager?

EW: Genuine and natural networking. All but two clients I've ever worked with came through a natural relationship. Even if you're shy, get out there and start meeting folks. Reputations often speak for themselves. We take on artists of all sizes, but in this era, there are so many ways to get some things going on your own that if you build it, management will come. First and foremost, however, the art of course has to be great.

SG: We all think that the manager's job is to make their client a star, but what makes someone a good client? Can you give us examples of how clients can help their managers make them more successful?

EW: A good client is someone who gets back to us within 24 hours but also respects holidays and weekends so we can have normal human breaks to recharge. As mentioned, we consider ourselves partners with the artists. I don't work for them and they don't work for me. But the faster artists get back to me on e-mails and phone calls, the faster we can move their careers forward.

SG: Let's talk about creative choices and the manager's role in helping the artist make them. I have a young client who is just graduated college and is now a background for a successful Bachata band, but she can also sing in English, and when she does she sounds like Beyoncé. What would you advise if you were her manager?

EW: She should do both. Diversify her career to get multiple avenues and revenue streams going while staying true to herself. Hopefully she can write as well! And if not, writing and recording are skills she should work on developing as they will benefit her in the long-term.

SG: How has the music industry and specifically the role of the manager changed in the digital age? What new opportunities and challenges have emerged for a music manager in the digital age?

EW: The role of manager in the new music industry has expanded for sure. It is our job to create and shape careers as opposed to find deals that might supplement career goals. Deals are still a large part of an artist's career, but a traditional label structure is something that cannot be counted on anymore. And again, with so many great direct-to-fan marketing tools out there, if the artist is great and the artist is willing to work hard, there's no reason why one can't start building a long-term fan base from day one (assuming the music is fantastic). I suppose the main challenge is that it's more work than ever, since the manager, agent, and attorney are generally the most consistent team members an artist will have. But management has always been a ton of work, so I suppose it's more that the type of work has changed as opposed to the amount. Regardless, if people think it's just about being in charge, being cool and hanging out, they will fail. Confidence is important, but that has to be backed up with knowledge and results. As far as being cool and hanging out? That might be 5 to 10 percent of it, but the rest is being a geek about one's inbox and staying on top of calls and e-mails. I clear my inbox daily and teach young managers modern office skills, as ultimately that's a huge foundation of what we do.

SG: There are tens of thousands of records released every year in the US alone. One stat is 75,000 records—but only 10,000 sell more than 1,000, and only 1,000 sell more than 10,000. Given that stat, is the holy grail, the only way to success, to find a leading record company to provide marketing, advertising, tour support, and radio play, as well as cover production costs?

EW: Not at all. The holy grail is to diversify oneself, making sure all possible revenue streams are looked after properly: touring, merch, publishing, sponsorship, sync strategy, direct-to-fan sales, and beyond. If one wants a hit, which many of us do, a major label is the best route; but there are other ways to have a successful career in which artists don't have to give up quite so many rights.

SG: Would you suggest that an artist have a written contract with a manager?

EW: Absolutely, as it clearly defines the relationship for both parties. A management agreement is like a pre-nup in a way. Figure out what should happen if a split were to unfortunately happen and then put it in a drawer and forget about it.

SG: Would you like to add any additional thoughts about the role of the manager in this digital age?

EW: Artist managers work on commission, which means we only make money if the artist does. Don't take that for granted. Many other team members in an artist's career charge fees up front and are paid no matter what. That is not the case with your manager, who is there for you and your career in every way. Nurture that relationship and it will only continue to grow to the artist's benefit.

Additional Resources

There are many books about music business and law. These are among the best:

Donald S. Passman, *All You Need to Know about the Music Business* (8th ed., Simon and Schuster, 2012)
Peter M. Thall, *What They'll Never Tell You about the Music Business: The Myths, the Secrets, the Lies (and a Few Truths)* (2nd ed., Billboard Books, 2010)
Jeffrey Brabec and Todd Brabec, *Music, Money, and Success: The Insider's Guide to Making Money in the Music Business* (7th ed., Schirmer, 2011)

These are the leading treatises on copyright law:

Melville B. and David Nimmer, *Nimmer on Copyright* (Matthew Bender, 2004)
Robert Clarida, *Copyright Law Deskbook* (BNA Books, 2009)

This is the best book for music industry contracts because it provides expert commentary on provisions in a variety of the most important agreements:

Donald Farber, ed., *Entertainment Industry Contracts: Negotiating and Drafting Guide*, vol. 4, *Music* (Matthew Bender, 2004)

Chapter 2

PRACTICAL ADVICE IN RESPONSE TO CLIENTS' MOST-ASKED QUESTIONS

This chapter addresses the questions that I hear most often when potential clients call me. Those questions are:

1. Somebody stole my song! What can I do? How much can I get? When can I get it, and how much will it cost?
2. How can I protect my name, or my band or label's name? Should I register the name, and how much will it cost?
3. How can a music lawyer help me? Will my lawyer shop my record, and how much will it cost?

In regard to (1) and (2), I enlisted the aid of leading experts who specialize in copyright litigation and trademark law. For the third question, I turned to veteran music attorneys Don Passman and Peter Thall.

Somebody Stole My Song! What Can I Do? How Much Can I Get?

In this interview, copyright attorney Robert Clarida gives a brilliant cost-benefit analysis of starting a legal action for copyright infringement specifically relating to music. Bob is a partner at the New York firm of Reitler Kailas and Rosenblatt LLC, and advises clients in a wide range of industries, including software, film, music, photography, and new media. He also serves as adjunct professor of copyright law at Columbia Law School. In addition to his JD, Bob earned a PhD in music composition. He is the author of the *Copyright Law Deskbook* (BNA, 2009) and also edited the first two editions of this book.

SG: Hi, Bob. Let's suppose that a potential client calls you, introduces himself, and says, "I heard a song on the radio and it is almost the same as my song!" Take us through the conversation you would have with the client. What would your preliminary questions be?

BC: First, I would want to hear the songs, but I see that's your next question, so I'll get to it in a minute. Assuming the songs are similar, it would be essential to establish that the client's song was actually somehow made accessible to the defendant. No matter how similar two songs are, there's no copyright infringement if the second song was created independently, without the artist ever having heard the first one. Copyright infringement requires copying, and you can't copy something you never heard. A lot of infringement cases fail on this basis, because frequently the client has not released his song commercially in a big way—maybe he's played it at a few gigs, or it was on the local radio station once, or maybe it's on his MySpace or Facebook page; maybe you can even buy it on iTunes. In those kinds of cases it can be very hard to establish that there was a "reasonable opportunity" for the defendant to hear the song, which is what the law requires. Sure, it's theoretically possible, but "mere possibility" isn't enough, and speculation isn't enough.

But if there was a "reasonable opportunity" for the defendant to hear the song, the case can go forward—even if the defendant claims he didn't actually hear the song (as of course he will). So let's say the client was an opening act for the defendant one night, and played the song at the gig, he has a video of it that his mother took, whatever. The defendant would clearly have a reasonable opportunity to have heard the song, even though he might say he was out in the tour bus relaxing while the opening act was on. That's just a credibility question, of whether you believe the defendant's story. Clearly he had a reasonable opportunity, and it will be up to the jury to decide whom to believe.

Frequently, the client will have sent demos of the song to various record labels, handed a demo to a producer at a party, things like that. In those cases, you really have to establish a connection, or a "channel of communication," between the person who got the demo and the creative team that made the record. Just sending something to the mailroom of a big label is not enough to establish access as to every subsequent record that label releases, or even any record by that label. The courts call this "bare corporate receipt," and it never succeeds in establishing access.

If there is "widespread dissemination" of a song, however, meaning extensive airplay, access is established. The George Harrison case over "He's So Fine" and the Michael Bolton case over the Isley Brothers' "Love Is a Wonderful Thing" are both examples of that—there's no way a defendant can plausibly say he or she never heard the earlier record, even though as I recall the Isleys' tune was not a huge hit.

SG: Of course, you would have to have to hear and compare the two songs, correct? How similar do they have to be for copyright infringement? It is often said there are a finite number of chords in pop music and there are always going to be some similarities to preexisting songs.

BC: First, there's a kind of sliding scale, related to access. If you have a very clear case of access, less similarity may be needed to show infringement, but if access is really far-fetched, the similarity has to be very compelling. There's even a concept of "striking similarity" some courts have used to say that if two songs are exactly alike in some unusual, quirky way, that can be enough to show access all by itself. For example, if our client had written a song with the word "supercalifragilisticexpialidocious" in it, before *Mary Poppins*, the mere presence of that word in *Mary Poppins* would be virtually impossible to explain, except to say it was copied. There's not really a good argument that it was independently created.

But even with a strong or "striking" similarity, there may be no infringement. To take the *Mary Poppins* example, if the only similarity was that one word, with no rhythmic or melodic or harmonic similarities, the second song would probably still not infringe. One "striking" word may be proof of copying, but that doesn't mean it's proof of infringement. What you need is "substantial similarity" with respect to the protectable elements of the client's song, and one word, even a made-up word, is probably not enough—I think everyone could go out tomorrow and use the word "supercalifragilisticexpialidocious" in a song and they'd be okay. What you can't do, though, is also take any significant portion of the melody and harmony and rhythm of the *Mary Poppins* song, because then you're going to have recognizable similarity as to protectable elements. There's a recent case called *Bridgeport v. UMG*, involving a hip-hop group called Public Announcement that had made a very inconspicuous use of the lyric and melody of "bow-wow-wow-yippee-yo-yippee-yay" from George Clinton's "Atomic Dog." They were held to be infringers: they took the melody, rhythm, and lyric of George Clinton's hook and used in their own song. That was too much, even as part of the background during the fade-out. Similarly with Michael Bolton, who was held to infringe the Isley Brothers' "Love Is a Wonderful Thing" in his song of the same name, although there's really not much similarity besides the lyric and title. There's a great website people should check out, started by Charles Cronin, that's got music clips from the actual songs at issue in virtually every music-infringement case ever decided; it's a joint project by Columbia and UCLA at cip.law.ucla.edu. The best way to get a sense of what infringes and what doesn't is to spend some time on that site and get familiar with what the courts have already done. It's hugely instructive, even though you might come away thinking the cases are all over the map, which they arguably are.

One big point I need to make, though, is that a lot of pop songs (and metal songs, and smooth jazz songs, and bluegrass songs, etc.) sound very much alike, simply because people are writing within certain shared patterns and conventions. Some melodic figures and chord progressions which may strike the client as unique and original (because they've never heard them before) are actually pretty common once you start looking for them, and another song with those same features will probably not be infringing, however much the client may feel it's a rip-off. That's why it's usually not enough to have a song that's kinda sorta the same; it's really got to be exactly the same, and for more than just a few notes, to be an infringement. Once you knock out all the commonplace stuff, which the court will do, there's often not much left of the claim. I got a PhD in music composition before I was a lawyer, and I can analyze melody and harmony better than most expert witnesses, at least judging from the expert reports I've seen, but no matter what kind of chart or graph an expert might make to show similarities, it's ultimately the ear of a layperson on the jury that has to make the call. If your client can play the two songs back-to-back for 10 total strangers, without telling them what result he's looking for, and nine of them call it a rip-off, you've got a case. If you need to show some color-coded chart made by an expert, think again before bringing the claim.

SG: Once you hear the two songs, and assuming you find there is sufficient similarity between the songs for copyright infringement, then whom would be the target be? Suppose the offending song was recorded and sung by "Johnny Rapper." Would you only go against Johnny, or his record company and music publisher, as well?

BC: Typically, you'd sue as many people as you can plausibly link to the sale of the infringing song: the artist, the label, the publisher, the producer; and there's often several publishers, and maybe several producers, so you'd put them all in the caption. Probably not iTunes or Walmart—although retailers are often sued in other kinds of copyright cases, like with fabric designs, for example, you don't see it so much in music claims. Clearly they are distributing the infringing work, though, and making money at it, so there's no reason the law shouldn't reach them. Maybe we'll start seeing more of that, since record sales are being concentrated in so few places now.

SG: I suppose the very next conversation with the client is "Is it worth it?" For instance, would you recommend sending a "demand" before filing a lawsuit, to save money, and if so, what would that letter say?

BC: Yes, I would send a demand letter in almost every case, unless there was some reason to think that the defendant would react by starting a declaratory judgment action in some distant place. Usually, the defendants in a case like this will not do that, because they will hope and expect that it can all go away either by ignoring it or throwing a little money at it, certainly less than they'd have to spend on litigating. So they probably won't start a lawsuit. The demand letter will basically say what your claim is: the client is the owner of copyright in a song called XYZ, registered in the Copyright Office no. PA1234567. If it's not registered, now is the time to register it; you may even want to register on an expedited "special handling" basis before you send out your demand letter, to make the letter more impactful. You will then go on to identify the infringing song, say that it is copied from and substantially similar to protectable elements of the client's song XYZ, and that it therefore violates the Copyright Act, 17 U.S.C. § 101 et seq. Then comes the demand: the defendants must stop all further use and exploitation of the song, account for all money received to date from exploitation of the song, and pay a sum not less than the amount they've made to date or they will act at their peril.

SG: In your experience, what is the likelihood that a strong letter will result in a tangible benefit for the client? Or is it most often the case that such letters are ignored and nothing will happen unless a lawsuit is filed?

BC: It depends on a lot of things. If you have a really strong case, and the defendants are being represented by a responsible grown-up, and you have a credible copyright lawyer writing the letter, there can be a quick settlement. I've certainly seen that happen; it never makes sense for defendants to pour a bunch of money into a lawsuit if they know they'll have to litigate and they know they'll lose. If the client doesn't seem to have the wherewithal to sue, however, or if the case is thin, or if the defendants are just ignoring the problem or reacting to it with bluster rather than rational thought, it will take more than a letter to get them thinking clearly about the spot they're in. There are middle steps between a demand letter and starting a full-blown lawsuit, though. If the song is on the web somewhere, you can send a DMCA notice to the host of the site on which it appears, and often the host will take it down. (If a defendant is hosting his own site, this will obviously not be effective, and even with a third-party host, the defendant could send a counter-notice and get the song put back up, but he may not want to bother to do so.) You can draft a complaint, and send it to the defendants with a letter saying we plan to file this in *x* days if we can't resolve our dispute. You can draft a complaint, file it with the court, but not formally serve it on the defendants, and say, "We have commenced this action, we will serve it on you in *x* days if, etc." This has the advantage of essentially precluding a declaratory judgment action, if you have reason to worry about that (for example, if the defendants are in California and you're in New York, you don't want them to beat you to the courthouse and file in California). Or you can go all the way, formally serve the complaint on the defendants with a summons, which starts their clock for having to hire a lawyer and respond within 20 days or they're in default.

SG: Suppose you send the letter but hear nothing back and a lawsuit must be filed—what would you tell the client as to how much money he is likely to recover and how long it will take? Let's focus on timing of recovery first; isn't it true the client may have to wait a long time to see any money? The "He's So Fine" case against George Harrison[92] took 12 years for a final decision on liability and damages! Is this standard?

BC: It can take a very long time to get a final result from a court: a year or more until you get to a jury; then maybe another year or more until an appeal is argued and decided, if someone appeals; and then maybe another proceeding on remand if the appeal doesn't resolve all the issues. But bear in mind that most cases settle at some point in the process, often fairly early through mediation or simple negotiation. Once the parties start paying tens of thousands every month in legal bills—and they will, if the case is being vigorously litigated—they quickly begin to see the value in settling even if they think they'd ultimately prevail.

SG: Couldn't you try for a preliminary injunction (PI)? That could take much less time, prevent the defendant from selling the song, and force a quick settlement.

BC: You could, but that would front-load the expenses in a big way. You'd have to spend those tens of thousands immediately to get a PI ready, and even if you won the PI you'd probably have to post a bond, which the court holds as security in case it turns out that you really don't win and the defendant's business has been halted for no good reason. Sometimes it's warranted, and the leverage can be great if you win, because a defendant may have to stop selling a record (or showing a movie with an infringing song in the soundtrack) just as it's taking off, but it's a very expensive proposition. I guess, like anything else, if you're willing to take a big risk you might get a big reward.

SG: Now let's talk about damages. Having registered the song doesn't mean the client will get the maximum statutory damages of $150,000, correct? What will the client have to prove to get that?

BC: Well, the statutory-damage number you mention, $150,000, is the top of the range for willful infringement. So the first thing you'd have to prove would be willfulness, basically meaning that the defendant knew he was ripping off your client and he did it anyway. If the infringement was something less than willful, like where the defendant credibly says, "I really didn't know what I was doing was a rip-off; it was just a tune that came into my head" (George Harrison said that, if you read his court transcript), the maximum for statutory damages is $30,000. For any statutory-damage award, willful or not, you'd also have to show some kind of connection between the number you're asking for and the actual harm suffered—statutory damages are not supposed to be a windfall. But if the defendant's song has been successful, the client would go for actual damages.

SG: Well, what about actual damages? If the song made a million bucks, and the client wins the case, how much does he get?

BC: Actual damages are basically the profits made by the defendant from the infringing song. That can be a huge number, and you don't have to show willfulness or anything, just that there was an infringement and the defendant made profits of *x*. "Profits" is basically gross revenue less the associated costs, including general overhead (unless the infringement is willful—there are some cases saying the defendant can't deduct general overhead for a willful infringement, so it would pay to prove willfulness even though you don't have to). The court doesn't necessarily award the whole profits number, though; it can only award the profits attributable to the infringement. Where a song is very substantially copied, the court would probably attribute the whole profits to the stolen material, but if the infringement is very short and fleeting, like the little George Clinton reference in the fade-out of the Public Announcement track, the court can and should apportion the profits and only award the amount it can reasonably attribute to the infringement.

SG: If the client registered the song, and he wins the case, will the court always award attorneys' fees?

BC: No, even if the client registered before the infringement. The best that plaintiffs can know for sure is that they are *eligible* for an award of attorneys' fees, not that they will automatically get it. (If they didn't register before the infringement, or within 90 days of publishing their work, they aren't even eligible for attorneys' fees.) Winning parties in copyright cases often get a fee award, but the main issue is whether the defendant's position is "objectively unreasonable." If the defense to an infringement claim is plausible enough to get to a jury trial, meaning that it survives a summary judgment motion, it is probably not objectively unreasonable. Also, the client needs to bear in mind that the defendant can get fees if he wins and the plaintiff's position is shown to be objectively unreasonable.

SG: Can you give us an idea of what it costs to start a lawsuit for copyright infringement?

BC: As I discussed earlier, there are several intermediate steps between a demand letter and serving a complaint, one of which is to "start a lawsuit" by filing the complaint but not formally serving it. That can often get settlement talks happening, and it gives the parties up to four months to work something out before they have to start litigating. You don't have to be rich to do that, but it might cost several thousand dollars to draft a complaint even if the case is very straightforward. A cease-and-desist letter is much cheaper but also puts essentially no pressure on defendants, and they can easily blow it off indefinitely if they so choose (again, if they have no responsible grown-ups around). Obviously, the best answer to almost every dispute is a settlement, which is why almost all cases settle. And a settlement is much easier for defendants with "deep pockets." So if you're asking for a $50,000 settlement from Goldman Sachs—maybe if they used the client's song on their website or something—that $50,000 is easier for them to part with than it would be for some formerly high-living musician who's now in bankruptcy. I think the depth of the defendant's pockets is more relevant to how much you settle for, rather than whether you take any action at all. Even if the infringer is broke, you still want him to stop using the client's music. Also, there are other ways to resolve a dispute besides money. Maybe the defendant is an established artist who would give the client credit as a cowriter or producer on the infringing track, or some future track, or agree to record several of the client's tunes on his next album, or something else that would be of value to the client but would not involve the defendant writing a big check. Often people don't think about these sorts of proposals until the lawsuit is under way and there's a mediation or settlement conference, but there's no reason to wait that long—unless you want to spend more money on your lawyer, which I certainly don't want to discourage.

How Can I Protect My Name or My Band's Name? How Much Will It Cost?

This interview answers the previously posed questions and goes well beyond to present one of the best trademark law primers for musicians, bands, and labels that I have seen. I want to express my thanks to James Trigg of Kilpatrick Townsend & Stockton LLP and Ashford Tucker of Fross Zelnick Lehrman & Zissu, P.C., two law firms often recognized among the leading firms in the world in the area of trademarks. They devoted a great deal of time and attention to addressing each of my questions. James is a partner whose practice focuses on copyright and trademark issues arising in the context of the Internet. Additionally, he has advised a variety of entertainers and creators on domestic and international trademark and branding issues, and he is an adjunct professor of trademark law at the University of Georgia School of Law. Ashford is an associate whose practice focuses on international brand protection, counseling clients in a variety of industries, including music, on trademark and copyright matters. Ashford also previously wrote for Pitchfork, the online music publication.

SG: Can you run down the basics? What is a trademark, and why is it important to artists and bands?

JT and AT: A trademark serves to identify the source of goods or services. When we see marks like COCA-COLA, MICROSOFT, BUDWEISER, and BMW, we instantly associate them with the products sold in conjunction with them, and we rely on these names to assist us in distinguishing one product or service from another. Thus, generally, trademark law seeks to prevent consumer confusion by allowing trademark owners to control the use of their marks so that consumers can rely on a trademark as an indication of a product or service's unique characteristics.

The law of trademarks applies to the fields of music, film, literature, and art just as readily as it does to soda, software, beer, and cars. Of course, most of us do not like to think of the arts as a "commodity," something that merely is bought and sold. Similarly, artists themselves at times may be reluctant to view their names or their creations as commercial trademarks that identify them to the public in exactly the same way that BUDWEISER identifies Anheuser-Busch. Nonetheless, by taking steps to protect their names, entertainers and artists can assume greater control of their identities and the way that those identities are perceived by the public.

Protectable Forms of Marks

Trademarks can assume innumerable forms, the only qualification being that they serve a source-identifying function for their owners. Naturally, there are traditional word marks: R.E.M., WEEZER, and NINE INCH NAILS all are trademarks that have been registered by their respective owners with the United States Patent and Trademark Office (PTO). Word marks can also take the form of personal names. For example, Madonna, Paul McCartney, and Faith Hill all have obtained trademark protection for their performing names.

Additionally, some artists and record labels (e.g., the Grateful Dead, Aerosmith, and Sub Pop) have developed and registered as trademarks distinctive logos and designs that serve to identify them to the public.

Notably, Kiss owns trademark registrations for its stylized KISS logo and the distinctive face paint worn by its members.

Quasi-Protectable Marks

Titles of literary and artistic works, while not completely unprotectable, receive limited benefits under trademark law. A band generally cannot register trademark rights in the title of a single album or song to prevent other artists from using it. A title of a single work, however, may be protectable, and indeed federally registrable, for use in connection with ancillary merchandise, such as toys or clothing. Also, a title may be protectable through litigation if the artist can show that it has achieved "secondary meaning"—in other words, show that consumers have come to exclusively associate that title with the artist or entity that originated the title.[93]

The general prohibition on registering titles does not apply where there is a series of works involved. For example, the singer Meat Loaf owns a federal trademark registration for the mark BAT OUT OF HELL, which he has used as the title of a three-album series.

SG: How does someone establish rights in a name?

JT and AT: Trademark rights in the United States can arise from use and from the trademark registration process, which we will describe. Under United States trademark law, a party can establish "common law" trademark rights simply by virtue of using the mark in commerce. Generally, "use in commerce" for the purpose of establishing rights means displaying the trademark to prospective purchasers in a manner that associates the mark with the mark owner's goods, services, or business.

Absent a federal registration, the trademark owner's rights in a mark are limited geographically to the scope of the owner's reputation. Therefore, absent a federal registration, it is entirely possible for two different entities to share rights in an identical mark for identical services if:

(1) the second party to adopt the mark offers its products or services in a geographic area so remote from that of the prior user that it is unlikely the public will be confused or deceived; and,

(2) the second party's adoption is in good faith (without knowledge of the prior user's use) and outside of the prior user's area of market penetration and "zone of protection."

In these circumstances, each user is entitled to prevent the other from entering into its "zone of protection" and both parties have the right to expand into "unoccupied territory" so long as their areas of operation remain remote. Thus, for example, a band in Atlanta, Georgia, with only a regional reputation in the southeastern United States can peacefully coexist with a band in Seattle, Washington, using the identical name. As long as each group stays within its zone of recognition, no confusion is likely. However, problems can begin to emerge if the Atlanta band signs a major-label recording contract that provides opportunities for nationwide touring and record distribution. In this event, the Atlanta group will need to resolve the potential trademark dispute with its Seattle counterpart, or else face the possibility of committing trademark infringement when it sells records and tours in the Pacific Northwest.

For any band beginning to enjoy a taste of success in the music business, it is worthwhile to check the PTO website's registration database (available at www.uspto.gov) and to do some targeted Google searches to ensure that their name is available for wider use.

The Benefits of a Federal Registration

SG: What is the benefit of a federal trademark registration, and how much does it cost? Is it necessary to hire a lawyer to do it?

JT and AT: Today, most artists and labels achieve recognition beyond mere regional exposure simply by posting music to the Internet. Online uses (offering streaming or downloads via MySpace or Bandcamp), online sales (selling MP3s via iTunes or Amazon MP3), and far-reaching concert events/tours are all common ways for musicians and labels to promote themselves. Accordingly, artists and labels may seek to avoid potential territorial squabbles like the previously described Atlanta/Seattle example by acquiring a federal trademark registration. Among other things, filing an application to register a mark constitutes nationwide constructive notice of the applicant's claimed rights in the mark. Although a federal trademark registration does not defeat the rights of a remote geographical trademark user who began using the mark prior to the application filing date, the registration provides its owner with superior rights as against any parties who begin using the mark after the filing date of the application.

The case of *Stuart v. Collins* demonstrates the benefits of a federal trademark registration in the music context.[94] The *Stuart* case involved a little-known rock musician named Thomas Stuart who performed in a group called the Rubberband. Although the group's primary area of operation was in the southeastern United States, Stuart procured a federal trademark registration for the band's name. Subsequent to the registration date of Stuart's mark, well-known funk bassist Bootsy Collins began to tour and release records under the name Bootsy's Rubber Band. Stuart filed suit and ultimately was awarded $250,000 after prevailing on his infringement claim. There is no question that Stuart's case was enhanced by his federal registration. Absent this registration, Stuart's rights would have been limited to his immediate zone of reputation, and the value of his claim would have been diminished accordingly.

The *Stuart* case may be contrasted with the case of *Sunenblick v. Harrell.*[95] In *Sunenblick,* a small jazz record label using the mark UPTOWN RECORDS without a federal registration brought suit against a larger R & B / rap label employing the same mark. The court found no likelihood of confusion between these uses, relying in part upon the small size of the plaintiff's label and upon the fact that the parties catered to different musical genres. It is worth querying whether the result of this case would have been different if the plaintiff had had the benefit of a federal registration. Indeed, had the plaintiff's mark been registered, it is possible that the plaintiff's claim to the mark would have been brought to the defendant's attention at an earlier time, and the defendant might have been deterred from adopting the identical mark in the first place.

The Application Process

JT and AT: A federal trademark application may be based upon the applicant's preexisting use of the mark in interstate commerce, or upon a bona fide intent to use the mark in interstate commerce at a future time. Effectively, the intent-to-use basis allows an artist to reserve an unused name for future use by filing a trademark application based on the artist's genuine intent to use the name in the future.

While not legally required, it is generally worthwhile to consult a trademark attorney to navigate the somewhat complicated federal trademark application process. A proper federal trademark application must be signed by the applicant and must include (1) a description of the goods and/or services the applicant seeks to protect, separated according to their proper class(es); (2) a filing fee of $325 per class of goods or services (assuming electronic filing); (3) a depiction of the mark; and, in the case of use-based applications, (4) specimens that evidence the mark's usage. Generally, musical artists applying for registration should seek to protect their sound recordings (Class 9) and entertainment services including concert performances (Class 41), at minimum. Additionally, they may consider protecting ancillary merchandise such as printed goods (Class 16) and clothing (Class 25). More sophisticated music retailers, be they artists, labels, or others, may seek to protect other services such as retail store services (Class 35) or online streaming services (Class 38). Accordingly, PTO filing fees for a trademark application may vary from several hundred dollars to thousands of dollars, depending on the variety of uses for which the applicant seeks to register the mark. Many trademark attorneys offer flat-fee per-class services that include PTO filing fees. Hiring an attorney to handle a two-class, use-based trademark application that encounters no serious complications in the review process generally will cost a band between $1,500 and $2,500, including PTO fees. Intent-to-use applications typically cost more because there are additional PTO fees involved. Also, conducting proper trademark searches can add to the cost of the process but can be well worth the expense.

Once on file, applications are reviewed by examining attorneys at the PTO, who compare the mark against prior registrations and applications to ensure that it is not confusingly similar to any previous marks. Examining attorneys also review the applications to make sure they do not consist of "merely descriptive" or "generic" terms, which are generally unregistrable. If the examining attorney deems the mark to be fit for registration, the application will be "published for opposition" in the PTO's *Official Gazette*. Interested parties then have 30 days from the publication date to oppose the application. Provided that the application survives the publication process, the mark will then become registered, if it is a use-based application, or it will be "allowed," if the application is based on intent to use. In the case of an intent-to-use application, the registration will not issue until the applicant has provided the PTO with proof that the mark is being used in commerce.

SG: Is it worth it? At what point should an artist or label think of registering a name?

JT and AT: Once an artist or label begins using a trademark in interstate commerce, theoretically there is no point too soon to apply for a federal registration. Practically speaking, however, paying rent and covering basic necessities (e.g., eating, maintaining a tour van) are major concerns for struggling musicians or small-label owners, so a trademark registration understandably may rank low on the priority list. But, on the other hand, if an artist or label achieves some measure of success and can afford to apply for a federal registration, the cost of doing so is money well spent.

Practically assessing the ongoing general decline in music sales, any performing artist hoping to make a living in the music business likely will sell ancillary merchandise such as clothing and posters. At first these sales may yield only gas money, but eventually they can create a substantial income stream for an artist. As was just described, a federal trademark registration puts the nation on notice of the rights the owner asserts in the trademark, thereby avoiding potential territorial squabbles over a mark going forward. The sooner a band or label does this, the better. In the end, a successful artist or label's trademark becomes an extremely valuable piece of property, and owning a registration serves to streamline enforcement procedures and provide a serious deterrent to counterfeiters. Artists who achieve widespread notoriety often have the opportunity to enter into lucrative merchandise-licensing contracts, and a party on the other side of such a deal will expect an artist to protect its trademark from counterfeiters. The most effective first step to protecting a mark is applying for a federal registration.

If a trademark owner fails to take protective measures, competing uses of similar marks can weaken the mark by diluting the distinctiveness of the owner's designations, thereby reducing the public's association between a particular mark and its owner. Large corporate trademark owners annually spend tens (sometimes hundreds) of thousands of dollars to register their marks, to police them in the marketplace, and, where necessary, to bring lawsuits to enforce their rights when other parties tread too closely. While most artists and labels typically do not spend at this level to police their marks in the marketplace, they should note that with the use and ownership of a trademark comes an obligation to protect the trademark. Even though a fledgling artist or label likely cannot afford the significant costs of litigation often associated with an aggressive trademark-enforcement strategy, registering a trademark is still a good idea because it grants a nationwide "zone of protection" and puts all other potential users of the mark on notice of the artist or label's use of the trademark. It is advisable to consult an attorney about a proper enforcement strategy, and in many cases a registration combined with a simple demand letter (crafted by or with the advice of an attorney) can be sufficient to deter infringing activity.

SG: How do courts analyze cases of trademark infringement?

JT and AT: Using trademarks, bands, artists, and record labels have the ability to distinguish their unique goods and services from their competitors in the marketplace. The test for determining whether a junior user's trademark infringes a senior user's rights is whether the junior party's mark is likely to cause confusion. This test applies regardless of whether the plaintiff's mark is registered. Courts examine a variety of factors in order to assess whether two marks are confusingly similar, including: (1) the strength or weakness of the plaintiff's mark;[96] (2) the similarity of the two marks in terms of sound, appearance, and meaning; (3) the similarity of the parties' products or services; (4) the similarity of purchasers and the channels of trade for the products or services; (5) the similarity of advertising media; (6) the degree of care that purchasers are likely to exercise; (7) the defendant's bad faith (or lack thereof); and (8) evidence of actual confusion among purchasers. (These factors vary slightly based on jurisdiction, but the differences are not significant.) A party who loses a trademark infringement suit can be forced to stop using the trademark at issue and to pay money to the other side, sometimes including the other side's attorneys' fees. The amount of money awarded in trademark damages may be significantly increased where the infringer acted willfully and/or used a counterfeit mark. Monetary damages are typically measured in terms of actual damages suffered by the plaintiff and/or in terms of the profits enjoyed by the defendant as a result of the infringing use.

Potential for a dispute exists especially where there is a possibility of confusion stemming from two bands using an identical or highly similar trademark/band name to offer identical or highly similar goods and services (e.g., recorded music and concert performances). For example, if we (James and Ashford) began selling our own original recorded rock music under the name Grateful Dead, there is a significant chance that any consumer purchasing our music would do so with the belief that we were the "real" Grateful Dead and would doubtless be disappointed to hear whatever we recorded instead of the original band. This likelihood of confusion would be increased if we also used the Grateful Dead's famous "steal your face" logo (shown previously). And if we marketed our rock band's concerts under the name Aerosmith, concertgoers probably would feel cheated when James and Ashford took the stage. For further illustration, note that if we used the name Airswift, standing alone, it might not infringe the AEROSMITH mark; but, if we used the Airswift name in conjunction with a "wing" motif and Aerosmith's unique typeface (shown next to the Grateful logo),, there could be an infringement problem. Trademark law should and generally would provide the Grateful Dead and Aerosmith with the ability to stop us from using their names or logos, or from using confusingly similar names and logos.

Accordingly, prior to investing time or money in developing a trademark, it is worthwhile to do a thorough online search for others in the industry using that trademark, to make sure to avoid the current or future possibility of a trademark dispute. And a trademark attorney can provide a more detailed domestic or international trademark search service, as well as a legal opinion on any potential trademark issues, for a party concerned about investing in a particular trademark.

SG: How can you protect your name in foreign countries?

JT and AT: Unlike copyright law, trademark law is territorial. The Berne Convention copyright treaty allows a US-based artist to enforce her copyright in a song in over 160 countries, including almost every market of general significance. By contrast, even if a party establishes trademark rights in the United States through widespread use and/or federal registration, that party's rights in the trademark end at the US border. Other nations regulate trademarks according to their own laws. Some countries—most notably, the United States, the United Kingdom, Canada, and Australia—allow a party to establish common-law rights based on use of a trademark. Many international trademark regimes are first-to-file regimes, so an artist seeking to protect her use of a trademark in these countries should apply for a trademark registration. We recommend meeting with an attorney to discuss international trademark protection options whenever international trademark issues arise.

Domain Names

SG: Let's start with basics: How does one register a domain name?

JT and AT: Domain-name registrars like Go Daddy (www.godaddy.com) and Network Solutions (www.networksolutions.com) offer domain-name-registration services, generally for between 10 and 15 dollars per domain name. The straightforward registration process involves filling out online forms and paying for the domain-name registration.

SG: What protection does registering give?

JT and AT: Registration of a domain name alone does not provide any kind of legal protection. Registering the domain name simply reserves it for use by the owner, effectively planting a flag in a piece of cyberspace ground. Practically speaking, registering and then using a domain name may establish common-law rights in a trademark incorporated within the domain name. But it bears noting that registering and using a domain name incorporating another's trademark can in some situations subject one to legal liability—just as planting a flag and building a tent in someone else's front yard could create trouble off-line.

SG: What if someone else has already registered the domain name an artist or label seeks?

JT and AT: The answer to this question depends in large part on whether the domain name includes a trademark in which the domain-name owner has legitimate rights. In such a case, there is generally little an artist or label can do to acquire the domain name, aside from making an offer to purchase the name. This option may be expensive, and it may be cheaper to come up with a creative variation on the desired domain name. Because of the many domain name extensions now available, registering a ".net" or ".biz" or ".tv" domain name may provide the best solution. Or adding the term "band" or "music" or "rocks" to the name may solve the problem.

If the domain name incorporates a trademark in which the artist or label already has established trademark rights, the artist or label may be able to take legal action to have the domain name transferred to it, especially in cases where the domain-name owner is merely squatting on the domain name and the artist or label has strong rights in the mark. One potential course of action is filing a suit in federal court under the Anticybersquatting Consumer Protection Act (ACPA). Notably, a party suing under ACPA may seek monetary damages. But litigation is expensive and generally not advisable for a party simply seeking transfer of a domain name.

A faster, cheaper option for recovery of a domain name is an arbitration mechanism created by the Internet Corporation for Assigned Names and Numbers called the Uniform Domain-Name Dispute Resolution Policy (UDRP). An action brought under the UDRP allows a complaining party to secure the transfer of a domain-name registration where she can establish: (1) that the domain name in question is identical or confusingly similar to a trademark or service mark in which the complainant has rights; (2) that the registrant has no rights or legitimate interests in the domain name; and (3) that the domain name has been registered and used in bad faith. It bears noting that the party bringing a UDRP action cannot seek monetary damages. But, while the amount of legal fees associated with a UDRP action varies based on a number of factors, filing a UDRP generally costs a mere fraction of what litigation in federal court typically costs. The crucial element in a UDRP proceeding is to establish that the registrant is a bad-faith "cybersquatter." This often involves convincing an arbitrator that the registrant has procured the name with the intent to sell it to the rightful owner, or with the intent to improperly profit from it, such as through online advertising or affiliate marketing programs.

SG: If they are available, should an artist or label acquire all the top-level domain names (TLDs) for its name—that is, <name.com>, <name.biz>, <name.net>, etc.?

JT and AT: Generally, yes. If they are available, an artist or label can probably purchase all of the major ones I just mentioned for less than a hundred dollars and easily should be able to redirect them all to its website. Note that it may be worthwhile to acquire country-specific TLDs in some scenarios. For instance, if an artist or label does a great deal of business in Japan, it is worthwhile to purchase the <name.jp>domain name. The relatively small costs of these domain-name registrations would seem extremely cheap in hindsight if, after an artist or label achieved great notoriety, a cybersquatter began using one or more of these domain names and forced the artist or label to take legal action.

SG: Obviously, people can register a domain name without a lawyer's help. When is it necessary to consult with a lawyer about domain names?

JT and AT: It is highly advisable to consult an attorney about a domain-name dispute. If someone has registered or is using an infringing domain name, or if an artist receives notice that its use of a domain name infringes another's trademark, an attorney should be consulted. Notably, an experienced attorney may be able to file one of the previously described UDRP proceedings on an artist's behalf for as little as a few thousand dollars.

Band Names

SG: Suppose you are in a band and someone leaves and continues using the band's name. What do you do?

JT and AT: The answer to this question depends first on whether the band has a contract that governs this situation. If a band agreement states that the exiting member has the right to use the name, then the remaining members likely have no claim against the exiting member. If the agreement states that the exiting member has no right to use the name, then the remaining members likely may bring a breach-of-contract claim and potentially a trademark-infringement claim against the departing member. Generally, remaining band members in such a scenario who feel they may have claims to bring against the leaving member should consult an attorney to determine the extent of their rights in the band name under the band agreement.

If there is no band agreement in place, these situations become far thornier. If the band's name is valuable, it is likely that the parties will hire attorneys to litigate over use of the band's name.

SG: Are there any notable cases about this issue?

JT and AT: The cases in this area demonstrate the default rule that trademark law will not prevent a former band member from making a truthful representation of former affiliation with her former band, so long as the former band member (1) does so in a manner that is not confusing and (2) has not agreed to refrain from such representations. In *Kassbaum v. Steppenwolf Productions, Inc.*,[97] the Ninth Circuit held that the former bassist from Steppenwolf was not barred by contract law or trademark law from using the phrases "Formerly of Steppenwolf," "Original Member of Steppenwolf," and "Original Founding Member of Steppenwolf" in promotional materials for a new band, provided that these phrases were less prominent than references to the new band.

In *HEC Enterprises, Ltd. v. Deep Purple, Inc.*,[98] the management company for the rock group Deep Purple brought suit to enjoin a former member of the band from using the names DEEP PURPLE and NEW DEEP PURPLE in connection with live musical performances. Notwithstanding the fact that the "original" Deep Purple had ceased performing several years prior to the former member's resurrection of the name, the court found that the mark DEEP PURPLE was still in use given that the group's recordings remained in distribution. Having established that the original group's management owned valid rights in the name, the court enjoined the defendants from making further use of the names DEEP PURPLE and NEW DEEP PURPLE and awarded damages and attorneys' fees to the plaintiffs.

In *Brother Records, Inc. v. Jardine*,[99] a corporation (BRI) formed by members of the Beach Boys and which owned the rights to the THE BEACH BOYS trademark sued Beach Boy Al Jardine to stop him from using the following names: Al Jardine of the Beach Boys and Family & Friends; the Beach Boys "Family and Friends"; Beach Boys Family & Friends; the Beach Boys, Family & Friends; Beach Boys and Family; and, simply, the Beach Boys. This case provides an example of a situation where a band used an agreement to create a corporation, the corporation owned and licensed the rights in the band's name, and the corporation was able to stop an unlicensed band member from using the band's name.

Most notably, the *Brother Records* court addressed the issue of nominative fair use, which Jardine raised as a defense. This doctrine allows a defendant to use a plaintiff's trademark to refer back to the plaintiff's goods and services in situations where (1) the product or service at issue is not readily recognizable without use of the trademark; (2) only so much of the trademark is used as is reasonably necessary to identify the product or service; and (3) the user does nothing that would, in conjunction with the mark, suggest sponsorship or endorsement by the trademark holder.[100] The court held that Jardine's use of his former band's name infringed BRI's trademark because Jardine's use indicated that the Beach Boys sponsored or endorsed his concerts. For example, some of Jardine's promotional materials displayed "The Beach Boys" more prominently than "Family and Friends," and Jardine's management testified that they had recommended using the THE BEACH BOYS name to create or enhance the value of the concert tour. Finally, the fact that some promoters and concertgoers were actually confused—they could not differentiate between a Jardine concert and Beach Boy Mike Love's nearby, licensed "The Beach Boys" concert—worked strongly against Jardine's case.

SG: Would you recommend a band contract, and if so, what do you recommend the contract say about the band's name?

JT and AT: For any band that has attained commercial success, or that is on the brink of such success, a band contract is advisable, and such a document should provide an explanation of who owns the band's trademarks as well as make provisions for ownership in the event one or more members should leave the band. Often these agreements allow former band members to promote themselves as "formerly of [band's name]," although typically there are limitations placed on how this can be done. For example, there may be a time restriction to how long this representation can be made, and there also may be limits placed upon the type size and font in which the band name appears.

SG: Without going into too much detail, because we could write a book on just this question alone, what other provisions should be in a band agreement?

JT and AT: Most crucially, a band agreement should provide how any conceivable band property or streams of income will be split among the band's members. Property includes tangible items like a van, a tour bus, or instruments and recording gear. And property includes intangible items like copyrights in the band's songs or in any visual designs used by the band, and trademarks in any band names or logos. Streams of income include record and publishing royalties, touring income, and merchandising income, among many potential others. Band agreements may also, among other things, establish the band as a particular type of business entity and delineate between actual members of the band and mere touring musicians. Much of the substance of a band agreement will depend on the negotiating leverage the different members bring to the table—for example, Johnny, who writes all the songs for a successful band, likely can dictate more terms than Jimmy, who just joined and can barely play his bass.

SG: Would you recommend hiring a lawyer for this? If so, do the other people in the band need their own lawyer, or can one lawyer be used for all the band members? And, if using just one lawyer, how does the lawyer avoid conflicts of interest?

JT and AT: Bands should consult an attorney to create any kind of band agreement. And, if they can afford them, band members certainly can hire their own individual attorneys. While hiring multiple attorneys maximizes each member's ability to protect herself in the agreement, it will be costly and it may not be conducive to reaching an agreement in a timely fashion. Generally speaking, a band can consult a single attorney about a band agreement as long as the attorney makes the band aware of the potential conflicts of interest in that situation. A conscientious attorney may require the band to sign a waiver stating, among other things, that the lawyer has explained the conflicts of interest at stake and the band agrees to proceed with the lawyer acting effectively as the band's clerk, memorializing the band's wishes and not intervening on behalf of any member's individual interests. In thornier band-agreement situations, such as when a band has had several members come and go, a band's everyday attorney may prefer to refer the band agreement to another attorney rather than be forced to help the band with an agreement that potentially could favor one member over another.

[Author's note: Clients whom I have worked with since the publication of the third edition inspired the following update by presenting trademark issues that I had not handled before. I am grateful to Ashford Tucker and James Trigg for sharing their expert knowledge once again.]

Special Update for 4th Edition

SG: One new situation that has come across my desk since I wrote the last book are bands and music companies who want to protect a logo as well as a name. If they are interested in protecting both the name and the logo, should they register them in separate applications or save the $275–$375 application fee by registering them in one application?

JT and AT: The answer to this question depends largely on the applicant's budget. The general recommendation is to file for a word mark first and consider filing for a logo at a later time. It is rare, but not entirely unheard of, that a logo is as important as a word mark.

Filing for a logo provides coverage for the specific logo itself, including any word(s) depicted in the logo; but it is important to understand that such coverage is limited to the depiction of the logo and stylized wording, if any, that is submitted in the logo application. By contrast, filing to protect a band/company name as a word mark protects any use of that name, on its own or with a logo. For smaller bands/companies, cost is a concern, and they want the broadest coverage for the name at the best value. Therefore, unless a stylized logo is an extremely important indicator of that company/artist, with as much importance as the name, it usually makes sense to prioritize filing an application for a word mark first, and consider protection for a specific logo if the remaining budget allows.

If an applicant can afford to file a separate application for a logo, doing so may be a good idea in some circumstances. For example, if an applicant always uses the same logo and fears that others will copy the logo without using the name, the applicant should seek to register the logo (e.g., consider the Grateful Dead skull mentioned earlier). It is important to remember that when a logo materially changes into a new logo, it becomes necessary to file another trademark application for the new logo. The logo applicant should also (1) ensure that he or she is authorized to use the logo from a copyright perspective (that is, that the applicant either created the logo from scratch or cleared the rights to use the logo from its owner/creator) and (2) consider registering the copyright in such a logo if it is an original work or used under an exclusive license.

SG: Should solo artists consider registering their names, and why?

JT and AT: Yes, because a solo artist's personal name is a trademark. That is, if a personal name serves a source-identifying function, it functions as a trademark just like any other trademark. Kanye West, Madonna, Kendrick Lamar, Paul McCartney, Miley Cyrus, and Faith Hill all have filed for US trademark protection covering music-related goods and services, and this is generally similar to the way beverage companies have filed to register COCA-COLA and DR. PEPPER. This point is worth understanding, because we tend not to think of musical artist names in the same way as we think of names in other fields. We have no difficulty thinking of names like Diane von Furstenberg, Calvin Klein, and Ralph Lauren as trademarks. Perhaps we think this way because designers' names are so clearly emblazoned on commodities on store shelves. But, although not as immediately intuitive, use of a performer's personal name with music, for example in the form of downloadable MP3s and/or live performances, serves just as important a source-indicating function to consumers.

Finally, as noted above, trademark law is territorial, meaning that it varies from country to country. US solo artists with international aspirations should take note that in Canada, a personal name is unregistrable without submitting evidence of somewhat extensive use of the name as a trademark in Canada. While such a showing can be made, and is routinely made, to the Canadian Trademark Office, it is worth being aware of this situation before filing in Canada, because being forced to make such a showing can add cost and delay to a Canadian application.

SG: The Trademark Office has various designations or "classes" for registration. Should a band or artist register as a "recording artist" or as a "live performer," or can they register for both in the same application?

JT and AT: If an artist is both a recording artist and a live performer, he or she should seek to register in both categories. A band or artist can register as both a live performer and a recording artist in the same application by covering multiple classes. Filing in Class 9 is important for any recording artist, because that class covers use with sound recordings including downloadable computer files, CDs, and vinyl records. Filing in Class 41 is important for musical artists, because that class covers use with entertainment services and live performances as well as services related to the production of records (to the extent an artist also acts as a record producer). As noted earlier, artists may additionally consider protecting ancillary merchandise such as printed goods (Class 16) and clothing (Class 25). And more sophisticated music retailers, be they artists, labels, or others, may seek to protect other services such as retail store services (Class 35) or online streaming services (Class 38). In the US, multiple classes can be covered in a single application, and more specifics concerning the application process are addressed earlier in the article.

When specifying goods and services in each class, there are upsides to using broad wording, but some countries including the US require use as a prerequisite to registration, so it can be inefficient to create an overbroad specification that does not reflect the actual use of the mark, which can create additional prosecution costs to eliminate non-core goods, or even potential vulnerability to a registration if use is claimed where it does not exist. By contrast, as noted earlier, filings in many territories outside the US, including the E.U., do not require use as a prerequisite for registration, so it is possible to obtain a registration for a broadly delineated goods specification, though evidence of use may be required after a certain period of time if such a registration is challenged.

SG: As a follow up to the previous question, part of the application process in the US involves providing a "specimen" showing that a mark has been "used in commerce." Often, it has been my experience, the Trademark Office Examining Attorney has a problem with the specimen. If a band or artist is trying to register their name as a recording artist or live performer what is the best kind of "specimen" to provide. Can they use the same specimen for both?

JT and AT: With respect to a specimen for sound recordings in Class 9, a US applicant will often be required to show that the name has been used as part of a series (because as noted earlier, registration of the title of a single work is not permitted unless the title is part of a series). So, for example, a band submitting a self-titled CD, bearing only the band's name, as a specimen likely would receive a rejection on this basis and may need to supplement with additional specimens in the form of other sound recordings bearing the artist's name. So, for Class 9, it is good practice to show that the name is used as part of a continuing series of releases. A good specimen for making such a showing in Class 9 may be a picture or group of pictures of multiple CDs, or a printout from iTunes showing that the band has multiple sound recordings for sale under its name.

For Class 41, current tour information is helpful, so a printout of the band's upcoming tour dates from the band's website, or a current tour flyer indicating upcoming dates, usually is sufficient for a band seeking registration for musical performance services in Class 41.

SG: In the last several years I have had several new clients who planned to launch music-based apps for the Android or/iPhone. Can you register the name of an app?

JT and AT: Yes. The name of a commercial software application generally is registrable as a trademark. Also, it bears noting that an app can be offered to consumers in different ways that might implicate different trademark classes. For example, downloadable files fall into Class 9, so this would be an important class for a downloadable app. Additionally, retail services (Class 35), streaming services (Class 38), website services (Class 41), or providing online, downloadable software (Class 42) may be important to cover, depending on the specific circumstances of how the app is offered and what the app actually does.

SG: As a follow-up to the previous question, could that company or any other music company register its name as a trademark even if it hasn't launched yet?

JT and AT: Yes. As noted previously, in the US, where use is required to obtain a registration, an applicant may file an intent-to-use application based on a bona fide intent to use the mark in interstate commerce at a future time. These types of applications often cost more than applications based on actual use because there are additional PTO fees and attorney time involved at the back end of the application process. In the case of an intent-to-use application, the registration will not issue until the applicant has provided the PTO with proof that the mark is being used in commerce.

Notably, in many countries, use is not a requirement. So, for example, an applicant could seek to register a trademark covering all of the member states of the European Union without encountering the issue of whether the mark is in use.

SG: After you get a registration, do you have to keep on using it actively to keep it valid, and do you ever have to deal with the Trademark Office again to keep it valid?

JT and AT: The short answer is yes and yes. To maintain a registration in the US, the owner must file a "Section 8" declaration with the Trademark Office between the fifth and sixth year following issuance of the registration, stating that the mark is currently in use with the goods covered by the registration. (A six-month "grace period" is available following the six-year anniversary, subject to payment of additional fees.) Additionally at that time, or at any time thereafter, the trademark owner has the option of filing a "Section 15" declaration of "incontestability," stating that the mark was continually used for the prior five-year period and that the mark has not been challenged or become generic. Although an "incontestable" registration is not entirely impervious to challenge, it is significantly more difficult to challenge than a non-incontestable registration. Incontestable registrations are generally susceptible to challenge only on the basis of being generic or having been obtained by fraudulent means. Subsequent to the Section 8 filing described above, the mark owner must again file a declaration with the Trademark Office between the ninth and tenth years following issuance of the registration, and basically every 10 years thereafter, stating that the mark remains in current use.

It is worth noting that trademark rights in the US can be abandoned if a mark is not used for a continuous period of three years. That said, abandonment is an extremely fact-intensive area of the law, and cases of abandonment in the US are rarely cut-and-dried. Brand owners should simply be aware of the fact that the failure to keep a mark in use can result in loss of rights.

How Can a Music Lawyer Help Me? Will My Lawyer Shop My Music, and How Much Will It Cost?

I sat down with Don Passman, author of *All You Need to Know about the Music Business*, and asked the following questions about lawyers:

1. When do you need one?
2. How do you find a good one?
3. How much will it cost, and, most importantly, what if you don't have a lot of money?

Here is his response:

> Lawyers in the music business can come in quite early if they like your music. A lot of them will help shop it. So if you have some recorded demos you can go to a lawyer who may actually help you get a deal. There are lots of ways to find one, which are set out in my book. But essentially, do some research—there are a number of websites that include lists of music lawyers. And there are other ways to access lawyers, including bar association referrals. After that, it's a matter of checking them out. If you find somebody you like, ask for references from other people who have worked with them. I believe the recommendations of other people involved in the music business who have worked with a particular lawyer are probably the best way of finding a good one, because they have had the experience of working with the lawyer they are recommending. In terms of the money, some of the younger lawyers will charge a relatively small amount up front and then take a percentage, and they'll roll the dice with you.
>
> Most well-connected and knowledgeable music lawyers are based in New York City, Los Angeles, Nashville, or Atlanta, because those cities are where the most successful labels, music publishers, and producers do business. Although you may not live in these cities, it is still possible to have an effective relationship with your music lawyer. Working with an attorney is not the same as, for example, a doctor, who needs to see you to evaluate and treat your medical issues. In terms of music law, your music and documents, which you can transmit online, by fax, or by snail mail, are the "body" that the lawyer is evaluating and assisting. In fact, many entertainment lawyers only see their clients well after they have started working with them, if they personally meet them at all.

I would add to Don's answers that sometimes if a manager, producer, or label thinks you are going to be successful and really wants to work with you, that person or company will pay a reasonable amount so you can hire a lawyer. I have had clients who are small labels and producers, who have footed the bill for a new artist to hire a lawyer. In the "old" days, when major labels signed scores of artists with huge advances, the lawyers would often review and negotiate the contracts for a percentage of the advance. This was a no-brainer, because the lawyers knew they were going to get paid. Now, however, many deals involve no money up front. Many indie labels and production companies expect the artist to provide a fully produced album or EP. Again, a good test to see if a label is serious about working with you, and willing to put time and resources behind selling your records and advancing your career, is whether they will allocate funds so you can hire a lawyer to review the contract they are offering you.

If you can't get the company or person who wants you to sign you to put up funds for legal fees, my suggestion is to do some research on the lawyer you want to use before you call him or her. Then contact the lawyer by e-mail to explain your situation. And only then follow up with a phone call. The lawyer will sense that you are a serious person and be more willing to work for you for a smaller than usual fee. Even if he or she can't work with you, the lawyer will be much more likely to take time on the phone to give you some useful advice.

Generally, entertainment lawyers will work on an hourly basis. Occasionally they will charge an all-in, i.e., all-inclusive, fee to handle a particular assignment like a trademark registration or to review an agreement. If you retain one on an hourly basis, don't be shy about asking for a detailed breakdown of the attorney's work. I like to use a retainer agreement that provides an hourly rate and states that I will keep my clients informed of the hours billed.

Don Passman correctly pointed out that lawyers can help shop records. Some music lawyers have very close relationships with powerful people in the music business, but the reader should be advised that the number of these lawyers is limited and not every lawyer has these connections. When I was working as a lawyer for Sony Music, we would deal with only about a couple of dozen law firms or solo practitioners on a regular basis. Those lawyers usually did have long-standing relationships with powerful people in the business, and the same lawyers still work with producers, production companies, and managers on a regular basis. Often a manager or producer will ask a lawyer to use his relationships to advance an artist's career. But if you are not represented by a successful producer or manager, chances are small that you will get one of these lawyers interested in shopping your music, unless you pay a retainer in advance. If you do get a lawyer interested in shopping your music, make sure that he has industry connections before paying anything, and never pay a lawyer to shop your music if he hasn't heard it! If the lawyer is credible, he needs to believe in your music before sending it to people in the business with whom he has strong relationships.

I asked veteran music lawyer Peter Thall about shopping music. In addition to authoring *What They Never Told You about the Music Business*, Peter has represented artists such as Miles Davis and Paul Simon.

> I no longer "shop" artists per se. I never liked that designation anyway. Some lawyers send out dozens of CDs to their A&R contacts at record labels to see if they "stick." They take a fee for "shopping." I never did that. I have always preferred to "present an artist" to a label. But that takes a team of people—often including the publisher, manager, agent, if any—and a presentation that is compelling. And it requires an understanding of the music, the community in which the artist is based, and the musical tastes and nature of the particular record label. It is not very often that a record label will take a lawyer's word that an act is worth listening to, but given the onslaught of incoming material, A&R people are happy

> to respond to lawyers' solicitations because the source is a trusted one. In addition, believe it or not, the A&R staff knows that the lawyers' contact information is stable and they won't be left holding a phone with no wire attached when they eventually try to contact the party offering the artist.
>
> My fees are more in line with New York lawyers'. Unlike California lawyers, we don't usually take percentages (how much more can an artist handle, after all?), or at least long-term percentages; but establishing a flat fee for "shopping" and another one when the deal is completed, when the act has no money, is very tricky for both parties. A lawyer should be paid for his or her time and for a particularly excellent result if the client agrees. Seeking a balance between that and zero in case the pursuit of a record deal fails is the result we always seek but do not always attain.

Peter's comments reflect a great deal of experience and wisdom. I would only add that it makes sense to target one or two goals, such as a particular record company or management firm, and let the lawyer shop your music to them for a specific fee. If you are satisfied that the lawyer is working diligently on your behalf and believes in your music, you can expand your search and increase the retainer to cover the additional time.

Chapter3

OVERVIEW OF DIGITAL MUSIC LAW

Introduction

This chapter is intended to provide a summary of digital music law. Chapters 4, 5, and 6 will explore the new rules in detail as they apply to downloading, interactive streaming, and noninteractive streaming. We start with an overview of the relevant statutes that, in addition to the Copyright Act, provide the basic rules for transmission of music on the Internet. We then define those delivery methods and outline how the rules apply to each.

Statutes Applicable to Distribution of Digital Music: AHRA, DPRA, and DMCA

Audio Home Recording Act of 1992

The Audio Home Recording Act of 1992 (AHRA) was the first piece of major legislation affecting digital music. The Act amended the United States copyright law by adding Chapter 10, "Digital Audio Recording Devices and Media." It imposes a levy on "digital audio recording device(s)" (such as a digital tape recorder) and "digital audio recording medium(s)" (for example, blank digital audiotapes or CDs) to compensate copyright owners and artists for sales lost due to copying. The payments are made to the US Copyright Office, which then distributes the royalties to copyright owners and creators, including labels, artists, music publishers, and songwriters. The income generated by the levy has been negligible, because the AHRA does not apply to new generations of technology, including personal computers and MP3 players, iPads, iPhones, etc.

Private Copying

People have been ripping music on blank CDs for decades, and now they use apps and software programs to rip music on any number of portable devices, as well as their computers. But is this legal? The AHRA states in relevant part: "No action may be brought . . . alleging infringement of copyright based on . . . the noncommercial use by a consumer of such a device or medium [i.e., a device or medium subject to the act] for making musical recordings." The statute therefore exempts personal copying for noncommercial purposes on devices and blank media covered by the Act. But a computer is not subject to AHRA. Neither are MP3 players. The Ninth Circuit stated in *RIAA v. Diamond Multimedia* (the "Rio" case) (9th Cir. 1999) that using a computer to make a copy of recorded music for private, noncommercial use was "entirely consistent with the purposes of the Act." But this statement was "dicta"; that is, it was not central to the ruling in the case, and is generally treated by other courts as extraneous material to which they need not be bound. We explore the case law on this issue in Chapters 15 and 16. For now, we can report that the RIAA has never pursued the issue of private copying.

The Digital Performance Right in Sound Recordings Act of 1995

The Digital Performance Right in Sound Recordings Act of 1995 (DPRSRA or DPRA) created a new right for owners of sound recordings (Section 114 of the Copyright Act, "Scope of exclusive rights in sound recordings"). Under the DPRA, owners of copyrights in sound recordings were given exclusive "public performance" rights for the purposes of "digital audio transmissions." This means that an online music service or other digital service (such as Sirius XM's satellite service) cannot play any prerecorded music that is protected by copyright without a license. As we pointed out in Chapter 1, sound recording copyright owners, whether they are record companies or unsigned artists, do not have a right to prohibit the public performance of sound recordings via terrestrial broadcast, including traditional radio. The recording industry has tried repeatedly to acquire such a right but failed, at least in part because the broadcast community has consistently rallied against it (see Chapter 6). But the labels were able to convince Congress to give them a public-performance right for digital transmission. They argued convincingly that digital transmissions can be reproduced without loss of quality, which could lead to massive copying and result in severe harm to the record business.

The Digital Millennium Copyright Act of 1998

The Digital Millennium Copyright Act (DMCA) of 1998 provided for a statutory license amending Section 114 of the Copyright Act, which grants certain digital-music providers, specifically noninteractive audio-only services that satisfy certain other conditions (see Chapter 6), the automatic right to use sound recordings in their noninteractive streamed programming. These services include "Internet radio" services such as Pandora, satellite services (Sirius XM), and normal radio stations that retransmit their signals digitally. This means that notwithstanding the new digital public-performance right in sound recordings under the DPRA, noninteractive audio-only digital services are entitled to use prerecorded music without the labels' specific permission, provided they comply with certain eligibility requirements and pay fees mandated by the Act. We discuss these requirements and fees as well as the role of SoundExchange, a not-for-profit organization established to oversee the administration, collection, and payment of the royalties to sound recording copyright owners and to the artists, in Chapter 6.

Note that there was no need to create a new public-performance right for songs, as the law was already clear that their public performance through any means of transmission, be it analog or digital, is protected. The same performing-rights organizations (ASCAP, BMI, and SESAC) that offer public-performance licenses to radio and TV stations also offer blanket public-performance licenses to Internet-based music services.

Distributing Digital Music: Downloading, Interactive Streaming, and Noninteractive Streaming

Downloading

Downloading music is accomplished through services such as iTunes, and more recently Amazon and Google Play, which are digital stores from which you can buy permanent downloads of songs or full albums. With regard to sound recordings, there is no compulsory license for permanent downloads. Such stores require the permission of the owners of the copyrights in copyrighted sound recordings. The copyrights in recordings of unsigned artists are generally owned by the artists themselves. But the copyrights of artists signed to labels are usually controlled by record companies. For start-ups, obtaining permission from major record companies can be difficult and very expensive. With regard to songs, a statutory license does apply. Under Section 115 of the Copyright Act, downloads of records embodying songs are referred to as *digital phonorecord deliveries*, or DPDs. These downloads are subject to the same rates applying to traditional copying of musical compositions on CDs or cassettes (currently $.091 for songs five minutes or less, or $.0175 per minute or fraction thereof per copy for songs over five minutes). As we discuss in more detail in Chapter 4, downloads do not constitute "public performances," so no public-performance license (from ASCAP, BMI, or SESAC) is required.

Interactive Streaming

Interactive streaming refers to real-time delivery of music where the listener has the ability to choose to hear any particular song. Limited-download subscription services such as Spotify's premium service, Rhapsody, and Beats Music incorporate this way of consuming music, but ad-supported Spotify and YouTube are examples of a pure interactive-streaming service: You can listen to anything you want when you want without downloading. "Limited downloads" (also referred to as "tethered downloads") refers to copies of songs that you can download and make into playlists, but which disappear once you stop paying the subscription fee.

Noninteractive Streaming, Including Webcasting and Satellite Radio

As the words suggest, noninteractive services, such as Pandora or Sirius XM, do not allow the user to listen to songs on demand. We noted that noninteractive audio-only services are entitled to a statutory license under the DMCA to transmit any copyrighted sound recording so long as they satisfy certain eligibility requirements and pay the required fees. A "public-performance license," which is available from the PROs, is required in order to stream the songs.

Application of the Copyright Law and the Statutes to Downloading, Interactive Streaming, and Noninteractive Streaming

Musical Compositions

1. *Downloading*. With the exception of musicians offering downloads of their own songs, providers of recordings for download must obtain a mechanical license to allow people to make copies of the songs. However, such providers are entitled to a compulsory license under which they must pay the statutory rate: 9.1 cents per song or 1.75 cents per minute or fraction thereof over five minutes. This license is available from the Harry Fox Agency for the publishers they represent and from unsigned writers directly. The leading download store, iTunes, requires that providers of recordings, including labels, obtain and pay for the requisite mechanical licenses. Downloads are not considered public performances, because a performance does not take place when a song is downloaded. ASCAP tried, but failed, to get two federal courts to conclude otherwise. These cases are discussed in Chapter 4.

2. *Interactive streaming.* Pure interactive streaming services such as YouTube and ad-supported Spotify require public-performance licenses for the use of the songs from ASCAP, BMI, and SESAC, and permission from the labels to use their masters and videos. Although streaming services that offer limited downloads, such as Rhapsody, Spotify's premium service, and Beats Music, allow people to make copies, those copies exist only for as long as the user keeps on paying subscriber fees. For a number of years, interactive services, including those that offered limited downloads, and publishers could not reach an agreement on exactly how much the services should pay the publishers. However, in 2008 the parties came to an agreement, later codified in the form of regulations by the Copyright Royalty Tribunal, that set mechanical royalty rates for interactive streaming and limited downloads, including for both subscription and ad-supported services. Limited download and interactive streaming services will generally pay a mechanical royalty of 10.5 percent of revenue, less any amounts owed for public-performance royalties payable to ASCAP, BMI, and SESAC. In certain instances, royalty-free promotional streaming is allowed; see Chapter 5 for details.
3. *Noninteractive digital streaming, including webcasting and satellite radio.* In order to stream songs not in the public domain or owned by the provider itself, noninteractive services must have a public-performance license available from the PROs: ASCAP, BMI, or SESAC. See Chapter 6 to learn in more detail how much these services must pay for public-performance rights. Noninteractive audio-only streaming services such as Pandora and Sirius XM do not need a mechanical license for the use of the songs, since no copies are made.

Sound Recordings

1. *Downloading.* Services offering sound recordings for download need permission from the copyright owners of the recordings—usually the record companies. See Chapter 4 to learn how much those copyright owners are paid, how much the artists are paid, and how much the publishers and writers are paid.
2. *Interactive streaming.* Interactive streaming services need permission from the owners of the music recordings—usually the record companies. See Chapter 5 to learn how much the record companies are paid, how much the artists are paid, and how much the publishers and writers are paid.
3. *Noninteractive digital streaming, including webcasting and satellite radio.* These services are entitled to a compulsory license for use of recordings if they comply with certain rules set forth in the DMCA as codified in Section 214 of the Copyright Act. The license is administered by the not-for-profit organization SoundExchange. There are a number of different rates that apply to different kinds of noninteractive services. For instance, the rate applicable to Pandora's Internet radio service is completely different from the rate that applies to Sirius XM's satellite radio service. The rules that make noninteractive audio services eligible for a compulsory license, the role of SoundExchange, and the various applicable rates are discussed in detail in Chapter 6. Also see Chapter 6 to learn how much the record companies are paid, how much the artists are paid, and how much the publishers and writers are paid.

Chapter 4
DOWNLOADING

Overview

In this chapter we discuss online stores that sell permanent downloads of songs and albums. iTunes still dominates the music downloading market with 63 percent of the market share in the US.[101] Amazon MP3, in second place, controls 22 percent.[102] Other competitors include eMusic and Google Play's music download store (as opposed to Google Play Music All Access, their interactive subscription-based service).

How Much the Services Pay for Copyrighted Music

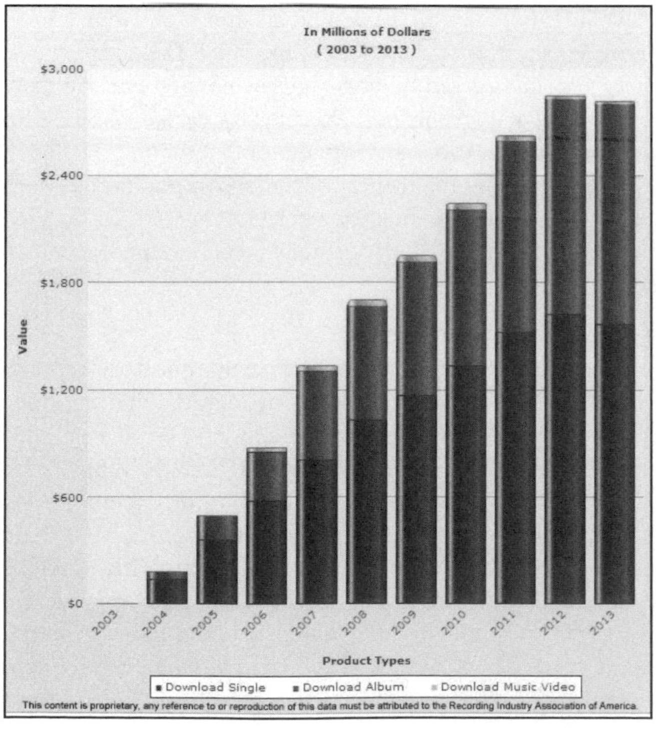

This chart shows that in 2013 downloading of recorded music generated approximately 2.82 billion dollars in the US.[103] This compares to 2.44 billion dollars generated by all physical sales including CDs (2.12 billion dollars), approximately 848 million dollars from interactive streaming, and 656 million dollars from non-interactive digital streaming.[104] This means that permanent downloads accounted for the biggest chunk of income for the recording business in 2013.

However, 2013 was the first year since iTunes launched in 2003 that income from downloading declined (from $2.85 billion in 2012). Moreover, the RIAA's *2014 Mid-Year Industry Shipment and Revenue Statistics* indicated that for the first half of 2014 revenues from permanent digital downloads declined another 12 percent compared to the first half of 2013.[105] Many blame this diminution on a dramatic increase in the popularity of streaming on-demand services, particularly Spotify. (We focus on those services in the next chapter.)

Downloading also generates money for music publishers and songwriters (see "How Much the Music Publishers Receive" later in this chapter). For every download of a song, the publishers and songwriters are generally entitled to the statutory royalty rate applicable to sales of any recorded music (currently the greater of 9.1 cents, or 1.65 cents per minute of playing time or fraction thereof).

How the Money Flows from the Services to the Labels, Artists, Publishers, and Songwriters

These three chapters on downloading, interactive and noninteractive streaming will use the Future of Music Coalition's "How the Money Flows" charts to analyze how the money flows from digital services to the stakeholders (i.e., labels, artists, publishers, and songwriters). The purpose is to tell you not only how much the digital services pay out, but who gets how much, and who may not be getting what they deserve.

How Much the Labels Receive

In the previous chart on download stores, the FMC distinguishes between (i) major record companies and their wholly owned affiliates, (ii) indie labels, and (iii) unsigned artists. According to the RIAA,[106] the major music companies "create and/or distribute about 85 percent of the music sold in the US," including downloading as well as physical sales.[107] The remaining 15percent is therefore going to indie labels who have direct deals with the download stores, and to unsigned artists who are placed with the stores by aggregators such as Tune Core and CD Baby.

iTunes started out paying 70 cents to sound recording copyright owners on each 99-cent download.[108] Most single downloads are $1.29 now; Apple pays 90 cents for each, and $8.39 for $11.98 albums, maintaining the 70 percent payout ratio. The recipient of that money, whether a label or an unsigned artist, is responsible for paying the owners of the copyrights in the songs (see "How Much the Music Publishers Receive" later in this chapter). But there is a difference between how much of this money the majors and their wholly affiliates receive, and how much indie labels and unsigned artists receive.

Major Record Companies and Their Wholly Owned Affiliates

As of 2014 the major labels consist of Universal, Sony, and Warner. When this book was initially published in 2005, there were two others, BMG and EMI. BMG was merged with and then bought out by Sony. In 2012 Universal acquired EMI in the United States and Warner gobbled up most of EMI's wholly owned labels outside the US, such as Parlophone Label Group.[109] The majors own a large number of well-known labels. This is just a partial list: Epic, Columbia, and RCA (Sony); Atlantic, Warner Bros., and Rhino (Warner); and Motown, Interscope, MCA, Def Jam, and Capitol (Universal). As just noted, the RIAA states that its members, which include the major labels, distribute 85 percent of recorded music sold in the US. However, as A2IM (American Association of Independent Music) points out, the "[i]ndependent music community . . . comprises over 34.5 percent of the music industry's market share in the United States based on copyright ownership."[110] Although the indies may own the copyrights in 34.5 percent

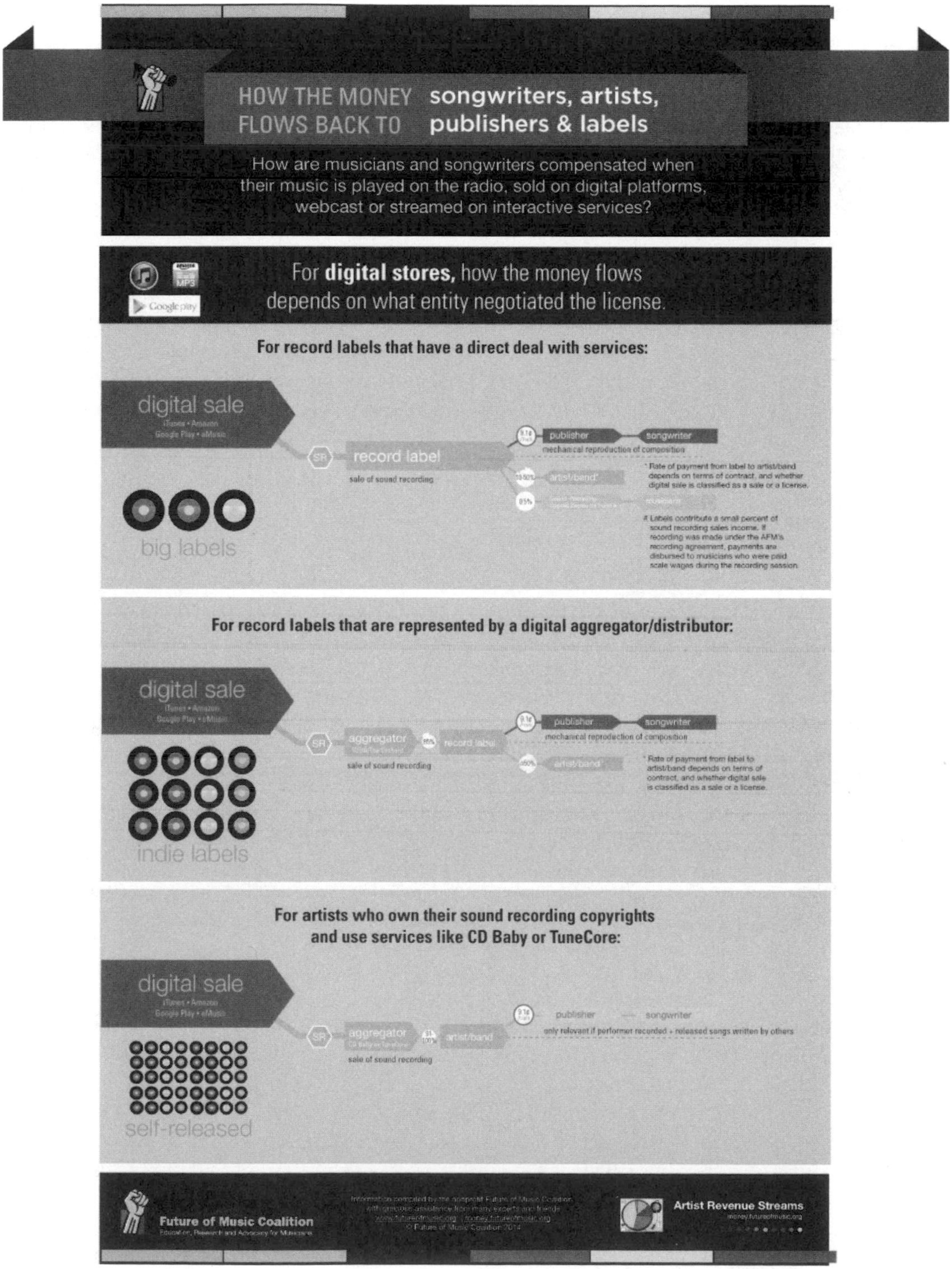
HOW THE MONEY FLOWS BACK TO
songwriters, artists, publishers & labels
How are musicians and songwriters compensated when their music is played on the radio, sold on digital platforms, webcast or streamed on interactive services?
MP3
Google play
For digital stores, how the money flows depends on what entity negotiated the license.
For record labels that have a direct deal with services:
digital sale
SR
record label
sale of sound recording
publisher
songwriter
mechanical reproduction of composition
10-50%
artist/band*
85%
* Rate of payment from label to artist/band depends on terms of contract, and whether digital sale is classified as a sale or a license.
# Labels contribute a small percent of sound recording sales income. If recording was made under the AFM's recording agreement, payments are disbursed to musicians who were paid scale wages during the recording session.
big labels
For record labels that are represented by a digital aggregator/distributor:
digital sale
SR
aggregator
record label
sale of sound recording
publisher
songwriter
mechanical reproduction of composition
artist/band
* Rate of payment from label to artist/band depends on terms of contract, and whether digital sale is classified as a sale or a license.
indie labels
For artists who own their sound recording copyrights and use services like CD Baby or TuneCore:
digital sale
SR
aggregator
artist/band
sale of sound recording
publisher
songwriter
only relevant if performer recorded + released songs written by others
self-released
Future of Music Coalition
Artist Revenue Streams

of recordings sold, which is more than any individual major, the three majors or their wholly owned indie label distribution affiliates (RED Distribution owned by Sony, Alternative Distribution Alliance or ADA owned by Warner, and Caroline owned by Universal), *distribute* many of the indies where the indies do not have direct deals with iTunes or Amazon. In addition, one of the leading digital aggregators for indie labels, The Orchard, is owned by Sony.

The majors and their wholly owned labels enjoy direct deals with iTunes and the other download stores. Therefore they receive the entire 70 percent payout on each download. How they pay their artists is another story entirely (see "How Much the Artists Receive" below).

Indie Labels

While certain indie labels have direct deals with iTunes, many distribute their music through the majors or their indie label distribution services, RED, ADA, and Caroline. Other indies may go through an aggregator such as The Orchard, INgrooves, or eOne Distribution, which will distribute their records to hundreds of digital services all over the world, including iTunes stores in various foreign countries. Labels that distribute to digital stores either through a major label distributor or through The Orchard or INgrooves must pay distribution fees, which generally range from 9 percent to 20 percent.

How Much the Artists Receive

Artists Signed to Labels

As reported in Chapter 1 (see "The Record Business"), the standard artist agreements provide a royalty of 10 to 15 percent of the retail selling price for sales of recorded music. But they also generally provide a royalty of 50 percent of any income generated by "licenses," such as licensing tracks for third-party compilation albums (e.g., *Sounds of the Seventies*, a multi-volume CD series issued by Time Life), or licenses for placing recorded music in commercials, movies, or TV programs. But prior to iTunes launching in 2003 it was unclear what royalty would apply to downloads. In the early 2000s the major record companies, as well as many indies, revised their standard contracts to include special new clauses that made "electronic distribution" of records subject to the artist's normal royalty rate. Here is an example of such a clause (with emphasis added):

> If [record company] sells **or licenses** to any third party the right to sell Electronic Transmissions of Records or Masters hereunder, the royalty rate will be the otherwise applicable Album royalty rate.

"Electronic Transmissions" is defined in this contract as "any transmission to the consumer, whether sound alone, sound coupled with an image, in any form, analogue or digital, now known or later developed (including but not limited to Streams, Limited Downloads, and Permanent Downloads)." Under the combination of the royalty provision and the definition, permanent downloads sold on iTunes, Amazon, Google Play, or eMusic (as well as interactive streaming and limited downloads, as discussed in the next chapter) are subject to an artist's normal royalty rate. Therefore, on a 99-cent download the labels will pay the artists their normal retail royalty of 10 to 15 percent. After deducting expenses, including the mechanical that the label pays for publishing (see "How Much the Music Publishers Receive" later in this chapter), and subject to reduction such as "net sales" (see "Standard Deductions to the Artist Royalty" in Chapter 1). The resulting penny rate (i.e., the amount the artist receives per download) will vary from contract to contract, but the amount will ultimately usually consist of only a few pennies per download.

Although the royalty that artists are entitled to under post 2003 contracts is clear, there is a great deal of controversy over what artists who signed older contracts that were not re-negotiated should receive. As discussed, under those older contracts there were just two kinds of artist royalty payments: normal retail sales and licensing. Many artists who entered into these agreements, and their lawyers, argue that the monies their labels receive from permanent downloads sold by third-party stores, including iTunes, should be treated as licensing income and that they are therefore entitled to 50 percent of the income that the labels collect.

Eminem's Lawsuit against Universal

This issue was presented by a lawsuit brought by Eminem's production company, F.B.T., against his record company, Universal Music. Universal treated monies received from downloads of Eminem's records as normal retail sales rather than licensing income. But the Federal Court of Appeals for the Ninth Circuit, which includes California, agreed with F.B.T. that the licensing provisions of Eminem's contract, rather than the sales provisions, applied to income from downloads, because the deals between Universal and iTunes and other online stores were indeed licenses.[111] The court found that Universal was not "selling" any records to iTunes; rather, they were licensing the tracks to them. The court also provided two grounds for the decision: First, it noted that "licenses" were not defined in Eminem's contract, and quoted the Webster's dictionary definition of a *license* as "permission to act." Declaring that Universal had "entered into an agreement that permitted iTunes, cellular phone carriers, and other third parties to use its sound recordings to produce and sell permanent downloads," it concluded that those agreements qualified as licenses. The second basis for the decision was that the case law interpreting the Copyright Act favored Eminem. Under that case law, the court found that it is clear that where a copyright owner retains title in copyright material, limits the uses to which the material may be put, and is compensated periodically based on the transferee's exploitation of copyrighted material, the transaction is a license. The court found that it was clear that Universal's agreements with the third-party download vendors were "licenses" to use the Eminem master recordings for specific authorized purposes—to create and distribute permanent downloads in exchange for periodic payments based on the volume of downloads, without any transfer in title of Universal's copyrights in the recordings. The court concluded: "Thus, federal copyright law supports and reinforces our conclusion that [Universal's] agreements permitting third parties to use its sound recordings to produce and sell permanent downloads . . . are licenses."[112]

The F.B.T. decision was a huge victory for artists with older agreements and very significant for major labels who still count on "catalogue" sales of legacy artists for a great deal of their income.

In the several years since the F.B.T. decision, a number of artists have presented claims to their labels seeking adjustments in their royalties from downloading from a few pennies to 50 percent of the label's income after paying for mechanicals (approximately 30 cents). These claims have mostly resulted in confidential settlements—no doubt in large part because since the F.B.T. decision any label would have to overcome the Ninth Circuit's decision in another court battle.[113]

Unsigned Artists

iTunes does not encourage direct deals with unsigned artists. Therefore, unsigned artists must generally go through aggregators who are paid a flat fee (for example, TuneCore) or a percentage of sales (for example, CD Baby) to place their records with download stores as well as other digital music services. See the FMC chart in the "The DIY Model" in Chapter 1 for a list of aggregators for unsigned artists and how each one works.

Because artists who are signed to labels usually earn only a few pennies from downloads of their records via iTunes and other download stores, it would seem that unsigned artists who only have to share a fraction of their income with aggregators do a lot better. In fact, the few pennies earned by signed artists are not even usually paid out. Instead, they are only "credited" to the artist's account because the artist usually owes the label money for unrecouped advances, production and marketing costs. On the other hand, although unsigned artists receive the entire 70 cents iTunes pays per download minus a small sum to an aggregator, unsigned artists sell very few units compared to artists signed with labels, particularly the majors or leading indies. There is a shocking stat from 2008 that there were at that time 10 million unsold tracks on iTunes,[114] that is, tracks that no one had ever downloaded—not even once. Unsigned artists have a problem selling on iTunes for all the reasons that we stated in Chapter 1 (see "Record Companies vs. DIY"). That is, the majors and successful indies not only provide advances and production, they also help artists get their music on broadcast radio and TV shows, help them finance live performances and tours at the beginning of their career, introduce them to and pay the most talented producers to work with them, etc. Aggregators such as CD Baby and TuneCore do none of these things. This is the reason why if you scan the *Billboard* charts, nearly all the best selling albums and single tracks are still distributed by the major labels or their affiliates.

How Much the Music Publishers Receive

Mechanicals: "DPDs" Are Subject to the Statutory Rate

As we previously discussed, a mechanical license is required to make a copy of a song embodied in a sound recording. The income that results from these licenses is referred to as *mechanical* royalties. Those royalties (currently the greater of 9.1 cents, or 1.65 cents per minute of playing time or fraction thereof) are paid to music publishers, who generally share 50 percent with the songwriter. As we explained in Chapter 1, the Copyright Act provides a compulsory license with regard to mechanical duplication of songs. This means the copyright owner cannot deny consent, provided that the song has been previously recorded and released to the public. This compulsory license also applies to downloading of songs. Section 115 of the Copyright Act refers to downloading as "digital phonorecord deliveries" (DPDs). The relevant language is as follows:

> When phonorecords of a nondramatic musical work have been distributed to the public in the United States under the authority of the copyright owner, any other person, including those who make phonorecords *or digital phonorecord deliveries*, may, by complying with the provisions of this section, obtain a compulsory license to make and distribute phonorecords of the work. A person may obtain a compulsory license only if his or her primary purpose in making phonorecords is to distribute them to the public for private use, *including by means of a digital phonorecord delivery*.

iTunes has always refused to pay for publishing; instead, they put the onus on those who supply music to them—whether they are major labels, indie labels, or aggregators who represent indie labels or unsigned artists. Generally, the majors and indie labels will pay the Harry Fox Agency the mechanical stat rate and Fox in turn pays its publisher members, who then share the money with their songwriters. Unsigned artists are supposed to take care of any mechanical royalties due to third-party writers. Of course, if they write their own songs they can keep the mechanical.

Downloads Are Not Subject to Public-Performance Royalties

As discussed in Chapter 1, ASCAP, BMI, and SESAC represent public-performance rights in the vast majority of all songs under copyright in the United States, and through their agreements with foreign performing-rights organizations, they represent virtually all the songs still protected by copyright that have been recorded and commercially distributed throughout the world.

In *United States v. American Society of Composers, Authors and Publishers*, (Applications of RealNetworks, Inc. and Yahoo! Inc.),[115] the Second Circuit addressed the question of whether downloads were a public performance for which download stores required a public-performance license. The answer is "no." At the time, Yahoo and RealNetworks sold music downloads and ASCAP demanded that they pay public-performance rights royalties. Yahoo and RealNetworks agreed that they should pay *mechanical* royalties for digital downloads, but not additional royalties for public performance. However, ASCAP argued that digital downloads are "public performances" as well as copies, and accordingly that the companies should compensate ASCAP with additional royalties for such "public performances."

The Second Circuit held that digital downloads do not constitute "public performances" because "[t]he downloaded songs are not performed in any perceptible manner during the transfers; [thus,] the user must take some further action to play the songs after they are downloaded."[116] In effect, the Court interpreted a "public performance" to be something that is "contemporaneously perceived by the listener" and since digital music downloads cannot be listened to during the actual electronic transfer, they do not meet that standard.[117]

The court pointed out that downloading for later playback is the same as buying a record. When you buy a record and listen to it at home, there is no public performance of music. When you play the music at home, it is considered to be a private performance.

Previews of Songs Are Subject to Public-Performance Royalties

The PROs license streaming previews at the likes of iTunes and other popular online retail destinations. This is because, although previews are only excerpts of full songs, they are still public performances which trigger a required license and payment. In an opinion and order dated January 30, 2009, the rate court ruled that previews, because they are not "transformative" and are performed for sales promotional purposes, are not a fair use.[118]

However, with regard to previews on streaming services, as opposed to download stores, the PROs are already collecting public-performance royalties, usually as a percentage of gross receipts, so there is no need to enter into a separate license or to charge separately for them.

How Much the Songwriters Receive

Generally, publishers pay 50 percent of mechanical royalty income to writers and another 25 percent if the writer entered into a "co-publishing" agreement (see "Music Publishing Contracts: Single-Song, Traditional-Term, Co-Pub, and Admin Deals" in Chapter 1).

If the writer is the artist and is not signed to a third-party publisher—is, therefore "self-published"—then he or she retains 100 percent of the mechanical. To be clear, when a singer/songwriter receives money from an aggregator for iTunes sales, he or she can keep all the money. Unfortunately, as discussed previously, unsigned artists sell relatively few downloads compared to artists who have support from labels.

Chapter 5

INTERACTIVE STREAMING

Overview

Interactive-streaming music services offer users the opportunity to listen to individual songs, music videos, or albums on demand. Some interactive services offer "limited downloads"—songs that users can download and listen to on demand on or off-line so long as they continue to subscribe to the service. Spotify's premium service, Beats Music, Google Play Music All Access, Rdio, and Rhapsody are all examples of interactive services that also offer limited downloads (sometimes also referred to as "tethered downloads"). Once you stop paying the subscription fee you lose access to any songs or playlists that you downloaded. With pure interactive services, like YouTube[119] and SoundCloud,[120] you can listen to any video or hear any song on demand, but you can't download them or watch or listen to them off-line.[121]

Since all these digital services are interactive, whether they offer limited downloading or not, they do not qualify for a Section 114 statutory license to perform sound recordings publicly (see the next chapter for a discussion of noninteractive services, including Pandora and Sirius XM). Therefore, these services have to negotiate with the owners of sound recording copyrights (usually major labels; indie labels; digital aggregators, such as The Orchard or INgrooves, which represent indie labels; or other aggregators, such as CD Baby and TuneCore, which represent unsigned artists).[122]

Besides the availability of limited downloads, the other important distinction in the interactive streaming market is between ad-supported and subscription (that is, pay-per-month) business models. Some services, such as Spotify, are both.[123] If you pay nothing, you can listen to any songs you wish on demand, but you will see or hear ads that play periodically. For $9.99 a month you can get rid of the ads, access the service on your smartphone and create playlists (limited downloads) that you can listen to off-line (for instance, in the NYC subway). You lose access to your playlists if you stop paying the monthly bill. Subscriber-based services usually cost $9.99 per month and are ad-free. On the other hand, interactive services that don't permit limited downloading are usually free and ad-supported. YouTube is an example.[124] In August 2014, SoundCloud announced that it will begin accepting advertising.

How Much the Services Pay for Copyrighted Music

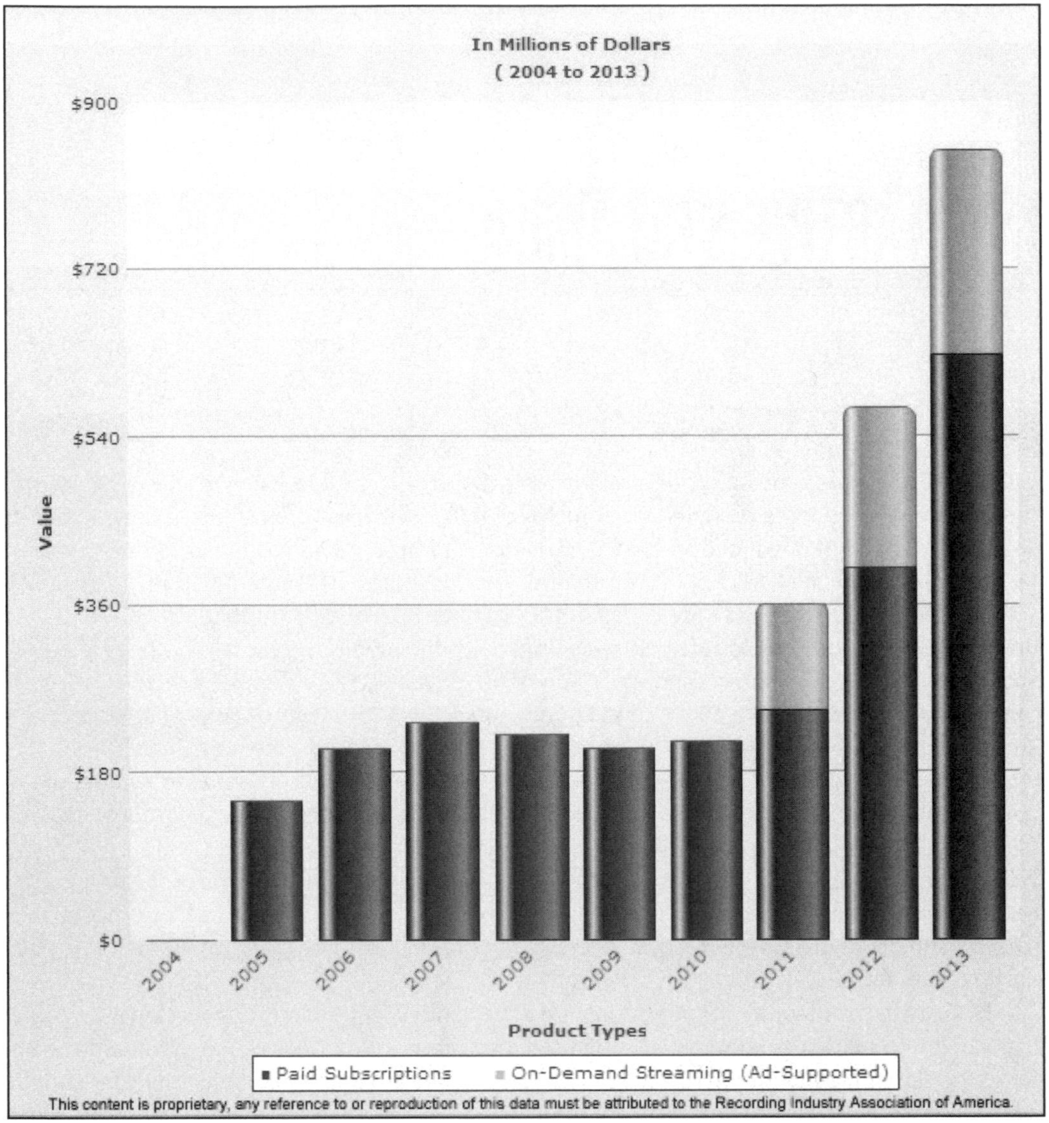

The chart above shows income paid to the sound recording copyright owners from both subscription-based interactive services, such as Spotify's premium service, Rhapsody, Beats Music, Google Play, and Rdio,[125] and from ad-supported interactive services, including Spotify's ad-supported interactive service and YouTube. It does not include income from services that operate under the Section 114 statutory license, such as Pandora and Sirius XM (see next chapter).

The chart shows that income paid by these services shot up from 570.8 million dollars in 2012 to 848.1 million in 2013. Most of this income, approximately $628 million,[126] was generated by $9.99 subscription services such as Spotify's premium service, Rhapsody, Google Play Music

All Access, and Rdio. In fact, paid subscription services grew the fastest of the digital formats, up 57 percent to $628 million in 2013.[127] Growth came not just in dollars, but in the number of subscribers as well, with the annual average totaling over 6 million subscriptions, up from 3.4 million in 2012.[128] Many commentators have seen this stark rise against the decline of income generated by permanent downloads as a sign that music fans care less about "owning" their music than they care about having instant access to any songs or playlists they wish to hear at any time.

YouTube and other ad-supported interactive-only (no limited downloading) services made only $220 million[129] in revenue for the music industry in 2013, about as much as vinyl records. The summer of 2014 saw a great deal of media coverage about YouTube's plan to start an advertising-free premium subscription version of itself[130] that would compete against Spotify, Beats Music, Rhapsody, and the other audio subscription services while retaining its video component. In early November 2014, YouTube launched the beta version of that service, Music Key. Similar to Spotify Premium and Rhapsody, Music Key will cost $9.99 per month. Music Key won't alter ad-supported YouTube, which draws more than 1 billion users every month. It will, however, group tracks by artist and albums in a more streamlined way (mostly eliminating cover versions). It will also allow users to toggle back and forth to the Google Play service, which includes an iTunes-style download store, and users will be able to make ad-free playlists that will be accessible off-line.[131]

How the Money Flows from the Services to the Labels, Artists, Publishers, and Songwriters

How Much the Labels Receive

Spotify claims that it pays approximately 70 percent of its revenue for music.[132] Of this amount, 10.5 percent is paid for publishing (see "How Much the Music Publishers Receive" later in this chapter). This leaves approximately 60 percent for labels and artists. Let's refer to this amount as the "revenue pool." How much is the value of each stream? The answer would seem to be that you divide the revenue pool by the number of streams that Spotify's users play. For instance, if the revenue pool in one month is $10,000,000 and there were a billion plays, each play would be worth 6/10 of one penny ($10,000,000 x 60 percent divided by $1,000,000,000). Theoretically, this would be the value of each play whether the money is flowing to major labels, indie labels, or unsigned artists. However, this may not be the case.

Major Labels and Their Wholly Owned Affiliates

The major labels' license agreements with Spotify and the other interactive services are, of course, confidential. However, it has been widely reported that the majors demand non-refundable advances or guarantees and that those advances or guarantees usually exceed the prorated royalty of each stream. If this is true, it bring down the value of each stream from our calculation, including streams of tracks owned by indie labels and unsigned artists.[133] For instance, assume again that the revenue pool is $10,000,000 for one month. Now assume that a major label's tracks were streamed 100,000,000 times. According to the previous math, each play would be worth .006. So the amount the major earned would be 100,000,000 x .006 = $600,000. However, if the major label demanded a $1 million advance or guarantee for each month, the service would have to reduce the revenue pool available to indies and unsigned artists, and that in turn would reduce the value of each stream.

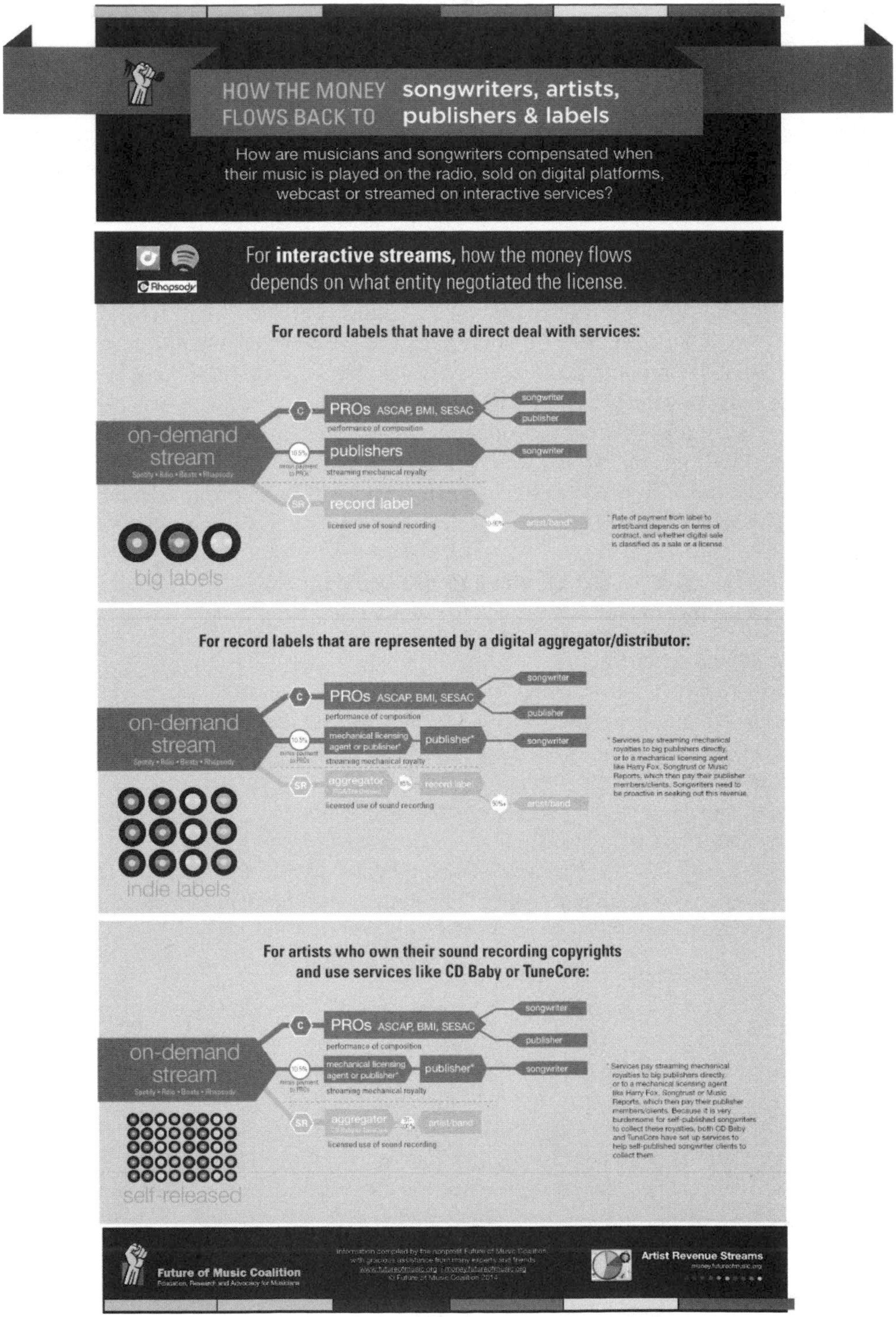
HOW THE MONEY FLOWS BACK TO
songwriters, artists, publishers & labels
How are musicians and songwriters compensated when their music is played on the radio, sold on digital platforms, webcast or streamed on interactive services?
Rhapsody
For interactive streams, how the money flows depends on what entity negotiated the license.
For record labels that have a direct deal with services:
on-demand stream
C
PROs ASCAP, BMI, SESAC
performance of composition
songwriter
publisher
10.5%
publishers
streaming mechanical royalty
songwriter
SR
record label
licensed use of sound recording
* Rate of payment from label to artist/band depends on terms of contract, and whether digital sale is classified as a sale or a license.
big labels
For record labels that are represented by a digital aggregator/distributor:
on-demand stream
C
PROs ASCAP, BMI, SESAC
performance of composition
songwriter
publisher
10.5%
mechanical licensing agent or publisher*
publisher*
songwriter
streaming mechanical royalty
SR
aggregator
licensed use of sound recording
* Services pay streaming mechanical royalties to big publishers directly, or to a mechanical licensing agent like Harry Fox, Songtrust or Music Reports, which then pay their publisher members/clients. Songwriters need to be proactive in seeking out this revenue.
indie labels
For artists who own their sound recording copyrights and use services like CD Baby or TuneCore:
on-demand stream
C
PROs ASCAP, BMI, SESAC
performance of composition
songwriter
publisher
mechanical licensing agent or publisher*
publisher*
songwriter
streaming mechanical royalty
SR
aggregator
licensed use of sound recording
* Services pay streaming mechanical royalties to big publishers directly, or to a mechanical licensing agent like Harry Fox, Songtrust or Music Reports, which then pay their publisher members/clients. Because it is very burdensome for self-published songwriters to collect these royalties, both CD Baby and TuneCore have set up services to help self-published songwriter clients to collect them.
self-released
Future of Music Coalition
Artist Revenue Streams

Indie Labels

Although some indies have direct deals with certain interactive digital music services through Merlin, an international rights agency that collectively licenses their repertoire,[134] many others go through aggregators such as The Orchard or INgrooves, which distribute to hundreds of digital services and stores, and others distribute through the majors or their distribution affiliates. Therefore the amount of money that indie labels receive from digital music services will often be subject to agency or distribution fees. Also, as we just pointed out, the advances and guarantees payable to the majors may reduce the value of each stream. (For the net value of each Spotify stream, see "Is Spotify Underpaying Indie Artists?" below). The bottom line is that the indies may be making less than the majors per stream, although artists signed to the majors may be doing even worse (see "How Much the Artists Receive").

Indie labels have spoken out against what they feel is the majors' disproportionate bargaining power. In June 2014 Darius Van Arman, cofounder of Secretly Group (a group of several indie labels whose acts include indie stars like Bon Iver) spoke before a House Judiciary subcommittee hearing on music licensing on behalf of the American Association of Independent Music (A2IM), a trade group representing approximately 330 indie US labels. In a statement supplied to the subcommittee in advance, Mr. Van Arman said that in the streaming age, "the three major recording companies have become proficient at extracting a disproportionate share of copyright-related revenue from the marketplace."[135] We discuss his comments in more detail in the next section.

How Much the Artists Receive

Artists Signed to Labels

Again, under most major label agreements entered into since 2003, artists will receive the same royalty rate from electronic streams and downloads as they receive from albums, that is, from 10 to 15 percent. Under such a deal, if a stream is worth .006 the label will credit its artists' accounts 10 to 15 percent of this fraction of a penny minus standard deductions (see "Standard Deductions to the Artist Royalty" in Chapter 1). However, artists signed to major labels may not be getting even that much.

"Breakage"—Are the Majors Paying Artists Properly?

Some critics have complained that major labels don't even pay their artists the small amount discussed in the last paragraph. Specifically, they have accused the labels of not crediting their artists anything for digital streaming by interactive services until "breakage," that is, until the major record company recoups the advances or guarantees that the services pay them. In his testimony before the House Judiciary subcommittee hearing on music licensing Darius Van Arman explained how this works:

> . . . if the major uses all of its bargaining power to maximize just the guarantee—with the intention that the guarantee is so high that it can't possibly be recouped in the period of time allotted for it—then the unrecouped portion of the guarantee is a significant boon to the major. It is revenue that cannot be attributed to specific recordings or performances, and thus the major does not have to share it with its artists . . . unless there are special contractual stipulations covering this kind of income (which is an accommodation that is attainable by only the largest and most

> established artists . . .). . . .This additional revenue that is earned from unrecouped advances, annual guarantees . . . can be referred to as "breakage."[136]

Van Arman conceded, however, that Warner Music Group currently has "a more progressive stance than the other two majors with regards to breakage, volunteering to share unrecouped advances and guarantees (but not equity) as a matter of policy with artists and with the independent labels that it fully digitally distributes." Universal Music to my knowledge has not denied the practice. But, soon after Van Arman testified, Sony Music publicly said that they do in fact credit artists with a fair portion of advance or guarantee money. However, one industry veteran complains that Sony shares "if that's in the artist contract, and how many lawyers put that in?"

Unsigned Artists

Unsigned artists must generally use an aggregator such as iTunes or CD Baby to place their tracks on an interactive service just as they must use them to place their music in download stores. You can see how much those aggregators cost unsigned artists in the FMC chart reprinted in "The DIY Model" in Chapter 1. In addition to this cost, the per stream value of tracks by unsigned artists may be reduced, just as those of indie labels are reduced, by the advances or guarantees obtained by the majors (see "Major Labels and Their Wholly Owned Affiliates" earlier in this chapter). Although the amount will always vary according to how much each interactive service receives during a given period of time, many unsigned artists report that Spotify's rate usually varies from .04 to .005 cents per song. That means if a track by an unsigned artist plays 10,000 times, the artist will only make between 40 and 50 dollars.

Is Spotify Underpaying Indie Artists?

There has been much criticism that Spotify underpays indie artists and labels because the fractional payout is so low. Zoe Keating is an example of an artist who feels that Spotify treats her unfairly.

> San Francisco–based Zoe Keating—a tech-savvy, DIY Amanda Palmer of the cello—has blown the whistle on the tiny amounts the streaming services pay musicians. Though she's exactly the kind of artist who should be cashing in on streaming, since she releases her own music, tours relentlessly, and has developed a strong following since her days with rock band Rasputina, only 8 percent of her last year's earnings from recorded music came from streaming. The iTunes store, which pays out in small amounts since most purchases are for 99-cent songs, paid her about six times what she earned from streaming. (More than 400,000 Spotify streams earned her $1,764; almost 2 million YouTube views generated $1,248.)[137]

Using these figures Keating's Spotify royalty is only $0.00441. In Spotify's defense: (1) if what it claims on its website is true, it is paying out 70 percent of its income for music, which is even more than what Pandora pays under a statutory license (see next chapter); (2) it is not Spotify's fault that even if a track is streamed 400,000 times, that is proportionately minute compared to the billions of streams that Spotify transmits; and (3) it values all streams the same (i.e., at the prorated amount resulting from dividing the revenue pool by the total number of streams).

On the other hand, if the majors are getting big advances or guarantees, as we discussed above, this may unfairly reduce the value of each stream, including the value of each one of Keating's 400,000 streams. Spotify might answer (if they talked about this, which they do not) that they have to pay the advances or guarantees demanded by the majors because the labels are under no obligation to grant them a license to play any of their records, and without their cooperation, Spotify could not compete with other services, and would indeed probably go out of business. Moreover, some people would say this is just how the capitalist system works, and the artists who complain are just whining. In fact, Part IV of this book presents the story of one indie artist who reports that he is happy with the money he makes from Spotify, and that in fact it represents a major portion of his income from the music business. (See "No One Wants to Talk Numbers When It Comes to Streaming Revenue. Well, Here Are Mine" by NYC-based independent artist Ron Pope.)

Another Controversy: The Majors' Equity Interests in Interactive Digital Services

Artist advocates point out that in addition to advances, it has been reported that the three major record companies now hold equity in certain interactive music services. For instance, it has widely been reported that the majors currently hold a collective ownership share in Spotify of approximately 20 percent. [138] These advocates point out that when Beats Music was sold to Apple for 3 billion dollars, Universal converted its 13 percent equity share in the company to cold hard cash to the tune of 404 million dollars.[139] Neither Universal nor its parent company, Vivendi, shared one penny with Universal's artists.

Of course, the labels could and do argue that they have no legal or ethical obligation to share their return on third-party investments with artists. After all, as one major-label business affairs executive told me, "if we lost money on an investment we would not make our artists share our losses."

But artist advocates argue that a major label's investment in a music service is different from other investments such as a purchase of real estate. They would point out that Beats' interactive music service, unlike its headphone business, would probably not have been able to launch in the first place had it not conceded to Universal's demand for equity. These advocates contend that records by the artists signed to Universal contributed to the success of Beats Music and made it attractive to Apple. Without their content, they argue, Beats would never have been able to get 3 billion dollars, even with the headphone business thrown in.

No doubt these controversies will continue and others will emerge. We will keep track of them in updates to this book, which you can read at www.futureofthemusicbusiness.com.

How Much the Music Publishers Receive

With regard to their use of musical compositions, as opposed to sound recordings, audio-only interactive services are entitled to a compulsory license under Section 115 of the Copyright Act and a statutory rate applies. YouTube and its new subscription service, Music Key, are not subject to this compulsory license because Section 115 does not apply to video services. Therefore, YouTube is required to negotiate direct deals with each music publisher. The deals between YouTube and the major publishers are confidential, but YouTube negotiated a deal with Harry Fox that allows Fox's indie publishers to "opt into." Under that deal those publishers who elect to participate share a one-time $4 million recoupable advance. The actual amount payable to each publisher depends on the aggregate market share of each publisher. After recoupment of the advance, YouTube pays a royalty of 15 percent of ad revenues associated with the songs controlled by the participating publishers in videos uploaded to the site.[140] HFA assesses an administration fee of 7.5 percent of the advance and any royalties payable by YouTube.

Statutory Rate Applicable to Audio Interactive and Limited Download Services

As we discussed in Chapter 3, in 2008, organizations representing the digital music services and the music publishers came to an agreement regarding rates payable by interactive audio services, and the Copyright Royalty Board adopted regulations under Section 115 of the Copyright Act that provided for a mechanical royalty rate pertaining to interactive streaming and limited downloading. These services, whether or not they make money from a service's revenues, will generally pay a mechanical royalty of 10.5 percent of "service revenue," less any amounts payable to the PROs (ASCAP, BMI, and SESAC) for performance royalties.

The NMPA website summarizes the rates as follows:[141]

- The agreement proposes mechanical royalty rates that cover both limited downloads and interactive streaming, including when offered by subscription and ad-supported services.
- The percentage rate structure in the agreement provides much-needed flexibility for new business models.
- The agreement permits the use without payment of certain kinds of promotional streams, in the interest of encouraging paid uses of musical compositions.
- The agreement confirms that the mechanical licenses issued under its provisions will include all reproduction and distribution rights necessary to provide the licensed limited downloads or interactive streams.
- Outside the scope of the draft regulations, the parties confirmed that noninteractive audio-only streaming services do not require reproduction or distribution licenses from copyright owners.

The Harry Fox Agency has published the chart on the final page of this chapter summing up the rates on its website. The first thing to recognize about this chart is that it applies to five distinct kinds of services. The first column is for subscription services that may only be accessed on a desktop and not on portable devices. The second column applies if that service provides limited downloads that disappear if the subscriber stops paying for the service. The third column is for portable subscription services that offer interactive streaming and limited downloads (e.g., Spotify premium, Rhapsody, and Beats Music). The fourth column is for services that are "bundled" with a device such as a smartphone or with a mobile phone service such as AT&T. The last column applies to free, advertiser-supported services (e.g., free Spotify).

If you take a brief look at the chart, it seems like rocket science to figure out what these services have to pay. It isn't. Generally, all these services have to pay 10.5 percent of their revenues minus the payments to the PROs. Since some deals that PROs make with digital services are confidential, it is impossible to state exactly what the PROs collect, although sources at the societies have informed me that generally the PROS collectively receive from 5 percent to 7 percent of revenues from most interactive music services.

Let's go through a test case: Assume a service with a million subscribers charges $10 per month. Its gross revenue is therefore $10 million per month. And let's assume that this service fits under the third column, i.e., it offers portable subscriptions, interactive streaming, and limited downloading. Assume it pays the PROs a total of 5 percent of revenue, and apply these figures tothe formula set forth in the chart.

Each service must pay the greater of the calculation in 1(a) or 1(b) minus payment to the PROs. In the example provided, 10.5 percent is the greater number:

Step 1(a): 10.5 percent x 10 million dollars = 1.05 million dollars ($1,050,000)

Step 1(b): 80 cents x 1 million subscribers = $800,000[142]

Step 2: 1,050,000 – $500,000 (5 percent x 10,000,000) = $550,000

Step 3: Greater of Step 2 ($550,000) or .50 x 1,000,000 ($500,000). Therefore this service would pay $550,000.

Step 4 provides how the money will be divided by the total number of plays of all musical works to yield a per-play allocation. For instance, if there are 1 billion plays, that would be divided by $550,000 = .055 cents per play.

How Much the Songwriters Receive

Public Performance

Songwriters receive the public-performance royalty part of the statutory rate directly from the PROs. Of the 10.5 percent, approximately 6 percent represents income payable to ASCAP, BMI, and SESAC.[143] The songwriters receive 50 percent of that after admin fees charged by the PROs. The publishers receive the other 50 percent directly from the PROs. In co-pub deals, the publisher will pay an additional 25 percent.

Mechanical

The mechanical component of the 10.5 percent (what's left after the services pay the PROs) is generally paid to HFA, which in turn pays its publisher members, who in turn pay 50 percent to their writers (and in co-pub deals 75 percent).

Calculation Steps for Subsection B of 37 CFR § 385 - "2008 Settlement"

OFFERING TYPE

	Standalone Non-Portable Subscriptions, Streaming Only	**Standalone Non-Portable Subscriptions, Mixed Use**	**Standalone Portable Subscriptions, Mixed Use**	**Bundled Subscription Services**	**Free Non-Subscription/Ad-Supported Services**
1. Calculate the All-In Royalty Pool, which is the greater of					
a) % of Service Revenue, and	10.5%	10.5%	10.5%	10.5%	10.5%
b) Service Type Minimum	lesser of: (i) $0.50 per subscriber per month, **and** (iia) 22% of service's payments to record companies for sound recording rights only, if not pass-through **or** (iib) 18% of services payments to record companies for sound recording and mechanical rights together, if pass-through	lesser of: (i) $0.50 per subscriber per month, **and** (iia) 21% of service's payments to record companies for sound recording rights only, if not pass-through **or** (iib) 17.36% of services payments to record companies for sound recording and mechanical rights together, if pass-through	lesser of: (i) $0.80 per subscriber per month, **and** (iia) 21% of service's payments to record companies for sound recording rights only, if not pass-through **or** (iib) 17.36% of services payments to record companies for sound recording and mechanical rights together, if pass-through	(i) 21% of a service's payments to record companies for sound recording rights only, if not pass-through **or** (ii) 17.36% of a service's all-in payments to record companies for sound recording and mechanical rights together if pass-through	(i) 22% of a service's payments to record companies for sound recording rights only, if not pass-through **or** (ii) 18% of a service's all-in payments to record companies for sound recording and mechanical rights together if pass-through
2. Subtract performance royalties paid in connection with the "Offering"					
3. Payable Royalty Pool ($ payable for all musical works used in the period)	Greater of 1. Step 2 result, and 2. $0.15 per subscriber month[2]	Greater of 1. Step 2 result, and 2. $0.30 per subscriber month[2]	Greater of 1. Step 2 result, and 2. $0.50 per subscriber month[2]	Greater of 1. Step 2 result, and 2. $0.25 per subscriber month[2]	Step 2 Result
4. Allocate Payable Royalty Pool based on the number of plays[3,4]	Allocation based on number of plays[3,4]	Allocation based on number of plays[3,4]	Allocation based on number of plays[3,4]	Allocation based on number of plays[3,4]	Allocation based on number of plays[3,4]

2. Subscriber month for all Offerings except bundled subscription services shall be calculated for the accounting period, taking into account all end users who were subscribers for complete calendar months, prorating in the case of end users who were subscribers for only part of a calendar month, and deducting on a prorated basis for end users covered by a free trial period subject to the promo royalty rate. For bundled subscription services, determine with respect to active subscribers (i.e., each end user who made at least one play of a licensed work during such month).
3. Per-Play Allocation: Divide the Payable Royalty Pool for an Offering by the total number of plays of all musical works made through the Offering to yield a per-play allocation and multiply the result by the number of plays of each musical work. See 37 CFR § 385.22 with respect to calculating "plays" of downloads.
4. The number of plays for a musical work with a playing time of over 5 minutes shall be counted so that each actual play is counted as 1 play plus 0.2 for each for each additional minute or fraction of a minute.

* NOTE: All calculations pertain to the current accounting period and exclude free trials or promotional uses authorized under the regulations

Chapter 6

NONINTERACTIVE DIGITAL STREAMING, INCLUDING WEBCASTING AND SATELLITE RADIO

Overview

As we discussed in Chapter 3, the Sound Audio Recording Act provided owners of sound recordings with the exclusive right to transmit their records on audio *digital* platforms. (As expressed in the upcoming discussion, they still do not have exclusive rights to publicly perform their records on terrestrial radio, or on broadcast or cable television.) The Digital Millennium Copyright Act 1998 provides audio digital music services that qualify a statutory license to publicly perform any sound recording. This means that although the sound recording copyright owners have exclusive digital public-performance rights, they cannot deny a license to services that qualify for the statutory license. The conditions for qualifying and the rates those services must pay are also set up by the DMCA as provided in Section 114 of the Copyright Act.

The best-known services that qualify under Section 114 are Sirius XM, the US satellite service, and "webcasters," including noninteractive stand-alone services such as Pandora, iHeart Radio, and Songza (also referred to as "Internet radio stations"), as well as radio stations that simulcast via the Internet (that is, they rebroadcast their analogue signals digitally so that they can be heard on any Internet-connected device). But other parties, including colleges, universities, individual podcasters, and background music services can also qualify for a Section 114 license.

In order to qualify, digital audio services must be noninteractive; that is, they cannot allow users to listen to individual songs or albums on demand, and they cannot allow any songs to be downloaded.[144] They must also comply with other conditions. The most important are referred to as the "sound recording performance complement." The service cannot, in any three-hour period, play more than three songs from a particular album (and no more than two consecutively), or more than four songs by a particular artist (and no more than three consecutively). The rationale of this condition was to prevent listeners from being tempted to record a digital transmission of, for example, a Sinatra album, or an hour of Elton John music. In addition, when performing a sound recording, a webcaster must identify the track, album, and featured artist. Advance song or artist playlists may not be published. Archived programs—those that are posted for listeners to hear repeatedly on demand—may not be less than five hours in duration, and looped or continuous programs—those that are performed continuously, automatically starting over when finished—may not be less than three hours in duration.[145] Certain other conditions apply. For the full list, see Section 114 of the Copyright Act.

But the most important obligation that a noninteractive digital audio service has under the DMCA is to pay the required fees (see "The Rates Payable by Various Noninteractive Streaming Services" later in this chapter). Those fees are payable to an organization called SoundExchange, which in turn distributes 50 percent of the monies directly to artists and 50 percent to the owners of the sound recordings, who are usually record companies. This statutory payment scheme eliminates a lot of the controversies we noted in the last chapter on how artists are paid (or not) for use of the records on interactive digital streaming services.

Even if a service qualifies for a compulsory license under Section 114, however, it must acquire an additional license for the public performance of the musical compositions represented in the sound recordings. ASCAP, BMI, and SESAC offer blanket licenses and negotiate fees with streaming services, then distribute the monies on a 50/50 basis to their songwriters and publisher members.

How Much the Services Pay for Copyrighted Music

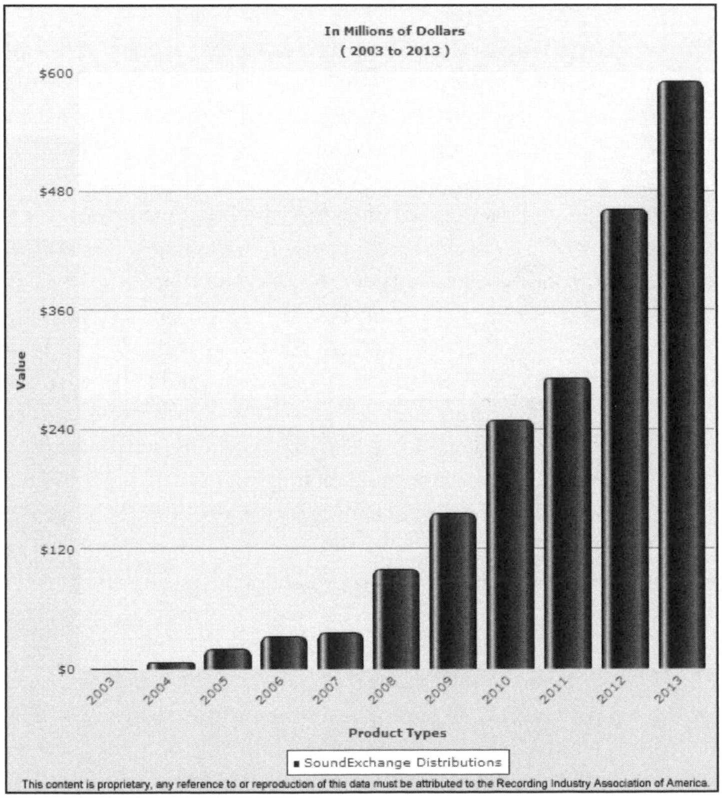

In regard to sound recordings, as noted previously, 100 percent of income payable to record companies and artists by services that qualify for a Section 114 license are paid to SoundExchange for redistribution to the labels and artists.[146] This chart shows that SoundExchange's payouts have soared in the last several years. The growth rate has been stunning—from 292 million dollars in 2012 to $462 million in 2012 to $590.4 million in 2013.[147]

The total amount collected by Sound Exchange in 2013 was actually 656 million dollars.[148] This compares to $507 million in 2012 and only $378 million in 2011.[149] According to SoundExchange's website, its administration fee is approximately 5 percent.[150] This means that SoundExchange is holding approximately30 million dollars either because they can't find the copyright owners or because there are legal disputes concerning the ownership of certain recordings.

The increase in both income and payouts through SoundExchange reflects the growing popularity of Internet and satellite radio. In fact, Pandora, the leading Internet radio service, and Sirius XM, the satellite service, pay approximately 90 percent of SoundExchange's income.[151]

Pandora was founded in 2000 in Oakland, California, by Tim Westergren, a Stanford grad and former musician,[152] and two partners. The company, which operates its Internet radio service in the United States, Australia, and New Zealand, developed a form of radio that uses intrinsic qualities of music to create stations that adapt playlists. You drop the name of one of your favorite songs, artists, or genres into Pandora and Pandora finds songs with interesting musical similarities to your choice. You can create up to 100 unique "stations."[153]

Pandora is the most successful Internet radio service operating in the United States today. It has approximately 200 million registered users and had 76.4 million active users in July 2014.[154] Pandora has approximately 70 percent share of the Internet radio market in the United States and streamed an average of 17.7 billion songs per month in the fiscal year 2013.[155] Total listener hours were at 5.05 billion in the second quarter of 2014.[156] In comparison with all other radio services, Pandora's market share in March 2014 was 9.11 percent.[157] In terms of profitability Pandora has always struggled and continues to do so.[158] Pandora is basically an ad-supported service and is free on both desktop and mobile devices. Although it offers an ad-free premium service for $4.99 per month, as of April 2014 it only has 3.3 million paying subscribers, which represents a small fraction of its overall user base.[159]

Pandora now accounts for nearly one-half of SoundExchange's total royalty collections.[160] According to its most recent 10-K filing (from mid-February 2014), Pandora paid 48 percent of its total revenues ($600.2 million) to SoundExchange for the last 11 months of 2013—which comes to over 288 million dollars. Since Pandora's figures were based only on 11 months of 2013 and SoundExchange's figures are based on the full calendar year of 2013, it is easy to conclude that Pandora's total royalties paid to SoundExchange for the full 12 months of 2013 would have been over $300 million.

Pandora often complains that profitability has been elusive because it pays too much for music rights,[161] although its total payout is over 50 percent for both songs and recordings, which is less than Spotify claims to pay. Spotify, however, has also struggled to be profitable.

Sirius XM is the only satellite radio service operating nationwide in the US. It's the result of the merger of two satellite radio services, Sirius Satellite Radio and XM Satellite Radio, in 2008. In 2014 Sirius XM reported that it has 26.3 million paying subscribers, a 5 percent increase over the year before.[162] According to *Forbe*s, in the first quarter of 2014, the satellite radio provider's subscription revenues jumped by 7.8 percent and overall revenues increased by 10 percent to $1.04 billion.[163] Sirius XM offers over 165 channels, including 72 commercial-free music channels,[164] at monthly fees ranging from $9.99 to $18.99 for access to all channels. Sirius XM's success is tightly aligned with its predominance in the automobile industry. The company has arrangements with every major automaker for installation of satellite radio in their vehicles and 60 percent penetration rate in regard to new cars. Of the customers who buy a car equipped with satellite radio, an astounding number (approximately 45 to 46 percent) convert to self-pay subscribers after the promotional trial runs out.[165] SoundExchange does not disclose the exact dollar amount that Sirius pays it. But in 2013 the rate that Sirius was required to pay SoundExchange was 9% of its gross revenues, and those revenues were 2.15 billion dollars.[166] So it is reasonable to conclude that Sirius paid approximately $200 million to SoundExchange.[167]

Of course, there are many other webcasters, including stand-alone digital webcasters such as iHeart Radio and Songza; simulcasters, i.e., terrestrial radio stations that simulcast their signal digitally; colleges and universities; and digital background music services. According to SoundExchange's website, more than 2,500 services are now paying SoundExchange.[168]

For the compositions embodied in the recordings that play on noninteractive services, the total aggregate payment to ASCAP, BMI, and SESAC is approximately 4 percent of each service's total income from advertising and subscription revenues. In Chapter 7 we will consider the contention of the music publishing community, including the PROs and the major publishers, that this amount does not fairly reflect the value of their songs, and look at the steps they have taken and continue to take to secure a greater share of monies, particularly from Pandora and other Internet radio stations.

How the Money Flows from the Services to the Labels, Artists, Publishers, and Songwriters

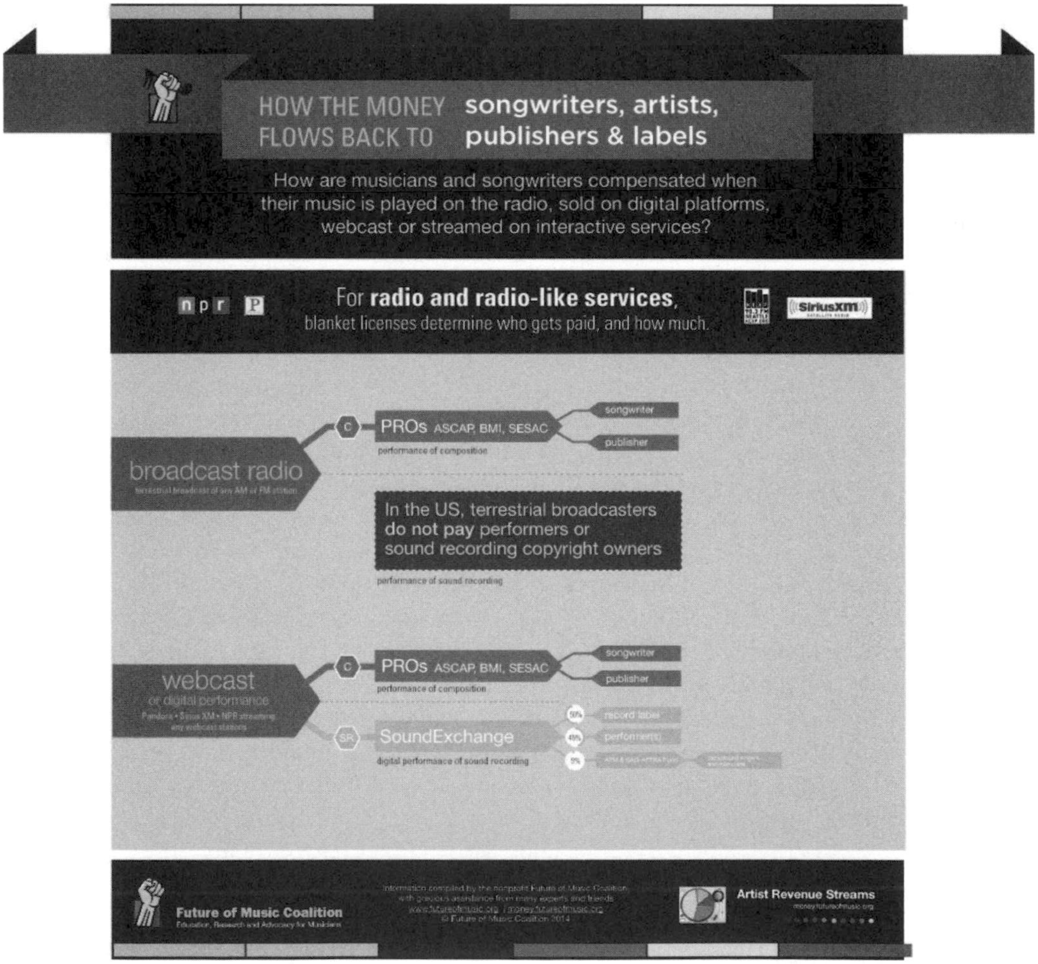

How Much the Labels and the Artists Receive

As the FMC chart emphasizes, terrestrial radio stations pay nothing to the labels and artists. The reason for this is basically that broadcast radio has the political and financial clout to persuade Congress to deny owners of sound recordings exclusive rights to perform their records except via digital transmission. (For more details, see "Why Radio Does Not Pay for Broadcasting Sound Recordings" in Chapter 1). But digital music services must pay for public performance and transmission of sound recordings. How much digital services who qualify for a Section 114 license have to pay is usually determined by a governmental body called the Copyright Royalty Board, or in some cases is negotiated directly with SoundExchange

The Services Pay SoundExchange and It Pays 50 Percent to Artists and 50 Percent to Sound Recording Copyright Owners

Originally a division of the RIAA, SoundExchange is now an independent nonprofit performance-rights entity jointly controlled by artists and sound recording copyright owners through an 18-member board of directors with nine artist representatives and nine copyright-owner representatives.

Of the 50 percent of monies payable to artists, 45 percent is paid to "featured artists" and 5 percent to "non-featured artists."[169] A featured artist "is an artist that is prominently featured on a track or album." A non-featured artist "is an artist who is not prominently featured on a track or album (i.e. a session musician or a back-up vocalist)."[170] Royalties for non-featured artists are covered by organizations such as the American Federation of Musicians (AFM) and the Screen Actors Guild and American Federation of Television and Radio Artists (SAG-AFTRA). But an organization called the AFM & SAG-AFTRA Fund administers these monies. In other words, SoundExchange pays them the 5 percent and they in turn pay the non-featured artists. The Fund then distributes 50 percent of that 5 percent as follows: 2.5 percent to entitled non-featured singers and 2.5 percent to non-featured musicians without regard to union membership. But musicians must register with the Fund in order to collect these royalties. In fact, if you are a working musician the Fund may be holding monies for you that you don't even know you are entitled to.

Featured artists receive direct payments from SoundExchange. If there is more than one featured artists (a band with two or more members, for instance), royalties are generally allocated on a pro rata basis, so if there are four members each would receive 25 percent of the 45 percent payout.[171] The beauty of this statutory system is that the featured artists who are signed to labels receive their money directly. This means that even if they are unrecouped, that is, they owe their label money because they have not earned enough through record sales to pay back advances, they receive their fair share of webcasting monies. In that way it resembles the system by which songwriters are paid by the PROs, that is, directly and bypassing the music publishers. This is crucial since so many recording artists signed to record companies are unrecouped.

How SoundExchange Calculates the Value of Each Performance

> SoundExchange generally allocates a service's royalties on a pro rata basis in accordance with the information provided in the service's reports of use. For example, if the net royalties (after deducting costs) paid by Service A total $100 for period X and Service A reported 10,000 discrete sound recordings during

> that period with identical usage reported for each track, then each distinct sound recording would be valued at one cent ($0.01) ($100 ÷ 10,000).[172]

SoundExchange is able to make these precise allocations for each performance because it requires its licensees to provide accurate reports of the identity of each track and how many times it was performed. Since all of its licensees are digital services, they are all capable of tracking the identity and the number of plays of each track. All royalties collected by SoundExchange are accompanied by extensive electronic play logs submitted by the licensee. These logs are "matched" to a database of unique sound recording information, and are in turn referenced to an owner of the sound recording and featured artist. This allows SoundExchange to accurately match unique performances with record companies and artists, and pay exactly what has been earned.

The Rates Payable by Various Noninteractive Streaming Services

Neither the DMCA nor Section 114 actually states the fees that licensees have to pay to publicly perform copyrighted sound recordings. Currently those rates, as well as other rates for statutory licenses under the Copyright Act including the Section 115 mechanical license rates, are determined by the the Copyright Royalty Board (CRB). The CRB consists of three copyright royalty judges appointed by the Librarian of Congress. The Board was created under the Copyright Royalty and Distribution Reform Act of 2004, which became effective on May 31, 2005, phasing out the Copyright Arbitration Royalty Panel (CARP). However, not all the current rates applicable to noninteractive services were determined by the CRB. In 2007 the CRB set new rates for certain services, including Pandora, that threatened to put some services out of business. Congress intervened and ordered SoundExchange to negotiate deals with webcasters including Pandora, National Public Radio, and others.[173]

Stand-Alone Digital Services, Including Pandora

The rate negotiated between Pandora and SoundExchange is the *greater* of 25 percent of gross income or 0.00130 per stream (that is, per song). In 2015 the penny rate increases to $0.00140.[174] Since Pandora has so many listeners (76.4 million active users in July 2014) who listen to so many songs (5.05 billion *hours* in the second quarter of 2014 alone), but relatively few listeners (approximately 3 million) who choose to pay $4.99 a month for premium service,[175] the per stream penny rate easily exceeds 25 percent of income. This is why Pandora's most recent 10-K filing, from mid-February 2014, shows that it paid 48 percent of its total revenues to SoundExchange. Pandora has often complained that its rate is too high, particularly when compared to the 9.5 percent of gross income that Sirius XM pays–and considering that AM/FM radio pays exactly nothing. SoundExchange agrees that it is unfair that normal broadcast radio pays nothing to artists or owners of recorded music. According to the president of SoundExchange, Michael Huppe, "It is an accident of history and politics that FM radio gets away with paying nothing for this primary input to their service."[176] But that's where the agreement between the two camps ends. In fact, Huppe and SoundExchange's position is that Pandora should be paying even more than it does now. Although Pandora has dramatically grown its listenership since its inception 14 years ago, Huppe believes it's the content providers themselves who deserve most of the credit. "Pandora would not exist if it weren't for the recordings that are provided to them through this process," he says, in somewhat of a chicken-and-egg argument. "We like what they do; it's a very exciting company. But if you remove the sound recordings from the mix, I would say the value proposition of Pandora drops off substantially."[177]

At the time this book is being submitted in January 2015, the CRB is in the process of determining new rates starting in 2016 for five years. The rates are supposed to be handed down no later than January 2015.[178]

Sirius XM Rate

As the only US satellite service, Sirius XM has its own rate with SoundExchange, paying royalties of only 9.5 percent of its gross income in 2014. The rate goes up to 10 percent in 2015 and thereafter by ½ point each year until 2018, when the CRB is supposed to provide new rates. As noted, Pandora complains that Sirius XM pays far less than it does and that this disparity is unfair. The counterargument is that all of Pandora's content is comprised of sound recordings, whereas Sirius XM has an enormous amount of non-music content, featuring everything from Howard Stern to sports events.

Broadcast Radio Services That Simulcast Their Signal

Similar to Pandora, radio stations that simulcast their signal pay a penny rate for each stream of a song; but this rate is higher: $0.0023 per performance in 2014, rising to $0.0025 per performance in 2015. The CRB is currently considering new rates that would go into effect in 2016.

Other Rates

There are a variety of other rates that apply to various kinds of services, including non-commercial services, educational webcasters (those operated or affiliated with an accredited school, college, or university), NPR and other public radio stations, small webcasters (those that make less than a certain amount or a small listenership, and background digital music services. For rates and terms that apply, see the "service provider" pages of the SoundExchange website, at www.soundexchange.com/service-provider.

How Much the Publishers and Songwriters Receive

Unlike either download stores or interactive streaming services that offer limited downloads, noninteractive digital services that qualify for a license under Section 114 do not pay any mechanical royalties. As with standard radio, listening does not involve making a "copy," even a temporary one, of any song. However, as with AM/FM radio, a public performance does occur. So these services need public-performance licenses.

Public-performance royalties payable by noninteractive services, particularly by Pandora, have recently generated some high-profile legal controversies. Pandora has recently engaged in court battles with both ASCAP and BMI. ASCAP sought more than the 1.85 percent of gross revenues (including advertising and subscription income) that had been collecting from Pandora, and Pandora wanted the rate reduced. The rate court—the special federal court in Manhattan that implements the consent decrees under which both ASCAP and BMI operate—decided to retain the 1.85 rate. This decision and a parallel proceeding involving BMI have initiated a flurry of legal maneuvering, including by major publishers, in an effort to amend the consent decrees with the goal of securing higher rates. We discuss these activities and the attendant legal and business issues in detail in Chapter 7. But it is appropriate to note here that the aggregate royalty presently payable by Pandora to all three

PROs is currently approximately 4 percent. In light of the fact that Pandora is paying nearly 50 percent of its income for playing music recordings, the PROs, the major publishers as well as, and many indie publishers and songwriters contend that Pandora is underpaying for playing their songs.

It is also useful to note here that all three PROs offer blanket licenses for anyone wishing to stream music, such as a music clubs that simulcast live performances on the Internet (see my interview with Spike Wilner in Chapter 27), a background music service that operates digitally, or a website that plays music. We discuss how to go about securing PRO licenses for these services in "How to Clear Music for Stand-Alone Digital Projects" in Chapter 13.

Performance Rights in Pre-'72 Recordings; Lawsuits against Sirius XM and Pandora

As we discussed in Chapter 1, federal copyright law applies to sound recordings but only to those produced on or after February 15, 1972.[179] Recordings produced prior to that date are subject to protection under the laws of individual states until 2067. A recent spate of lawsuits has raised the issue of whether Pandora's Internet radio service and Sirius XM's satellite service have the right to play sound recordings produced prior to February 15, 1972, without permission from and payment to the owners of the copyrights in those recordings or the artists performing on them. Pandora and Sirius XM are currently not paying SoundExchange for pre-'72 recordings. They contend that since federal copyright law does not apply to such recordings, they are entitled to play them without paying the royalty required by federal law (specifically, the DPRA and DMCA—see Chapter 3).

Pre-'72 recordings include some of the most iconic records of all time, featuring such artists as Billie Holiday, Frank Sinatra, Elvis Presley, Miles Davis, Johnny Cash, and countless others. Pre-'72 recordings account for about 5 percent of plays at Pandora and 15 percent at Sirius XM.[180] So this is an important issue for both Pandora and Sirius XM.

As of the submission of this manuscript in January 2015, there are six lawsuits questioning Sirius XM and Pandora's position that they do not have to ask for permission or pay for pre-'72 recordings. These include four lawsuits brought by Flo & Eddie, Inc., a corporation created in 1971 that is owned by Howard Kaylan and Mark Volman, two of the founding members of the music group the Turtles. They filed three lawsuits against Sirius XM in California, Florida, and New York and initiated another one against Pandora in California. The recording industry, led by Capitol, a wholly owned label of Universal Music, is suing Sirius XM in California[181] and Pandora in New York.[182]

Of these six cases, as of January 2015, there have been two decisions, both in favor of Flo & Eddie and against Sirius XM. In September 2014 a California federal court found that a California statute enacted in 1982 specifically designed to protect pre-'72 recordings created a public performance right in such sound recordings. The relevant statute is Cal. Civ. Code § 980(a)(2), which reads in relevant part:

> The author of an original work of authorship consisting of a sound recording initially fixed prior to February 15, 1972, has an exclusive ownership therein . . . as against all persons except one who independently makes or duplicates another sound recording that does not directly or indirectly recapture the actual sounds fixed in such prior recording . . .[183]

Judge Philip Gutierrez found that this statute gave authors of pre-'72 sound recordings exclusive public performance rights as well the exclusive right to copy or distribute them. The primary basis for his decision was that there is nothing in the statutory language that would preclude performance rights in pre-'72 sound recordings. He inferred from this "that the legislature did not intend to further limit ownership rights, otherwise it would have indicated that intent explicitly."[184] Judge Gutierrez concluded that "copyright ownership of a sound recording under § 980(a)(2) includes the exclusive right to publicly perform that recording." Shortly after the court issued its decision, Sirius XM announced that it will appeal Judge Gutierrez's decision.

Flo & Eddie scored another victory against Sirius XM in New York. In November a New York federal court found that although New York had no statute protecting sound recordings, the state's common law (that is, judge-made law) protected a public performance right in sound recordings. Judge Colleen McMahon of the Southern District of New York denied Sirius XM's motion for summary judgment against Flo & Eddie's complaint, alleging that Sirius XM Radio committed common-law copyright infringement by publicly performing pre-'72 sound recordings of the Turtles.[185] McMahon found that "general principles of common law copyright dictate that public performance rights in pre-1972 sound recordings do exist."

The judge based this conclusion on a series of New York court decisions that afforded public-performance rights to holders of common-law copyrights in works such as plays and films. She acknowledged that "the conspicuous lack of any jurisprudential history confirms that not paying royalties for public performances of sound recordings was an accepted fact of life in the broadcasting industry for the last century." But she discarded that history by observing,

> . . . acquiescence by participants in the recording industry in a status quo where recording artists and producers were not paid royalties while songwriters were does not show that they lacked an enforceable right under the common law—only that they failed to act on it.

The decisions in both New York and California have broader implications than just whether Sirius XM or other digital services must pay for pre-'72 recordings. Even though both decisions only involved Sirius XM, both decisions imply that terrestrial radio and venues such as nightclubs, bars, or any other place that publicly performs records must seek the permission of the owners of the copyrights in pre-'72 recordings, because both decisions are based on laws and cases that were passed or decided before digital transmission of music even existed. If these laws and cases require digital services to secure permission to publicly perform sound recordings, they would logically require terrestrial radio and physical venues to secure permission.

Of course, this would change the fundamentals of music licensing, at least in California and New York. Indeed, the decisions could be the basis of a class action on behalf of copyright owners of recordings by legacy artists against terrestrial radio stations and physical venues in New York and/or California. Whether the major labels who own most of these copyrights pursue this course remains to be seen. However, the possibility of such an action could be used in the longstanding battle by the recording industry to induce broadcast radio stations to finally pay them for playing their records, especially if the courts' decisions are upheld on appeal. The record industry, as represented by the RIAA, could agree to forego launching lawsuits against terrestrial radio stations in California and New York for playing pre-'72 records without permission in exchange an agreement by the terrestrial radio industry, represented by the National Association of Broadcasters, to finally pay a reasonable royalty for the performance of all sound recordings.

The decisions could also provide momentum for the passage of special legislation introduced in Congress in May 2014, titled "Respecting Senior Performers as Essential Cultural Treasures" or the RESPECT Act. This bill, which is supported by the RIAA, and which has been opposed by Sirius and Pandora, would amend the federal copyright law by specifically requiring noninteractive digital radio services, including Pandora and Sirius XM, to pay royalties for pre-'72 recordings. The bill, if passed, would also immunize such services from legal action if they paid SoundExchange "in the same manner as they pay royalties for sound recordings protected by federal copyright that are fixed after such date."[186] Since the law would head off any future lawsuits against Sirius XM and Pandora, Flo & Eddie's legal victories may influence Sirius and Pandora to stop opposing the bill.

Aside from requiring noninteractive streaming services to pay for pre-'72 recordings, the Act would not "federalize" pre-'72 recordings; that is, it would not apply any other provisions of the federal law to those recordings. Thus, the termination rights discussed in Chapter 1 would not be available for pre-'72 recordings.

Since the bill was not reported out of the Judiciary Committee, it will have to be reintroduced in 2015. But supporters of the bill are hopeful that it will and that it will be passed and approved by both houses of Congress.

For new developments concerning the case law regarding pre-'72 sound recordings and the RESPECT Act, please visit www.futureofthemusicbusiness.com.

Chapter 7
THE DIRECT-LICENSING CONTROVERSY
Will Publishers Be Able to License Public-Performance Rights to Digital Music Services Directly (Instead of through the PROs), and What Are the Consequences for Songwriters?

Direct licensing" refers to a license to use music that is secured directly from the owner of that song or music recording. For instance, as we discus in Part II of the book, in order to secure the right to use a song in a movie or TV program, it is necessary to secure a "sync" license directly from the company that owns or controls the copyright in that song, usually a music publisher, be it a major such as Sony/ATV or Universal Music, an indie, or a self-published songwriter.

Collection Societies

However, because of the complexity of licensing music to all possible users for all possible uses, over time, copyright owners in the music business all around the world have set up what are referred to as "collection societies." These groups are authorized to license and collect money on behalf of the music copyright owners for certain purposes.

The PROs

As we discussed in Chapter 1, songwriters and music publishers founded the American Society of Composers, Authors and Publishers (ASCAP) in 1914 to license and collect money for the public performance of music. Broadcast Music Incorporated (BMI) was set up by broadcasters to essentially compete against ASCAP in 1940, and the Society of European Stage Authors and Composers (SESAC) was created in 1930 to represent contemporary European classical music. Each of these performing-rights organizations (PROs) are authorized by their publisher and songwriter members to license public-performance rights for their music to radio and TV stations, concert halls, bars, nightclubs, restaurants, stores, amusement parks, bowling alleys, and anywhere else where music is publicly performed.[187] Although this is a huge job, the PROs historically have not licensed any other rights than the right to publicly perform music. For instance, they are not authorized to issue "sync" licenses, so you cannot call them to acquire permission to use a song in your movie. And they do not represent "mechanical" rights, so you cannot acquire a license from them to include a song on your record.

As the public performance of music moved to the Internet, the PROs started to license songs for use on platforms such as Pandora, YouTube, and Spotify. At first, the music publishers were content to let the PROs license public-performance rights to these new platforms. But in 2007,[188] certain publishers, particularly the major publishers such as Sony, started experimenting with direct licensing of performance rights. These publishers were dissatisfied with the amount of money that the PROs were receiving from digital platforms. They were particularly irritated that their industry cousins, the record companies, were doing much better in the digital music space than they were. For instance, Pandora pays approximately 50 percent of its revenue to record companies and artists, but only approximately 4 percent to the music publishers and songwriters through licenses with the PROs. According to the *New York Times*, these percentages translate into approximately $313 million dollars and $26 million dollars respectively.[189]

Unfortunately for the publishers, both ASCAP and BMI are in a relatively weak bargaining position because they both operate under government-imposed "consent decrees," which limits their bargaining power. (SESAC, which is much smaller than ASCAP and BMI, is not subject to a consent decree.)

Consent Decrees and the "Rate Court"

In the late 1930s, ASCAP's general control over most music and its membership requirements were considered to be in restraint of trade and illegal under the Sherman Anti-Trust Act. The Justice Department sued ASCAP in 1941, and the case was settled with a consent decree. BMI, which was formed in 1940, also signed a consent decree in 1941. Among the most important points in the decree is that ASCAP and BMI cannot "discriminate" between users of music who have basically the same requirements. For instance, they must treat all bars and restaurants in a similar manner. Also, and even more importantly, ASCAP and BMI cannot deny anyone a public-performance license. If the parties cannot agree on a rate, the consent decree provides a mechanism whereby either party may petition the United States District Cour t for the Southern District of New York (the "rate court") for determination of a reasonable fee. The ASCAP and BMI rate courts are each overseen by a federal district court judge. Rate court proceedings are essentially non-jury trials.

Major Publishers Make a Move but the Rate Court Rebuffs Them

To circumvent the consent decrees, some big publishers tried to limit their relationship with ASCAP and BMI, forcing digital services like Pandora to negotiate directly with them. In 2011, EMI Music Publishing, which later merged with Sony/ATV to become the largest music publisher in the US, was the first of the major publishers to pull from both the two major PROs (first ASCAP, and soon after BMI) the right to license its songs to certain "new media services" in order to gain leverage in direct license negotiations with services like Pandora. Because copyright owners enjoy exclusive control of their musical works and are not constrained by consent decrees, they can withhold the right to use their songs for any reason and can negotiate higher royalty rates than the PROs. In late 2012, Sony/ATV—which had followed EMI's lead and withdrawn digital rights from the PROs—successfully negotiated a deal with Pandora for its repertoire at a rate of 5 percent (prorated by the amount of Sony's songs played on Pandora) of Pandora's revenue; this rate was 25 percent higher than the approximate 4 percent that the PROs were receiving from Pandora at that time. But the publishers' withdrawal strategy appeared to backfire in two separate decisions by the ASCAP and BMI rate court judges in proceedings initiated by Pandora around the time of the Sony/ATV-Pandora direct license.

The ASCAP-Pandora Rate Proceeding and Judge Cote's Summary Judgment Decision (September 2013)

In 2010, before withdrawal from PROs began to occur, Pandora terminated the license with ASCAP under which it was paying 1.85 percent of its gross income for the right to perform any or all of the songs in the ASCAP repertoire. At the behest of its major publisher members, ASCAP modified its rules so that publisher members could negotiate exclusive direct licenses for "new media services" such as Pandora. Prior to such changes, all of ASCAP and BMI's arrangements with their members (both publishers and songwriters) were non-exclusive, allowing either ASCAP or a publisher to negotiate licenses with music users. As a practical matter, therefore, there had rarely been an incentive for publishers to pursue direct licenses so long as music users could fall back on ASCAP licenses.

As mentioned earlier, the first publisher to withdraw digital rights from ASCAP was EMI Music Publishing in May 2011. Upon learning of EMI's action, Pandora started negotiating with EMI. During the course of that negotiation Sony/ATV acquired EMI's music catalogue. Subsequently, other major publishers, including Warner Chappell, Universal, and BMG, announced their intention to withdraw their digital rights from the PROs, and Pandora started negotiations with them as well. In 2012 Pandora, faced with rate hikes demanded by the "withdrawn" majors, filed a summary judgment motion in the ASCAP rate court proceeding asking for a determination that ASCAP was required to license all the songs in its repertoire under its consent decree. Pandora complained that it had been put in "absolute gun-to-the-head circumstances" in negotiations with Sony and other big publishers. It also argued that treating digital services differently from other licensees, such as terrestrial broadcasters, by only offering part of their repertoire was discriminatory toward new media services and violated the consent decree. The court sided with Pandora. Judge Cote stated in her September 2013 decision that:

> Because the language of the consent decree unambiguously requires ASCAP to provide Pandora with a license to perform all of the works in its repertory, and because ASCAP retains the works of "withdrawing" publishers in its repertory even if it purports to lack the right to license them to a subclass of New Media entities, Pandora's motion for summary judgment is granted. [190]

Pandora argued that the rate should be 1.7 percent, which is what terrestrial radio stations pay ASCAP for their normal broadcast and digital simulcasts. ASCAP asked that the rate be set at 1.85 percent for the first two years (this is the same rate Pandora had been paying), 2.5 percent for 2013, and 3 percent in 2014 and 2015. Instead of giving ASCAP the rate increases it asked for the last three years, the court maintained the 1.85 percent rate in a decision made in 2014.[191]

The BMI-Pandora Rate Proceedings and Judge Stanton's Summary Judgment Decision (December 2013)

In a parallel proceeding to its action against ASCAP, Pandora also asked for a determination that BMI had to license its entire repertoire even though the big publishers had withdrawn digital rights from BMI just as they had with ASCAP.

The BMI rate court judge, Louis Stanton, ruled that publishers seeking to withdraw digital rights from BMI had to completely withdraw all songs and all rights—throwing the entire publishing business into a state of confusion. The decision meant that Sony, Universal, Warner, BMG, and other big publishers could continue doing direct deals, but only if they did them with *all* users of music, not just digital platforms. This would have meant that tens of thousands of "general" licenses in effect with stores, bars, hotels, and concert halls, automatically renewed annually, would cease to include the repertoire of major publishers—accounting for nearly half the market. In the ASCAP case, Judge Cote found that publishers are "all in" unless they resign from ASCAP completely; conversely, Judge Stanton decided that publishers were "all out" if they persisted in withdrawing new media rights from BMI.[192]

Universal had announced it would withdraw digital rights from BMI beginning January 1, 2014. As a result of the BMI decision, Universal entered into a short-term deal with BMI for its entire catalogue to remain a part of the blanket license offered by BMI to all music users. Universal's deal with BMI is short-term because, like other major publishers, the company hopes that the Department of Justice will agree to amend the consent decrees so that digital rights can be withdrawn.

The Publishers' New Strategy: Amend the Consent Decrees

Martin Bandier, president of Sony/ATV, which is partly owned by the Michael Jackson estate, is attempting to secure higher rates from digital services than ASCAP and BMI have been able to achieve. Bandier said in a statement, "In the current digital environment, it is critical that we reform the system, which does not fairly compensate songwriters and composers." Against that backdrop, the large publishers like Universal as well as Sony/ATV have approached the Justice Department about getting the consent decrees amended to allow for partial rights withdrawal so they can negotiate directly with Internet radio services such as Pandora, Songza, and iHeart radio.

The PROs are "regulated by an antiquated consent decree with the Justice Department that was last amended before the introduction of the iPod," UMPG chairman/CEO Zach Horowitz said in a statement. "The decree is ill-suited for the changes in the digital marketplace. A recent court ruling would require us to withdraw our repertoire from BMI for all purposes in order to retain the right to directly negotiate with mobile and online music services. We don't believe that the consent decree should work this way."

In cutting short-term deals, publishers now have time to see what rates are set and if the Justice Department is willing to negotiate amendments to the consent decrees. Staying with the PROs in the short term deals "gives us time to reflect—we can look at the rate court decisions and for alternatives if need be, including whether the DOJ can see its way clear to amend the consent decree," Bandier says.

If publishers don't like the rates established by the courts, or if it appears that the Justice Department is dragging its heels on amending the consent decrees, publishers will then have the option of completely withdrawing from the PROs. In the meantime, they have more time to prepare for that day, should it come.[193]

Why Direct Deals May Be Horrible for Songwriters

Songwriters as well as publishers have expressed frustration with the present state of affairs. For instance, in 2012, several very successful songwriters testified at congressional hearings. They reported that hit songs they had written for stars like Beyoncé and Christina Aguilera that had been performed more than 33 million times by Pandora had yielded just $587.39 in royalties for the songwriters. These reports of millions of plays equating to very little in songwriter royalties have become very common. In April 2014, Bette Midler complained she had over 4,175,149 million plays on Pandora but only received $144.21.[194]

However, to be fair, those meager payouts come from ASCAP, BMI, and SESAC, not from Pandora. Pandora pays the PROs, not the publishers or songwriters. The PROs collect all the money for public performance from Pandora. *They*, not Pandora, then determine what a play on Pandora is worth. The PROs would argue that they would pay their writers more if they received more from Pandora. Still, their role in determining payouts is often overlooked, as are certain other relevant facts:

Many Writers Are "Unrecouped"

Well-heeled publishers, including the majors, generally offer the songwriters they wish to sign (commercially successful ones who write "hits") "advances" to convince them to sign with their company. These advances can range from tens of thousands to millions of dollars. Advances are essentially loans; after receiving the advance the writers do not receive any royalties unless and until their songs earn enough money to pay back the advances. Many writers never "recoup"; therefore they may never receive any royalties. For these writers the only money they may make after the publishing advance is their payment from a PRO. This has become what is known as the "ASCAP check," although BMI and SESAC writers depend just as much on their payments from these PROs. ASCAP, BMI, and SESAC all pay writers and publishers each 50 percent of the total royalty earned by a song performance. The 50 percent payable to songwriters, what is known as the "songwriter's share," is paid directly to the songwriter. In fact, many writers never see another dollar from the exploitation of their songs except for the checks they receive from ASCAP, BMI, or SESAC. Publishers only pay royalties (generally 50 percent to 75 percent for sync and mechanical royalties) after recoupment, that is, after repayment of the advance. (It is worth noting that ASCAP was set up by powerful songwriters such as Irving Berlin, Jerome Kern, and John Philip Sousa as well as their publishers—so they set up a system that was very favorable to songwriters compared to other parts of the music business. BMI and SESAC followed the same system of paying writers 50 percent directly when they were created in order to compete against ASCAP in signing up the most successful songwriters.) With a direct license, the publishers receive all the money from a licensee. They are supposed to turn over a portion of those monies to the writers—unless the writer is unrecouped.

Publishers Generally Do Not Have to Share Advance Monies with Their Songwriters

In 2007 Sony negotiated a direct deal with DMX, the digital background music service. In doing so, it received an advance payment of 2.7 million dollars. It is doubtful whether Sony's writers received any portion of this money. Individual music publishing contracts vary depending on the bargaining power of individual writers or the negotiating skills of their lawyers (among other reasons), but almost all agreements have a provision similar to this one:

> In no event shall composer be entitled to share in any advance payments, guarantee payments or minimum royalty payments which Publisher may receive in connection with any sub-publishing agreement, collection agreement, licensing agreement or other agreements . . .

The rationale for this clause is that if a publisher secures an advance for all of its songs it should not have to share that money with each songwriter. But the clause did not contemplate direct licenses by publishers for performing rights. Around the world, writers are usually paid performance fees directly by performing-rights organizations (for example, PRS in England, JASRAC in Japan, and GEMA in Germany as well as ASCAP, BMI, and SESAC in the US). However, if publishers were allowed to enter into direct licenses this clause would allow publishers to avoid paying writers.

Direct Deals Could Hurt Independent Publishers and Songwriters

The above factors could have the most negative impact on writers signed to major publishers. The reason is that major publishers are more likely to pursue direct licenses than the indies. That's because the majors feel they can get better rates than ASCAP and BMI. But small publishers will be more hesitant to withdraw digital rights from the PROs. They have much less bargaining power because they are small. They are also more likely to want ASCAP and BMI to negotiate on their behalf because they will be negotiating as part of a group. However, even writers signed to indie publishers may suffer if the majors do direct deals. The loss of the majors would diminish ASCAP and BMI's bargaining power, which in turn would decrease the amount of money that these organizations could secure from digital services; this would have the effect of diminishing the payouts to the writers of the songs that remained with the PROs. And, if the big publishers secure advances from licensees in exchange for lower royalties, this could have the effect of driving down the rates ASCAP and BMI can negotiate with the same licensees. Indeed, this is exactly what happened with ASCAP and BMI's licenses with DMX after its aforementioned deal with Sony.

DMX provides background music via digital means to approximately 100,000 locations, including restaurants, bars, clubs, retail stores, and chains. When DMX and BMI failed to agree on the price for a blanket license, DMX initiated an action in rate court asking the court to reduce the amount that BMI sought to charge. BMI sought a blanket license fee of $41.81 per location. DMX argued that it had secured "direct licenses" from 550 different publishers at the rate of $25 per location, and that that amount should be used as a "benchmark" for the true market value of BMI's blanket license. The court agreed, and significantly reduced the fee DMX would have otherwise had to pay BMI. The judge held that the blanket license fee for use of BMI songs should be only $18.91 per location. BMI's then president and CEO, Del Bryant, said in a statement, "Our writers and publishers should not be expected to lose more than half of their income from DMX based on the court's erroneous holdings, which substantially reduce the value of their creative efforts." In a subsequent action against ASCAP (December 2010), DMX was also successful in significantly reducing ASCAP's per location rate to $13.74.

BMI had argued that of the 550 "direct licenses," there was only one license with a major publisher, Sony/ATV. The court found that the $25 per location fee was a good benchmark for the real marketplace value of a license for all the songs DMX plays. However, the court did not consider it relevant that DMX had paid a $2.7 million advance to Sony. BMI maintained that Sony would never have entered into the direct license and accepted the $25 rate unless it had received the advance, and that DMX had used the deal with Sony to persuade many of the 549 other direct licensees to accept the $25 per location rate. BMI also pointed out that DMX had not told the other direct licensee publishers about the advance payment to Sony, and instead had assured them "they would be the same as a sophisticated major publisher who had accepted the same deal." Finally and most tellingly, the $2.7 million represented approximately 150 percent of all royalties Sony received from both ASCAP and BMI for one year.

This case shows that the major publishers, if freed up to make direct deals, may force licensees to pay advances in exchange for lower royalties, and that this may negatively affect the songwriters who are represented by indie publishers.

A Proper Solution to Avoid Screwing the Writers

I talked to the president of an indie publisher who was also a lawyer and he understood the issue under discussion above. He told me he had revised his deal with songwriters so that if his company did a direct deal for public-performance rights, he would pay them 50 percent of anything the publisher received off the top without deducting any unrecouped advances. If the consent decrees are amended to allow for partial withdrawals from the PROs, hopefully the DOJ will require the same level of writer protection.

Final Note: Even if the Consent Decrees Are Amended and Major Publishers Withdraw Digital Rights from ASCAP and BMI, Certain Songs in Their Catalogues, Including Huge Hits, May Be Excluded

Amanda Harcourt is an English attorney and former law professor who helped me write the next chapter of this book. As we discuss in more detail there, reciprocal contracts between the PROs are key to licensing public-performance rights from foreign songwriters. If major US publishers withdrew completely from ASCAP and BMI, they would not be able to license songs by songwriters signed to foreign societies—such as the Beatles songs written by Lennon and McCartney, and Rolling Stones songs by Jagger and Richards—an issue largely overlooked by media in the US, and certainly in public statements by US PROs or music publishers.

Chapter 8
INTERNATIONAL DIGITAL MUSIC LICENSING

In Chapters 3 through 7 we discussed how digital music licensing works for downloading, interactive streaming, and noninteractive streaming, but only with respect to the United States. In this chapter we discuss the rules that apply to digital music services operating in foreign countries.

Overview of the Global Digital Music Business

The information in this section is drawn from a 2014 *Digital Music Report*[195] from the International Federation of the Phonographic Industry (IFPI), a trade group similar to the RIAA, but that represents the recording industry worldwide.

According to the IFPI report, the recording industry's digital revenues grew by 4.3 percent in 2013 to US$5.9 billion even as sales of CDs continued to drop. Overall total global revenues fell 3.9 percent from 2012 to approximately $15 billion[196] (compared to $38 billion in 1999). As in the US, both subscription and ad-supported digital music services grew dramatically in terms of both user numbers and income, while income from downloading remained relatively stable. [197]

Subscription services saw the greatest growth of any digital medium worldwide. Revenues from music subscription services grew 51.3 percent in 2013, exceeding $1 billion for the first time. Global brands such as Deezer and Spotify, according to FPI, "are reaping the benefits of geographical expansion, while other services such as Rdio and Rhapsody continue to expand around the world."[198] Paid memberships to subscription services rose to 28 million in 2013, up 40 percent since 2012 and up from only 8 million in 2010. It is interesting to note that Pandora has not elected to open in Europe, probably because of the high cost and sheer difficulty of foreign digital music licensing, and Sirius XM does not choose to enter into other countries because, according to executives there, they fear the difficulty of appealing to mass audiences who speak different languages.

Revenues from advertising-supported streaming services, including YouTube, which operates in many countries throughout the world, have also grown globally—up 17.6 percent in 2013.[199] Music video revenues in particular increased as the industry extended the monetization of YouTube to more than 50 countries, adding 13 territories in 2013. According to IFPI,

> Record companies have adapted their business to a model increasingly based on access to music, and not only ownership of music. This reflects in the growing share of subscription and streaming revenues as a percentage of digital revenues globally. The industry now derives 27 percent of its digital revenues from subscription and ad-supported streaming services, up from 14 percent in 2011.
>
> The digital download model remains a key revenue stream, however. Downloads still account for a substantial two-thirds of digital revenues (67 percent globally) and are helping to propel digital growth in certain developing markets such as South Africa, Hong Kong, Philippines, and Slovakia. Downloads have seen a slight decline in overall value globally. . . . Revenues from downloads globally fell slightly by 2.1 percent in value, the decline being offset by increases in streaming and subscription revenue to generate overall digital revenue growth in the majority of markets.

This parallels the trend in the US, where income from streaming grew dramatically in 2013 while income from downloading declined for the first time.

Introduction to Global Digital Music Licensing

To explore international digital music licensing, I interviewed a renowned copyright and music law expert, Amanda Harcourt.[200] That interview is set forth in the next section.[201] As part of that discussion, Ms. Harcourt identifies the collection societies that provide licenses for both broadcast and digital music performance rights in Europe and other countries, how to go about securing such licenses, and the rates that apply. Although a comprehensive discussion of how digital music licensing works and how much it costs in every country outside the US is beyond the scope of this book, this chapter provides an overview of the challenges facing those who wish to operate digital music services abroad.

We start by describing some key differences between music publishing in the US and Europe and how those differences impact the authority of US publishers to make direct licenses with any potential licensees, including digital services—an issue largely ignored by the US media, PROs, and music publishers. We also discuss how terrestrial radio stations in Europe obtain licenses to publicly perform sound recordings, how much they pay to publicly perform them, and to whom they make those payments. We then discuss how a digital music service operating outside the US would go about licensing music, and how that process differs from how it works in the US (as discussed in Chapters 3–6).

Interview with International Copyright and Music Attorney Amanda Harcourt

Distributing Digital Music

AH: Before I start answering your questions about how to go about licensing music for the various digital music services, I think that your readers may find it useful if I highlight some differences between the music rights landscape in the USA and the rest of the world. Understanding, for example, the European position for writer/publisher splits, or how the law treats

Internet dissemination, means the answers to your questions will make more sense. I will start with songwriters and composers (and their partners, music publishers).

Firstly, composer splits: Songwriters' contracts outside the USA, broadly speaking, unless they predate the '70s or relate to some television or all library music, are *not* 50/50 deals. The split is much more likely to be 70/30, 75/25, 80/20 in the writer's favor. (At one stage in the 1990s when interest rates were high, one English supergroup managed to negotiate a 110 percent/10 percent writer/publisher split, as the publisher was earning so much in interest during the accounting period that the writers shared the benefit. Ah, those were the days). The splits may be 50/50 for usage such as synchronization fees, but by and large a modern music publishing contract will see the lion's share of revenue going to the writer (subject of course to all those discreet sleights of hand that benefit the large corporations and that one sees in any accounting computation for music and film!).

So a music publisher in the UK passes a percentage of the 50 percent revenue share paid to them by the UK's PRS for Music (the equivalent of America's ASCAP/BMI/SESAC) to the writer at the regular accounting intervals of the publishing contract.

SG: This is not *that* different from the US. For many years the standard was that the writer would assign 100 percent of the copyright to the publisher and the publisher would take half the income. But in recent times the standard publishing deal has been replaced by the "co-pub deal," where the songwriter and the music publisher are "co-owners" of the copyrights in the musical compositions, and the writer retains 100 percent of the "writer's share" and 50 percent of the "publisher's share" for a total of 75 percent of the song. ASCAP/BMI/SESAC pays the writer 50 cents for every dollar, 25 cents to a publishing company owned by the writer, and the other 25 cents to the writer's publisher. In England, it seems you are saying, PRS pays 50 percent to the publisher; and then the publisher kicks back half of that to the writer per the publishing agreement. But the result is the same.

Also, in an "admin" deal, a writer will typically receive 80 percent or more of all revenues, although generally only the most successful writers can get those deals.

AH: This is the key difference: the nature of the performing-right assignment to the societies is different. Composers and songwriters assign their broadcast and performing right to their local society on an exclusive and a global basis. Only their local society can exercise this right, and worldwide performing rights flow through the collecting society network under the reciprocal contracts.

So a music publisher has a contractual right to share the income generated by the performing right but does not own that slice of the copyright. A publisher will not actually own or control the public-performance right in a writer's songs under the publishing contract unless the writer resigns membership in his or her local society and *only* then.

This is a very important difference from the US position, where the authors' societies have a non-exclusive assignment and in some (but not all, depending upon the wording of individual publishing contracts) writers' contracts the publisher is empowered to issue licenses direct to potential music users.

The contracts between the US societies and societies elsewhere in the world as a rule state that the rights are being passed to the USA for exercise (licensing) *only* by the society that is party to the reciprocal agreement. Some contracts (e.g., the one from PRS for Music) expressly state that the agreement is personal to the US society and prohibit that US society from devolving the licensing function to a third party (such as a publisher purporting to issue a direct license).

Impact of Foreign Publishing Business Practices on Direct-Licensing Controversy in the US

This legal position of global exclusivity has been widely ignored in the USA of late. All US music services should be extremely wary of US publishers purporting to issue licenses for the global repertoire of songs. These US publishers *do not* control the performing right in any works by writers who are direct members of authors' societies outside the USA. In effect, there can be no lawful direct licenses issued in the USA for the Beatles, the Stones, Coldplay, Adele, Leonard Cohen (Canada), Jean Michel Jarre (France), etc. This subject has been covered repeatedly on the European copyright blogs. As the US has a statutory damages regime for copyright infringement, this is a serious, and potentially expensive, risk for US Internet music services.

SG: This is a crucial issue that the media that cover these issues in the US seem to have missed.

AH: If you can help this become the public scandal in the US (and elsewhere) that it should be, there will be thousands of grateful songwriters out there. Taxpaying songwriters, at that!

The US courts are still mulling over the question of rights withdrawal, but what needs to be said is that for writers who are direct society members outside the US, these rights cannot be withdrawn—however much the monopoly publishers might wish! And remember, lump sum monies rarely, if ever, get shared with writers by their publishers—their contracts state that they only get money if it is "directly and identifiably" attributable to the work.

SG: With regard to the Beatles catalogue—even though Lennon–McCartney seemed to have signed with PRS per the BMI database, the songs are owned by Sony/ATV. That being said, Sony/ATV still cannot direct license the Beatles songs. That seems inconsistent with the notion that Sony "owns" the Beatles' catalogue; or did they not get these rights from Michael Jackson because he didn't have them in the first place?

AH: Sony/ATV owns the strands of the copyrights *excluding* the performing right in the Beatles catalogue. Lennon and McCartney assigned that strand in the bundle of rights in a copyright to PRS, which has been mandated to send the US rights to a US society *and only a US society* [Author's note: "US society" refers to ASCAP, BMI, and SESAC]. Sony/ATV has no right to issue a license for that aspect of the work. That's the whole point.

SG: Same question with all the Stones (Jagger/Richards) songs administered and "owned" by ABKCO . . .

AH: Now you get it.

Terrestrial Radio

SG: Let's discuss traditional radio and how music licensing in the US differs from the rest of the world. With regard to musical compositions, as opposed to sound recordings, standard terrestrial radio stations in the US have to secure licenses from ASCAP, BMI, and SESAC, who collect a percentage of their ad revenues on behalf of their songwriter and publisher members. However, radio stations in the US do not pay record companies or artists, because owners of sound recordings do not have public-performance rights in the US except for digital transmissions. I know this is different from most of the rest of the world. In fact, to my knowledge, every other country makes radio pay for sound recordings except Rwanda, Iran, Iraq, and North Korea.

AH: That's a great place to start. Prior to World War II, the International Labour Organization (ILO) prepared a draft text of an international treaty that was intended to give performers a right to remuneration akin to that enjoyed by songwriters via their performing-right organizations. In recognition of the fact that a performer (a singer or musician) has an interpretative function and is not the actual creator, these rights are known as neighboring rights—the clue is in the name. A neighbor to the authorial right. World War II interrupted and in the process magnetic tape was invented—the military always lead the field for sexy inventions. As a result broadcasters and record companies wanted to be recompensed in an equivalent manner for the use of their broadcasts and recordings. Thus, the text became the Rome Convention, which was first signed by the initial countries in 1961—and the text of which you can find on the WIPO website here: http://www.wipo.int/treaties/en/text.jsp?file_id=289757.

This Rome Convention is in effect in its signatory countries. In addition, the European Union has enshrined its terms in European law via a Directive (92/100 EC, since repealed and replaced). The terms are to be found in "Directive 2006/115/EC of the European Parliament and of the Council of 12 December 2006, on rental right and lending right and on certain rights related to copyright in the field of intellectual property, (codified version)" or 2006/115/EC. Catchy title, huh?

Performers are given the right to authorize or prohibit the recording or fixation of their performances. But there is an important additional right. Put very simply, the effect of these instruments (no pun intended) is that record labels and performers have a right to be "paid by the user, if a phonogram published for commercial purposes, or a reproduction of such phonogram, is used for broadcasting by wireless means or for any communication to the public, and to ensure that this remuneration is shared between the relevant performers and phonogram producer"—Article 8 2006/115/EC.

And: "If a phonogram published for commercial purposes, or a reproduction of such phonogram is used directly for broadcasting or for any communication to the public, a single equitable remuneration shall be paid by the user to the performers, or to the producers of the phonograms, or to both. Domestic law may, in the absence of agreement between these parties, lay down the conditions as to the sharing of this remuneration" —Article 12 Rome Convention 1961.

So a network of collecting societies, under the aegis of the International Federation of the Phonographic Industry (IFPI), has grown up since 1961 to issue licenses to broadcasters and places where sound recordings are performed to collect fees and administer this revenue stream. The money is shared between labels and performers.

And before we leave this introductory bit for recordings, we should mention data. Composers, music publishers, and authors' societies have been working on the Global Repertoire Database (GRD). While not without its political difficulties, part of the (some might say overambitious) GRD project is the establishment of a single global database and record of the ISWC codes.

There is an equivalent of the song's ISWC number, which was intended to be used for recordings—the International Standard Recordings Code or ISRC code. While the record company/performer societies try and ensure that the record companies allocate unique ISRC codes to individual recordings, these efforts have not been a great success. The codes are in, frankly, a mess. Unbelievably, there is no single data resource that holds these ISRC codes, the allocation of numbers has been patchy, and this is a source of huge frustration to composers, songwriters, societies, and music users.

SG: Do you know approximately how much standard broadcast stations have to pay for the right to play sound recordings and from whom they need permission in Europe and other parts of the world?

AH: In the UK a terrestrial radio broadcaster will pay Phonographic Performance Ltd (PPL)—the society—between 2 percent and 5 percent of annual advertising and sponsorship revenue. For satellite radio it is £2300 per annum or 20 percent. The BBC's license fee to PPL is unknown but is the largest single contributor to PPL's annual £69 million in broadcast revenue.

As far as where one goes for permission, this is a very vexed question. In most countries where this right exists—well, actually pretty much everywhere but in the UK—the right to remuneration is vested equally in the labels and the performers. So there are hybrid societies of joined performer/label groupings that negotiate the fees together with user groups. In Germany, an anomaly, the record labels, as a matter of law, have to assert the right to their share of money against the performers.

For the powerful English-speaking rock and pop catalogue created in the UK, this right to claim remuneration is framed so the performers must seek it from the record companies. Thus every musician risks the revenue being used for recoupment—if their lawyers are not awake in negotiations. And, when it comes to the respective allocation of digital revenues between label and artist, a scandal lies waiting to erupt. Of which, more later.

For costs in other parts of the world, I suggest a trawl through the other society websites—best sourced via PPL's website (www.ppluk.com). We can't do all the work for your readers! As Alfred Korzybski said, "The map is not the territory."

Digital Music Streaming

SG: Okay, we have discussed how it works on normal terrestrial radio; now let's focus on what we call in the US "streaming services." And first, let's discuss musical compositions.

AH: As a broad principle one needs to secure two licenses: a license to copy a song, colloquially known in the industry as the "mechanical" license, as well as a license to communicate it to the public—the communication right, i.e., to broadcast or publically perform. I understand that for some inexplicable reason in the US, no mechanical license is required for noninteractive audio streaming. The copying of a copyright work is an act restricted by copyright and requires a license. So this US position appears to me to ignore both the letter of the law and the physics of streaming.

SG: I asked a knowledgeable person at the Harry Fox Agency this question, more specifically why Pandora does not pay for the reproduction of songs that it has to make for its server. His answer was "commercial forbearance." The copyright owners do not demand a payment for this, because if they did a court might hold that making one copy is a fair use "necessary to implement" public performances, for which Pandora does pay license fees. But outside the US it sounds like a mechanical license is required as well as a public-performance license.

AH: In each country of operation both these licenses will need to be secured. If one's first port of call is the performing-rights society, the society will advise whether they are mandated also to address the mechanical licensing process or whether direct approaches need to be made to publishers.

SG: And how does it work in Europe specifically?

AH: Europe? Well Europe is an interesting beast. Here goes . . .
Before 2005 in Europe, licensees—however annoyed they might have been by this fact—had to go to the authors' societies in every country in the EU for licenses for the communication right and for the mechanical right.

In the UK, PRS for Music, which was bolted together with the mechanical licensing body (MCPS), a licensee would issue a copying (mechanical) license via MCPS and a performance license via PRS. The same procedure took place across the European Union—one visit per country. Two licenses per country—copying and performance. Dreary? Yes. Unduly complex? No, not really.

Then, in 2005, the European Commission, in its infinite wisdom, decided that freeing up the marketplace would be a great plan. Difficulties arose because two interested parties own (there is that word again) the two rights involved in digital exploitation—the societies, who own the communication to the public right, and the publishers, who own the mechanical right. In the UK, for example, the MCPS operates as an agent for licensing; the company does not actually own the mechanical right.

In response to the European Commission's recommendation of October 18, 2005, on cross-border licensing, major music publishers terminated the agency mandate to the mechanical societies for mechanical rights. And, as a result, licensing for digital music has become more complex.

Major music publishers, a collective of independents and PROs, have been granting multi-territory licenses from a series of collaborative entities set up specifically for the purpose of granting online and mobile licenses throughout the EU (the communication right via the

PROs and the reproduction right via the individual publisher or their collaborative entity). These include IMPEL (licensing of Anglo-American repertoire owned by independent music publishers on a pan-European basis); PAECOL (license of Sony/ATV's Anglo-American repertoire); CELAS (EMI's—now part of Sony/ATV—Anglo-American repertoire); PEL (a Sony/ ATV/ SGAE initiative for the Latin-American repertoire); and DEAL (Universal's Anglo-American repertoire and SACEM's catalogue).

Benefit has primarily attached to the powerful Anglo-American catalogue, but regrettably, as demonstrated, it has also increased the number of entities that a would-be licensee must approach to secure lawful access to the entire global catalogue on a pan-European basis. A would-be licensee must seek licenses from every collaborative venture for the mechanical license for some of the global repertoire of songs—the mechanical societies across every country in the EU for the rest of the repertoire as well as every PRO in every EU member state to get a license to communicate songs to the public.

This drives up transaction costs for users, particularly for SMEs. [Author's note: "SME" stands for small and medium-sized enterprises—as defined in EU law.] Temptations arise to focus upon the Anglo-American catalogue, and this does not necessarily act to the advantage of smaller member states' musical works and cultures. Nor does it give assurance to a music service of its having lawful access to a unified global catalogue of musical works. And we have already flagged up the dangers of not licensing the global repertoire of songs thoroughly.

Dreary? Yes. Unduly complex? You bet! However, some societies will offer a pan-European license for communication to the public for songs direct from the one place. PRS for Music, in the UK, is one such society. And it is matter of public record that some 300 music services are now operating on a pan-European basis from this source.

One final point should be made about data. The societies are working to ensure they all use the same unique identifier system for the songs in the global repertoire—the International Standard Works Code (ISWC—see http://www.iswc.org/). But sadly, music publishers do not always use the same identifier as the societies!

Surely we can all agree that it must be in the best interests of creators, owners, and music users for the same identification number to be applied to a work, right throughout the world. It promotes efficiency in usage reporting and data management by users and administrators alike. It also, one has to assume, optimizes the chances of the right composer being allocated the correct revenue for his or her work.

SG: The total costs of licensing songs for an Internet radio service in the US are the fees payable to ASCAP, BMI, and SESAC, which total approximately 4 percent of gross revenues. Can you give us an idea of the costs of licensing songs for Internet radio outside of the US?

AH: If you look at, say, the website of PRS for Music where they show their digital licensing costs, your question is answered for all but the pan-European licenses.

Online music licensing information is here:

http://www.prsformusic.com/users/broadcastandonline/onlinemobile/Pages/default.aspx
and mobile music licensing information is here:

http://www.prsformusic.com/users/broadcastandonline/onlinemobile/Pages/default.aspx.

You will see that for a pan-territorial license, a licensee must negotiate directly with the society. This is to be expected. Tariffs for different song usage vary from country to country in the European Union, so this is a much more complex discussion than it is in the USA, where the rate court rulings and the consent decrees have federal effect. Europe is not federal.

The societies in other countries in the world should publish equivalent information—and in Europe, as a result of a new law that came into force in March 2014—societies are going to be obliged to be more transparent about costs and procedures.

The Australian society APRA AMCOS publishes guidelines for online and conventional broadcast on its site (www.apraamcos.com.au/).

SG: Many terrestrial stations in the US simulcast on the Internet, and they pay ASCAP, BMI, and SESAC an extra fee for that. How does that work outside the USA?

AH: In the same way. A broadcast tariff is calculated and paid in one fashion and an extra fee is charged for the simulcast or interactive function.

SG: In the US under the DMCA, certain streaming services, such as Internet radio stations, are entitled to a "compulsory" license to perform any master recording provided that it complies with certain limitations. The most important of such limitations is that it be noninteractive. That is, the webcaster cannot allow a listener to choose which songs to listen to. In addition, these services must comply with the "sound recording performance complement," which prohibits them from transmitting more than a certain number of songs from the same album or by the same artist within a period of time (see Chapter 6 for more details). If they qualify for the license, they pay a rate implemented by SoundExchange. The benefit of this system for webcasters is that it makes it unnecessary for them to negotiate with the three major labels and the thousands upon thousands of smaller labels and indie artists.

To your knowledge, does any other country have a similar system? And if I were an American webcaster who qualified for a SoundExchange license in the US and I wanted to operate in Europe, for example, how would I go about licensing masters for that territory? And what would the costs be?

AH: In continental Europe there are societies in every country that will issue the licenses for the labels and the performers for local repertoire.

In the UK, as stated, the law is framed slightly differently from the way in which it works in the rest of the EU and other countries that are signatories to the Rome Convention. The right to remuneration is, by UK statute, asserted against the record company—so the performers have to seek this license revenue from the label with which they contracted.

The collective management organization is Phonographic Performance Ltd—http://www.ppluk.com. But for digital delivery the record labels in the UK withdrew their digital rights, and the effect has been that online music services have to negotiate directly with the labels—individually with the majors, via a consortium called Merlin [http://www.merlinnetwork.org/whowelicense] for the independent labels, and with the aggregators for unsigned artists.

How much does a license cost? There's a great question, one to which many artists would love to know the answer. The deals are covered by NDAs, the bane of the creators' lives when it comes to assessing their revenues. Spotify, for example, according to Swedish corporate filings, has given the major labels a shareholding stake in the company as part of the license fee deal for sound recordings.

Where labels and performers in the UK share revenue collected by PPL for the right to communicate to the public, the split is 50/50. But for online usage, the revenue is treated differently by the labels. Notwithstanding the fact that the making-available right is a subset of the communication to the public right (administered by PPL), the labels' approach is to regard the revenue as constituting a sale—particularly where consumers can assemble a playlist to retain on their computer. As a result the labels allocate the revenue to the performers in accordance with the percentage identified in the individual record contracts for a "sale." For heritage acts this can be as low as 7 percent or 8 percent; for later recording artists slightly more but unlikely to be in excess of, say, 25 percent.

SG: The leading Internet radio station in the US is Pandora. But outside this country they only serve users in New Zealand and Australia. Do you think Pandora operates in so few foreign countries because it would be too expensive or too difficult to get appropriate licenses, or both?

AH: For Australia and New Zealand the webcasting license is secured via the Phonographic Performance Company of Australia (PPCA). Online licenses, with territorial limitations, are granted collectively—see http://www.ppca.com.au/music-users-/webcastlicensing/. Music services can avail themselves of collective licensing tariffs and provide usage data to the society.

Pandora is in itself a large topic. I am pretty sure Pandora believes that acquiring licenses for music in Europe will be too expensive because the labels will be setting fees outside the collective licensing framework. While I am not exactly charmed by the way the labels allocate the revenue, I look upon Pandora with a similarly jaundiced eye. Without music, an iPod, or other personal device, is just a metal box emitting a buzzing sound. A conventional retail operation pays 65 percent or more of turnover to suppliers for its products. So for Pandora to be complaining about the percentage of its turnover it has to pay for its only and indispensable product, i.e. music, seems disingenuous to me. So I can see why the labels might be holding out.

SG: In the US, licensing songs for interactive streaming and tethered downloading (see Chapter 5 for definitions) has come under a relatively new compulsory license created by the Copyright Royalty Tribunal. As previously discussed in this book, the rate is 10.5 percent minus what the service has to pay the PROs (approximately 4–5 percent). Is there any comparative compulsory license in any foreign countries?

AH: One of the characteristics of collecting societies is that they cannot refuse a license. But in Europe the rates that users pay are set by periodic collective negotiation.

SG: How would services such as Spotify that involve both on-demand streaming and tethered downloading secure licenses? Who do they have to deal with, and approximately how much would they pay?

AH: The Spotify service involves the right to copy (as a matter of physics—and as applies in conventional broadcast) and the making-available right. Where a user can assemble a playlist there are also the twin acts of copying and making available. But the revenue is allocated differently for different dissemination methods. The PRS will split royalty income 50/50 between the copying element and the communication to the public element for streaming usage. Where it is a webcast, 75 percent of the license fee is allocated to the communication to the public and 25 percent to the copying element.

We have already addressed the where—the how much is answered in two parts. For UK downloads I would direct your readers to the PRS website:
http://www.prsformusic.com/users/broadcastandonline/onlinemobile/Pages/default.aspx

Pan-territorial licenses will be subject to individual negotiation as shown there.

Where the societies are issuing these licenses in the EU, the applicable society should show this information on its website. Since the adoption by the European Parliament of the Directive on Collective Licensing in March 2014, this information will be legally required to be made public.

SG: In the US there is no compulsory license to pay for on-demand streaming of masters or tethered downloading. Services such as Rhapsody and Spotify, which offer both, must deal with each major record company (Warner, Sony, and Universal) plus indie labels and aggregators such as INGrooves and the Orchard. These deals are private, but Spotify for example claims that it pays approximately 70 percent of its revenues to music copyright owners. Since they are paying 10.5 percent for the songs, this means that they are paying approximately 60 percent of their income for the masters.

AH: Does this accommodate the labels' shareholding entitlements? Just asking . . . Spotify's licensing arrangements have already been covered. And as a matter of law, we are still dealing with the restricted acts of copying and communication to the public (including making available).

Of course, one can ask why the comparative fee levels for writers/publishers as opposed to labels/performers are so skewed. There should, in my view, also be some rebalancing of the respective shares of the services' total license fee liability. This would have to be resolved within the music industry—and with so much horizontal integration it is unlikely to occur.

There is plenty of information available from writers and artists as to how much music is valued at when the license fees trickle down to the talent. But in the face of the rash of NDAs that cover the licensing deals, it is difficult to identify exact license values.

Increasingly the major publishers in the UK are attempting to issue direct licenses to digital music users—or at to least negotiate the value of the performing right—but they cannot purport to control or actually issue the performing-right license. The writers have, as previously stated, exclusively and globally vested the communication/making-available right to their society, and the publishers only have a right to revenue. This will, I think be an interesting process to watch. Sadly, the large companies seem to be trying to erode the collective administration system—which, while not perfect, does actually provide convenience for the would-be music service.

Major companies operate a separate works identification system (for songs) and an incomplete one for recordings, and they cannot claim to have the data accurately to allocate revenues to the correct parties. This has to be seen as a barrier to their driving the licensing process in the future. That pesky "directly and identifiably" wording means revenues are unlikely to reach creators—something that should be of huge concern to policy makers (and music services with a genuine concern for the music they seek to make available to audiences).

Downloading

SG: In the US, music licensing for inclusion in a download store is straightforward. Downloading services such as iTunes have to pay the statutory set rate of 9.1 cents, which applies to sales of discs and vinyl as well as digital downloads. For this purpose most of the publishers in the US and all the majors (Sony ATV, Universal, BMG, and Warner Chappell) use Harry Fox to collect the pennies. How does it work in other countries?

AH: The copying element of download is covered by licenses issued by the societies. Many continental European societies are genuine hybrids, managing both copying and the communication/making-available right—for example, SIAE in Italy and GEMA in Germany.

Mechanical (copying) licenses in the UK are issued by the MCPS (a company allied to PRS for Music) and both the copying and communication/making-available rights are issued together by PRS for Music. Copying for a physical product is calculated by reference to its wholesale price—in the UK 8.5 percent of dealer, elsewhere in Europe, over 9 percent. Fees for a download are 8 percent of gross or between 2 pence and 5 pence per song and vary according to the nature of the service. Seventy-five percent of revenue is allocated for the copying and 25 percent for the making-available element.

SG: In the US the rate that a downloading service must pay to the owners of sound recordings is subject to negotiation. But iTunes, by far the leading download service, pays 70 cents on every 99-cent download and a commensurate amount for differently priced songs. Most other downloading services pay a similar amount. All of this money goes to the owners of the sound recordings (usually labels) minus the 9.1 cents payable for the songs. How does it work in other countries?

AH: The share of the download price paid to publishers is not necessarily paid directly to them. It varies according to country and catalogue. The money goes through the societies that administer the mechanical right in some countries, and directly to the publishers for certain catalogues via the pan-European licensing collectives such as Armonia.

The download services keep 30 percent of the price per unit downloaded. Then the other 70 percent of the price is paid to right owners and shared between labels and artists, and between publishers and writers via the publishers' collectives and the societies. The lion's share (85 to 90 percent of the 70 percent) is allocated to the recording.

Downloading a sound recording is in effect a sale and artists are remunerated according to their sale percentage in their contract. But in my view the label and artist should be sharing 50/50. It is arguably a license. The labels do not have the costs associated with manufacture, storage, and delivery of product. As a matter of fact, a single copy is required to be delivered to the music service for digital sales to take place. This is the subject of challenge in the US courts, and one should expect the rest of the world to follow suit—that is, this is a license and revenues should be split equally between label and recording artist [Author's note: This issue is addressed in Chapter 4].

PART II
MUSIC CLEARANCES

"Music clearances" means licensing songs that have already been written and musical recordings that have already been produced and commercially released. It does not pertain to original music written for a particular project.

Although I have negotiated numerous "composer agreements" for the development of new music, a significant portion of my practice consists of clearing music for producers who are seeking well-known songs and recordings, or music that fits a particular project—for instance, pop music from the '80s for a feature set in that era, or music by a particular musician in a documentary about that artist.

For over 10 years I was a lawyer and director of business affairs at Sony Music, where I specialized in TV and video. I did all the legal work for the production of every music video, long-form concert program, and music-based documentary produced by Columbia and Epic Records for artists such as Michael Jackson, Bruce Springsteen, Billy Joel, Bob Dylan, Mariah Carey, Lauryn Hill, Céline Dion, Pearl Jam, and many others. In addition, I did all the legal work for Automatic Productions, Sony Music's in-house production company. Automatic produced several TV series, including *Live by Request* (A&E) and *Sessions at West 54th* (PBS). Part of my job was "clearing" the music in every one of the TV programs and videos that Sony and Automatic produced.

In my current practice, I continue to represent producers of audiovisual music content. But, unlike my time at Sony, I now work with a huge variety of projects, including motion pictures, musical theater, advertising campaigns, audio compilations, parody albums, sample clearances, as well as stand-alone digital projects such as music-based apps and websites, online promotions, and digital sheet music.

The first three chapters in Part II (9–12) focus on music clearance issues involving audiovisual works such as films, documentaries, and television; audio-only projects such as compilations and music sampling; and special projects such as musical theater and fashion shows. These chapters provide an overview of standard business terms and practices for licensing music for these projects and explain how digital distribution has changed the standard terms and conditions applying to them. Chapter 13 focuses on stand-alone digital projects, including websites and apps. Chapter 14 contains tips for clearing music for any project.

Part II ends with my Commentary for *Billboard* magazine about why copyright owners should give special consideration to producers of music-based documentaries.

Chapter 9

INTRODUCTION TO MUSIC CLEARANCES

Songs vs. Masters

To secure the right to use music in various projects, producers need to consider that there are two distinct copyrightable "works" that are in involved in clearing music:

1. "musical works," that is, songs and other musical compositions, and
2. "sound recordings," that is, the recordings of those songs

A song or musical composition is the underlying music embodied in a sound recording. These recordings are also sometimes referred to as "masters." To use a recording of a song, both of these "copyrights" have to be cleared. For example, if you wish to use Aretha Franklin's recording of the classic pop hit "Walk On By," you have to clear both the recording and the underlying song.

Copyright Owners: Music Publishers and Record Labels

To continue with this example, in order to clear the song, you will have to identify the songwriters. This information can sometimes be found on album packaging or through research. In this case, Burt Bacharach and Hal David wrote "Walk On By." You should not, however, try to contact the songwriters. Instead you would contact their representatives, who are generally music publishers. In this case you would contact Universal Music, which administers on behalf of Mr. Bacharach, and BMG Music, which administers on behalf of the estate of Hal David. You will need the permission of both. If the approval of Mr. Bacharach and the estate of Hal David are required, the publishers will secure it. But generally, only the music publishers, in this case Universal and BMG, may issue a license for you to use the song. In music clearance parlance, BMG and Universal are "co-publishers" of the song. With respect to royalties or fees, they will indicate in written quotes what their percentage of ownership is, and the actual amount of money payable to each will depend on this percentage. For instance, if each publisher controlled 50 percent of the song, and the fee for this particular project were $1,000, $500 would be payable to each publisher.

Now let's focus on Aretha Franklin's recording. Although she may have recorded the song for other record labels, or as a guest on various TV shows, her most famous recording of this song was as a recording artist for Columbia Records. The performance of the song was initially released by Columbia on an album called "Jazz to Soul." Generally, recording artists such as Ms. Franklin transfer their rights in their performances on a "work for hire" basis to the record company in accordance with standard terms in most exclusive recording agreements (see "The Record Business" in Chapter 1). In this case, she would have transferred any rights she may otherwise have had in the recording to Columbia Records. Columbia is now owned by Sony Music. Therefore, you would have to receive authorization from Sony to use this recording.

Sync License vs. Master-Use License

A license for the use of a song in an audiovisual project such as a movie or a TV show is referred to as a "sync license." The origin of this term stems from the fact that the producer is synchronizing the song to a visual image. The license to use the *particular recording* of the song that the producer chooses for the movie is usually referred to as a "master-use" license to avoid confusion, that is, to indicate that the license is for the use of a recording rather than the underlying song.

When You Don't Need to Clear the Master

New Recordings: If you are producing a concert video, that is, an audiovisual recording of a live performance of musicians playing various songs, you don't need to secure a master-use license. As the producer of the recording, you are creating new masters of the songs.

Rerecords: Also, if you rerecord a song, you will not have to clear the original master. Suppose you hire a singer to perform "Walk On By" for your TV commercial. You will need a sync license to use the underlying musical composition written by Bacharach and David. But you will not have to contact Columbia Records or Sony Music. They would have no interest in your new recording of the song. (But see "Sound-Alikes" in the section on advertising in Chapter 11.)

Footage: If you use audiovisual footage of a performer singing a song, as discussed previously, you will have to secure a sync license in the song. But if the owner of the footage is not the record company, with certain exceptions (see "Labels' Blocking Rights"), you will not have to secure the record company's permission. However, you will have to secure a license to use the footage containing the performance. Suppose, for instance, you wish to use footage of the Beatles' performance of "I Want to Hold Your Hand" on the old *Ed Sullivan Show*. You would still have to clear the song—in this case written by Lennon–McCartney and controlled by the publisher, Sony/ATV. Instead of securing rights from a record company, you would need a "footage license" from the owners of the *Ed Sullivan Show*.

Footage Licenses

The rest of this chapter is devoted to standard terms and business practices for licensing songs and masters for various projects. Often my clients—especially those who make documentaries, but sometimes producers of feature movies, TV shows, installations and exhibits, and even musical theater—will wish to use footage of a musical performance rather than the original audio-only master recording. Using the example above, if a producer wished to make a doc about the "British Invasion" and wanted to use the Beatles' performance of "I Want to Hold Your Hand" from the *Ed Sullivan Show*, he would have to secure a license from Sofa Entertainment, which controls the rights in that show, rather than the company that controls the original audio recording, Apple Records.

Footage licenses are much simpler and more straightforward than licensing songs and masters, but they can also be more expensive. As we discuss in the balance of this chapter, the basic structure of licensing agreements for songs and masters and their financial terms vary depending on the nature of the project. For instance, both the rights and the financial terms applicable to documentaries are usually vastly different from those negotiated for feature motion pictures. In contrast, footage licenses are generally structured as "buyouts"; that is, the license permits the use of the footage in the project in all media for a period of years, and the fees payable generally do not change from project to project. So the terms, and the fees, for licensing footage for any project will usually not vary as much as they do for licensing a song or master. Generally, the duration of a footage license is 10 years, but some owners insist on a shorter term, and others charge a premium for perpetuity.

The fee payable usually depends upon the source of the footage and the amount of footage required rather than the nature of the project for which the footage is sought. For example, use of TV news footage is generally licensed on the basis of a "rate card" and can cost from \$50 to \$100 per second depending on the source. Footage from a Hollywood movie can cost from \$5,000 a minute to \$10,000, although discounts may be available from certain studios for very brief excerpts. Licensing footage from old TV series such as *Soul Train*, *The Dick Clark Show*, or the *Ed Sullivan Show* also varies depending on the owner. Generally, the price is fixed by that company's rate card based on timing. It is true that discounts can sometimes be obtained by limiting the media to one or two forms of release, such as only PBS and home video, but even then the discount will usually not be significantly less than an all-media buyout. It may be possible to negotiate "bulk" discounts if a great deal of footage is used from one source. For instance, if a producer is making a doc about famous prewar musicals that were released by a particular Hollywood studio, that studio may provide a discount depending on how much footage the producer wishes to use.

Finally, clearing footage from Hollywood movies and sometimes TV shows may require additional clearances. For instance, a license from a major US motion picture studio for the use of footage will usually require the licensee to secure any required clearances from actors appearing in the film as well as any required clearances from guilds such as the DGA, WGA, and SAG/AFTRA. The necessity for securing these clearances depends on a number of factors, including the year the movie or TV show was released or broadcast. Fortunately, there are clearance professionals who have knowledge of these rules and specialize in securing the necessary permissions.[202]

Labels' "Blocking Rights"

There is a caveat about releasing projects containing new recordings of songs, or using footage that contains original recordings of songs. Although the labels would not own the recordings of these songs (unless they owned the footage), they still might have "blocking rights." In any standard contract between an artist and a label, the label generally acquires the exclusive right to "distribute any recordings that an artist makes during the term, whether or not coupled with a visual image, for home or personal use." The reason for this provision is that if an artist or any third party produced and distributed records featuring the artist, those records would compete against the records produced by the label. Therefore, producers who record new performances of artists who are signed to a label have to be careful about releasing their programs as CDs, DVDs, or downloads. Even if the artist consented, the labels would still have a cause of action known as "interference with contract."

One example of how blocking rights work in practice occurred when I worked in the business affairs department at Sony Music. MTV recorded a series of shows called *Unplugged*, featuring acoustic performances by such artists as Mariah Carey and Bob Dylan. They would not release CDs or DVDs of the shows without our consent, because they knew Sony enjoyed blocking rights in the music performances of those artists, even though MTV owned the recordings of those performances. Ultimately, we worked out deals with MTV to acquire the right to distribute those recordings as CDs or DVDs ourselves.

Lip Syncs

Another worm that could infest the clearance process is "lip syncing." Clearing footage from the TV series *Soul Train*, for example, can be more complicated than other clearances. Usually footage of an artist performing live will include an original recording of the master. But most of the artists who performed on *Soul Train* sang "to track." That is, they were lip syncing to the original master. So if a producer wanted to use *Soul Train* footage she would have to (1) clear the song with the owner of the song, usually a music publisher; (2) clear the footage with the owners of Soul Train; and, finally, if the performer was singing to track, (3) clear the recording with the owner of the sound recording, usually a record company that owns the underlying master.

Public Domain

If you want to use classical music in your movie, the underlying music may be in the "public domain" (PD). For instance, anything by Mozart or Beethoven is PD. (See "Duration of Copyright" in Chapter 1.) However, a particular *recording* of the music may still be protected by copyright. In that case, the producer will still have to clear the master. As a rule of thumb, songs published in the US prior to 1923 are PD, but sound recordings that are even older may still be protected by state statutory or common law. For tips on identifying PD songs, see "Research Techniques" later in this chapter.

Special Rules for Public Broadcast Stations Are Favorable to Producers

The Copyright Act provides special rules for use of copyrighted materials, including music, on public broadcasting stations. Generally, producers are not obligated to clear songs or masters for programs produced for PBS or other public broadcasting stations.

In regard to songs, Section 118 of the US Copyright Act provides for a compulsory license for the inclusion of musical compositions in programs that air on public broadcasting stations. The fees applying to these licenses are pre-negotiated by the public broadcasting stations and the publishers. In practice, if your show airs on a public broadcasting station, PBS will pay that pre-negotiated fee to the relevant publishers. All you need to do is provide a "cue sheet." (See

"Public-Performance Licenses and Cue Sheets" later in this chapter.) Section 118, however, does not provide for a statutory license for any other purpose than broadcasting the show on public broadcast stations. Therefore, producers have to acquire sync licenses to release the program in any other medium, including as a CD, home video, or on foreign television or on video on-demand services such as Netflix. In my own practice, I am frequently called on to clear shows that originally aired on PBS and that the producer wishes to subsequently exploit in these other distribution outlets. Even if the home video of the program is distributed by PBS (usually as a "free" gift in return for a pledge), the songs must be cleared.

In regard to masters, Section 114(b) of the Copyright Act reads in relevant part:

> The exclusive rights of the owner of copyright in a sound recording . . . do not apply to sound recordings included in educational television and radio programs . . . distributed or transmitted by or through public broadcasting entities . . . Provided that copies or phonorecords of said programs are not commercially distributed by or through public broadcasting entities to the general public.

Therefore, no payment is required for use of masters in programs on public television. But, as with songs, if the program is released in any other media, the producer *will* have to secure master-use licenses if music from records was used in the program.

Charitable Projects

Occasionally, I clear music for projects produced by not-for-profit organizations for a charitable purpose, such as a public service announcement (PSA) intended to raise money for a shelter for homeless animals, or a concert to raise money for victims of a natural disaster. The rest of this chapter discusses standard terms and practices for clearing music for all kinds of projects. But keep in mind that it may be possible to secure reduced rates for projects with a charitable purpose. For instance, I was able to secure a gratis license to use a hit song in the PSA, and vastly reduced rates for worldwide television.

Most-Favored-Nation Clause

A most-favored-nation (MFN) clause, in the context of music clearances, means that all copyright owners should be treated equally. If you grant more favorable terms to one copyright owner over another for a particular project, you must grant the same, more favorable terms to other copyright owners. For instance, if you offer to pay Party A \$1 and Party A agrees, but Party B insists on \$2 and you agree to pay B \$2, you have to pay A an extra dollar. However, it is essential to recognize that MFN is not a statute, nor is it required by any governmental body or judicial decree. Instead, it is a contract provision. A copyright owner who wants it must include it in the license. If an MFN clause is not included in the license, then there is no duty to provide MFN treatment to that party. Here is a typical MFN clause from a license for use of a song in a documentary:

> Most Favored Nations ("MFN"): In the event Licensee grants more favorable terms including, without limitation, additional consideration in any form, to the co-publisher of any Composition(s) licensed hereunder, the party(ies) granting

> rights to use the master recording(s) thereof, or any third party licensing the right to use any musical composition and/or master recording in the Program for similar use and duration as granted herein for the Composition(s), Licensee shall notify Licensor thereof, and this Agreement shall be deemed amended to incorporate same as of the date when such higher fee is paid or such more favorable terms are granted to such third party, and to continue for the duration of the period which such more favorable terms are granted.

This clause would require the licensee to pay the same amount of money to the licensor as the licensee pays for any other song or master in the doc. You usually find these types of MFN clauses not only in licenses for documentaries, but also in licenses for projects such as concert programs, where every song is played in its entirety by a live artist or band. But not all MFN clauses are the same.

For feature films, the MFN clause in licenses to use songs and masters will usually pertain to one particular song or master in the film. That is, the license for the song will state that MFN applies to the master containing that song, and the license for the master will state that MFN applies to the song contained in that master. If the MFN clause is written in that fashion, the licensee can pay more for *other* songs and masters without violating the MFN clause; the clause is there to ensure that copyright owners of the same song or master are compensated equally. Here is a typical example of an MFN clause for use of a song in a movie. It is from the same publisher that included the previously quoted MFN clause in a license for a song in a doc:

> Most Favored Nations: In the event Licensee grants more favorable terms including, without limitation, additional consideration in any form, to the co-publisher(s) of the Composition or the party granting rights to use the master recording thereof (if applicable) in the Motion Picture, Licensee shall notify Licensor thereof, and this Agreement shall be deemed amended to incorporate same as of the date when such higher fee is paid or such more favorable terms are granted to such third party, and to continue for the duration of the period which such more favorable terms are granted.

Under this MFN provision, the producer must provide equal treatment only to other copyright owners of the song (i.e., co-publishers) and to the copyright owner of the masters. The MFN clause in a music license for a movie is usually limited in this way because publishers and labels generally recognize that some songs and masters are more valuable than others, and may be more or less prominent in a given film depending on how they are used. For instance, in a feature, you may only hear a song playing in the background for a few moments (an actor tuning a radio on and then changing the station), and in a later scene you may see an actor singing an entire song (e.g., Diane Keaton's memorable performance of "Seems Like Old Times" in Woody Allen's *Annie Hall*). In contrast, a concert video usually uses all the songs in their entirety. Docs with music-based themes, for example, a doc about the songs of the civil rights movement, or another concerning the career of a particular artist, will usually use each song in a similar manner, i.e., brief excerpts of an artist's performance of a song heard in the background over talking heads or brief excerpts of footage of an artist performing the song. In any event, the custom and practice is that copyright owners will use the broader MFN language in licenses for concerts and docs, and the narrower MFN language in licenses for features.

Approvals

Generally, both music publishing and recording agreements provide that the publisher and the label have the *exclusive* right to grant sync or master-use licenses. They usually, but not always, also provide that the publisher and the label, as the case may be, have the right to license songs and masters without the approval of the writer or the artist. Standard exclusions include X-rated movies and ads for tobacco or feminine hygiene. However, often a publisher and a label will go back to the writer or the artist (or their estates, if they are deceased) out of courtesy and in order to maintain cordial relationships. Copyright owners will rarely tell you whether they are legally required to secure the creators' permission, and will usually only let you know that the song or master is "out for approval" without telling you exactly who the "approver" is.

Credits

Generally, a written quote containing rates or fees for use of a song or a master will also indicate the exact form of credit that should appear in the end credits. A publisher such as Sony/ATV, which now also administers EMI Music's catalogue, may be the copyright owner, but the credit may be more involved due to the copyright owner's contractual obligations or policies. For instance, this is the credit Sony/ATV wanted for "Let's Get It On":

> "Let's Get It On" by Marvin Gaye, Ed Townsend
> Courtesy of EMI [Jobete Music Co. Inc. (ASCAP), Stone Diamond Music Corp. (BMI)

The original record of "Let's Get It On" was released by Motown Records. Universal Music, which acquired Motown, wanted the following credit:

> Performed by Marvin Gaye
> Courtesy of Motown Records under license from Universal Music Enterprises

Public-Performance Licenses and Cue Sheets

As discussed in Chapter 1, owners of copyrighted works, including musical compositions, enjoy the exclusive right to publicly perform their copyrights. Generally, though, music clearances do not involve securing the right of public performance. The reason is that TV networks, independent stations, and free and pay cable services are all already licensed by the PROs, i.e., ASCAP, BMI, and SESAC. They obtain licenses from, and pay the associated fees to, the PROs for the public performance of any music on their broadcast stations and services, including foreground use in concert programs or background use in movies, news programs, etc. But the PROs have to know what music is being used in which movie, TV show, or TV ad campaign at what times on what dates, in order to determine how much to pay the publishers and songwriters. To implement this system, music publishers generally require producers to create "cue sheets."[203]

A cue sheet is a document that lists all music used within an audiovisual program, including a TV show, documentary, concert program, or movie. It includes the song title, writer and publisher information, and duration and type of use (e.g., "background" or "foreground"). Here is a typical clause from a sync license:

> Cue Sheet: It is a material condition and requirement of this Agreement that Licensee shall provide Licensor with a cue sheet of the Program as soon as practicable, but no later than sixty (60) days following the first broadcast of the Program.

The publisher submits the cue sheet to the relevant PRO, together with information on where and when the program will be aired, so that every time it's broadcast, the publisher and its writers receive credit for the performance. An example of an accurately filled-out cue sheet can be found in the "Creators" section of BMI's website (BMI.com).

Research Techniques

There are various databases that music clearance specialists use to identify the copyright owners of songs and masters. The US PROs, i.e., ASCAP, BMI, and SESAC, all list the publishers and writers of all the songs in their repertoire on their websites. Harry Fox provides Songfile.com, which lists songs represented by Fox, including publisher and writer information. There are also books that may be helpful in determining whether a song is PD. One such book is *Variety Music Cavalcade 1620–1969* by Julius Mattfeld (Prentice Hall, 1971). Another resource for identifying PD songs is www.pdinfo.com. In regard to masters, AllMusic and, yes, Wikipedia can also be helpful in identifying record companies that own particular masters. In certain cases, it may be advisable to do a search of the Copyright Office to identify the current owners of a song or master. Recent copyright registrations can be found on the Copyright Office's website. Those prior to 1978 must be examined in person at the Library of Congress. There are experts that will perform the search at reasonable hourly rates, or you can pay the Copyright Office itself to do a search ($200 per hour, with a two-hour minimum for searching records and preparing an official report).

What if You Can't Find the Copyright Owner?

But what if, after checking the available resources, you can't identify the publisher of a given song or the label that owns a particular master? A song published prior to 1923 is PD, but a sound recording may still be protected by copyright even if it was released prior to 1923 (see "Duration of Copyright," Chapter 1). If a song or master cannot be confirmed as PD, and you cannot determine the copyright owner after performing a "due diligence" search, the risk of a copyright owner filing a complaint is relatively small, but you are not insulated from potential liability. There has been proposed legislation that would amend the copyright law to eliminate or reduce the penalties for copyright infringement of "orphan works," but no such proposals have been adopted into law. At this point, you should consult with a copyright attorney to access the legal and business risks of using such a song or master.

Chapter 10
AUDIOVISUAL PROJECTS

Movies

Standard Terms and Practices

The standard practice for licensing music for movies is to separate the right to use the music into two categories: "festival rights" and "broad rights." Festival rights generally give the producer the right to show the movie at movie festivals such as Sundance or Tribeca Film Festival. Broad rights mean the right to use the movie in all media throughout the world in perpetuity.

Naturally, broad rights are much more expensive than festival rights. (Festivals offer filmmakers the chance to find a distributor and to show their work to an audience, but they generally do not compensate them financially.) In general, feature producers should request festival rights with an *option* for broad rights. By making broad rights an option, which by definition does not have to be exercised, the producer ensures that if she can't find distribution, at least she will not have to pay for rights she cannot use.

Alternatively, if a filmmaker does not expect to find a distributor who will release the film theatrically and in all other media, he can ask for festival rights with options for the specific media for which he thinks he will be able to find a deal. For instance, if he does not expect to get theatrical distribution but thinks he may get an offer from a cable TV service or a home video distributor, he can ask for separate options for each of these windows. Each option will be less expensive than broad rights, and no particular option has to be exercised if a deal for that window is not found. I had a client who did precisely this and we saved a great deal of money by limiting the options to just those media that he really needed.

Price

The price of clearing music for movies will be primarily determined by three factors:

1. Whether the movie is an "indie" production or a studio picture
2. The identity of the song and master
3. The kind of use that is made of the music in the movie

Whether a film is an indie or a major studio product is a key distinction because copyright owners recognize that the budgets of most indie filmmakers are modest compared to those of major motion picture studios. Often the copyright owner will inquire as to what the budget of the movie is when calculating a fair price.

Another key factor in determining price is the identity of the music you wish to use. A monster hit by a major recording artist will almost always be more expensive than a song that was never a hit and was recorded by an obscure artist.

The precise manner in which the music is used in the movie will also be a factor in pricing. Generally, use of music over the opening or closing credits will be more expensive than using a piece of music in the movie itself. Also, a "foreground use" is generally considered more valuable than a "background use." A foreground use is when a character in the movie is seen performing the music. An example of a background use would be when characters in the movie talk as they are driving a car with the radio on. In addition, if a piece of music is used multiple times in a movie, the price will increase. The copyright owner may want the same fee for each use. This factor is more important when negotiating rights for a big-budget movie, where one use of a popular song can easily reach six figures.

Notwithstanding all of these factors, if the producer wants music by an emerging songwriter or artist, the price can be absolutely free. Sometimes the writer or artist may be satisfied with a credit that can be used to garner future work. But the price of securing broad rights for a song that has had commercial success or was written by a well-known writer or performed by a successful artist may range from $5,000 to $25,000 (for each component, the song and the master). The good news (for producers) is that if copyright owners agree to license a song or master, they will generally charge $500 for festival rights whether the song was obscure, moderately successful, or even a monster hit.

This is the quote I recently received for a successful pop song performed by a well-known artist that was used in the background of a low-budget feature motion picture:

> Festival use: $500 for one year world
> Option for broad rights: Flat fee of $10,000 for worldwide broad rights.

If the picture had been a major studio production, the fee for broad rights would have been significantly higher.

Most copyright owners will want a synopsis of the movie and as well as a description of the scene(s) in which the song is used. The owners of many commercially successful songs are protective of their copyrights and will not license the song unless they approve of the subject matter of the movie and the manner in which the music is used. It's important to keep in mind in choosing music for your movie that a copyright owner can deny permission to use a song or master for any reason and is not obligated to tell you why.

Step Deals

Sometimes copyright owners will structure their quotes as "step deals." This means the price will ultimately depend on the financial success of the movie. The following is a quote that I received for another indie movie:

> RIGHTS:
> Film Festival/One (1) year/ World $500

OPTION
All Media Broad Rights Step Deal:
Media: All media now known or hereafter devised
Initial Fee: $2,500

With Steps of $2,000 at $3M, $5M, $8M, $10M, $12M and $15M worldwide gross receipts based in ALL forms of exploitation (including but not limited to theatrical, all videograms/DVD, all TV media, and Internet streaming and downloading).

This quote, which reflects a typical step deal, provided for a moderate initial payment of $2,500 and only required additional payments if the movie became financially successful.

MFN's Application to Features

A music publisher will usually insist on MFN treatment with the owners of the master containing that song. The label will also usually insist on MFN treatment with the song. But, as discussed in the previous chapter, producers can avoid MFN treatment between different songs and masters. Both labels and publishers recognize that the use of an entire song or master over the credits, for example, is much different than the use of a brief excerpt in the background of a scene. It is just as well recognized that the use of a monster hit such as "Jumpin' Jack Flash" by the Rolling Stones or "Stayin' Alive" by the Bee Gees is a great deal more valuable to a filmmaker and much more likely to help make a movie successful than an obscure song by an unknown artist.

Trailers: In-Context, Out-of-Context, and Other Promotions

Generally, but not in all cases, if granting broad rights in a song or master, a copyright holder will provide a gratis license to the producer to use that music to advertise the movie, but only "in-context." In-context means the same use of the music in the trailer as it is used in the movie itself. Generally out-of-context use, e.g., using the entire song during the trailer, will trigger an additional fee. Sometimes a filmmaker will wish to use a song that is not even in the movie at all, and this will call for a negotiation that will include all the same factors as using a song in the movie itself.

Relationships and Music Clearances

In clearing music for movies or other projects, a producer may wish to use personal relationships she has with writers or artists. However, if the writer or artist is already represented by a music publisher or label, the writer or artist will generally not have the right to grant a sync or master-use license. But a writer or artist who wants his or her music in your movie can significantly influence that publisher or label to make the clearance process much faster and a "yes" much more likely. Ultimately, the price of the license will usually be determined by the copyright owner, which means one should not expect a cheap price just because the writer or artist likes the movie. After all, he or she presumably entered into that music publishing or record company agreements to make money.

Also, your clearance professional may have relationships with copyright owners that may be helpful. For example, I have a good working relationship with a company that represents both the publishing and recordings of a certain superstar recording artist / songwriter. Recently,

I represented a filmmaker who wanted to use a song written and recorded by that artist. But the budget for the entire movie was less than $150,000 and his budget for music was only $20,000. Generally, a song and master by the artist in question would cost at least five figures each. But I was able to secure a gratis license. The company knew my client could never afford their normal fee. They granted permission because the star liked the synopsis. But the license would not have been free without my relationship with them.

Television

Standard Terms and Practices

Historically, producers of shows that appeared on network TV have always preferred securing all rights in all media for their programs, because if the show was a hit, it might have gone into "syndication" and repeated for years on local broadcast stations. In today's world, however, even a mediocre show on network, cable, or pay TV (e.g., HBO) may become available for VOD viewing or download in the US or throughout the world—virtually forever. So it's even more important for owners of these shows to secure as many rights and the longest term as possible. For instance, I recently re-cleared all the songs and masters for the home video release of a dramatic television series from the late '80s. The publishers and labels had granted home video rights in the show for seven years, but the term had expired. Because there were over 500 songs and masters in the show, it cost almost 1 million dollars to secure the home video rights to release the show on DVDs and as downloads.

Prices

A normal buyout price for a song for a TV show will depend on a number of factors. The most important one is the identity of the song. Unknown songwriters may find themselves faced with a deal that pays them absolutely nothing up front, but allows a company such as Viacom, which clears for MTV and VH1, to play their song(s) on any of their shows or promotions. The only money a writer can make by entering into this deal comes in the form of royalties payable by his PRO (i.e. ASCAP, BMI, or SESAC). But the royalties will be marginal unless the song is used a ton of times. If you are offered this contract, the only good reason to sign it is to enhance your resume with a credit so that you can actually make some money the next time someone wants to use your music.

At the extreme end of the spectrum, it was widely reported in 2012 that Lionsgate, the studio that produces *Mad Men* for the basic cable service AMC, paid about $250,000 for the recording and publishing rights for the Beatles' "Tomorrow Never Knows." The song was used at the end of one episode of *Mad Men*. Mathew Weiner, the creator of *Mad Men*, felt the high cost was worth it because the song was thematically and chronologically consistent with the setting of the show, which takes place in the mid-'60s. Most popular songs made famous by successful bands or artists are licensed to television programs for under $100,000. The Beatles rarely authorize use of their tracks for any commercial purpose.

It is worth noting that the average price of a "sync" for a network TV or cable program has, according to most knowledgeable people, decreased in the last 10 to 15 years. TV shows such as *Sex in the City* or *The O.C.* used to pay two or three times as much as comparable shows now pay. The reason is that budgets have come down, and the competition to place music for "sync" has soared as income from selling recorded music has declined.

Documentaries

Standard Terms and Practices

Clearing music for documentaries is a much more subtle process than clearing music for movies or TV shows. I often work with producers with extremely limited budgets. Their projects are not backed by TV networks or Hollywood movie studios, and they simply can't afford to pay the same fees. Publishers and labels recognize this reality. Sometimes, but not always, they also acknowledge that many documentaries that focus on musical topics, such as a particular artist or genre, directly promote their music and can lead to sales of catalogue that generate additional money for both publishers and labels. For instance, I worked on docs about the songs of the civil rights movement, and about the work of great songwriters and artists such as Pete Seeger, James Brown, and Joan Baez. All of these programs have the potential of spurring sales of catalogue. Record labels make more money from these sales, and publishers make more money from mechanical royalties that flow from them. Therefore, both music publishers and record companies benefit from these kinds of docs. (For more on this, see "Music Documentary Filmmakers Deserve a Break…" in Chapter 14.) However, often publishers and labels will take the position that a filmmaker shouldn't use their music if the fimmaker can't afford it.

In any event, rates for music in documentaries are generally lower than rates for network or cable TV shows, or for feature movies. However, if a documentary producer asks for the same terms as a producer for feature films and TV shows (i.e. all media buyouts), she is going to get a quote that she probably will not be able to afford. For example, I worked on a documentary about a well-known choreographer who worked with some famous performers, including Michael Jackson and Madonna. There were approximately 10 songs and 10 masters in the documentary. All the songs were fairly well-known pop tunes. The producers asked one of the publishers who controlled several of these songs for a quote to use the songs in "all media throughout the world in perpetuity." The quote was $10,000 per song. Had the project been a network drama or HBO comedy, the quote would have made sense. However, my client could never afford to pay that much money. Under the operation of MFN , as discussed in Chapter 9, the producer would have had to pay $10,000 for each song and $10,000 for each master, for a total of $200,000. But the budget for the entire doc was only $150,000.

Strategies for Saving Money

The strategy that a documentary filmmaker who wants to use music has to employ (if, like most indie producers, she has a limited budget) is to think in terms of clearing only the rights she will actually need. For instance, there is no need to clear music for PBS. As discussed in Chapter 9 (see "Special Rules for Public Broadcast Stations…"), with regard to public television, producers of any shows, including documentaries, do not need to pay for the music. PBS has a blanket deal for the broadcast of music on their stations, and the Copyright Act exempts public broadcasting stations from having to pay for masters. Since public television may be the only vehicle for a documentary, it would be absurd to ask copyright owners for all rights in all media in perpetuity.

In fact, I have cleared music for many documentaries that initially appear on PBS. My job is to clear the music for other "windows." In this context, a "window" means another medium for distributing the documentary, such as home video, foreign TV, and Internet video on demand (such as Amazon Prime). For instance, if a documentary airs on PBS, local stations may wish to "give away" DVDs in exchange for pledges to the station. PBS will ask the filmmaker to clear home video rights. The filmmaker will make money by selling units to PBS, but will have to clear the home video rights with the copyright owners of the music used in the film.

Home Video

Generally, for music used in a documentary to be released on home video, you will have to pay 10 to 15 cents per song and per master, per DVD sale or download. It usually does not matter whether you use excerpts or full songs, although discounts are sometimes possible for use of very brief excerpts. And, unlike the music cleared for TV shows or movies, the price usually does not vary depending on the identity of a song. A song by a famous writer or recorded by a famous artist is usually the same price as every other song. This is the standard business practice among copyright owners for licensing music for documentaries. Of course, it is always possible that a filmmaker will receive a "no," for any reason. For instance, I cleared home video rights for a doc celebrating ethnic diversity in America, and a famous songwriter refused to let his publishers grant a license because he perceived the documentary as "political." Fortunately, most songwriters—even famous ones—are not *that* finicky. And, depending on the writer's contract, a publisher may have the authority to grant a license even without the writer's approval.

Usually a copyright owner will require an advance as well as a penny rate. For instance, the publisher or label may require an advance of $300 against 2,500 units, including DVDs and downloads.

Other Windows

A filmmaker may wish to release her doc on a cable TV service rather than PBS, and seek a foreign TV deal and also license the doc to a VOD service such as Netflix. If that producer has already secured a cable deal, I will secure the cable TV rights for that window, e.g., basic cable, and secure "options" for other windows. An "option" in this context is gaining the right to show the doc in a certain medium (such as home video or foreign TV) without the obligation to pay for those rights *unless* the producer chooses to exercise the option.

US cable and foreign TV rights will generally be subject to a flat fee. That fee will usually range from $1,000 to $1,500 depending on a number of factors. The most important factors are how the songs are used (in full or excerpted), the identity of the songs (obscure songs may be cheaper), the identity of the copyright owner (some are more flexible than others), and the number of songs in the program (volume discounts are sometimes possible). Although some copyright owners may agree to lower rates, the operation of MFN, which usually applies to all songs and masters in a doc, may drive the cost up. On the other hand, MFN can also be used to pressure copyright owners who want exorbitant fees to agree to what everybody else has agreed to. Generally, the duration of a license is limited to three to five years, but most TV stations do not insist on a longer term. Cable and Internet VOD are also usually subject to a flat fee for a limited term.

In a typical case, if I am clearing a documentary that will be initially released as a home video, I may ask each copyright owner for the following rights and options:

> Home Video
> Royalty: 10 cents PBS Pledge only OR 12 (to 15 cents) for commercial DVD and downloads of full programs

Advance: 2,500 units
Territory: US[204]
Term: 7 years

OPTION 1: Basic Cable or Pay Television
TERRITORY: United States and Canada
Term: 3 [to 5] years
FEE: [flat fee] per song (or master)

OPTION 2: Foreign Television
TERRITORY: World excluding United States and Canada
Term: 3 [to 5] years
FEE: [flat fee] per song (or master)

OPTION 3: Internet Streaming Services (e.g., Hulu, Netflix)
TERRITORY: World
TERM: 1 year [with options for additional years]
FEE: [$flat fee] per song (or master)

OPTION 4: Airplane and Closed Circuit
TERRITORY: World
Term: 3 Years
FEE: $[flat fee] per song (or master)

Discounts for Very Obscure Music

Occasionally it is possible to negotiate special deals for documentaries featuring very obscure music. For instance, I worked on a doc about the history of American gospel music that featured songs that were not PD, but which no one outside the gospel world would have ever heard of. I was able to secure buyouts of all rights for a very reasonable fee. I managed the same result for a doc focusing on a famous dance troupe that performed to esoteric European jazz compositions from the 1930s. It is interesting that although the music in both of these **docs was extremely** obscure, most of it was owned by the major publishers and major record companies thanks to the consolidation that has occurred over decades both in music publishing and in the recording business. The major record labels like to gobble up niche record catalogues to increase their market share. There are currently only three major labels, and they control an incredible number of recordings. Similarly, the major publishers have acquired catalogues of songs in niche genres over the years. Yet the major publishers and labels that I bargained with all provided discounted rates because they recognized that these copyrights were less valuable, from a financial perspective, than their other more commercially successful songs and masters.

Concert Programs

Standard Terms

Clearing music for concerts is similar to clearing music for documentaries. Like documentary filmmakers, producers of audiovisual concerts usually operate on tight budgets, and copyright owners are generally willing to agree to more affordable terms than for feature films or network TV shows. I employ the same approach to help concert producers save money as I do with producers of documentaries. We ask for rights for an initial distribution window that the producer has already made a deal for or is at least aiming to get, such as home video or US cable, and I will ask for options for additional windows such as foreign TV and VOD. The rates for each window that applies to the docs just set forth will usually apply to concerts.

The key difference between clearing music for concerts and for documentaries is that the concert producer does not have to clear masters unless the performer sang "to track," i.e., lip synced the performance to a master recording. In that case, he or she must clear the underlying master, which is usually owned by a record company.[205] Also, producers of concert programs must keep in mind that a record label may assert "blocking" rights. As explained in Chapter 9, record companies usually have the exclusive right to distribute an artist's musical recordings including audiovisual recordings, and a producer who releases an artist's recordings as CDs, DVDs, downloads, or even on-demand streams may be interfering with a label's blocking rights. This is especially an issue to consider seriously if the entire concert features a single artist. For instance, I knew a European entrepreneur who acquired home video rights from a German TV station for a concert of a well-known hip-hop artist. When the major record company to which the artist was signed found out about the imminent home video release of this concert program, the record company prevented the release of the DVD, even though the producer had paid both the TV station and the artist for the home video rights. Unfortunately for the entrepreneur, the company that he contacted to press and distribute DVDs of the concert turned out to be owned by the artist's label.

Another difference between clearing music for an audiovisual concert program and for a documentary, movie, or any other prerecorded audiovisual project is that the producer does not need to clear sync rights if the concert is broadcast live. During a live performance, the music is not being synchronized to a visual image and therefore no sync license is required. This is also the case even if the concert is streamed live on the web—so long as it is streamed live. However, if the concert is repeated, made available on demand, or broadcast only after it is edited (e.g., the Victoria's Secret Fashion Show), then a "fixation" of sound and image does occur and sync licenses for the songs are required.

Producers and promoters of live concerts should know that although sync licenses are required for a live concert, the venue may not have PRO licenses or may require the producer or promoter to acquire them. (See "The PROs" and "How Much Various Users Pay the PROs" in

Chapter 1 as well as "Licensing Music for Fashion Shows" in the next chapter.)

For rates that apply to showing a concert in various windows such as TV, foreign TV, and Internet streaming on demand, see the rates that apply to documentaries in the previous section. The home video rates that usually apply to docs also apply to concerts. That is, the home video release of a concert is subject to the same penny rate as docs. Sometimes, though, the producer of a concert program may think that he will sell more home video units than a documentary, particularly if the performers are well known. In that case, the producer may ask for a "buyout" for the home video rights by offering, for example, $1,500 per song for an unlimited number of units. In effect, the producer is making a bet that he will sell enough units to lower the rate per unit below the penny rate. Assume, for instance, that the producer could secure a license for 10 cents a unit with a small advance of $250 against 2,500 units. He may offer the publishers

$1,500 up front for an unlimited number of units if he thinks he can sell more than 15,000, because if, for instance, if he sells 30,000 units, his effective penny rate will come down to 5 cents. The advantage for publishers in this deal is that they receive their fee up front.

Discounts for Benefit Concerts

As stated in Chapter 9, music sync fees for concerts produced by not-for-profit charitable organizations and designed to raise funds for a charity such as disaster relief can be a fraction of the cost of clearing songs for a normal concert. Music publishers recognize that the concert was produced to support a good cause and may discount their normal rates.

Advertising

A Brief History of Music in Advertising

For the first several decades after the invention of television, music in advertisements generally consisted of jingles. I grew up with catchy product-related jingles like "See the USA in Your Chevrolet." Clearances were not required because the jingles were written by songwriters who were on the payroll of advertising companies or jingle houses. Eventually, jingles faded in popularity, and by the 1980s, a commercial landscape developed in which advertisers used well-known songs to catch the attention of potential customers. The use of previously recorded pop songs in television advertisements began in earnest in 1985 when Burger King used Aretha Franklin's original recording of "Freeway of Love." Then, in 1987, Nike used the original recording of the Beatles' "Revolution" in an advertisement for a new line of sneakers.[206] The floodgates for using pop music in television ads had been opened.

By the 1990s, audiences around the country were used to hearing some of their favorite songs in television ads. But it still made news when Microsoft paid the Rolling Stones a rumored $8 million to $14 million to use "Start Me Up" in their Windows 95 campaign.[207] The Microsoft campaign was one of many examples of a commercial not only piggybacking on the popularity of well-known songs, but also milking the audience's memories and desires, and selling them back to us.

In 1999, Moby released *Play*, an electronic-techno album layered with samples, gospel, and house music. It was a mild success at first. Then he decided to license every track—all 18 of them. Suddenly, *Play* was on TV, it was in movies, it was in advertisements. Since then, it has sold 10 million copies worldwide and is widely perceived to have obliterated, once and for all, the wall between popular music and advertising.

The relationship between popular music and advertising has continued to evolve. While many musicians long believed that any artist helping to sell a product was "selling out," that attitude has changed, especially among younger artists. The main reason for this may be that sync has become an increasingly important source of income as revenues from record sales continue to decline.

Standard Terms and Practices

Generally, licensing for a TV commercial will include the right to use the music in one commercial for a specific territory for a period of time. Here is a specific example of quotes for use of a hit pop song. The licensee was a major US health insurance company. Note the amount of the fee.

Your request is approved as follows, subject to a final approval on the TV commercial storyboard once available.

Licensee: ______ Inc.
The campaign is currently scheduled to start in February or March 2013.

Song Title: _________ ("Composition")
Writer(s): _________
Publisher: _________
Society: BMI

Rights:
To record and synchronize an excerpt of the Composition in timed-relation with one (1) spot of up to sixty seconds (0:60) in duration for background vocal use. Free TV and Basic Cable TV without limitation as to number of airings.

Exclusivity on all life insurance campaigns for TV.

Term: 1 year
Territory: United States
Fee: $350,000

Option (to be exercised prior to the expiration of the initial term)
1 year renewal of terms at a 13 percent increase

"MFN": In the event Licensee grants more favorable terms including, without limitation, additional consideration in any form, to the party granting rights to the use of the master recording(s) (where applicable), Licensee shall notify Licensor thereof, and this Agreement shall be deemed amended to incorporate those more favorable terms as of the date when such higher fee is paid or such more favorable terms are granted to such third party.

Rights and Fees

Note that the rights to use the song in the previous example are limited to one spot—network and basic cable TV only—for one year, and only in the US. The price seems huge—$350,000 (although far less than the uses of the Beatles and Stones songs already noted), but this quote is not unusual for an immediately recognizable song in a national television campaign. Moreover, the fee would have been even higher if additional rights had been requested (such as an additional 30-second spot or a companion radio spot); if the territory requested had included other countries; or if the licensee had wished to use the commercial on the Internet and social media.

In this case, the licensee wished to use the original master recording, and the quote from the record company that owned the master was also $350,000. This was not an accident. Almost always, the label will agree to the same amount of money that the licensee has negotiated with the publisher. Note that the MFN clause in the publisher's quote would have required the licensee to pay the publisher more money if they agreed to pay the label more money. So the total cost to the client was $700,000. One way to have reduced the total expense would have been to re-record the song. That would have cost only a few thousand dollars and the client would not have had to pay the label. Indeed, the same client rerecorded another hit song from the '70s and saved $175,000 (the fee payable for the song).

In contrast to a national television campaign for one year, here is a quote for the use of another hit pop song in a commercial designed to promote car shows in small markets:

Use: 60 seconds
Media: TV/Radio
Term: 8 days in each territory
Territory: Phoenix, Arizona, Milwaukee, Wisconsin, and Baltimore, Maryland
Fee: $5,000 MFN

The fee was only $5,000 mainly because the spot was to run for only eight days in five small markets. Again, the record company wanted the same money as the publisher, so the total cost for the client was $10,000.

The rates for both of these examples could both have been radically reduced by not using hit songs, although the power of the ads would have been diluted. But a client who is seeking music to just create a mood or set a tone, rather than to capture attention with a well-known pop hit, can save a great deal of money by using a music library. (See my discussion of music libraries in Chapter 1 as well as my interview with the president of APM, one of the largest music libraries in the US.) Another alternative to hit songs are indie performers or "baby bands" who may not be signed to a major label or have a big radio hit, but have a great sound. There are many sources for this music, including indie song reps such as ZYNCH Music, Terrorbird, and LoveCat Music. Finally, ad agencies will often ask an indie producer to submit a "demo" for a spot, and if they love it they will hire that producer to develop the music and deliver a final version. The cost of a demo is usually low four figures, but if the music is used for a national campaign the sync fee could range from an additional $5,000 to $25,000, or more.

Other Factors in Determining Price

In addition to the identity of the song itself, whether a library is used or an indie producer is hired, there are other factors that will be examined when negotiating a reasonable fee. The most important are:

Manner of use: If the licensee only needs a song to play in the background for a few moments, the price may be reduced, particularly if the lyrics to a song are not used.

Radio and other media: A publisher of a well-known song will usually demand an extra 5 percent to 15 percent for use of a song in radio spots. This charge is usually negotiated as an option to run concurrently with the television advertisement. However, for obscure, catalogue, or baby-band songs, it may be possible to include radio without an additional charge.

Territory: As illustrated in the second example quote above, limiting the territory to certain cities, regions, or TV markets can dramatically affect the price an advertiser will have to pay for music, especially for hit songs. Publishers will generally try to negotiate an additional charge of 10 to 20 percent for the use of commercials in Canada. If a song is less than a major hit or a pop standard, it may be possible to negotiate Canadian rights into the basic fee, or at least to reduce the standard increase.

Options for extending the term: As illustrated in the first example quote, copyright owners will sometimes ask for a higher fee (usually from 5 percent to 15 percent) if the advertiser wants an option to extend the term during which the advertiser can play the commercial. Conversely, advertisers can save money by paying for only the time they definitely intend to use the ad and structuring any extension as an option that they don't need to exercise or pay for in case they decide to stop using the spot.

MFN, Exclusivity, and PRO Licenses

The MFN quote from a publisher will almost always require the advertiser to pay more to the owner of the master (usually a label) containing the song. As previously mentioned, an advertiser may wish to rerecord a song to avoid having to pay a label altogether. That may not be free, but it will generally be a lot less expensive than using the original master.

The first example quote included this provision: "Exclusivity on all health insurance campaigns for TV." The license itself provided more details:

> (b) The License Rights granted herein are non-exclusive, and Licensor shall be free to use, or grant others the right to use the Composition in any manner or media whatsoever throughout the world. However, Licensor agrees not to license the Composition for use in commercial advertising for a Related Product, as determined by Licensor using Licensor's reasonable business judgment, within the Territory during the Term. "Related Product" shall mean health and medical insurance companies.

The licensee (the insurance company) requested this provision so that the song for which they were paying so much money would not be used by a competitor, at least during the one-year term of the license. They secured the same concession from the record company for the master.

Sync licenses from publishers will also usually include a provision titled "Public Performance," which requires any service playing the spot, including any broadcast TV, radio, or Internet service, to be licensed by the PROs. The reason for this provision is that the publisher is paid a royalty in addition to the sync fee for the public performance of the song. But that royalty is paid by the PRO, not the advertiser. In order to receive this royalty, the broadcaster or Internet service that plays the spot must be licensed by the PRO. Almost all broadcasters in the US and around the world do have such licenses, as do established digital players such as YouTube, Yahoo, and Amazon. In addition, a license for the use of a song in an advertising campaign will usually require the advertiser to provide initial broadcast dates and Competitrack codes that allow the songwriter's PRO to track each broadcast of the commercial containing a particular song, so that the publisher and songwriters can be properly credited and paid for each performance of the spot. A license to use a master in an ad campaign usually does not demand this information because owners of sound recordings are not entitled to public performance royalties except for digital audio transmissions (see "The Exclusive Rights That Copyright Affords" in Chapter 1).

Sound-Alikes

An advertiser that rerecords a song and tries to make the new recording sound as much like the original as possible—referred to as a "sound-alike"—may be taking a legal risk. In 1988, singer

Bette Midler sued over a sound-alike version of her recording of "Do You Wanna Dance," which was used in a Ford commercial. She won. The Federal Court of Appeals decided:

> We need not and do not go so far as to hold that every imitation of a voice to advertise merchandise is actionable. We hold only that when a distinctive voice of a professional singer is widely known and is deliberately imitated in order to sell a product, the sellers have appropriated what is not theirs and have committed a tort in California. Midler has made a showing, sufficient to defeat summary judgment, that the defendants here for their own profit in selling their product did appropriate part of her identity.[208]

The court found it relevant that the advertising company, Young & Rubicam, had asked Midler if they could use her voice, and she had denied permission. Then they had asked one of Midler's backup singers if she could make herself sound "as much as possible" like the Bette Midler recording of "Do You Wanna Dance." Midler won the case even though Young & Rubicam secured a license from the copyright owner of the song and owned all the rights to the new recording.

Legendary singer-songwriter Tom Waits, who has steadfastly declined to license his music for commercial use, has filed several lawsuits against advertisers who tried to imitate his distinctively raspy voice without his permission. Waits' first lawsuit was against Frito-Lay for imitating his voice to sell chips. The Ninth Circuit Court of Appeals affirmed an award of $2.375 million in his favor.[209] As in the Midler case, the advertiser had asked Waits to perform one of his songs in an advertisement, Waits had declined the offer, and Frito-Lay had then hired a Waits impersonator to imitate Waits's style and manner. The Midler and Waits cases show that an advertiser should proceed with caution in producing a commercial using a "sound-alike" recording.

Practical Tips for Clearing Music in Ads

The following advice is intended for representatives of an ad agency or sponsor that is seeking to use a well-known song for a commercial campaign.

Remind the publisher about public-performance royalties: When clearing songs for commercials, it's important to remind publishers that they, and the writers they represent, are paid *twice* if an advertiser uses their song. The advertiser pays for the sync license. In addition, as previously noted, the publisher's performing-rights organization (ASCAP, BMI, or SESAC) pays the publisher, and the writer, each time the ad is broadcast. Public-performance income can be substantial. If a publisher declines to license the song, the publisher and the writer the publisher represents have that much more to lose.

Give them a budget: Some publishers will work with you if you let them know how much you or your client is willing to spend. Ask for a quote for a catalogue song and the publisher may start with $100,000 or more for a national campaign. But, if you tell publishers that you only have $50,000 to spend, they may take it, or at least steer you in the direction of a song in that price range.

Approach the creator first: If a song was recorded and written by a band, it may make sense to approach their manager directly—even if they have a deal with a label, publisher, or licensing rep. The band may be more eager to make a deal for a song than their publisher or label, because publishers and labels represent many other writers and artists whose work may bring in higher fees. Even if the label or publisher has exclusive authority to make a deal, the band can exert pressure on them to negotiate an affordable deal.

Consider using library music or a jingle house: If you are not looking for a recognizable song, you may be better off not approaching a music publisher or label at all. There are many music libraries and jingle houses that may be able to provide music composed on a work-for-hire basis that will work for your commercial and be much less expensive. They are also more likely to control the masters.

Consider emerging artists and their reps: As with libraries, you can save money but also tap into current trends by working with reps who license music by new artists such as the ones previously mentioned in "Rights and Fees."

Consult an expert: There are music-clearance professionals who are extremely experienced in negotiating these deals. You may wish to avail yourself of that expertise.

Instructional Videos

Some of my clients produce and sell DVDs of professional musicians teaching viewers how to play guitar or other instruments. Licenses for recorded music are generally not required because the performers featured in the video are not using the original recordings of popular songs. With regard to the songs, my experience is that the publishers are generally cooperative and will grant reasonable terms. A standard license would be 10 to 12 cents per song per unit sold, with an advance of 5,000 units for a duration of five to seven years. However, newer songs (and even some older songs, especially if they were huge hits) may be more difficult to clear, because some writers may not want their songs to be associated with an instructional video. Nothing is lost by requesting a license, though. If the producer of an instructional video wishes to build a website instead of selling DVDs, publishers may accept a flat fee for a limited term such as one to three years, or they may seek a percentage of revenues if the website charges a subscription fee.

Special Event Videos

I receive a number of calls from professional videographers or family members who want to use music in a video for a special occasion such as a wedding or birthday. They tell me that they only want to make a few dozen copies and ask whether they need permission. The answer is that they do if they use copyrighted music, even if they give the videos away for free. And many owners of popular songs will not want their music associated with someone's event. On the other hand, I have had success in licensing some popular songs for fees around $500 for a limited run of copies. This is particularly doable for "non-approval" songs. These are songs that a music publisher can license without the permission of writers or their estates. The more recent and commercially successful the song, the more likely it will be subject to approval. If the original recording is desired, then it will also be necessary to obtain the approval of the owner of the master, usually a record company. Those who want to use music in a wedding video should consider a music library from which they can license or buy music in all kinds of genres for a small fee.

Of course, millions of people upload videos containing third-party music to YouTube. YouTube has a content ID system that is supposed to identify copyrighted material, including songs and masters, and notify the copyright owners—usually record companies and music publishers.[210] The copyright owner is then supposed to tell YouTube to either take the video down or to "monetize" it. If the owner chooses the latter, YouTube is supposed to pay a percentage of ad revenues in connection with the video to the copyright owners.[211] Although this system is not designed to immunize uploaders from liability, the practical effect is that the worst-case scenario for most people who upload third-party copyrighted music without permission to YouTube is that the video will be taken down.

Exhibits and Installations

I do a number of short-term exhibits where videos are included. I clear music in footage and sometimes promo music videos for various clients, generally not-for-profit museums or other institutions. Here is a typical quote for the use of a song in an exhibit for which no separate admission was charged:

> Project: _____________
> Licensee: _____________
> Song title: _____________
> Media: Audiovisual clip on monitor in the ______ Museum only. Any additional rights (online, TV, film, etc.) must be cleared separately
> Start Date: June 2014
> Term: 6 months
> Fee: $350 (based on 100 percent)

The fees, as in this example, can be as low as a few hundred dollars, depending on the term. In this case, the term of use was only 6 months. A term of 10 or more years could cost $1,000 or more.

Chapter 11

AUDIO-ONLY CLEARANCES, PARODY, AND FAIR USE

Audio Compilations

Compilation albums are usually recordings that have been previously released, such as "greatest hits" or "best of" collections, gathering together an artist's or a band's best known recordings. Other compilations can be genre-based (classical, rock, pop, etc.) and can be a lucrative way of selling old music in new packages. Time Life, for instance, sells hundreds of different compilations with themes designed to attract baby boomers, such as *Legends: The Ultimate Rock Collection* and *The Ultimate Love Songs Collection.* Still other compilations are collections of recordings that were not only previously released, but also included in a particular movie or TV show. Recently, for instance, I cleared a dozen songs for a CD compilation; each song was originally included in a documentary, called *Airplay,* that focused on the history of American DJs. Music licensing for compilations is fairly straightforward.

Songs

Under the US Copyright Act, the right to record a song for distribution to the public is one of the copyright owner's exclusive rights. However, Section 115 of the Act states that once a song is recorded and distributed to the public, anyone can rerecord that song and/or distribute "phonorecords," i.e., audio copies containing that song. This provision is referred to as a "compulsory" license because the owner of the copyright in the song cannot deny permission. The rate for this compulsory license (9.1 cents for recordings of a song five minutes or less, and 1.75 cents per minute or fraction thereof for those over five minutes) is set by a government body called the Copyright Royalty Board (see "Mechanical Rights and Royalties" in Chapter 1 for more details concerning this and other compulsory licenses). This rate is commonly referred to as the "stat" rate, and the license itself is often referred to as a "statutory" mechanical license. It applies to distribution of physical records, including CDs and permanent downloads. If a compilation consists of songs that have previously been released, as most compilations do, the producer of the compilation is entitled to this compulsory license for each song contained in the compilation.[212] The Harry Fox Agency (HFA), as we discussed in Chapter 1, is set up to issue statutory mechanical licenses. For details on how to acquire an HFA license, please read the upcoming section on covers.

Masters

In order to secure permission to use previously recorded masters in a compilation, you must negotiate with the owner of each master, which is usually a record company. Unlike songs, there is no compulsory license and no statutory rate for masters, so clearing each master is subject to negotiation. However, the "standard" rate, i.e. the rate most labels will accept, is 10 to 12 cents per track, but any label can insist on more money. In addition, most labels will require advances. For instance, an advance of 10,000 units is common. Sometimes a more difficult problem than negotiating a rate is getting permission for usage at all. Record companies are extremely reluctant to license new tracks. They fear the compilation may compete with their own records. Also, for this reason, labels will almost always require that compilations be sold as albums only to prohibit single downloading.

Finally, each record company will usually ask for MFN with other tracks. So if label X demands 15 cents, and all the other labels have already agreed to 12 cents MFN, you will have to pay 15 cents to all of them. Of course, one solution is to delete X's track. A better solution, assuming you really wanted X's track, would be to convince X to reduce its rate by arguing that all the other labels have agreed to the MFN rate.

Covers and Parodies

Covers

In popular music, a "cover version," "cover song," or simply "cover" refers to a new recording of a previously recorded song, by someone other than the artist who made the first recording. Some covers are much more successful than the original recording. Examples are Whitney Houston's version of Dolly Parton's "I Will Always Love You," Sinead O'Connor's recording of "Nothing Compares 2 U" (originally recorded by Prince), and "I Love Rock 'n' Roll" by Joan Jett (originally recorded by band called Arrows).

Compulsory License

As we discussed in the last section, the right to record a song for distribution to the public is an exclusive right of the copyright owner, but once a songwriter has recorded and distributed a song or permitted another to do so, a "compulsory" license is available to anyone else who wants to rerecord the song, provided they pay the "stat" rate. This applies to downloads as well as CDs and other physical formats.

The compulsory license under 115 also prohibits changing the "basic melody or fundamental character" of the song.[213] It's not always clear if the new version of a song has changed its "fundamental character," but changing the words or basic melody would be the line that you cannot cross to take advantage of the compulsory license.

The Harry Fox Agency

As introduced in Chapter 1, HFA was established as an agency to license, collect, and distribute mechanical royalties on behalf of music publishers who then share the monies with their writers under publishing or administration agreements. In order to secure a compulsory mechanical license to record and distribute a song that has been previously released, you can ask Fox for a license. They represent all the major publishers and a majority of important indies. But to make sure that Fox represents a particular song before you apply, you can use their public database, called Songfile (http://www.harryfox.com/public/songfile.jsp). If Fox represents the song, you can set up an account and acquire the license online through their website. In the rare instance that HFA does not represent a particular song, you can follow the instructions set forth in Section 115 of the Copyright Act: "Scope of exclusive rights in nondramatic musical works: Compulsory license for making and distributing phonorecords," although it would be easier to secure a license from the publisher by requesting a mechanical license directly from them.[214]

If you plan on making fewer than 2500 copies or selling fewer than 2500 permanent downloads of your recording, HFA suggests you request your licenses using HFA Songfile. However if you use Songfile, you will have to pay up front and it will only cover the number of copies or downloads that you indicate you will manufacture or download up to 2500 units. If you manufacture or download more than the units specified, you will need another license; and if you manufacture or copy fewer, you don't get a refund. Still, Songfile is a bit easier to use than the normal compulsory licensing procedure, as you can avoid the necessity of preparing quarterly accounting statements (royalties on a normal license are due within 45 days after the close of each calendar quarter). For either a Songfile or a normal compulsory mechanical license, you will need to set up an account at www.harryfox.com, fill out the online forms provided by Fox, indicating the names of the songs, the writers, and the publishers along with some other basic information such as the name of the album (if any) and the release date. After providing this information, HFA will generate a license that can be signed electronically. You never even have to print out the licenses.

Audiovisual Covers

It is important to note that the Section 115 compulsory license does not apply, and Fox does not issue licenses for, audiovisual recordings of a song. In that case, a "sync" license will be required from the music publisher. Of course, millions of people take videos of themselves performing pop, R & B, hip-hop, and every other conceivable kind of song and upload them to YouTube. As discussed in "Special Event Videos" in the previous chapter, YouTube has a content ID system that is supposed to identify these video "covers" and notify the copyright owners—usually music publishers and record companies.[215] The copyright owner is then supposed to tell YouTube to either take the video down or "monetize" it. If the owner chooses the latter, YouTube is supposed to pay a percentage of ad revenues in connection with the video to the publisher.

It is worth noting that one publisher, Sony/ATV, initiated "We Are the Hits," an online video network that allows musicians to create, syndicate, and monetize cover songs—legally. WATH was formed in 2011 and currently has over 200 artists who generate thousands of videos and over millions of views a month on YouTube alone. WATH was the first video network to allow the cover artist to participate in the advertising revenue. WATH (which is now independently owned by Larry Mills, who started the company within Sony/ATV as an employee) has millions of songs available, including the catalogs of Sony, Universal Music Publishing, and Kobalt. By becoming a member of the WATH network, artists are able to get a license, share in advertising revenue, and have their content syndicated to multiple online platforms including YouTube.

Parodies

Merriam-Webster defines "parody" as "a piece of writing, music, etc., that imitates the style of someone or something else in an amusing way." One of my clients decided to write and record a parody album using classic pop songs to poke fun at the baby boomers that grew up with them. For instance, he wanted to change Jerry Leiber and Mike Stoller's lyric

From: "You ain't nothin' but a hound dog. Cryin' all the time"

To: "You ain't nothin' but an *old* dog. Cryin' all the time."

You get the idea. The Section 115 compulsory license that we just discussed obviously does not apply, because parodies change the lyrics and therefore the "fundamental character of the work." In that sense, they are derivative works, defined by Section 101 of the Copyright Act as follows:

> A "derivative work" is a work based upon one or more preexisting works, such as a translation, musical arrangement, dramatization, fictionalization, motion picture version, sound recording, art reproduction, abridgment, condensation, or any other form in which a work may be recast, transformed, or adapted.

Under Section 102 of the Act, the owner of copyright has the exclusive right "to prepare derivative works based upon the copyrighted work." Therefore, parodies (unless the parodist secured permission) would appear to violate the rights of copyrights of the song they are parodying.

The party from whom permission is required is usually a music publisher. If the publisher grants permission, it will usually demand not only 9.1 cents per copy but also the ownership of the copyright in the new lyrics. This means they would receive one percent of any performance rights royalties (e.g., if the parody played on the radio) and could use the new lyrics for any purpose themselves. Moreover, the publisher can always deny permission—for any reason. In the example just presented, we cleared 12 of 16 songs.

Are Parodies Protected by Fair Use?

Although a parody is a derivative work, it *may* be protected under the fair-use doctrine (see Chapter 1 for a discussion of fair use). That is, it's *possible* that you don't need permission at all. For instance, the Supreme Court of the United States decided in *Campbell v. Acuff-Rose Music, Inc.* 510 U.S. 569 (1994) that 2 Live Crew's parody of Roy Orbison's song "Oh, Pretty Woman" could qualify as a fair use within the meaning of the Copyright Act.

Here are the facts of the case: The members of the rap music group 2 Live Crew—Luke, Fresh Kid Ice, Mr. Mixx, and Brother Marquis—composed a song called "Pretty Woman," a parody based on Roy Orbison's rock ballad "Oh, Pretty Woman." The group's manager asked Acuff-Rose Music (now owned by Sony/ATV Music Publishing) for a license to use Orbison's tune for the ballad to be used as a parody. Acuff-Rose Music refused to grant the band a license, but 2 Live Crew nonetheless produced and released the parody. Almost a year later, after nearly a quarter of a million copies of the recording had been sold, Acuff-Rose sued 2 Live Crew and its record company, Luke Skywalker Records, for copyright infringement. The District Court ruled in favor of 2 Live Crew, holding that their song was a parody that made fair use of the original song under Section 107 of the Copyright Act. The Court of Appeals disagreed, holding that the commercial nature of the parody rendered it presumptively unfair. But the Supreme Court reversed the Court of Appeals decision. It held that 2 Live Crew's commercial parody may be a fair use within the meaning of Section 107 even though the parody had a commercial purpose. They found it important that although the parody did make fun of the original, at the same time it was "transformative" of the original by using a song about a "pretty woman" to tell a story about, according to Judge Souter, "nameless streetwalkers."

Judge Souter wrote in relevant part:

> This is not, of course, to say that anyone who calls himself a parodist can skim the cream and get away scot free. In parody, as in news reporting . . . context is everything . . . It is significant that 2 Live Crew not only copied the first line of the original, but thereafter departed markedly from the Orbison lyrics for its own ends. 2 Live Crew not only copied the bass riff and repeated it, but also produced otherwise distinctive sounds, interposing "scraper" noise, overlaying the music with solos in different keys, and altering the drum beat.

Unfortunately for parodists, the fair-use doctrine's applicability to parodies, as the quoted language demonstrates, depends on the facts of a particular case, and even the Supreme Court did not conclude that 2 Live Crew's parody actually *was* a fair use. They remanded the case back to the trial court "for further proceedings consistent with this opinion." On remand, the parties settled the case out of court. According to press reports, under terms of the settlement, 2 Live Crew agreed to license the parody of the song and Acuff-Rose stated that they were paid, although they did not disclose the terms.

So whether musical parodies are fair use is still an extremely "gray" area of law. Moreover, the costs of litigation, particularly legal fees that a parodist who is sued by a well-heeled copyright owner would have to pay to defend the case, could be ruinous *even* if the parodist wins the lawsuit. Perhaps this is the chief reason why "Weird Al" Yankovic, who has been making parodies of famous songs and artists for decades, has always secured permission.

For a comparison between Roy Orbison's original "Pretty Woman" lyrics ans 2 Live Crew's parody, see the court case summary of Campbell vs. Acuff-Rose Music, Inc., 510 U.S. 569 [1994] at: https://supreme.justia.com/cases/federal/us/510/569/case.html.

Sample Clearances

Sampling Defined

Some people think that sampling only applies when using an excerpt of the original master recording, but generally, if you use lyrics or music from a musical composition, you also need to clear the underlying song. Here is a good definition of music "sampling":

> Sampling is (1) the use of prerecorded material within another recording, which requires a master-use right, and/or (2) the use of a portion of a musical composition that you don't own or control within another recording, which also requires permission from the owner.[216]

As the definition states, sampling involves taking a piece of the original master and/or musical composition. Of course, if you don't sample the actual recording, you don't have to clear the master. For example, Biz Markie used the three-word hook from Irish singer/songwriter Gilbert O'Sullivan's song "Alone Again Naturally." He did not use O'Sullivan's recording of the song, just the words "alone again naturally." But Markie and his record company were still sued—by O'Sullivan's publisher. We discuss the result of the lawsuit in the next paragraph.

Brief Legal History

From a legal perspective, sampling has been an area of contention. Hip-hop artists were the first to experiment with sampling. Early sampling artists simply used portions of other songs and recordings without asking for permission. But once hip-hop and rap became commercially successful, the original artists began to take legal action, claiming copyright infringement. Artists and record labels have become more diligent about clearing samples ever since a judge admonished "Thou shalt not steal" in 1991, when rapper Biz Markie and his record company, Warner Records, were sued over a sample of Gilbert O'Sullivan's "Alone Again Naturally" in Markie's "Alone Again."[217] As discussed above, Markie only used the three-word hook of O'Sullivan's song, but he repeated it throughout "Alone Again." This case had a powerful effect on the record industry, with record companies becoming much more concerned with the legalities of sampling, and demanding that artists make full declarations of all samples used in their work. On the other hand, the ruling also made it more attractive to artists and record labels to allow others to sample their work, knowing that they would be paid—often handsomely—for their contribution. Today, most mainstream acts obtain prior authorization to use samples, a process known as "sample clearance." Clearing samples usually requires paying an up-front fee as well as royalties to the original publisher and/or label. Independent artists and bands lack the funds and legal assistance to clear samples, leaving them at a disadvantage.

Sample Clearance Process

To give you an idea of how to go about acquiring permission to use a sample, here is an example of a "sample request" form from a major publisher:

_________ Publishing
Sample/Adaptation Clearance Form

*Please complete all fields

Requester's Name:	
Position:	
Company:	
Address/City/State/Zip:	
Phone/Fax:	
E-mail Address:	

NEW SONG Title:	
Artist:	
Label/Distributor:	
Proposed Release Date:	
Quantity to Be Pressed / Promo Details:	

Territories of Release:	
Composer(s):	
Publishers:	
Description of Sample Usage:	
Are there any other samples used in this recording? If so, please list and give details of clearance.	
Has there already been a Promotional Release anywhere on the web, radio, or on a mix tape, etc., and where can we access it?	
If approved, will the New Song be sold, released as a Promotional Release (online, mix tape, etc.), or synchronized with TV/film/online video?	

Details of the ORIGINAL SONG:

Title:	
Original Artist:	
Composer / Authors:	
Publishers:	

It may take weeks (if not longer) for a publisher to ingest this information and let the "approvers" at the publishing company decide on the request. The process could take even longer if use of a master is also required, that is, if you sampled the master as well as the song. So those seeking a sample clearance should start early. In fact, because many sample requests are rejected, or the fees demanded may be just be too high, it is preferable to clear the sample before you even use it.

I recently cleared a sample of a well-known song that was used in the entire chorus of a new recording. My client, the sampling artist, who is also a songwriter, did not use the original master. Most of the new song's lyrics were different, but the client did use the original words from the sampled song in the chorus. The publisher granted consent but demanded $3,000. This is a typical quote, although sample quotes can be somewhat lower or a great deal higher, depending on the song, the publisher, and the original writer.[218] In addition, the publisher demanded 50 percent of the copyright in the new song, including the new material created by my client. This demand is also not uncommon, although, if a brief sample is used or if there are multiple samples, a publisher may be satisfied with a smaller percentage of the copyright in the new song.

In addition to the up-front fee and the ownership interest in the copyright, the publisher wanted 50 percent of any monies attributable to the new song, including performance royalties payable for radio play or other public performance of the song, plus 50 percent of mechanical income from CD sales or downloads. These payments would be due after recoupment of the $3,000.

When Is Sampling "De Minimis?"

The "de minimis" doctrine has provided some wiggle room for music samplers. Unlike fair use, which is an exception to a copyright owner's exclusive rights, "de minimis" means that the use of the original was so slight or trivial that it does not amount to copyright infringement in the first place. As seen in the following discussion, some courts (particularly in California) have dismissed copyright infringement cases against samplers when their use of another song and/or master is so insignificant as to be de minimis; other courts (particularly the one that decided the case discussed next) have not been so generous to those who sample.

The Bridgeport Case

In *Bridgeport Music, Inc. v. Dimension Films* (6th Cir. 2004), the US Court of Appeals for the Sixth Circuit, which includes one of the capitals of the recording and music publishing business, Nashville, decided that no use of a musical recording, no matter how brief or insignificant, could qualify as de minimis. The court ruled that *any* sampling of prerecorded sounds is an infringement of the sound recording copyright in the original master, no matter how little was used or even whether the original was recognizable. The court stated:

> If you cannot pirate the whole sound recording, can you "lift" or "sample" something less than the whole? Our answer to that question is in the negative.
>
> Get a license or do not sample.

They added, "We do not see this as stifling creativity in any significant way." The *Bridgeport* case effectively eliminated the de minimis doctrine as a defense to sampling recorded music in the Sixth Circuit. The court justified its decision by relying on a provision of the Copyright Act that states that owners of sound recordings can sue for copyright infringement only if the new work actually took elements of the recording itself rather than re-creating the sound embodied in the original recording. The court reasoned that this implies that taking any part of the recording is copyright infringement. Many copyright scholars disagree with this analysis. They point out that the language relied on by the court is actually a limitation on the right of sound recording owners to claim copyright infringement. It was not intended to confer greater rights on owners of sound recordings than owners of other copyrighted works. Whether the case was rightly or wrongly decided, it's still the law in the sixth circuit.

The Beastie Boys Case

In contrast to *Bridgeport*, the Ninth Circuit, which includes Los Angeles, found that taking only three notes from a song was de minimis. In *Newton v. Diamond* (9th Cir. 2003), the Beastie Boys obtained a license to sample six seconds of a record containing three notes. The song was recorded and composed by an accomplished jazz flutist, James W. Newton. Although the Beasties licensed the recording from Newton's label, they did not get a license to sample the underlying musical composition.

The district court granted summary judgment to the Beasties. It held that no license to the underlying composition was required because, as a matter of law, the notes in question—C–D flat–C, over a held C—lacked sufficient originality to merit copyright protection.[219] But the district court also held that even if the sampled portion of the composition was sufficiently original to merit copyright protection, the use that the Beasties made of the sample was de minimis.[220] The Ninth Circuit affirmed.

Notwithstanding the different outcomes, *Bridgeport* and the Beastie Boys cases can be reconciled because in the latter case, the Beasties did secure a license to use the master recording, and *Bridgeport* only dealt with the master sample. It is conceivable that if the Beasties had not licensed the master, the court could have ruled in favor of the plaintiff.[221]

The Madonna Case: Conflict between Jurisdictions

In a 2013 case, Madonna and producer Robert "Shep" Pettibone were alleged to have illegally sampled both a recording titled "Love Break" and the underlying musical composition in Madonna's 1990 international hit "Vogue." The case resulted in a ruling in favor of the defendants.[222] The decision in this case is in direct conflict with *Bridgeport.*

The plaintiff, VMG Salsoul, owned the "Love Break" song and master. VMG alleged that Madonna and Pettibone had violated these copyrights by using a single chord played on a horn (referred to by the court refers as the "Horn Hit") 11 times in "Vogue." The district court found:

> Having listened to the sound recordings of . . . "Love Break" and "Vogue," the Court finds that no reasonable audience would find the sampled portions qualitatively or quantitatively significant in relation to the infringing work, nor would they recognize the appropriation. The Court finds that any sampling of the Horn Hit was de minimis or trivial.

The plaintiff argued that the decision in *Bridgeport* supported their position, but the court responded that "This case is not applicable . . . the Sixth Circuit's bright-line rule has not been adopted by the Ninth Circuit."

Caution Advised

Even though California recognizes some wiggle room with regard to sampling, since all major record companies maintain offices in Nashville and LA, they are likely to clear *all* samples that they can identify. The law pertaining to jurisdiction is complex, and it is possible that if a record containing a sample is offered for sale in Tennessee, then even an unsigned artist or indie record company in another state could be subject to jurisdiction there. Also, every case depends on its individual facts, even in California and other states. The law is, in fact, deeply "gray" in this area, and the music sampler is always taking a risk in the absence of a license. Plus, as we discussed in the first chapter, possible statutory damages of up to $150,000 and attorney's fees apply to copyright infringement. The point is simple: if you wish to sample a copyrighted piece of music, get a sample license if you can afford it; otherwise, be aware of the business and legal risks.

Chapter 12
SPECIAL CASES

Musical Theater

Grand Rights

With the success of *Jersey Boys* and other jukebox musicals like *American Idiot*, more and more producers are dreaming of bringing a musical based on pop hits to Broadway. Over the past several years, I have been called on to clear songs for half a dozen musical-theater productions. Several of them were based on the life and music of famous artists; another was based on a comic book about musical debutant "warriors" from Texas; and another was about a fictional music video TV channel. In each case, I cleared at least a dozen and sometimes more than two dozen songs.

Although each of these musicals featured the live performance of musical compositions, and the PROs offer blanket licenses for the public performance of songs, I could not use them to clear the songs. Unlike other live performances, such as concerts, musicals are "dramatic" performances, and the PROs do not license such rights. Clearing music for theatrical musicals involves so-called "grand rights," also sometimes referred to as "dramatic rights." The ASCAP website provides useful information regarding this point:

> ASCAP members do not grant ASCAP the right to license dramatic performances of their works. While the line between dramatic and non-dramatic is not clear and depends on the facts, a dramatic performance usually involves using the work to tell a story or as part of a story or plot. Dramatic performances, among others, include:
>
> (I) performance of an entire "dramatico-musical work." For example, a performance of the musical play *Oklahoma!* would be a dramatic performance.
>
> (II) performance of one or more musical compositions from a "dramatico-musical work" accompanied by dialogue, pantomime, dance, stage action, or visual representation of the work from which the music is taken. For example a performance of "People Will Say We're in Love" from *Oklahoma!* with costumes, sets, or props or dialogue from the show would be dramatic.
>
> (III) performance of one or more musical compositions as part of a story or plot, whether accompanied or unaccompanied by dialogue, pantomime, dance,

stage action, or visual representation. For example, incorporating a performance of "If I Loved You" into a story or plot would be a dramatic performance of the song.

(IV) performance of a concert version of a "dramatico-musical work." For example, a performance of all the songs in *Oklahoma!* even without costumes or sets would be a dramatic performance.

The term "dramatico-musical work" includes, but is not limited to, a musical comedy, opera, play with music, revue, or ballet.

ASCAP has the right to license "non-dramatic" public performances of its members' works—for example, recordings broadcast on radio, songs or background music performed as part of a movie or other television program, or live or recorded performances in a bar or restaurant.

Dramatic and grand rights are licensed by the composer or the publisher of the work.

The key reason that publishers and writers do not authorize the PROs to license grand rights is that they want to retain the right to prevent particular songs being used in musicals that they do not like. ASCAP and BMI operate under a government consent decree under which they cannot deny permission to anyone who wishes to license their repertoire. If their publisher and writer members granted them dramatic or grand rights, any producer of any musical could use any song he or she liked. Indeed, in almost every case of the half-dozen musicals that I have cleared, we received at least one rejection, and most of the time more than one. Generally, the publishers don't explain their reason for denials. But when they do offer an explanation, it's usually that they or the writers that they represent do not like the subject matter of the play or do not want to have their songs mingled with others. The reason is usually not financial because, as we shall see in the upcoming discussion, the financial model for licensing songs in musicals—although not subject to any mandatory terms—is well established.

None of the theater projects that I have worked on used original masters. In all cases, the songs were performed by cast members. So we did not approach any record companies for licenses.[223] However, in one production, we did license some BBC footage consisting of the actual singer who was the subject matter of the play, performing a song, and I had to clear the footage (from an agent who represented the BBC for footage requests) as well as the song. (For more on this type of clearance, see "Footage Licenses" in Chapter 9).

Standard Terms and Practices

If permission to use a song is granted, the standard financial arrangement (which is well established) is much more favorable to the theatrical producers than are the terms that producers of documentaries, feature films, or TV programs can expect. One difference is that theatrical producers usually do not have to pay any advances. In other words, there is no up-front cost. The standard business practice is simply to pay the publishers a percentage—usually four to five percent—of box-office gross receipts. That percentage is then prorated among all the songs in the musical. For instance, if there are 10 songs, each song is credited with one-half of one percent of gross box office receipts. The price does not go up even if more songs are added. This is also obviously extremely favorable to theatrical producers.

In order to secure a license, the following information will generally need to be provided:

Identity of the producer
Synopsis of the musical
Scene description of music use
Start date
Length of production term
Performance territory
Total number of scheduled performances
Theater size (number of seats)
Ticket price (USD)
Duration of music/timing
Version of song used (i.e., live, CD)/artist recording (if applicable)
Lyric change (if applicable)
Total number of songs used in project

Here is a typical quote for a song to be used in a musical:

> Your request for use of the below song(s) in ________________ is approved on the following terms; All Terms MFN w/ Master (If Used) and All Songs of Similar Use:
>
> Song: "_________"
> Writers: _________
> Publisher: _________
> Ownership percent: 100 percent
> Licensee: [producer]
> Name of Production: __________
> Use: Visual Vocal, Up to Full Use Per Song
> Media: Live Stage
> Term: 3 Years
> Territory: United States
>
> Royalty Rate: 5 percent Gross Box Office Pro-Rata MFN w/Masters and All Songs.

Publishers will generally limit the term to no more than three years and only to the US. They want to see that the producer is actually mounting the production and pays them the royalty on a regular basis before granting a longer term or a worldwide license.

Licensing Music for Fashion Shows

This section is designed to provide a legal road map for designers and producers of fashion shows who wish to use music for live shows, TV programs, and the Internet. A designer or producer of live shows can play CDs or hook up an iPod to speakers without having to worry about clearing the records. As we discussed in the first chapter, owners of sound recordings don't have public-performance rights except for digital transmissions.[224] And you don't need a sync license for the songs unless you are producing an audiovisual recording of the show for later playback for television or the web. But it is necessary to clear the public-performance rights in the songs. Unlike musical theater, fashion shows require a license from the PROs because the use of music in such shows is not considered to be a dramatic performance. So, for instance, you can play Lady Gaga's recording of "Bad Romance" without permission from her label, and you don't need a sync license for the song, but you will need permission to publicly perform the song.

PRO Licenses

Some venues where fashion shows take place, including most nightclubs, will already have ASCAP, BMI, and SESAC licenses, so the producer of the show doesn't have to worry about getting a license. However, some venues won't have a license, like the temporary structures set up for Fashion Week in New York City. Also, some venues that occasionally, or even regularly present live music shows, such as arenas, will insist that the producer or promoter of the live event secure a PRO license for that specific event—in order to place the economic burden of paying the PROs on the promoter. Each PRO has a license that would apply to fashion shows.

LICENSE FEE SCHEDULE

SCHEDULE A EVENTS WITH PAID ADMISSION			
Seating Capacity			**% of Gross Ticket Revenue**
0	to	2,500	0.80%
2,501	to	3,500	0.60%
3,501	to	5,000	0.40%
5,001	to	9,999	0.30%
SCHEDULE B FREE OR BENEFIT EVENTS			
Seating Capacity			**Fee Per Benefit Event With No Charge**
0	to	250	$16.00
251	to	750	$19.00
751	to	1,500	$29.00
1,501	to	2,500	$48.00
2,501	to	5,000	$70.00
5,001	to	7,500	$94.00
7,501	to	9,999	$132.00

Minimum Annual Fee is $222

Here are the rates that apply:

ASCAP: If prerecorded music is used instead of a live band, ASCAP charges $97 per day. For live music or a DJ, ASCAP's fee is based on a percentage of "Live Entertainment Costs" including fees paid to the musician(s) or DJ (1.75 percent if admission is charged, and 1 percent if the event is free). There is a minimum of $126 per year.[225]

BMI: For shows that don't charge admission fees, BMI charges $16 per show for venues with 250 seats or less (and slightly more for larger venues.) For shows that charge admission, BMI's fee is based on a percentage of gross ticket sales starting with 0.8 percent for venues with up to 250 seats (and slightly more for larger venues). Either way, there is a minimum annual fee of $222. This chart is from BMI's license for venues with fewer than 10,000 seats:

SESAC: The fee is currently $82 per day.

How to Avoid the PROs

If the venue is not licensed and the designer and producer want to play music at the live show, they can still avoid having to secure the PRO licenses and pay the accompanying fees by hiring a live band that writes its own music. Even if the members of the band who wrote the music are signed to one of the PROs, they retain the right to permit any third party to publicly perform their music.

Licensing Music for Fashion Shows for Television

The *Victoria's Secret Fashion Show* has been a widely watched event on network TV for over a decade. Aside from the models and sexy lingerie, the show features an abundance of music, including songs by leading artists of the day such as Kanye West, Jay-Z, Rihanna, Maroon 5, Nicky Minaj, Lady Gaga, and Beyoncé. But Victoria Secret's lawyer does not have to worry about PRO licenses for the public performance of the songs. All of the networks (including CBS) that currently air the show have licenses with the PROs.

However, since the *Victoria's Secret Fashion Show* is prerecorded (rather than broadcast live), the music is "fixed in time relation" to the visual images, so sync licenses are required. In addition, since some of the original master recordings are used in the show, master-use licenses are also required. Unlike PRO licenses, every sync or master-use license is subject to negotiation; there is no preset rate, and the license fees can vary wildly from being very cheap for a music documentary to being extremely expensive for national TV commercials. Sync licenses for network television shows like *Victoria's Secret* fall somewhere in between. A normal network license can range from $1,500 to $3,000 for one to three years.[226] However, if a show only runs once, like *Victoria's Secret*, the producer can negotiate for a reduced fee. As with other projects, if a master license is also required, the label will usually ask for the same amount as the publisher.

Licensing Music for Fashion Shows for the Web

Public Performance

If the producer uploads footage containing music on YouTube or Vevo, there is no need to secure licenses from ASCAP, BMI, or SESAC. These sites already have licenses from the PROs. But in order to legally play the footage on the producer's website, the producer must acquire a public-performance license. These licenses may be obtained directly from ASCAP.com, BMI.com, and SESAC.com. The rates and terms depend on various factors such as the size of the website (for instance, ASCAP provides low-cost expedited licenses for small websites with little income and traffic); whether music is the primary function of the site (for instance, BMI offers "The Corporate Image Website Music Performance Agreement" if the website's primary function is to promote a business or corporate image and generates little or no direct revenue from music), and whether the website allows for interactive streaming of individual songs (ASCAP has a special license for this). Generally, however, these licenses are available for advances of a few hundred dollars against an aggregate royalty of a small percentage (four to six percent for all three) of the site's gross income. (See Chapter 5 on interactive streaming for more details.)

As we've discussed, owners of the copyright in sound recordings do not have public-performance rights for live performances and normal broadcast, but they do have them for digital transmission. If the producer uploads the show to his or her own website, and the show includes prerecorded music, the producer will usually negotiate the public performance of the master as part of the master-use license.

Sync and Master-Use Licenses for the Web

Since the songs will be synchronized to a visual image, the producer must negotiate a sync license for each song—just like a TV show. The prices, too, will depend on many of the same factors we discussed in connection with a TV show, including how the song is used, the term of the license, etc. My recent experience is that one can expect a quote of approximately $500 to $1,000 for one to three years. Again, most record companies will go along with the music publisher's quote. However, the producer should pre-clear the songs and the masters, because a publisher or label may decline to license a particular song or master if, for instance, a writer or artist does not wish to be associated with the show.

Chapter 13

HOW TO CLEAR MUSIC FOR VARIOUS STAND-ALONE DIGITAL PROJECTS

Artist Websites

Most serious unsigned artists have their own websites to promote their music, records, live performances, merchandise, etc. They usually include pages where fans can listen to their tracks in whole or in part and watch their videos. Of course, if they write and record their own music, there are no music clearance issues.

Audio Covers

However, an artist or band covering a song (that is, recording a new version of a song that was previously recorded and released by another artist), should read the section on covers in Chapter 11. As discussed in more detail there, in order to offer permanent downloads of a cover (even if there is no charge for the download) the artist needs to secure a "mechanical" license. That license, which will require the artist to pay 9.1 cents each time the song is downloaded, can be obtained for most songs from the Harry Fox Agency. If HFA does not represent the song, you can ask the publisher for a license directly; even if they do not respond, you can follow the procedures set up in Section 115 of the Copyright Act[227] and pay the 9.1 cents to the publisher pursuant to the statute.

If you would like to allow your fans to simply listen on demand, HFA also offers a license for interactive streams for one cent ($0.01) per stream via the "Songfile" section of their website (http://www.harryfox.com/public/songfile.jsp). Licenses are available for a minimum of 100 and up to 10,000 interactive streams per song licensed[228] and are valid for one year. Unfortunately, even if you obtain this license, you still have to secure a public-performance license. All three US performance rights organizations, or PROs (ASCAP, BMI, and SESAC), offer website licenses, and each charges a small percentage of income or a small minimum yearly fee. For rates, see the next section on music websites. In order to license just one or two songs, it may be more efficient to approach the publishers of those songs directly for both the mechanical and public-performance licenses. Although most leading publishers authorize HFA to license mechanical rights and the PROs to license public-performance rights, they also reserve the right to make such deals directly.

Video Covers

If you are an artist or band who decides to make a video of a third-party song and show it on your website, you must acquire a sync license even if you show the video for free. The cost will depend on the identity of the song and the publisher, as well as a series of other factors, including how long (i.e., how many months or years) you wish to use the video and whether you want to make it available for downloading. To give you some idea of the general cost, I have negotiated these kinds of licenses for $500 for one year. But keep in mind that a publisher can always deny permission and does not have to give a reason. Uploading "cover videos" to YouTube has been made much more efficient than securing a sync license yourself. See "Audiovisual Covers" in Chapter 11.

Music Websites and Blogs

How to Avoid Clearance Issues Altogether

I acted as the attorney for a major music blog/website that wanted to develop the "TV" section of the site. We developed an agreement geared toward unsigned rock bands who wrote their own songs. We would shoot the band performing a series of songs—usually in a studio or on a rooftop in Brooklyn. Under the agreement that we presented to them, we would acquire promotional rights to play the footage on our site. In return, the band received the right to use one song on their website, YouTube, or any other social media. However, we always advised the band that we would only record performances of songs that they or someone in the band had written, and our agreements with the band, which each member would sign, stated that they gave us permission to use the songs; thus we avoided the need to acquire PRO licenses.

Music Websites

For websites that do not produce their own recordings and do not license the songs directly from songwriters, the music clearance issues that arise will depend on the nature of each site, the identity of the songs and masters the site wishes to use, and the particular uses the website makes of music. For instance, download stores will require licenses from the labels for their masters and mechanical licenses for each song. Interactive streaming sites and apps will require licenses from the labels: public-performance licenses to play the songs and special mechanical licenses designed just for interactive streaming and temporary downloading. Finally, Internet radio sites and apps will require special SoundExchange licenses for masters as well as public-performance licenses to perform songs. All of these licenses are explained in detail in Part I, in the chapters on downloading, interactive streaming, and webcasting.

Music Blogs: A "Gray" Area of Law

Many music blogs actively use music by artists and writers who already have label and publishing deals. Many of these blogs operate in a legal gray area. If they only offered streams of brief excerpts, commented on the songs, and invited readers to comment in turn, they would be doing exactly what the fair-use doctrine was designed to protect (see Chapter 1). However, music blogs often offer free permanent downloads. Occasionally, marketing personnel at record companies will encourage the blogs to offer the free downloads in hopes of creating a "buzz" for new songs. There have been instances where the lawyers at these companies don't know that the marketing people have provided the music and will ask the RIAA to send them a cease-and-desist order. [229]

But many MP3 blogs post copyrighted material as a free download without permission. Although this is illegal, record companies often turn a blind eye. Other blogs will offer free streaming with links to iTunes and other authorized stores where readers can buy the track (along with other tracks) by the same artist. Again, the labels may not go after these blogs because the blogs are helping them sell downloads. Music publishers, whose copyrights are also involved, may not have the time and resources to go after these sites, either.

Simulcasting

Some venues, such as Smalls Jazz Club in NYC, simulcast live music at the venue on the Internet so that people who can't attend the show in person can still see and hear the show (see my interview with Spike Wilner, owner of Smalls Jazz Club, in Chapter 27). Smalls simulcasts a video feed of performances at the club seven days a week. Even though the simulcast is audiovisual, a sync license is not required because the simulcast is live and there is no "fixation" of any song to a visual image. However, two different kinds of public-performance licenses are required—one for the live performances in the club, and one for the Internet simulcast. Smalls has licenses from all three PROs for both kinds of public performances, explained in more detail below.

Public-Performance Licenses

Live Performance: The fee for an ASCAP license for "Restaurants, Bars, Nightclubs, and Similar Establishments" is based on a number of factors, including seating capacity, whether there is an admission charge, and the number of nights the club features live music. BMI and SESAC's club licenses are similar. All three PROs have a minimum of several hundred dollars.

Internet Simulcast: All three PROs also offer a license for simulcasting. ASCAP's rate is the greater of 1.85 percent of gross income from the site, including advertising and subscription or an amount determined by a formula based on the number of visits to the site by all users. The minimum license fee is $288 per year (note that this is cheaper than ASCAP's "Agreement for Interactive Services," which is the greater of 3 percent or a formula based on usage and a minimum of $340). BMI's rate is 1.75 percent with a minimum of $342. SESAC's rate is .061 percent and the minimum is $242 for six months.

Live Streaming Services

Some people use services such as Livestream or Ustream to simulcast their own performances or shows. They don't have the resources to webcast from their own websites because broadband costs money. Instead, they upload their simulcasts to services such as these. However, you can't necessarily count on these services to do music clearances for you. For example, Ustream warns in its user agreement:

> 4. Copyrighted Materials: No Unauthorized Use.
>
> You will not use the site or services to transmit, route, provide connections to or store any material that infringes copyrighted works or otherwise violates or promotes the violation of the intellectual property rights of any third party.

So, if you use these services and want to comply with the strict letter of the law, and with the sites' user agreements, the solution is easy—sign or perform only songs that you or your band have written.

Webisodes and Web Series

Indie vs. Well-Funded

Depending on how one uses the word, "webisode" could refer to a network or cable TV show that is also available on demand at Hulu, Amazon Prime, Netflix, Google Play, or some other Internet VOD service. It also may refer to programs, short segments, and promos produced in conjunction with an existing television series, or it might refer to a series, such as Netflix's *House of Cards*, that was as expensive to produce as any typical network or HBO dramatic series.

But for the purposes of this section, we are focusing on indie content distributed exclusively through the Internet. These exclusively web-based shows and series are becoming an increasingly popular way for producers, directors, writers, and actors to gain experience, hone their skills, get some attention, and even, occasionally, make money. In fact, some shows now on broadcast and cable TV started as webisodes. For example, when he was only 15 years old Lucas Cruikshank introduced his "Fred" character, a 6-year-old boy with a high voice, a dysfunctional home life, and some "anger management" issues. The series and the character became so popular that it led to *Fred: The Movie*, which aired on Nickelodeon in 2010. Nickelodeon subsequently produced a sequel, *Fred 2: Night of the Living Fred* in 2011. In 2012 Nick aired 24 episodes of *Fred: The Show*, as well as a third movie, *Fred 3: Camp Fred*. Another example is *Childrens Hospital*, a satirical comedy that lampoons medical drama shows, created by and starring actor/comedian Rob Corddry. The series began on the web with 10 episodes, roughly five minutes in length, all of which premiered in 2008.[230] Adult Swim picked up the rights to the show in 2009 and began airing episodes in 2010.

Although a webisode may appear on a stand-alone website, producers who may only be kids like Cruikshank, or who are working with tight budgets, usually try to avoid bandwidth costs and seek a broader audience by using YouTube or sometimes some other website such as Hulu. For instance, *Dorm Life*, a mockumentary web series created by former UCLA students about the fictional lives of students in a dorm, is one of Hulu's most popular web shows.

Clearing Music for Indie Webisodes and Web Series

With regard to music clearances, platforms such as YouTube and Hulu do have blanket licenses that would cover the public performance of any songs in the shows—but those licenses do not apply to the synchronization of the songs with a visual image, and they do not cover the use of any prerecorded tracks. So, basically, the same business practices that apply to securing sync and master-use licenses for TV shows (discussed in Chapter 10) would apply. The only difference is that generally the producer of a TV show, who may be backed by financing from a network or cable service, will usually seek "buyouts" for all media so that the TV show may be aired in any medium (including the Internet and home video) without having to re-clear the music. If the producer of a webisode or web series limits his or her request to airing the show only on the web, or, even better, on only one platform such as YouTube, he or she will probably be able to secure rights in a song or master, as the case may be, for a fraction of the price that a buyout would cost.

However, even a few hundred dollars may be too much for a web producer on a tight budget. These producers may be well-advised to think about using "catalogue" or library music. As I discussed with Adam Taylor, president of APM Music, in Chapter 1, music libraries license pre-cleared music for very low rates. There are large libraries, such as APM, that handle almost every conceivable genre of music, and smaller libraries that specialize in certain niche areas such as Latin jazz or heavy metal. Many major TV services and motion-picture studios, as well as individual producers, depend heavily on these music catalogues for many of their shows. This is because even network and Hollywood studio budgets are not unlimited. They may include several hits by major artists and use library music to fill out the rest of the show. Of course, none of this music will be instantly recognizable like a hit song. But many of the libraries and music reps will work closely with producers to find the music that best suits their project and most resembles the mood that the producer wants to conjure up.

Crowdfunding Video Promos

Rates and Terms

I represented a filmmaker who wished to use Kickstarter to raise funds for a movie about the history of punk rock music in Washington, DC. To initiate the campaign, as with practically any crowdfunding campaign, the producer needed to make a video about the project. He asked a local band with whom he was friends with to record a punk song associated with the city. The band agreed to allow him to use the recording gratis in the Kickstarter promo, but they hadn't written the song. So the producer hired me to clear the song for the promo. This is the relevant portion of the letter that I prepared to clear the song:

> I am writing today on behalf of a producer wishing to raise funds on Kickstarter for a documentary to be called "__________" (the "Film"). The doc, as the title suggests, is about the punk music scene in Washington, DC, in the early '70s. As you know, Kickstarter campaigns require a video teaser ("Teaser"). My client would like to use some footage that he shot of a local band performing "_______" by ________ (the "Song"). BMI indicates that your company is the publisher. The entire teaser video will be approximately five minutes. The producer would like to use approximately 45 seconds of the Song in the Teaser.
>
> The goal for the campaign, which represents our sole source of financing, is $50,000. All of the funds raised will be used for the production of the Film. We would like to offer you $500 for the sync rights for the use of the Song in the Teaser. The duration of the Kickstarter campaign is four to five weeks starting early April, 2014.

The publisher confirmed that the $500 was acceptable on an "MFN" basis; that is, with the understanding that we did not pay more money for any other song in the teaser.

Internet PSAs

Rates and Terms

I've cleared music for two different Internet-only public service announcements. One was for a nonprofit group that provided shelter for homeless dogs in Seattle. In that case, I was able to secure a gratis license of a then current radio hit. Presumably the band who both wrote and recorded the song wanted to be associated with a good cause.

In another case, an affluent county in Ohio wished to use a well-known pop song to promote its business-friendly reputation. We were able to secure rights in the song and the master for a very reasonable price by limiting the use to the county's own website. The price would have gone up and the request might even have been declined had the county wanted to use the PSA on social media.

Music-Based Mobile Apps

Introduction

After publishing the first edition of this book in 2005, I started working with clients who were launching digital start-ups involving music and video. But "apps" did not even exist. Now, there are over 1 million apps on the iPhone App Store alone, and approximately as many on Android phones.

Since Apple launched the iTunes App Store in 2008 the app business has exploded. In just a few short years, apps have transformed interaction with mobile devices and have generated many successful businesses.[231] The following is a list of the total number of apps available in the App Store at given dates up to 2014.[232] The list is based on Apple announcements and the numbers are approximate:

June 2014: 1,200,000
June 2013: 900,000
June 2012: 650,000
June 2011: 425,000
June 2010: 225,000
July 2009: 65,000
July 2008: 800

As of June 2014, there were approximately 1,254,000 apps available on Android phones.[233] Tens of thousands of new apps roll out every month on both IOS (Apple) and Android systems. A report by the Gartner Group research firm found that by the end of 2013, mobile app downloads reached 102 billion, up from 64 billion in 2012, and total revenue in 2013 was $26 billion, up from $18 billion in 2012.[234] Gartner predicted that downloads of all apps would increase to 138 billion in 2014, 179 billion in 2015, 224 billion in 2016, and 268 billion in 2017.[235] Free, ad-supported apps currently account for approximately 91 percent of total downloads.[236] Apple takes 30 percent of all revenue generated from apps in its App Store, including ad- and fee-based apps, and 70 percent goes to the app publisher.[237]

Music-based apps are among the most popular apps on IOS or Android systems, including Internet radio (e.g., Pandora), interactive music streaming (e.g., Spotify), music recognition (e.g., Shazam), and a mind-numbing variety of free and paid apps featuring everything from music for the deaf (think vibrations) to music-based games, music concerts (e.g., Qello, Songkicks), and ringtone makers, to apps that let you listen to and/or watch music videos from YouTube or Vimeo, as well making unlimited playlists. Some of the apps falling into the last category are absolutely free (e.g., Music Tube) and others have a small price of a dollar or two (e.g., Instatube).

Major-Label Blanket Licenses Are Expensive

The clearance issues that arise in connection with music-based apps depend on the way each such app uses music. However, any app seeking a blanket license to use commercially popular music should recognize that it's like shopping at Tiffany's: a fat wallet or a deep line of credit is required.

I recently worked with a client developing a free phone and SMS texting service. The client wished to use contemporary commercially successful music as part of the service to differentiate it from similar apps. The vast majority of commercially successful songs are either owned or distributed by the three major record labels, Warner, Sony, and Universal, or their affiliates. So we solicited quotes from each of those companies. Before hiring me to set up meetings with the majors and negotiate deals, the client had spent a great deal of time, effort, and money to develop the app.

We met with digital music business development executives at each label. Each one was impressed with the app, which was produced by a leading developer. After waiting several weeks, we received two offers. Below are the summaries of the offers:

MAJOR LABEL 1:

Term: One (1) year.

Territory: US only.[238]

Advance: $50,000 advance payable on signing.

Minimum Guarantee[239]: $250,000 for one year to be paid as follows: Q2: $50,000; Q3: $75,000; Q4: $125,000. The Advance counts towards the Minimum Guarantee.

Royalty: (i) 70 percent of gross price of downloads of the label's masters; plus (ii) 70 percent of any of any other gross revenues such as advertising and subscription income, prorated by the number of the label's masters divided by all the masters used in the App.

Publishing: The Label will pay for required mechanical payments to publishers of songs contained in the masters.[240]

MAJOR LABEL 2:

Term: One (1) year.

Territory: US only.

Advance $350,000 advance payable upon execution.

Additional $20,000 "content prep fee" also payable upon execution.

Subject to Label's agreement to extend the Term, additional advances of $30,000 would be due at the beginning of each month.

Royalty: The greater of 50 percent of retail price of each master or $1.00 per master.

Publishing: App must pay mechanicals or any other payment due for use of underlying songs in each master.

Presumably, these offers included a blanket license to use any track released by the labels, since that is what we discussed at our meetings with the digital business development executives. However, neither written offer made it clear what tracks the labels would actually deliver.

My client had invested approximately half a million dollars in developing the app and did not have another half a million plus to pay two major labels, let alone to pay additional advances and/or guarantees to the third major.[241] So the app launched without major label music.

Instead, the service used tones provided by a catalogue company and paid a few dollars for each tone. In addition, they acquired a license to use thousands of songs from a leading music library. The library deal was no money up front and 45 percent of revenues associated with the library's tracks. The moral of this story is that, as Richards and Jagger famously wrote, "No, you can't always get what you want; but if you try sometime, you just might find you get what you need." In all seriousness, though, the major labels' strategy for digital licensing continues to be to cooperate only with major companies such as Apple, Google, and Amazon. They don't have an interest in dealing with start-ups unless they can secure large advances or guarantees.

Online Lyrics Sites

There has been a lot of controversy about sites, and now apps, that provide access to song lyrics. These sites provide all of the lyrics of a song to music fans who may want to get the words to their favorite songs, find a word that Bob Dylan may have slurred, or figure out what their favorite rapper is actually saying. The National Music Publishers Association (NMPA), a trade association for the American music publishing industry and the lobbying and legislative arm of the Harry Fox Agency, claims that more than 5 million searches for "lyrics" occur every day on Google and that more than 50 percent of lyric page views are on unlicensed sites.[242]

Why Permission Is Required

Copyright owners enjoy these exclusive rights, among others:

(1) the right to reproduce the copyrighted work in copies or phonorecords; and
(2) the right to prepare derivative works based upon the copyrighted work

Making copies of the lyrics of a song would seem to violate both of these rights. Making a copy of the words would be equal to making a copy of at least a substantial portion of any non-instrumental song. Although this is not copying the complete song (as sheet music does), it is acknowledged to be copying a substantial portion of the song. "Substantial similarity" is the test for copyright infringement. That is, if the new work is substantially similar to the original, the new work violates the copyright in the original. In addition, copyrighting only the words would seem to be a derivative work. That term is defined in Section 101 of the Copyright Act as follows:

> A "derivative work" is a work based upon one or more preexisting works, such as a translation, musical arrangement, dramatization, fictionalization, motion picture version, sound recording, art reproduction, abridgment, condensation, or any other form in which a work may be recast, transformed, or adapted.

Some would argue that lyric sites should not have to ask permission because they are providing a service for fans who wish to know more about songs by their favorite artists, and that even if the sites are not paying the songwriters or publishers, they are promoting interest in the songs that could lead to royalties from additional record sales. Most copyright owners would disagree. NMPA has expressed appreciation that fans get to know more about songs from these sites and apps, but it also points out that most of these sites include paid advertising, and that its members—the publishers and writers—are not receiving any part of this income.

NMPA sent takedown notices to the top 50 sites hosting song lyrics without a license in November of 2013.[243] NMPA president and CEO David Israelite stated: "This is not a campaign against personal blogs, fan sites, or the many websites that provide lyrics legally. NMPA is targeting 50 sites that engage in blatant illegal behavior, which significantly impacts songwriters' ability to make a living."[244] In May 2014, the NMPA announced that it has filed lawsuits against SeekLyrics.com and LyricsTime.com, two unlicensed lyric sites that it says have refused to license or remove infringing content.[245]

Rap Genius and the Fair-Use Argument

Rap Genius, one of the 50 sites listed in the NMPA's initial takedown notice, differs slightly from most lyrics sites in that it is built to allow and encourage line-by-line annotation from its online community. Cofounder Ilan Zechory issued the following statement after receiving the NMPA's initial takedown notice:

> We can't wait to have a conversation with them about how all writers can participate in and benefit from the Rap Genius knowledge project. Rap Genius is so much more than a lyrics site! The lyrics sites the NMPA refers to simply display song lyrics, while Rap Genius has crowdsourced annotations that give context to all the lyrics line by line, and tens of thousands of verified annotations directly from writers and performers. These layers of context and meaning transform a static, flat lyric page into an interactive, vibrant art experience created by a community of volunteer scholars.[246]

Although Zechory seemed confident that his site is unique because the annotations "give context" to the lyrics, the problem remains that the original lyrics still appear. Outside of the user's ability to scroll over the lyrics and see annotations from artists or fans, the lyrics appear unchanged in any other sense. Therefore it was not surprising that less than a week after Rap Genius was hit with the takedown notice, it "[began] the expensive process of doing it all legal, securing a licensing agreement with Sony/ATV Music Publishing, who have over 30 percent of the global song rights share."[247] By January 2014, Rap Genius had also secured a license agreement with Universal Music Publishing and was negotiating with other publishers.[248]

How to Acquire a License

After issuing the takedown requests, which were a precursor to filing the two copyright infringement lawsuits, David Israelite announced that the NMPA wants to facilitate licensing deals rather than shut them down: "We simply want those that are making money off lyrics to be business partners with the songwriters who created the content that is the basis of the sites."[249] The Harry Fox Agency will grant lyric licenses on a case-by-case basis through their business development department. Also, the publishers have authorized two companies, LyricFind and MusiXmatch, to be "aggregators." According to Israelite,

> Most lyric sites choose to go through lyric licensing aggregators LyricFind or MusiXmatch. These are free market negotiations—there is not a statutory rate or consent decree process that governs the negotiation. We have been told by both LyricFind and MusiXmatch that most of their agreements with lyric sites require the sites to pay on a per-page-view basis (usually a fraction of a penny per page view) or a percentage of revenue.[250]

Digital Sheet Music

I have had a couple of clients who operated instructional music websites—one taught piano, and another taught guitar. Both offered specialized instruction in these instruments online, and both sought to secure rights to offer downloads of digital sheet music that subscribers could use in connection with their lessons. Unlike lyric sites, these clients desired the music notation in addition to the words of the songs.

Rates and Terms

Physical sheet music was, a very long time ago, the heart of music publishing. Now it is only a small part of the business; many commercially successful publishers have farmed it out to companies that specialize in publishing and distributing paper sheet music. But as the rest of the music business has shifted to digital media, so too has sheet music. Many leading publishers, but not all, have authorized the same physical sheet music companies to sell or authorize others to sell digital sheet music. I approached one of these companies on behalf of the piano teacher, who had given me a list of 16 songs. The company agreed to license 12 of the songs on these terms: advance of $100 per song against a royalty of 25 percent of the retail selling price. With respect to the four other songs, they told me that I had to approach the publishers of two of the songs directly, and that the other two songs were declined. They didn't give a reason for the rejections. The takeaway, besides considering the financial terms for the songs that were approved, is that if you would like to sell digital sheet music, you may not be able to get everything you want from one company, and there are some songs you may not be able to get at all.

Ringtones and Ringbacks (Ain't What They Used to Be)

The first thing to know about ringtones and ringbacks is that they have dramatically declined in popularity and the income generated from sales has plummeted. This graphic from the RIAA shows their fall:

The chart "Product Types: Ringtones and Ringbacks" shows income from sales of ringtones and ringbacks[251] in the US from 2005 to 2013. At their height in 2007, income from sales of ringtones and ringbacks exceeded 1 billion dollars in the US alone. Worldwide income was over 4 billion dollars.[252] By 2013, income from sales in the US had sunk to only 97 million dollars. The popularity of ringtones and ringbacks has dropped in the rest of the world as well.[253] There are two principal reasons for this decline: (i) similar to disco, ringtones and ringbacks simply fell out of fashion, and (ii) audio-editing software emerged that makes it easy to create ringtones from songs that users have already downloaded (whether done legally or not).

The decline of ringtones has hurt both the recording industry, which licensed their masters, and the music publishing business, which made money from mechanical royalties from the use of their songs. However, since the ringtone and ringback business is still nearly a hundred-million-dollar business in the US, it is still worth knowing what the standard business terms and practices are.

Licensing the Masters

Although the business has tanked, major labels and indie labels will still license the right to sell ringtones if you ask them. Generally, the record companies ask for 40 to 50 percent of gross revenues with a floor price of 50 cents to a dollar per sale. Of the money that record companies receive from ringtone revenues, they are responsible for any payment due to the artist.

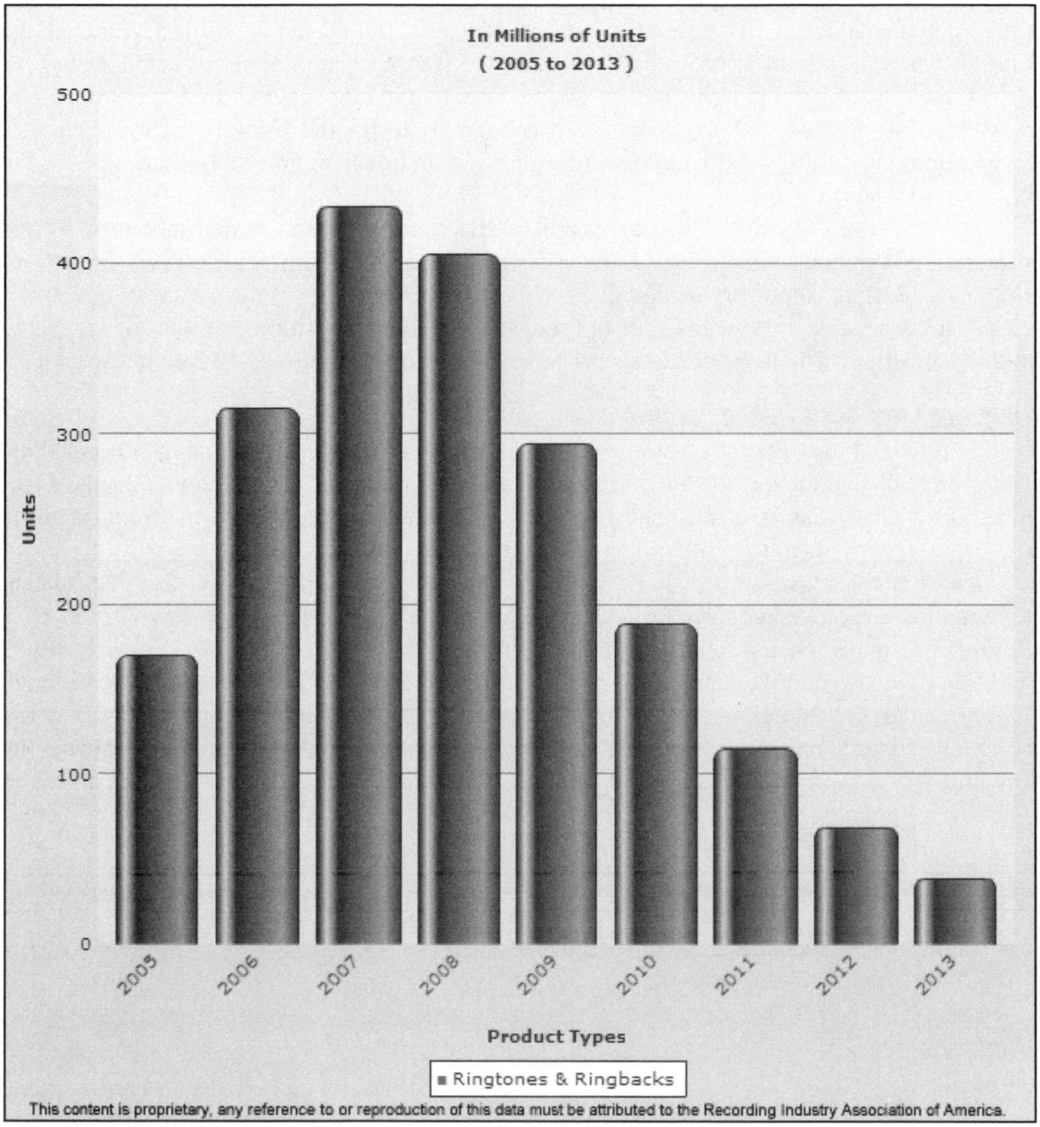

Compulsory Licensing for Songs

At the height of ringtones' success, the carriers would try to make the record companies responsible for clearing and paying the publishers. That led to a great deal of bickering between labels and publishers regarding what percentage of income should go to the publishers. Usually the publishers ended up with approximately 10 percent. After several years of continuous negotiation between the labels on one side and the music publishers on the other, the labels petitioned the Copyright Office to determine whether ringtones were subject to Section 115. In October 2006, the Copyright Office (*In the Matter of Mechanical and Digital Phonorecord Delivery Rate Adjustment Proceeding, Docket No. RF 2006-1*) concluded that the sale of ringtones did fall within the definition of "digital phonorecord delivery" (DPD) in Section 115. Although the rate for a normal sale of a record under Section 115 was 9.1 cents, in her decision, Marybeth Peters, the register of copyrights at that time, did not fix the rate for ringtones at the same rate as downloads. Instead, she concluded, "[I]t is appropriate for the Copyright Royalty Judges to determine royalties to be payable for the making and distribution of ringtones under the compulsory license."

In 2008, the Copyright Royalty Board (CRB), a three-person panel appointed by the Librarian of Congress whose function is to set rates under the Copyright Act, set the rate for ringtones under a compulsory license at 24 cents per ringtone sold—almost three times the statutory rate applicable to downloads of full songs. The music publishing community was elated at this outcome.[254] The licensee can secure a license at this rate from the Harry Fox Agency.

Ringtones Are Not a Public Performance

Until the federal district court that oversees rates set by ASCAP (the "rate court") decided the matter in 2009 and the Second Circuit affirmed *United States v. ASCAP* (2nd Cir. 2010), it was not entirely clear whether publishers were entitled to a public-performance fee from ringtones as well as a mechanical royalty. Both courts decided that they are not.

As we just discussed, the sale of ringtones already requires the seller to pay mechanical royalties to the publisher. But ASCAP claimed that when a ringtone is downloaded by a customer or plays when a mobile phone rings, this constitutes a public performance and an additional license and payment are required. Judge Denise Cote of the rate court disagreed. She ruled that the sale of a ringtone did not implicate a public performance under US copyright law. Judge Cote reasoned that a ringtone purchaser does not actually hear a ringtone when he or she pays and downloads it. In other words, a *data* download isn't a performance. She also concluded that because the transmission is sent to a single individual, by definition, it's not public. But what about when the phone rings and music is heard? The judge wrote, "Customers do not play ringtones with any expectation of profit. The playing of a ringtone by any . . . customer in public is thus exempt under 17 U.S.C. § 110(4)[255] and does not require them to obtain a public-performance license." The Second Circuit subsequently upheld the district court's decision.

Video Games

The worldwide video game marketplace, which includes video game console hardware and software, online, mobile, and PC games, reached $93 billion in 2013, up from $79 billion in 2012, according to Gartner, Inc. Driven by strong mobile gaming and video game console and software sales, the market is forecast to reach $111 billion by 2015.[256]

Music and sound effects have always played an important part in the success of the video game industry. For instance, for many years video games have incorporated music in the background, over the credits, or at certain points in the action of the game. But much of this material is composed in house or outsourced on a work-for-hire basis. Certain games such as *Grand Theft Auto* have and continue to feature prerecorded music and often songs by emerging artists as well as more established talent. Unfortunately for big labels and superstar artists, music-based games such as *Guitar Hero* and *Rock Band* have faded in popularity.[257]

Licensing Parameters

Fees for use of music in video games such as *Grand Theft Auto* that use prerecorded music from both well-known and emerging artists are usually for use in the game only. Fees can start at several thousand dollars and rise from there depending on the popularity of the song or the artist and the budget of the game developer. A "buyout" will allow the game publisher to use the music without paying royalties based on unit sales. Sometimes the licenses will prohibit the copyright owners from licensing the same music in other video games for a period of time, or at least in other video games that fall into the same genre and that directly compete with the licensee's game.

Note that the compulsory-license rate of 9.1 cents per song per copy does not apply to the use of musical compositions in a video game because, as with movies and television, these are audiovisual uses, and the compulsory license applies solely to audio-only uses.

Chapter 14
TIPS AND COMMENTARY

Practical Tips for Clearing Music for Any Project

This interview originally ran in the journal *Entertainment Law & Finance* (ELF) and its content remains applicable today.

ELF: What kinds of projects do you work on?

Steve Gordon (SG): TV, movies, documentaries, compilation albums, DVDs, and Internet-based projects. I recently worked on several interesting jobs in cooperation with Universal Media Inc. [a company specializing in finding footage and music]. These projects included a documentary on Latin jazz for the Smithsonian Institution, a companion record album for Smithsonian Folkways Recordings, a network TV special featuring the music of Elvis Presley, and a PBS special featuring Frank Sinatra's duet performances from his old TV series, to be released as a home video and on foreign TV. Currently, I'm working on an independent movie about a serial murderer who targets punk-rock fans, containing more than two dozen songs and masters. I also represent a publicly traded Internet content provider that is continually securing rights in all kinds of content, including music, videos, and computer games.

ELF: What is the process for securing copyright clearances?

SG: The process is basically the same for any kind of project. Research the songs, strategize with the client, negotiate the terms, and review or, in certain instances, prepare the licenses. In regard to the last item, music publishers and labels will usually provide their own licenses. However, occasionally a small label, publisher, or unsigned artist will request that you draft the license.

With respect to research, the kind of material to be cleared will dictate the nature of the research to be performed. For instance, for musical compositions, the ASCAP and BMI databases are excellent sources for identifying the writers and music publishers. Each of these databases may have to be explored, because each performing-rights organization provides information only on the songs in its own repertory. SESAC also administers certain songs that will not be included on the ASCAP or BMI sites. In addition, the Harry Fox Agency provides information concerning songs that it represents [see www.Songfile.com]. If your client is using musical recordings, the packaging and liner notes can supply information such as the name of the record company and artist and the release date. If the client is using excerpts of TV, movie, or video footage, someone should view the credits from the original TV program, movie, or music video to determine the TV service, studio, or record label that controls the copyright in the footage. The musical artists, actors, and other persons (or their estates) appearing in the footage may also have to be cleared depending on various circumstances, including whether there is a musical performance in the footage.

Once you have identified those who control rights in the material to be used, you are almost ready to approach the owners and negotiate terms. But first you must strategize with the client. This conversation should include what rights will be required, that is, media, territory, duration; what you think it will cost; and what to propose to the licensors. This process is the real "art" of licensing. With knowledge of the applicable business practices and pricing, you can advise your client on the approximate amount of money he or she will have to pay for clearances; alert him or her to potential problems, such as material that may be too expensive and may have to be replaced; and develop a letter addressed to the owners accurately reflecting the precise rights that your client needs and proposing the lowest reasonable fee or royalty. The proposed payment, which obviously must be approved by the client, should be as low as possible and include a cogent explanation of the reasons that the owner should accept such a rate. At the same time, the proposal should not be so out of whack with standard business practices that the owner feels insulted.

The negotiation process involves a discussion with the copyright owner or its representative about the project, plus continual follow-up. Many of the projects on which I work will not make a great deal of money for any individual copyright owner. For that reason, many of these requests usually are low-priority items to the people from whom I am seeking permission. To do this work, therefore, a combination of courtesy and persistence is recommended.

Ultimately, if the licensor doesn't accept your terms, you will have to negotiate compromises or even advise the client to drop the desired music. For instance, trying to get a hit song for an independent movie may not happen, because the song owner may not like your client's project, or may not wish to license it to anyone at any price, or may propose a fee well beyond your client's ability to pay.

Finally, the owner will send the license, and it is my responsibility to make sure that the terms in the license exactly match the understanding between my client and the owner.

ELF: What issues arise specifically in the case of independent movies?

SG: From a clearance point of view, the most important difference between an independent film and a major studio production is that an independent producer usually has a lot less money to spend on anything, including music. Therefore, an independent filmmaker may have to curb his or her desire for securing "name-brand" talent. For instance, if your client wants to use "Satisfaction" under the opening credits, that is going to cost big bucks indeed, unless he or she happens to be a personal friend of Mick Jagger, and even then, don't assume a huge discount.

Even if Mick Jagger is your client's best friend, the people who administer the Stones' copyrights may never have heard of your client. Music publishers and labels generally will adjust their rates downward based on the size of a movie's budget. But don't expect to pay a nominal fee for a hit song just because your client's budget is modest. Independent film producers should also understand that no matter how popular or recognizable the music in a movie is, people don't watch movies to listen to music. A lawyer or clearance person can work with a savvy producer to create a great soundtrack without busting the budget. For instance, many music publishers, labels, and managers may be eager to place new songs written by "baby bands" that will be more reasonably priced than songs written by established acts. Another alternative is a "stock" music house. Generally, these firms can license both the song and the master, and therefore offer one-stop shopping as well as low prices. Finally, a composer or songwriter/producer can be hired to write music for specific scenes, or a complete score. There are many talented but hungry songwriters who would be happy to work on a client's project for a credit and a reasonable fee.

Another way to work within a client's budget is to set up the quote request as a series of options. Generally, a film festival license can be secured for a small fee, because music publishers and labels recognize that festivals are not commercial enterprises. Additional rights, such as theatrical, free TV, cable, and home video, can be requested as options. Each one may be exercised by paying a specific fee. "Broad rights"—which include theatrical, TV, and home video—can be expensive. In case your client does not succeed in securing commercial theatrical distribution, these options will allow him or her to gain exposure for the movie (on cable TV, for instance) for a reasonable fee without paying for unnecessary rights.

ELF: Please describe the deal points (e.g., term, territory, royalties, or fees).

SG: The term will vary depending on the nature of the project. Of course, you always would like to secure perpetual rights for your client. But that may not always be possible. For instance, in regard to a TV project, music publishers and labels will customarily limit the term to three to five years. A longer period will cost a lot more money. One way to accommodate future uses is, again, to set up options. The original term can be three years, with an option for another three. That way, your client doesn't have to pay the additional fees unless he or she actually exploits the program for a longer term. Movie and TV producers will generally seek worldwide to maximize the audience for, and income from, their projects. Producers of album compilations, on the other hand, may wish to target the North American market only. So the scope of the territory provision will depend on the business interests of your client.

Of course, the most important item in virtually all clearance licenses will be the money. Generally, flat fees will be required for TV and movies, because that is the standard business practice. On the other hand, if you license a song or master for an album or a home video, you can expect to pay a penny rate per unit. How much you pay will depend primarily on the nature of the project. In regard to a compilation album, although there are exceptions, the owner of the track (generally a record company) will require a per-unit penny rate against an advance. If the penny rate is 10 cents, then an advance payment of $1,000 may be required, with a "rollover" payment of another $1,000 for sales exceeding 10,000, and additional rollover payments after that for each block of 10,000 units. The underlying song will be subject to a statutory mechanical license, currently 8 cents per unit [Author's note: the rate is now 9.21 cents], although it may be possible to secure reductions from such rate in certain circumstances (if a charitable purpose is involved, for example). Clearing music for a motion picture is a whole different ball game, because there is no compulsory license for use of musical compositions in audiovisual works. The money demanded for even a never-quite-famous song can easily reach six figures for a movie to be distributed by a major studio. The owner of the master, usually the record company, probably will want at least an equal amount for the master recording.

ELF: What is meant by the phrase "most favored nation"?

SG: Also referred to as "MFN," this is a business practice that can affect all the terms of a license. It means that you cannot treat the owner or licensor of content less well than any other owner or licensor of content used in a similar manner. The practice is very common in regard to concert TV programs featuring a dozen full-length musical performances. No one who licenses any song for such a program wants to get less money or give more rights than any other licensor. MFN also plays a big role in audio compilation albums. It exists but is less common in regard to clearing music for movies, because in a movie each piece of music is often used in a different way. For instance, one song may be used over the credits, another song may be used for only a few moments in the background of a scene, and another song may be heard as a theme throughout the movie.

ELF: What are some reasons that a copyright clearance cannot be secured?

SG: Money is the most common reason. In regard to a movie, although some baby bands, composers, or songwriters may love the exposure that your client can create, established artists and bands may not need the exposure. They already have it. Therefore, the price can be prohibitively high. To give a recent example from my own practice, we could not get the price of a Bee Gees song down for an independent movie. So we replaced it with a new song composed by my client. Another problem is that the copyright owner, or his or her representative, may not wish to be associated with your client's project for whatever reason. I once had a problem with getting permission to use "Macarena" for a Chipmunks video. Apparently, the composers did not relish the idea of their song being performed by cartoon characters.

ELF: What are the possible penalties if copyright clearances are not secured?

SG: Perhaps the worst-case scenario is an injunction, which is available as a remedy for copyright infringement. Your client's project could be shut down completely. If it's yanked out of distribution, not only are potential profits lost, but there also could be serious expenses incurred in retrieving the product from warehouses or retail outlets (as there would be if a DVD were involved). Of course, copyright owners have other remedies available to them, including statutory damages and attorney fees, if they properly registered their works. Therefore, the price of using a copyright without permission can be quite steep indeed.

ELF: What is the role of a music supervisor?

SG: A good music supervisor can identify music that could enhance your client's project. But, due to budget constraints, experienced music supervisors make their living working with big studio productions. When they can be afforded, they have knowledge and contacts that could prove valuable, especially when it comes to finding new, cutting-edge music. The client can't depend on lawyers or clearance people to be his or her "ears." Depending on the budget, therefore, the client may have to be his or her own music supervisor, although a knowledgeable lawyer with good industry contacts can be very helpful.

ELF: What is involved in licensing music for Internet-based projects? How is it or other new technologies an emerging area for clearances?

SG: New technologies, including the Internet, have created new uses for all kinds of content. New business practices and forms of licensing have also emerged. The issues and rules can be quite complex, depending on what you are trying to do (e.g., webcasting, streaming, or downloading) and the kind of content you are trying to clear (interactive games, music, etc.). Perhaps the fastest-growing areas of music licensing are interactive webcasting and video on demand. Already, satellite systems and digital-cable modem services are offering content on demand. Concert specials accommodate themselves beautifully to these new technologies. Eventually, concert videos may also be available on the web on an on-demand basis. Therefore, in addition to clearing a concert special for TV and home video, clearance people will find themselves clearing for on-demand uses. This will entail educating the licensor as to the new technologies and, in the case of webcasting, assuring copyright owners that your client will protect the owners' copyrights with encryption technologies to prevent piracy.

Billboard Commentary: Music Documentary Filmmakers Deserve a Break on Licensing Fees

It's appropriate to end this section of the book with a commentary that I published in *Billboard* on music-based documentaries.[258] Although it is several years old, all the views expressed are ones I still hold today. The commentary explains the value to copyright owners of the work of my clients who produce music-based documentaries, and appeals to copyright owners to consider that value when they issue quotes.

> I believe in copyright and the right of artists and songwriters to make a decent living. But as a lawyer who represents the makers of music documentaries, I also believe that the owners of music copyrights should exercise greater flexibility when dealing with my clients.
>
> Unlike feature films, which license music to enhance scenes, my clients often celebrate the music itself, and usually shoot their documentaries on limited budgets. Examples of recent projects I've worked with include *Big Pun: The Legacy*, a documentary about the first Latin rapper to go platinum; *Let Freedom Sing*, a movie celebrating the music that inspired the civil rights movement; *Punk Attitude*, a survey about the punk era; *And You Don't Stop: 30 Years of Hip-Hop*, a multipart series about the history of hip-hop for VH1; and two documentaries about Elvis Presley for network TV, *Elvis Lives* and *Elvis by the Presleys*.
>
> Because music documentaries can be an effective means of introducing new generations of audiences to legacy artists, labels and publishers should recognize that they're good for business. When I worked at Sony Music, Ken Burns' *Jazz* series on PBS spurred sales of our jazz catalog titles. For *Elvis by the Presleys*, what was then known as Sony BMG released a companion CD because the label recognized the power of the documentary to move the product.
>
> But too often, owners of music copyrights fail to recognize the promotional value of such works, forcing producers of music documentaries to always weigh the value of using as much music as possible against the cost of doing so. Generally, labels and publishers charge less for use of their music in documentaries than

in feature films because they know that documentary budgets are typically much smaller. But greater flexibility is needed.

Complicating matters is the fact that labels and publishers nearly always insist on "most favored nation" treatment, meaning that if the producers pay more money for one song, they must pay that higher amount to the owners of all the other songs in the film. Recently I was clearing the music rights for a documentary on the history of gospel music. Although most of the songs in the program were so old that they were in the public domain and didn't require payment, about a dozen other songs were still protected by copyright. One of them was more widely known than the others, but fortunately the song's owner agreed to license it at a reasonable rate. This was essential to the project because if the owner had asked for more, we would've had to pay the same amount for all the other non-public-domain songs, which would've exceeded our budget.

Under US copyright law, producers of documentaries for PBS or other public broadcasting stations aren't obligated to pay for publishing rights or the use of master recordings for music they use in their works. Instead, PBS, with funding from the Corporation for Public Broadcasting, pays copyright owners the relevant licensing costs.

But this provision of US law doesn't exempt PBS documentary producers from having to pay for the cost of licensing compositions and master recordings when their documentaries are released on DVD or in foreign territories. This is important because PBS stations often like to give away DVDs of music documentaries during pledge drives in return for contributions and filmmakers usually want options to distribute their work on foreign TV or other media to recoup production costs.

As a clearance professional, I always try to get the most reasonable rates and the most expansive rights for my clients' documentaries, even as I remain conscious and respectful of the value of the music as well. Publishers and labels, however, should recognize that these celebrations and histories of their music are great promotional tools and should enable documentary filmmakers to make the best work possible.

PART III

THE RECORDING INDUSTRY IN TRANSITION

A Brief History of Digital Music, Current Status of the Battle Against Unauthorized "Free" Music, and Current Controversies and Trends

Income from sales and licensing of recorded music has dwindled to less than 35 percent of what it was in 1999, accounting for inflation. Part III focuses on the recording industry's struggle to come to grips with the digital era and recover from its precipitous decline. Chapter 15 provides a brief history of how the industry has reacted to new technologies since the original Napster.

Chapter 16 offers an update on its continuing battle against digital piracy, the continuing tension between tech and content, and why the recording industry's most powerful "partners," including both Apple and Google, may be the biggest obstacles to its making a comeback.

Chapters 17 and 18 report on current controversies and developments, and Part III ends on a hopeful notewith a discussion of the possibility of monetizing the greatest potential market in the world,the People's Republic of China.

Chapter 15

A BRIEF HISTORY OF THE RECORDING INDUSTRY'S STRUGGLE WITH DIGITAL MUSIC

Introduction: A Business Affairs Conference at Sony Music in 1999

In his memoir, *Howling at the Moon: The Odyssey of a Monstrous Music Mogul in an Age of Excess*,[259] the former president of CBS Records, Walter Yetnikoff, reported that when he joined the company in the early 1960s as a young staff attorney, the most popular artists on the roster were Mitch Miller and Jerry Vale. Gross sales were only $250 million. When he left in the late 1980s, sales exceeded $2.5 billion. From Elvis to the Beatles, rock 'n' roll captured the public's imagination, then captured their wallets. Superstars, led by Michael Jackson, were selling tens of millions of records. The payoff for a successful album was spectacularly lucrative. For instance, Michael Jackson's *Thriller* sold over 30 million CDs. At approximately $7 wholesale, they made a fortune for Jackson's label, Epic Records. In the '90s, other artists such as Madonna, Mariah Carey, Bruce Springsteen, U2, Pearl Jam, and many others regularly sold almost as many. A business that had consisted of dozens of strong independent companies, such as Atlantic, Motown, Arista, and many other familiar names, was largely gobbled up by a handful of multinational corporations (currently Universal, Warner, and Sony). The accountants and the money men saw cash in the record business and rushed in to reap the profits. What had been a colorful group of music business entrepreneurs such as Ahmet Ertegün and Jerry Wexler (founders of Atlantic, later purchased by Warner), Berry Gordy, Jr. (founder of Motown, purchased by MCA and ultimately by Universal Music), and Clive Davis (founder of Arista, which was acquired by BMG and is now owned by Sony) came under the supervision of the "suits." But the new corporate owners had the good sense to keep most of these music men at the helm of their new properties, and everyone made a lot of money (that is, the executives and those artists who became household names with the help of the labels. Artists who were less successful rarely saw any money beyond their original advances because the labels recouped production and marketing costs from the artists' recording royalties).

But then came Napster. As a young business affairs executive at Sony Music in 1999, I attended an international business affairs conference at the Four Seasons Hotel in New York City. In attendance were about 250 attorneys and business affairs executives from Sony Music's various offices in all parts of the world, including London, Paris, Tokyo, Berlin, and Sydney as well as New York and Los Angeles. There were many presentations, including mock recording-agreement negotiations, updates on new contract provisions, etc. But the last presentation was on something called "Napster." Many of us had not even heard of it. But millions of kids (mostly college students) knew what Napster was and loved it. That presentation was unusual in that it was given by someone from the litigation department (the reason for that will become obvious soon). The first thing that she did was flash the iconic cat-wearing-headphones logo of the original peer-to-peer (P2P) service on a large screen. Then she asked the audience for the name of a song, any song. Someone suggested "Hey Jude" by the Beatles. She typed the words on a keyboard, and up on the screen popped not only the Beatles' version, but every cover of "Hey Jude" ever recorded by any other artist or band.[260] And then the other shoe dropped. She clicked on the Beatles' version, and as it started to play, she told us that anyone could play the song and could download it FOR FREE! That was the first time we heard about "free" music. Then she continued: Not only did you not have to pay, you could burn the song to a blank CD or e-mail it to all your friends. Of course this seems commonplace today, but in 1991 it was big news! The presentation then became truly depressing. She showed us how Sony intended to "compete." She clicked on the Sony music website, found Mariah Carey's home page, clicked through a couple of other screens . . . and finally the titles of two songs came up. You could download these songs, but for $3.99 each! Even if you paid this amount, since the songs were coded with DRM (digital rights management), they would reside on your desktop only. You could not make copies, burn the songs to a CD, or share them with anyone else. It seemed ridiculous compared to Napster. But then the litigator reassured us that Sony and the other majors had started a lawsuit to shut Napster down, and said that our lawyers were confident of success. We all let out a collective sigh of relief. But after the presentation, I recall the head of the legal department saying, "If we don't crush this thing, I'll see you on the unemployment line." He was both right and wrong.

Labels vs. P2P File Trading: Why the Record Industry Supreme Court Victory against Grokster Actually Hurt Its War on Piracy

Sony and its sister major labels did crush Napster. But it really didn't matter. As of 2014, it is clear that though the business won multiple legal battles against digital piracy, it never won the war. They beat Napster in court,[261] but it was soon replaced by other P2P services, including Grokster, Morpheus, and Kazaa. These services were less legally vulnerable than Napster. Ultimately, the legal battle with P2P culminated in a ruling by the Supreme Court that had mixed consequences for the recording industry.[262]

The Legal Battle with Napster

Napster was cofounded by two programming prodigies, Sean Fanning and Sean Parker (the latter also had major roles in developing Facebook and Spotify), in 1999. Napster specialized in MP3 files of music and a user-friendly interface. At its peak, the Napster service had about 80 million registered users.[263] Napster made it easy for music fans to download copies of current hits as well as songs that were otherwise difficult to obtain, including older songs, unreleased recordings, and concert bootleg recordings. In the legal action that followed the rise of Napster's popularity, it was very important that the music traded between Napster's users was stored on Napster's servers.

In 1999, the Recording Industry Association of America (RIAA), which represents all the major labels and most of the large indies, sued Napster and alleged both contributory and vicarious copyright infringement. As publicity around the trial grew, so did Napster; soon millions of users (many of them college students) flocked to it. The Ninth Circuit Court of Appeals in California found that Napster had knowledge of its users' infringing activity and materially contributed to it. The court did not disagree with the trial court's finding that that Napster was in fact overwhelmingly used for acts of infringement (downloading copyrighted songs and masters without permission). But the heart of its analysis was that Napster was able to control, access, or block infringement by end users, but it chose not to. The court found that since the names of songs and masters resided in an index on Napster's server, and gave users the opportunity to research which songs they wished to download, Napster was under a duty to police it.[264] On remand, the district court ordered Napster not to engage or allow users to engage in copying, downloading, uploading, transmitting, or distributing copyrighted sound recordings.[265] Following this injunction, Napster closed down. It reopened about a year later under different management as a legal service. However, it never regained its former popularity and eventually was bought by Best Buy, which merged it into Rhapsody in 2011.

While the record companies were litigating Napster to death, new and even more powerful variations of P2P technology burst onto the scene, typified by services such as Grokster, Morpheus, and later Kazaa. Like Napster, these services allowed people to trade copyrighted music files without paying a cent. Unlike Napster, they proved more resistant to the labels' legal firepower because these services did not control a central database or index where every song was catalogued for users to identify and share with each other. Instead, they simply provided software that allowed users to locate and trade files directly with each other. Unlike Napster, Grokster, Morpheus, and Kazaa,[266] all allowed users to trade their own songs with each other without the assistance of a central database identifying each song.

Once again the record business went to court, and once again the case wound up in the Ninth Circuit. But this time the Ninth Circuit ruled against them, confirming the trial court's decision[267] that the defendants, Grokster and StreamCast (which owned Morpheus), did not violate copyright law ever though many users of these services used them to trade copyrighted music files.[268] And, as we will see, even a reversal of this decision by the United States Supreme Court[269] had at best mixed consequences for the recording industry. When additional digital tools emerged that made it easy to obtain free unauthorized music, the Supreme Court's decision in *Grokster* actually made it more difficult to shut them down.

In the first round of the legal battle with Grokster and Morpheus, a California federal district court ruled that because Grokster and Morpheus (unlike Napster) did not control a central database indexing the identity of each music file,[270] they did not violate copyright law. The court reasoned that since Grokster and Morpheus could not block the trading of copyrighted music files even if they wanted to, these new file-sharing services were lawful. The court relied on the Supreme Court's decision in the *Betamax* case; that is, if a device or service has "commercially significant non-infringing uses" the creators of the distributors of that device cannot be held liable for copyright infringement.[271] Like a videocassette recorder (such as Betamax), the district court reasoned, Grokster and Morpheus simply provided a tool (P2P software) that customers could use to trade legal or public-domain materials as well as copyrighted materials. They could not be held responsible for their customers' illegal activity, since they ultimately had no control over the traded content. The Ninth Circuit affirmed the lower court's ruling on appeal, holding that peer-to-peer software developers were not liable for any copyright infringement committed by users of their products, as long as they had no direct ability to stop the acts.[272]

In October 2004, the plaintiffs in *MGM v. Grokster*, representing virtually every major record company and Hollywood studio, petitioned the US Supreme Court to overturn the Ninth Circuit's ruling. In early December 2004, the Supreme Court announced that it would review the Ninth Circuit's decision. And on June 27, 2005, the Supreme Court ruled against Grokster and its fellow defendant, StreamCast Networks (maker of Morpheus). The Supreme Court found that Grokster and Morpheus violated federal copyright law because they promoted, encouraged, and induced swapping copyrighted songs and movies. Justice David H. Souter wrote for a unanimous Court, stating, "We hold that one who distributes a device with the object of promoting its use to infringe copyright, as shown by the clear expression or other affirmative steps taken to foster infringement, is liable for the resulting acts of infringement by third parties." Unlike in the *Betamax* case, which turned on the commercially significant non-infringing uses of a device, the Supreme Court in *Grokster* ruled that P2P firms could be held responsible for infringement if they are marketing their products toward infringement. Souter wrote, "There is substantial evidence in MGM's favor on all elements of inducement." Following the ruling in favor of the plaintiff labels and studios, Grokster almost immediately settled the case and announced that it would no longer offer its peer-to-peer file-sharing service.

Although the decision was a victory for both the MPAA and the RIAA, effectively putting both Grokster and Morpheus out of business, it also confirmed that P2P technology was itself legal—so long as it is not marketed and promoted in such a way that encourages copyright infringement. In fact, the *Grokster* case established that a website or any other technology that allows users to secure free unauthorized copyrighted content may not be liable so long as it does not induce or encourage copyright infringement.

In regard to each defendant in this case, the Supreme Court easily detected a bad actor. The court complained:

> The record is replete with evidence that from the moment Grokster and StreamCast began to distribute their free software, each one clearly voiced the objective that recipients use it to download copyrighted works, and each took active steps to encourage infringement.[273]

The Court pointed to three things that Grokster and StreamCast did that showed the intention of promoting illegal activity. (1) They both advertised their software to former users of Napster and specifically stated that their software could be used to trade copyrighted movies, music, and software programs. The court also pointed to various incriminating internal documents, such as this one written by StreamCast's chief technology officer: "The goal is to get in trouble with the law and get sued. It's the best way to get in the new[s]." (2) They completely failed to attempt to develop filtering tools to diminish infringing activities. (3) They directly profited from illegal use by getting bigger ad fees as their subscriber base increased due to illicit copying.

But it is crucial that Judge Souter stated that without evidence of intentionally "promoting" unlawful activity, Grokster would not have been liable:

> Mere knowledge of infringing potential or of actual infringing uses would not be enough here to subject a distributor to liability . . . The inducement rule, instead, premises liability on purposeful, culpable expression and conduct, and thus does nothing to compromise legitimate commerce or discourage innovation having a lawful purpose."[274]

He hammered the point home in what is now a famous footnote:

> Of course, in the absence of other evidence of intent, a court would be unable to find contributory liability merely based on a failure to take affirmative steps to prevent infringement, if the device otherwise was capable of substantially non-infringing uses. Such a holding would tread too close to the Sony safe harbor.[275]

Therefore, a website that enables P2P does not have to monitor traffic on the site so long as it does not promote, encourage, or induce users to trade unauthorized content. However, a gentleman named Bram Cohen made things even worse by creating an open-source P2P software protocol known as BitTorrent, which he gave to the world for free.[276] BitTorrent is P2P on steroids, because it allows sharing massive files such as movies, as well as songs, faster than any prior P2P technology. Under the Grokster decision the industry can do nothing to shut down the BitTorrent protocol, nor can they shut down a site that simply allows for BitTorrent sharing without encouraging users to share copyrighted files. All they can do is pursue sites, such as Pirate Bay, that encourage users to employ BitTorrent to trade copyrighted files.

Moreover, the Grokster decision gave more legal armor to other technologies, such as software and apps, that can be used to get free unauthorized music but have legal purposes as well. So long as there is a legal purpose and the software or app does not actively encourage or induce users to steal copyrighted contact, there is little the industry can do about them, thanks to the Supreme Court's decision in Grokster.

In the balance of this chapter, we present an overview of the industry's frustratingly disappointing efforts to curb free unauthorized music, including its failed effort to get the electronics business to cooperate in efforts to battle piracy (SDMI); its effort at sabotaging new technology itself (the Rootkit disaster); its lawsuits against music fans who used the P2P services; its lame attempts to compete against the pirates (MusicNet and PressPlay); its giving into Steve Jobs' demand that they allow iTunes to sell singles instead of albums, thereby turning the record business into a singles business whose customers can cherry-pick songs they like without paying for entire albums; and, finally, its attempt to legislate piracy to death (SOPA), which failed because, as we discuss in more detail in Chapter 16, there are very powerful forces—companies much richer and therefore more influential than the record labels—that benefit tremendously from "free" music.

Labels vs. the Consumer Electronics Industry and the Failure of the Secure Digital Music Initiative (SDMI)

This section deals with the labels' failed attempt to place a "digital lock" in computers to stop unauthorized distribution of music. The Secure Digital Music Initiative (SDMI) was a forum that brought together more than 200 companies and organizations representing the major record labels, consumer electronics and computer manufacturers, security technology, information technology, and Internet service providers (ISPs). It started functioning in earnest at the beginning of 1999. According to its website, SDMI's charter was to develop "technology specifications that protect the playing, storing, and distributing of digital music such that a new market for digital music may emerge."[277] The open-technology specifications released by SDMI were supposed to "reflect . . . the legitimate needs of the record labels for security of digital music." The website stated:

> Record companies have identified the lack of a . . . standard for security as the single greatest impediment to the growth of legitimate markets for electronic distribution of copyrighted music. Likewise, technology companies developing computer software, hardware, and consumer electronics devices that will handle new forms of digital music have realized that an important part of these devices is the presence (or absence) of adequate security for electronic music.

Evidently, the electronics companies ultimately preferred the absence of standards, because in 2001, SDMI went out of business. The SDMI website concluded: "Based on all of the factors considered by the SDMI plenary, it was determined that there is not yet consensus for adoption of any combination of the proposed technologies. Accordingly, as of May 18, 2001, SDMI went on permanent hiatus."

What happened? In a nutshell, the content owners could not get the electronics industry to play ball. The labels wanted electronics makers to voluntarily include in their computers and CD burners codes that would prevent transmission and downloading of content that was not authorized by the content providers. Ultimately, this would have made those computers and other devices less appealing to consumers. One of the problems is that the content owners themselves were partially owned by the electronics business. Specifically, Sony Music was owned by one of the world's leading manufacturers of gadgets, including computers, blank optical discs, and all kinds of digital devices to record and copy music. You can imagine how difficult it must have been for the Sony Music executives to strongly advocate for systems that could make their parent company less profitable.

Labels vs. Technology: The Rootkit Disaster

With the failure of the electronics business to cooperate, the labels got desperate enough to try to manipulate technology themselves. In 2005, what was then Sony BMG Music embedded copy protection software in 52 new CD releases. The software included a "rootkit" designed to hide the copy protection so that no one could defuse it, but the rootkit also created holes through which malware, worms, and viruses could enter and attack host computers.[278] When consumers tried to play the CDs on their computers, the rootkit was automatically installed on the Windows desktop, creating security vulnerabilities that led to thousands of PC owners reporting that their computers lost functionality or stopped working completely. Sony BMG reacted by offering a software utility that was meant to remove the rootkit component from affected Microsoft Windows computers, but this removal utility was soon revealed as only exacerbating the security problems, resulting in even more sick or dying PCs. Thousands of parties filed lawsuits against Sony BMG; class actions were commenced in California and New York, the Texas attorney general started a lawsuit, and the Federal Trade Commission started a formal investigation. The company ended up settling all the lawsuits after spending untold millions, recalling all the affected CDs, and never trying to embed code on CDs again. The disaster showed that without the consumer electronics industry's cooperation, the content companies—specifically the record labels—could not shut down free copying and CD burning.

Labels vs. Fans: RIAA's Lawsuits

Shortly after the *Grokster* decision, facing ever steeper declines in CD sales and income, the record industry did the unthinkable: they started suing their own customers. As Cary Sherman of the RIAA said about the industry's dramatic loss in income in the last several years, "You worry more about survival and a little less about popularity."

Among the defendants in the first round of lawsuits were a 12-year-old and a grandmother. The RIAA's suit against the grandmother was eventually dropped when her son-in-law, an attorney, was able to demonstrate that the RIAA had made a mistake: her computer was incapable of downloading or uploading the songs that she had been accused of stealing. In Chapter 10, we will report on the latest group of lawsuits by the RIAA against music file sharers, and we will discuss whether they have achieved the RIAA's goal of reducing unauthorized music file sharing.

Although the labels would love to have made the Internet service providers (ISPs) shut down P2P services such as Pirate Bay, ISPs (which are controlled by companies much bigger than the labels) are immune from liability under the Digital Millennium Copyright Act of 1998 (DMCA). Section 512 of the DMCA provides that ISPs are immune from liability in regard to any content that is transmitted on their service at the direction of their users or for linking users to websites or services that contain infringing content. Therefore, even though the ISPs provide access to sites like Pirate Bay, they are not responsible for their activities. Some believe this is unfair and argue that the ISPs should take down or block such unauthorized services.

Labels Enter the Digital Music Business: MusicNet and Pressplay

When the record companies started hemorrhaging money and litigation failed, they launched their own legal alternatives to the pirates. Warner, EMI, and BMG started MusicNet, and Sony and Universal launched Pressplay. Both were introduced in 2002, and both were miserable failures. They failed because (1) neither allowed the user to download any music; (2) neither allowed customers to transfer the music to any other device; (3) each service offered music only from its label parents (so Pressplay, for example, contained only Sony and Universal music); and (4) even from those catalogues, a lot was missing, either because major artists had not consented or because of restrictions in guest-artist contract and sampling licenses.

Universal and Sony sold Pressplay. MusicNet continues in a different form today, having changed its business model to aid other online music stores in securing licenses to use music from labels. Unfortunately, the labels were not focused on creating the future when they birthed MusicNet and Pressplay. They were too busy trying to kill the future.

Labels Give Away the Store: The Birth of iTunes

When I was a lawyer at Sony Music in the early 2000s, Steve Jobs approached us. He met with the head of the company, Tommy Mottola, and his trusted comptroller, Mel Ilberman. A financial guru and a master of record-business economics, Mel had been with Tommy at Champion

Entertainment before Tommy became chairman of Sony Music. Jobs came in offering a digital music store that would provide greater revenues, on a wholesale basis, than any label had ever received before. Instead of 50 percent wholesale, which was standard, Jobs offered a whopping 70 percent. After their meeting, Ilberman was reported to have said, "That guy is a donkey."

iTunes launched in 2003 to great fanfare, while the labels licked their chops. The problem was that instead of selling albums, iTunes was selling singles. Instead of making $8 wholesale for every CD, the labels made only $0.70 for every $0.99 download. Music fans, it turned out, were much more interested in cherry-picking the songs they liked than in buying complete albums. iTunes became another nail in the coffin of the old record business. Although Jobs has sold over 10 billion songs, income from recorded music has plummeted by more than 50 percent, as reported in the introduction to this book. The replacement of album sales by singles, facilitated by iTunes, only worsened the crisis created by free file sharing. But Jobs made a fortune—not from music, but from devices. Sales of iPods skyrocketed in the mid-2000s. By September 2010, Jobs had sold 275 million iPods. With the introduction of the iPhone, which incorporated the iPod's capacity to play music, his fortunes increased even more spectacularly. By June of 2010, iPhone sales had climbed to almost 60 million since their launch in June of 2007. Although Ilberman was right that Jobs could not make money from selling music, Apple made a fortune from selling the devices that played the music. Perhaps Jobs was not a "donkey" after all.

Recording Industry Pushes Antipiracy Legislation but Tech Industry Pushes Back: The Failure of SOPA

The Stop Online Piracy Act (SOPA) was proposed legislation introduced by US Representative Lamar S. Smith (R-TX) in 2011[279] and backed by the major labels. SOPA was intended to crack down on copyright infringement by restricting access to sites that host or facilitate the trading of copyrighted content. If enacted, SOPA would have would have allowed the US Department of Justice as well as individual copyright owners to seek court orders to stop online ad networks and payment processors from doing business with foreign or domestic websites that "engage in, enable, or facilitate" copyright infringement.[280] The requested court orders could have barred search engines, including Google, from linking to the allegedly infringing sites; ordered ISPs to block subscriber access to sites accused of infringing; and required domain name registrars to take such sites down.[281] The proposed law would also have expanded existing criminal laws to include unauthorized streaming of copyrighted content, imposing a maximum penalty of five years in prison.

Proponents of the legislation, and of the corresponding Senate bill, the PROTECT IP Act (PIPA), including Hollywood movie studios as well as major record labels, said it would not only protect their intellectual property, but also preserve thousands of jobs for people who worked in the record and movie business and whose livelihood was threatened by piracy. They claimed the Act was necessary to bolster enforcement of copyright laws, especially against foreign-owned and -operated websites who could evade US law. But by targeting such powerful players as Google, the credit card companies, and the Internet service providers (such as Verizon, Comcast and AT&T), SOPA made some extremely powerful enemies.

Opponents of the Act, including Google, claimed that SOPA threatened free speech and innovation, and that it would enable law enforcement to block access to entire Internet domains even if the site itself did not encourage copyright infringement and there was minimal trading of unauthorized content. They also expressed concerns that SOPA would bypass the "safe harbor" protections from liability presently afforded to websites by the Digital Millennium Copyright Act (see the previous section, "Labels vs. Fans: RIAA's Lawsuits"). Other opponents declared that requiring search engines to delete domain names violated the First Amendment and could begin a worldwide arms race of unprecedented Internet censorship. The copyright community perceived such arguments as a smokescreen for what they considered the real motive of SOPA's opponents, that is, money. The credit card companies, ISPs, and Google all benefit directly or indirectly from the same websites that SOPA was designed to shut down.

In November 2011, tech behemoths including Google and Facebook lodged a formal complaint letter to lawmakers, saying, "We support the bills' stated goals. Unfortunately, the bills as drafted would expose law-abiding US Internet and technology companies to new uncertain liabilities [and] mandates that would require monitoring of web sites."[282]

On January 18, 2012, Google and Wikipedia, plus an estimated 7,000 other smaller websites, coordinated a service blackout to raise awareness. Other protests against SOPA included petition drives, with Google stating it had collected over 7 million signatures; boycotts of companies and organizations that supported the legislation; and an opposition rally held in New York City. The bills lost some of their congressional backers as a result of the backlash.[283]

In response to the protest actions, the Recording Industry Association of America (RIAA) stated, "It's a dangerous and troubling development when the platforms that serve as gateways to information intentionally skew the facts to incite their users and arm them with misinformation," and "It's very difficult to counter the misinformation when the disseminators also own the platform."[284]

Access to websites of several pro-SOPA organizations, including the RIAA, CBS.com, and others, was impeded or blocked with denial-of-service attacks that started on January 9, 2012. Self-proclaimed members of the "hacktivist" group Anonymous claimed responsibility and stated the attacks were a protest of both SOPA and the United States Department of Justice's shutdown of Megaupload, a popular cyberlocker discussed in the next chapter, on that same day.[285]

On January 20, 2012, House Judiciary Committee Chairman Smith postponed plans to put SOPA to a vote in Congress. This postponement became permanent and SOPA died a lonely death, although the official statement was: "The committee remains committed to finding a solution to the problem of online piracy that protects American intellectual property and innovation . . . The House Judiciary Committee will postpone consideration of the legislation until there is wider agreement on a solution."[286] A "wider agreement on a solution" has yet to happen.

The death of SOPA meant a retreat by the copyright community, including the movie and recording industries, from legislative solutions to piracy. We will see in Chapter 16 that non-legislative solutions have not worked, either, and the frustration with Google, especially by the record industry, remains as high as ever.

Chapter 16

UPDATE ON PIRACY

The Recording Industry's Battle with "Free Music"

Introduction

Since the late '90s, there have been two basic ways that people acquired unauthorized recorded music using digital technology: (1) pirate sites, peer-to-peer file sharing, and, more recently, cyberlockers (also referred to as a file-hosting service or cloud storage service); and (2) private sharing through ripping, burning, instant messaging, e-mailing music files, and USB and hard drive sharing. However, in the last several years, a horde of software programs and apps have emerged that facilitate unauthorized music consumption on both PCs and smartphones. These programs and apps are perhaps the most insidious threat to any possible comeback that the recording industry could make for two reasons: (a) many of these programs and apps are potentially legal; and (b) many of them are making unauthorized listening and downloading available on mobile phones, opening an entirely new front in the battle against free unauthorized music. In fact, piracy on mobile phones is one of the greatest obstacles to growing subscription-based services such as Rhapsody or Spotify Premium.

On top of all this, the industry's digital "partners," such as Google (which owns YouTube, Google Play, and now Songza), and even Apple (which owns iTunes, iRadio, and now Beats Music), arguably make even more money directly or indirectly from unauthorized free services than from the authorized ones that they own, and therefore lack the will to shut them down. Also, the ISPs, such as AT&T, Verizon, and Comcast, who have or are in the process of forming "partnerships" with the record business, continue to have powerful incentives to allow people to access to free unauthorized music.

Pirate Sites; P2P and BitTorrent; and Cyberlockers

Pirate Sites

In July 2014 the BBC News and Technology site ran an article titled "Russia's anti-Internet piracy law faces backlash." It reported that President Putin had signed the antipiracy bill into law in June of 2014. The bill was praised by content owners as a new weapon to defend content makers, but decried by others "as a blunt tool that could extend censorship of the Net." The article quoted Natalia Malysheva of the "Russian Pirate Party" as saying,

"Access to online content should be free and global, because it is people's right to freely receive and distribute information, as well as it is their right to consume art."[287]

The US recording industry has been fighting the attitude exemplified by Ms. Malysheva's statement for years.[288] And to some extent they have had success. Russia's new antipiracy law is a step in the right direction, although it remains to be seen how well Russian authorities will enforce the law.[289]

Despite all of the industry's efforts, if you use any major search engine to find the name of an artist followed by "MP3" you will immediately find scores of pirate sites offering indexes containing links for downloading any popular song you may wish.[290] Many of these sites, most of which make money from advertising,[291] operate off shore.[292] SOPA, which was designed to allow US law enforcement authorities and copyright owners to pursue them, as we discussed in the last chapter, failed to become law largely due to the lobbying efforts of those very same search engines, particularly the wealthiest and most powerful, Google.

P2P and BitTorrent

BitTorrent is now the most popular P2P format for trading unauthorized music and movies, although it can be used for trading legal files as well.[293] The BitTorrent protocol enables trading large files faster than other P2P formats because it allows users to join a "swarm" of hosts to download and upload from each other simultaneously.[294] It is important to distinguish BitTorrent, the open-source protocol for peer-to-peer file sharing that Bram Cohen invented to enable the transfer of large files, from Bit Torrent Inc., the company that Cohen heads. BitTorrent, the company, has long sought to partner with content owners, particularly Hollywood studios.[295] But the BitTorrent technology that Cohen invented continues to be used largely for piracy of copyrighted content, including movies, TV shows, and games as well as music. For example, Bruno Mars had 641,000 paid album downloads in the United States through December 22, 2012 according to Nielsen SoundScan. It is estimated that eight times this number of albums were downloaded via BitTorrent.[296]

Following is a list of the top 20 BitTorrent artists in 2013, as tracked by data analysis firm Musicmetric:[297]

1.	Bruno Mars	5,783,556	11.	One Direction	2,920,445
2.	Rihanna	5,414,166	12.	Maroon 5	2,857,652
3.	Daft Punk	4,212,361	13.	Zedd	2,828,764
4.	Justin Timberlake	3,930,185	14.	Nicki Minaj	2,681,177
5.	Flo Rida	3,470,825	15.	Adele	2,594,275
6.	Kanye West	3,199,969	16.	Avicii	2,562,151
7.	Eminem	3,176,122	17.	David Guetta	2,441,235
8.	Jay Z	3,171,358	18.	Linkin Park	2,352,385
9.	Drake	3,139,408	19.	Pharrell Williams	2,336,996
10.	Pitbull	3,138,308	20.	Katy Perry	2,318,740

The industry has been engaged in litigation against the operators of two of the most popular BitTorrent sites—The Pirate Bay and isoHunt. Both have millions of users trading a vast catalogue of music, films, and TV shows. But the legal action against both sites shows the difficulty of shutting down an online pirate site even when the law is squarely on the side of content owners.

The Pirate Bay, unlike other more "neutral" sites that may also be used to secure free content, openly advocates piracy and perceives copyright in the context of the Internet as "censorship."[298] But no matter how hard the movie and recording industries have tried, the site, which launched in 2003, remains fully operational. As early as 2006 the website's servers in Stockholm were raided and taken away by Swedish police. Three days later, the website went back online. Since that time The Pirate Bay has been in a constant game of cat and mouse with legal authorities from around the globe. Government agencies have often tried to shut the site down or thwart people from reaching it, even sending its operators to jail[299]—only to see the site retaliate with new doorways to allow people to access BitTorrent files. Over the years the Pirate Bay site has undergone many changes to survive, including moving its servers to the cloud and changing its domain names, after court orders to block the site.[300] The Pirate Bay is currently censored in Iran, North Korea, the United Kingdom, the Netherlands, Belgium, Finland, Denmark, Italy, and Ireland. But last year people involved with The Pirate Bay released a free web browser, called "Pirate Browser," that allow people in countries where The Pirate Bay is currently blocked to access the site. Moreover, in late July 2014 The Pirate Bay debuted a new mobile version of itself ("The Mobile Bay") designed to make it easier to download the same content that can be obtained from a desktop.[301]

Originated in 2003, isoHunt describes itself as "the most advanced BitTorrent and best P2P torrent search engine."[302] In February 2006, the Motion Picture Association of America (MPAA) issued a press release stating they were suing isoHunt for copyright infringement. After seven years of litigation a settlement with MPAA was reached in 2013. It stipulated $110 million dollars in reimbursement to copyright owners and the site's closure followed on October 21, 2013. But less than two weeks later, on October 30, 2013, a group of people claiming to be dedicated to isoHunt's continuance brought a near-identical site online, accessible via isoHunt.to.[303] This website is still up and active.

Although BitTorrent sites are still alive and drawing millions of users, they have become less popular in recent years according to a report published in late 2013 by Sandvine, a broadband network company. Sandvine noted that file sharing now accounts for less than 10 percent of all Internet traffic in the US, down from 31 percent in 2008. In 2004, file-sharing took up more than 70 percent of total Internet bandwidth. "As observed in previous reports, BitTorrent continues to lose share and now accounts for just 7.4 percent of traffic during peak period and file-sharing as a whole now accounts for less than 10 percent of total daily traffic,"[304] the report noted. "This demonstrates a sharp decline in share. Long are the days when file-sharing accounted for over 31 percent total daily traffic, as we had revealed in our 2008 report."[305]

Some experts are attributing this drop in BitTorrent and P2P to the proliferation of legal services, whether Netflix, YouTube, or any number of similar competitors across music, television, or movies. These commentators argue that antipiracy efforts, whether suing pirate sites or proposed legislation, are having a marginal impact. "If this trend continues I think it can most likely be explained by the increase in legal alternatives people have in the United States," *Torrentfreak* founder Ernesto van der Dar told the BBC. [306] "In Europe and other parts of the world, it's much harder to watch recent films and TV shows on demand, so unauthorized BitTorrent users continue to grow there."[307]

The Sandvine report specifically found that as peer-to-peer file-sharing is sliding in popularity,[308] real-time authorized entertainment options, particularly YouTube and Netflix, continue to grow. The report provided the following ranking of all Internet traffic during peak periods in North America in the second half of 2013:

Application: Share[309]
Netflix: 28.18 percent
YouTube: 16.78 percent
HTTP: 9.26 percent
BitTorrent: 7.39 percent
iTunes: 2.91 percent
SSL: 2.54 percent
MPEG: 2.32 percent
Amazon Video: 1.48 percent
Facebook: 1.34 percent
Hulu: 1.15 percent
Total Share: 73.35 percent

Some experts believe that P2P piracy will further decline the more legal alternatives emerge. According to these experts, "There's a clearly established relationship between the legal availability of material online and copyright infringement; it's an inverse relationship."[310]

Cyberlockers

Although P2P may not be as popular as it used to be, file swapping is not dead. In fact, the use of cyberlockers to share unauthorized music, movies, and other copyrighted content has been rising in popularity. In terms of visitor traffic, cyberlockers have overtaken BitTorrent.[311] Cyberlockers, also known as file-hosting or cloud storage service, are Internet hosting services specifically designed to host user files. They allow users to upload files that can then be accessed over the Internet from a different computer, tablet, smartphone, or other networked device. Most cyberlocker services are aimed at private individuals, offering "network storage" for personal backup, file access, or file distribution. Users can upload their files and share them publicly or keep them password-protected. Cyberlockers are often used for completely legal transactions, such as a filmmaker sharing his work with select individuals. And companies with household names are in this business, such as Dropbox and Google Drive.

However, because cyberlockers are so convenient and are sophisticated enough to house large movie and music files, it is a common practice for people to share copies of popular movies and songs through their cyberlockers.[312] And, unlike BitTorrent file-sharing, which may be traceable, cyberlockers are very hard to monitor, as they employ one-to-one connectivity, which is essentially invisible to surveillance tools. Because of this convenience and anonymity, cyberlockers are an ideal tool for trading pirate movie and music files.

One of the most popular cyberlockers that was used by many people to trade copyright content was Megaupload, founded by the infamous Internet entrepreneur and former hacker Kim Dotcom (born Kim Schmitz). At the height of its success, Meguapload had 150 million registered users.[313] But in January 2012, action by the US Department of Justice in collaboration with local law enforcement authorities in New Zealand led to a raid of Dotcom's mansion home and his arrest and subsequent closure of Megaupload.[314] The entertainment industry, including the major labels and Hollywood studios, it seems certain, will continue to pursue enforcement action against the operators of other similar services. However, as is the case with the software programs and apps discussed in the next section, cyberlockers may generally not be vulnerable to legal attack unless they deliberately and publicly encourage users to use their storage facilities for illicit purposes.

In Megaupload's case the encouragement to use the site to trade copyrighted files started almost as soon as it was launched in 2005. Megaupload announced an "Uploader Rewards" program, offering money and cash prizes to people who uploaded content to the site. [315] "This makes Megaupload the first and only site on the Internet paying you for hosting your files," Megaupload said at the time. "You deliver popular content and successful files. We provide a power hosting and downloading service. Let's team up!"[316] These premium users first had to pay Megaupload a subscription fee ranging from a few dollars a day to $260 for lifetime membership. To earn rewards, users had to put up files—and the material had to be popular enough to generate at least 50,000 downloads within three months. Megaupload initially offered cash bonuses of up to $5,000 for uploaders who generated the most downloads, later increasing it to $10,000. One uploader made $55,000, the indictment says. Obviously, this led to massive trading of unauthorized content, particularly blockbuster movies as well as copyrighted songs and albums. But not all cyberlockers that are used for file trading of copyrighted content are as obvious.

For instance, in 2011 the Swiss-German file-hosting service RapidShare was accused of being the leading "digital piracy" site, with over 13 billion yearly visitors.[317] At its peak Megaupload only had 5 billion yearly visits. As far back as 2010 the US government's congressional international antipiracy caucus declared the site a "notorious illegal site," claiming that RapidShare was "overwhelmingly used for the global exchange of illegal movies, music, and other copyrighted works."[318] The RIAA (Recording Industry Association of America) blames RapidShare for carrying huge amounts of pirated content. It wanted the firm to install filters to police the illegal content changing hands via its site.[319] RapidShare refused. But in the 2010 case, *Atari Europe S.A.S.U. v. Rapidshare AG*,[320] the Düsseldorf higher regional court reached the conclusion that "most people utilize RapidShare for legal use cases"[321] and that to assume otherwise was equivalent to inviting "a general suspicion against shared hosting services and their users which is not justified."[322] The court also observed that the site removes copyrighted material when asked, and does not provide specific search facilities for illegal material. The court concluded that the proposals for more strictly preventing sharing of copyrighted material were "unreasonable or pointless,"[323] and that the company couldn't be held responsible for the actions of its users. This case, although not an expression of US law, runs parallel to US cases such as *Grokster* that hold that a site has a legal purpose, so long as it does not encourage or induce piracy, it may be immune from legal prosecution even if it is widely used for illicit purposes.

Private Sharing: Ripping, Burning, Instant Messaging, E-mailing Music Files, USB, and Hard Drive Sharing: A Bigger Source of Unauthorized Free Music than P2P and Cyberlockers Put Together, but One Which the Industry Can Hardly Do Anything to Stop

While music piracy via BitTorrent and cyberlockers is still rampant, off-line trading and private sharing is probably an even bigger source of illegal music acquisition than online trading, including P2P or cyberlockers.[324] The RIAA's website itself gives the following examples of how people should *not* share music without authorization:

- You transfer copyrighted music using an instant-messenging service.
- You have a computer with a CD burner, which you use to burn copies of music you have downloaded onto writable CDs for all of your friends.
- Somebody you don't even know e-mails you a copy of a copyrighted song and then you turn around and e-mail copies to all of your friends.[325]

It turns out that these "old school" methods of sharing copyrighted music, when added to other off-line techniques of sharing music such as USB or hard-drive sharing, are a bigger problem for the record industry than P2P and cyberlockers combined. A confidential RIAA report in 2012 that was leaked to the media showed that 65 percent of all music files are "unpaid" (that is, only 35 percent of recorded music is acquired legally), but the vast majority of that unauthorized acquisition is obtained through off-line swapping. The report showed that private sharing accounted for 46 percent of ALL music acquisition, whereas P2P and cyberlockers accounted for less than 20 percent.[326] The reason the report was confidential, according to Torrent Freak, a blog dedicated to reporting the latest news and trends on the BitTorrent protocol and file sharing, was that, although off-line sharing is technically illegal, there is practically nothing that the RIAA can do about it. Although the RIAA used to sue people who swapped files via Kazaa and Limewire, they never pursued people for burning CDs of their favorite songs or even for sharing a USB containing thousands of songs. "Education" ***à la*** the RIAA website is about the best they can do. But such messages seem unlikely to have any significant impact. It is just an unfortunate result of the Internet, and new technology in general, that people can move music around almost at will without having to pay for it.

Stream-Ripping Programs

If you search on Google for "YouTube to MP3," you will see over 1 million entries. Here is a typical slogan on the home page of a typical service that pops up:

> . . . you can download your music for free and convert your favorite videos from YouTube, Dailymotion, Vevo, and Clipfish online to MP3, MP4, and more. It´s fast, free, and there is no registration needed.

This kind of ripping service is a popular way people can and do create collections of playlists and never have to spend a penny to have them. There are also ripping programs that allow you to capture individual tunes on Pandora or Sirius XM or any of the authorized digital services. In addition, there are multitudes of services that allow you to create your own ringtones. For years the recording industry has turned a blind eye to most of these software programs and apps, because they are not necessarily illegal. In the *Betamax* case the Supreme Court of the United States found that although the Betamax (now replaced by set top boxes supplied by your cable company) allowed people to make unauthorized copies of copyrighted TV programs and movies, it could not be prohibited because Betamax had a "substantial legal purpose," that is, time-shifting programs for later private viewing. [327] All the software programs and apps I've just described arguably also have "substantial legal purposes." For instance, you could use the programs that convert YouTube to MP3s to make copies of your own video of a song that you wrote yourself, or to copy scores from silent movies that are now PD. Therefore, if the recording industry were to pursue legal action against these services or software programs, they could well lose. And that would create a precedent that might encourage even more software programs and apps.

Piracy Goes Mobile

In March 2014, the tech news site Re/Code reported,

> The music industry faces a new front in its long-running battle against piracy: the smartphone. Mobile applications have eclipsed file-sharing services, online storage sites known as "digital lockers," and stream-ripping software as the most widely used source of free music downloads, according to a 2014 study by the research firm NPD Group.[328]

NPD determined that approximately 27 million people in the US alone have used mobile applications to download one or more songs in the past year, and that many of these downloads were from pirate sites. "In the beginning, we had feature phones with ringtones and very slow networks," according to NPD head Russ Crupnick. "As the technology improves, it becomes a free-for-all for someone who wants free music files."[329]

The Google Play store offers approximately 250 apps that can be used to download MP3 files to Android-powered smartphones. The most popular of these is Music Mania, which has been downloaded more than 10 million times. The RIAA claims that this app enables piracy and has demanded that Google take it down, but as of January 2015 the app was still available. Mobile phones were once considered safe from piracy because of the limitations of the early phones and mobile networks. "All you were going to do is buy a ringtone for $2.99," said Crupnik.[330] That changed as the devices became more sophisticated and the networks grew more robust.

According to music industry antipiracy executives that I interviewed for this book, Apple is more cooperative with them in removing from the iTunes store apps that may be used to obtain unauthorized music. However, even on the iTunes store you can download apps to create playlists from YouTube that can be played commercial free. One of my interns built an entire collection of music from using one of these apps and told me that she didn't listen to music any other way. The total amount that she spent in acquiring thousands of songs was $2.99 to download the app.

As was just reported, a recent addition to regulators' worries is the Pirate Bay's new site for mobile devices.[331] The mobile Pirate Bay offers a much more usable interface to browse the torrent site on mobile devices. When visitors loaded the normal version of the Pirate Bay site on their smartphones, the site would appear smaller, which made it harder to use. The mobile version, called "The Mobile Bay," offers easy-to-tap buttons to search, browse, and view recent torrents or the top 100. Many in the industry were hoping that mobile listening of copyrighted music could revive the business. But the appearance of a mobile version of The Pirate Bay is an ominous sign that this dream may not come true. As the *New York Times* put it, "People can complete all sorts of tasks with a smartphone now—order tickets, check the weather, or call a taxi. Starting Thursday, people will also be able to easily steal copyrighted content on their mobile phones."[332]

The Forces Amassed against the Recording Industry: Google, Apple, and Other "Partners"

Certain multinational corporations have been benefiting from piracy for years. In 2003, I wrote a Commentary article for *Billboard* pointing out that the ISPs, such as Verizon, AT&T, and Comcast, as well as the electronics industry, are major beneficiaries of free unauthorized music.[333] Since "free" unauthorized music is not really free—you need to pay for a computer, tablet, smartphone, or other device to trade copyrighted music, as well as a high-speed Internet connection—I suggested that the recording industry try to secure compensation from these companies (particularly the ISPs, with their ability to block pirate sites) for the terrific losses that it has suffered due to piracy. But the collective power of these companies relative to that of the recording industry made this impossible. Instead, as we have discussed, the content owners felt they had no choice except to play legal whack-a-mole with services such as The Pirate Bay and even sue individual music fans (see "Labels vs. Fans" in Chapter 15). Both of these approaches, as we have seen, have had marginal success, if any. As an alternative approach, in the recent past, particularly after the failure of SOPA in 2012, the record labels have shifted their focus to trying to coax the tech sector, particularly Google and Apple, to work with them collaboratively. After all, both companies are distributing legal music services. Unfortunately for the recording business, however, both of those companies have conflicting interests. As pointed out at the beginning of this chapter, although Google owns YouTube, Google Play, and now Songza, and Apple owns iTunes, iRadio, and now Beats Music, they arguably make even more money directly or indirectly from unauthorized sites and apps than from the authorized services they own, and therefore lack the will to shut them down. For instance, both companies make money from apps, including those which facilitate piracy, based on a percentage of income received by the app from sales or advertising, and Google makes money from advertising associated with searches, including searches for pirate sites.

In its *Digital Music Report 2014*,[334] the International Federation of the Phonographic Industry reported that 74 percent of consumers are introduced to pirate sites through the top search engines, including Google, Yahoo!, and Bing. The report stated:

> Search engines have pledged to do more to tackle online piracy, but there is still a long way to go. In August 2012, Google announced that it was altering its algorithm to take account of notices received from rights holders to place infringing sites lower down in search results. Unfortunately, this seems to have had little impact. A search for the name of any leading artist followed by the term "MP3" in the leading search engines still returns a vast proportion of illegal links on the first page of results.

The report provided the following percentages representing links to pirate sites on the first page of search results by artist name and "MP3":

ARTIST	GOOGLE	YAHOO!	BING
Pharrell Williams	80 percent	90 percent	80 percent
Katy Perry	100 percent	80 percent	80 percent
Jason Derulo	80 percent	90 percent	90 percent
John Legend	100 percent	70 percent	80 percent
Beyoncé	90 percent	90 percent	90 percent

In the US an offshore pirate site, mp3skull, usually comes up first. As of August 2014, more than 67 percent of total mp3skull.com traffic in the last 3 months came from search, and of that approximately 90 percent came from Google.[335] FPI's report also noted that by January 2014, the global recording industry had sent more than 100 million requests to Google to remove links to infringing content, an amount that would have been even higher were it not for the cap on the number of requests that Google imposes on individual rights holder groups. The report complained:

> While Google has taken some steps to develop licensed services and improve its reaction to antipiracy notices from rights holders, the music industry believes it has the technological expertise to do more. In January 2014, IFPI issued a statement calling on search engines to take a number of measures: including fulfilling the promise to demote sites receiving extensive numbers of piracy notices and ensuring that the "take down" of a song is effective and does not mean temporary removal—to be replaced two seconds later.[336]

Another area of concern is that the apps that Google makes available through the official app store for the Android operating system. Dawn Chmielewski explained on Re/Code,

> Apps undergo an automated process that screens for malicious behavior before developers can upload the software to the Google Play store, and its developer guidelines expressly prohibit copyright infringement—but Google states that it relies on copyright holders to flag apps that enable piracy. One music industry executive, speaking on condition of anonymity for fear of reprisals, said that since 2010 his label has issued some 3,000 requests to remove apps that enable piracy—with the "vast majority" found on Google's Android platform.[337]

In testimony before the House Judiciary Committee, RIAA Chairman Cary Sherman said the industry has sent Google more than 2 million notices of infringements from mp3skull.com.[338] But as recently as March 10, 2014, at least 10 applications available through the Google Play store claimed some connection to the pirate site, Sherman said.[339]

But Google is not the only industry "partner" that is actually facilitating unauthorized consumption of free music. Chmielewski noted that "Apple takes a curated approach to software offered through its App store, and can reject an app that enables piracy. As the world's largest music retailer, it has been more aggressive than Google in policing its apps, say music industry executives."[340] But, even though Apple is still a leading source of revenue for the record business with iTunes, it also facilitates free music. As of the time this manuscript the App Store carries apps such as Instatube or Music Tube that allow you to make portable playlists of any video on YouTube or Vimeo.

IFPI's *Digital Music Report 2014* points to "progress" that the industry is making against piracy by citing a few European court decisions favoring content owners. Industry professionals I have talked to, including antipiracy executives at major labels, say things are improving because Google and Apple are becoming more cooperative in terms of removing blatant pirate apps. But in the face of the avalanche of free music and tools that make it accessible, it seems that this "progress" is almost like whistling in the dark. Moreover, in addition to the pirate sites, BitTorrent, cyberlockers, and a myriad of legal, illegal, and semi-legal digital tools and apps that provide means of obtaining unauthorized music, and superpower tech companies that have divided interests in the war against piracy, perhaps the biggest hurdle to overcome, as expressed by one antipiracy executive at a major record company, is:

> We now have a generation of people that think music is free and doesn't have a monetary value. I think that's why you see such a slow adoption of streaming services. They're just all used to getting music and movies for free and aren't interested in paying for the service.

On the other hand, there are now strong alternatives to piracy available on both computers and smartphones that offer millions of virus-free tracks of every imaginable type of music—including popular services like Spotify, Pandora, Sirius XM, and YouTube. This is a profoundly better picture than the early days of the digital era when there was no good alternative to free in terms of digital offerings. And *that* is real progress.

Chapter 17

NETWORK NEUTRALITY

What Is It? Will It Survive? And the Consequences of Its Demise for the Music Business

A Brief Overview

Network neutrality (or net neutrality) is the principle that Internet service providers (ISPs) should treat all content on the Internet equally, not block content, charge differentially by user or type of content, or deliver content at different levels of speed or quality. Just as phone companies can't check who's on the line and selectively degrade or block the service of callers, everyone on the Internet should start on the same footing: ISPs shouldn't slow down services, block legal content, or charge particular providers more money to deliver their content faster than a competitor's. But in January 2014 a federal circuit court in Washington, DC, which has jurisdiction over the Federal Communications Commission (FCC) dealt a major blow to network neutrality. The federal appeals court threw out the FCC's rules that required ISPs to give all traffic equal access through their networks. The decision could pave the way for Internet service providers like Verizon, AT&T, or Comcast to charge content companies (for instance, ESPN, Netflix, Facebook—or music services such as Spotify or iTunes) to deliver their content to consumers at a faster speed. This would leave small content companies or start-ups on a "slower track" than their wealthy competitors—and allow an ISP to block a content provider entirely for any reason.

The FCC tried to prevent those deals by issuing a set of rules in 2010 known as the "Open Internet Order." But the court found that those rules were invalid. So these deals may be coming soon. In challenging the 2010 regulations at issue in the case, Verizon told the court that if not for the FCC rules "we would be exploring those commercial arrangements."

Dangers of Eliminating Network Neutrality

Notwithstanding its ruling, the three-judge panel pointed out the dangers of eliminating net neutrality:

> Proponents of net neutrality—or, to use the Commission's preferred term, "Internet openness"—worry about the relationship between broadband providers and edge providers. They fear that broadband providers might prevent their end-user subscribers from accessing certain edge providers altogether, or might degrade the quality of their end-user subscribers' access to certain edge providers, either as a means of favoring their own competing content or services or to enable them to collect fees from certain edge providers. Thus, for example, a broadband provider like Comcast might limit its end-user subscribers' ability to access the *New York Times* website if it wanted to spike traffic to its own news website, or it might degrade the quality of the connection to a search website like Bing if a competitor like Google paid for prioritized access. But circuit judge Tatel, writing on behalf of the court, concluded that its hands were tied because of a prior determination by the FCC itself.

The FCC's Classification of ISPs

The court found that the FCC's network neutrality rules could not be applied to ISPs because the FCC itself had, in 2002, decided not to classify them as "common carriers." At that time, and under the Republican administration of George W. Bush, Chairman Michael Powell (son of former secretary of state Colin Powell) deemed ISPs to be subject to Title II of the Telecommunications Act of 1996. Title I of the Act provides rules for common carriers such as telephone companies, and Title I services are subject to much tighter regulation. Under Title I, for instance, telephone companies cannot discriminate against various users by charging more than others. The rationale is that telephone companies are public "utilities" that are crucial to the general public, similar to electricity. Bur Chairman Powell decided not to classify ISPs in the same category as telephone companies. One reason for his original decision, Mr. Powell said in an interview, was that in 2002 the Internet needed enormous capital investment, which would have been deterred by tighter regulations.

The Right but Not the Will to Reclassify

The circuit court said the FCC has the authority to change the classification of ISPs from Title II "information providers" to Title II common carriers. Moreover, the current chairman of the FCC, Tom Wheeler, has expressed his strong support for basic fairness on the Internet, declaring, "As a result of the importance of our broadband networks, our society has the right to demand highly responsible performance from those who operate those networks."

But the chairman also made it clear that he had no intent to reclassify the ISPs as common carriers. The reason is probably political. Although Barack Obama has expressed support for network neutrality (in 2007, in response to a question at a town-hall meeting sponsored by MTV, Mr. Obama said he was "a strong supporter of net neutrality"), and progressive commentators have called for reclassification, such a move could create a huge storm among Republicans in Congress who are strong supporters of free enterprise and "innovation" on the Internet. The backlash could be proposed legislation permanently banning network neutrality or any other rules restraining the ISPs from discriminating between users.

Therefore, instead of reclassifying the ISPs, the FCC has decided to use a bit of "wiggle room" in Judge Tatel's decision. Although the court found that the regulations preventing discriminatory deals were invalid, it stated that the commission did have some basic authority "to promulgate rules governing broadband providers' treatment of Internet traffic." It also upheld agency rules requiring broadband companies to disclose how they manage their networks.

Current Controversy: The New Proposed Rules and President Obama's Call for the FCC to Reclassify Internet Service under Title II

Using this opening, Wheeler announced that he intended to promulgate new rules that would make the ISPs subject to "commercial reasonableness." This sparked a great deal of controversy. As the debate continues, and you can find updates on this controversy in my blog at www.futureofthemusicbusiness.biz/.

On Thursday, May 15, 2014, the FCC proposed new rules for public debate. According to Chairman Wheeler, the new rules would "preserve an open Internet" by preventing ISPs from slowing the transmission of content. However, the rules, if adopted, would allow content providers to pay for a guaranteed "fast lane" of service. Opponents of the plan argue that allowing some content to be sent along such a so-called "fast lane" would discriminate against other content. Supporters of net neutrality argue that the proposed rules would seem to give the ISPs a financial incentive to create a fast lane for those who can afford the "tolls," thereby making it more difficult for indie or start-up content providers, including music services, to succeed.

On the other hand, the FCC also specifically requested public comments on whether and by how much the commission should tighten regulation of Internet service providers. For example, the commission asked whether it should reclassify high-speed Internet service as a utility-like application, subject to stricter regulatory controls than now apply, and if it should ban certain practices that might impede consumers from getting equal access to all legal online content through their chosen Internet service provider. President Obama, who campaigned in 2008 promising to enact net neutrality, said through a spokesman that the administration "will be watching closely as the process moves forward in hopes that the final rule stays true to the spirit of net neutrality." The public had until September 10 to file comments replying to the initial discussions. The new rules became a lightning rod for criticism. More than 3.7 million comments about the policy have flowed to the commission. Many of them argued that Mr. Wheeler's plan does not go far enough to protect an open Internet.

On October 9, President Obama said that he was "unequivocally committed" to net neutrality and firmly opposed to any proposal that would let companies buy an Internet fast lane to deliver their content more quickly to consumers. These statements, at a town-hall meeting in Santa Monica, California, were designed to give a strong signal to Mr. Obama's Democratic appointees on the Federal Communications Commission, including Mr. Wheeler, that he wants them to heed the overwhelming public sentiment to protect net neutrality.

In early January 2015, as this book was undergoing final editing, Barack Obama called on the FCC to "implement the strongest possible rules to protect net neutrality." Obama was surprisingly specific about what he hoped Wheeler and the F.C.C. would do: apply Title II of the 1996 Telecommunications Act to the ISPs, reclassifying these companies as public utilities.

As the debate continues, you can find updates on this controversy at www.futureofthemusicbusiness.com.

Impact on the Music Business

The most obvious impact on the music business if network neutrality does not survive is that entrenched players and well-heeled players in the music space such as Apple, with billions of dollars of cash in reserves, will be able to buy a fast lane. Of course, paying for bandwidth is basically how online enterprise works, including music services. If a music service operates a site, it will cost a certain amount of money to apportion bandwidth to do what the site wants to do, and the company pays for that, similar to paying for a domain name and server host. What the service would not have to worry about, if net neutrality applied, is that an ISP is going to charge them more money to deliver content to the user who chooses to access it, beyond what they have already paid in bandwidth. Established services such as Pandora, or services owned by financially powerful companies such as Beats Music and iRadio (both owned by Apple) or Google Play could afford to pay for a fast lane, but start-ups such as the simulcast streamed by Smalls Jazz Club probably could not. (See Chapter 27, "How a Jazz Club Is Using the Internet to Reach a Worldwide Audience and Create a New Income Stream for Artists Who Play There").[341]

Some commentators such as Charles Sanders, outside general counsel to the Songwriters Guild of America, Inc., and former general counsel for NMPA, argue that the ISPs need to freedom to discriminate amongst content providers so that they can disrupt music piracy:

> Most informed music creators, led on this issue by songwriter and SGA president Rick Carnes, have long considered the term "net neutrality" as synonymous with the concept of blocking the ability of a broadband network to protect itself—through reasonable network management initiatives—from devolving into a copyright thieves' paradise. Such unfair constraints on filtering and other management tools result in huge expenses to the company and devastating damage to creators, but provide massive benefits to search engine proprietors, criminals and freeloaders.[342]

Supporters of net neutrality, such as Casey Rae, head of the Future of the Music Coalition and adjunct professor of law at Georgetown University, point out that the original network neutrality rules that the DC court struck down in early 2014 applied only to *lawful* content. He notes that "[t]he rules explicitly allow[ed] rights holders and Internet companies to take action against illegal content, including music distributed or accessed without permission."[343]

The issue is whether imposing net neutrality would harm the music business by preventing ISPs from disrupting piracy. As Casey Rae points out, though, rules imposing network neutrality could carve out music piracy, thereby allowing ISPs to block pirate sites. Furthermore, there is no guarantee that the ISPs, in the absence of net neutrality rules, would do this. In fact, they could charge pirate sites fees to continue to use their networks, thereby preserving piracy while making additional profits for themselves, or they could charge music providers more money for a "fast lane" to their users.

Net Neutrality and Mobile Broadband Services

Even when the FCC spelled out its Open Internet Rules in 2010, it was very careful to carve out broad exceptions for wireless in order to encourage further innovation.[344] In June 2014 T-Mobile took advantage of those exceptions to launch a new initiative called Music Freedom. Under this program a handful of music services will be blessed by the carrier so that they don't hit subscribers' monthly data allowances. (T-Mobile doesn't charge overage fees, but it throttles data speeds once users reached prescribed limits.) The list of Music Freedom–compatible services currently includes Pandora, Rhapsody, iHeartRadio, iTunes Radio, Slacker, Spotify, Samsung's Milk, and the forthcoming streaming service from electronic music destination Beatport.[345] It'll also be taking votes from customers through its website and on Twitter for other services to add to the list of exemptions. According to one commentator:

> It sounds wonderful—and right in line with the "uncarrier" image that firebrand CEO John Legere has worked so hard to cultivate—but it's a terribly slippery slope: T-Mobile has decided, arbitrarily, that some of the data traveling over its pipes should count against a cap, while other data should not. What's to stop it from using data cap exemptions as a punitive measure against content providers that aren't on good terms with T-Mobile (or its parent company Deutsche Telekom)?
>
> But T-Mobile points out that all that it's doing is letting its users listen to music without charging them for data and that it is not charging music services for the privilege of being exempt from the caps. On the other hand without neutrality rules, it could if it wanted. In addition there is nothing to prevent T-Mobile from excluding any other music service from "Music Freedom."[346]

Please visit www.futureofthemusicbusiness for the latest developments on network neutrality and the music business.

Chapter 18
CURRENT CONTROVERSIES, TRENDS
and Developments Discussion with Glenn Peoples, Senior Editorial Analyst at Billboard *Magazine*

This chapter is based on a Q&A with Glenn Peoples, senior editorial analyst for *Billboard* magazine. We conducted the interview in March 2014. Because of the speed at which changes in the music business are happening, some portions of the conversation may seem dated by the time you read this. For that reason I invite readers to go to www.futureofhtemusic-business.com for updates.

Vinyl Makes a Comeback

SG: For the first time since the iTunes store launched in 2003, sales of digital tracks and albums declined last year (i.e., 2013), and sales of CDs declined as they have every year except one since 1999.

Meanwhile, one format quietly posted huge gains: vinyl records. At their height in 1978, more than 440 million LPs were sold in the US. After cassettes (early '70s) and CDs were introduced (1984) the numbers nosedived to around only 2 million per year throughout the '90s and 2000s.

But in 2013 LP sales were up an amazing 32 percent from 2012, continuing an improbable growth trend that began in around 2007. The numbers are still relatively small compared to the industry as a whole: only 6 million units or about two percent of all album sales in the United States. Still, the recent growth of vinyl has been startling, as you can see in the following chart.

Some experts say as digital music has migrated from compact discs onto hard drives—and, increasingly, the cloud—collectors interested in a physical copy of their favorite albums no longer see a reason to prefer CDs. In fact, many prefer records, whether for the sound quality, the nostalgic appeal, or simply the beauty of the vinyl record as a design object. CDs and cassettes had their virtues as media, but aesthetics was not among them. What do you think?

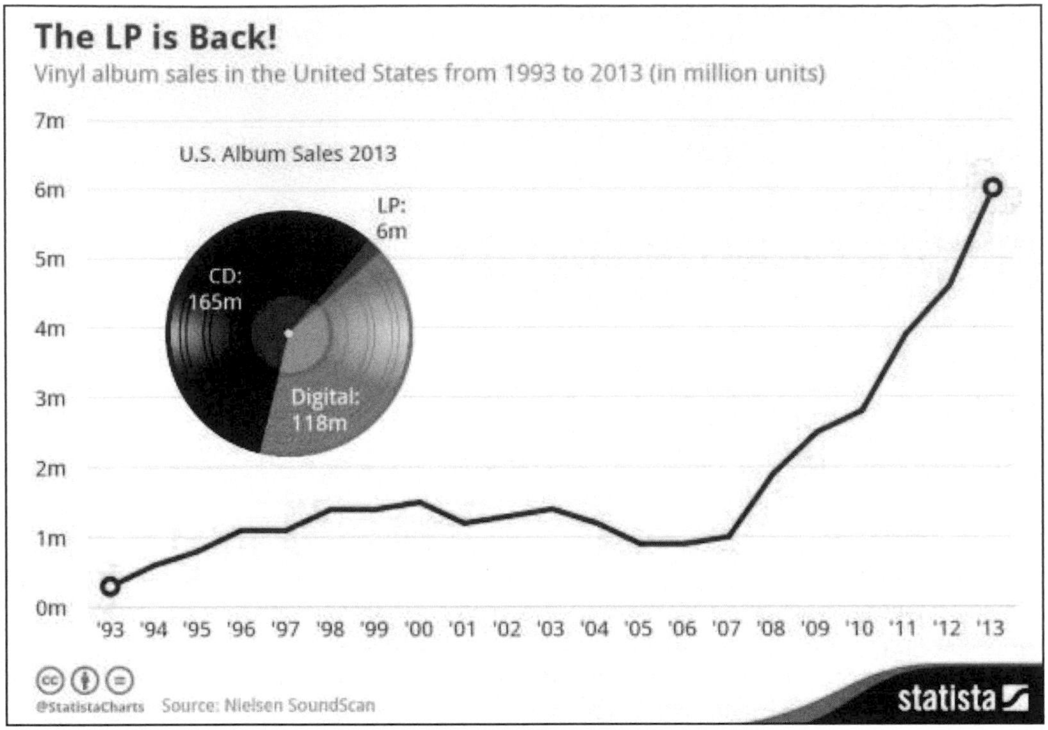

GP: Let's examine vinyl record sales in two ways: what they represent and what they do not represent.

The upswing in vinyl sales has been positive for the music business. First and perhaps most importantly, vinyl sales have helped provide stability for a beleaguered indie record store community. Most vinyl sales come from indie retail, whereas mass merchants such as Walmart and Target represent the biggest share of CD sales. These newfound sales have undoubtedly allowed many indie retailers to remain in business, and they have spurred the creation of some vinyl-only retailers. Record Store Day, and the hundreds of labels and artists that have supported it, have played a vital role in vinyl's rise at indie retail.

Vinyl's resurgence has helped pull consumers back to the physical format. Perhaps these music lovers have found digital music not to have lived up to the utopian promises. Perhaps they just like holding music in their hands and have far less interest in the CD format. Or maybe people just think today's vinyl records are cool. Whatever the case, Jack White was right when he started Third Man Records: Music lovers want a kind of a listening experience and scarcity that digital formats can't deliver.

But vinyl trends need to be put in context. Vinyl sales are a tiny fraction of overall music purchases and represent an even smaller share of total recorded music revenues when subscription and advertising-based business models are taken into account. The mainstream consumer is content with digital music and, decreasingly, CDs. Indie retail, the dominant force in vinyl sales, has a single-digit share of US album sales. All that is to say that vinyl is a niche and is unlikely to become anything more than a niche.

Will Streaming Kill Downloading?

SG: In 2013 music streams grew by 32 percent to 118 billion music streams, but download sales declined for the first time since iTunes launched. Will streaming kill downloading?

GP: Yes, streaming is helping to kill the download. I use the word "helping" because I think the download would have run out of momentum without the incredible growth of streaming—there is a limited and seemingly finite number of consumers that want to buy downloads. But streaming seems to have already helped push the download toward its inevitable decline.

Until 2013, there was a good deal of uncertainty amongst record labels about exactly how much impact streaming was having on downloads. People who studied the numbers didn't see an impact. But by the end of 2013, it became clear that streaming was having an impact. By the beginning of 2014, we could see download sales had fallen sharply in 2013. Track sales were down 5.7 percent in 2013 after growing 5.1 percent the prior year. Digital album sales dropped 0.1 percent after rising 14.1 percent in 2012.

The manner in which downloads finally showed the impact of streaming makes perfect sense intuitively. First, there would be a delay in the decline of download sales because early adopters are more likely to both buy downloads and subscribe to music services. Early adopters are the heaviest spenders. Next, growth in subscription services would eventually harm download sales. There's no reason to expect consumers to both pay for unlimited services and continue their download-buying habits unabated. The former is an adequate replacement for the latter. (You may ask how streaming revenues can grow if people will be encouraged to spend less. The potential lies in the size of the market: Far more people will need to use and pay for subscription services than have purchased digital downloads.)

It may be that streaming services often change purchases rather than replace purchases. We can't overlook the value streaming services provide in informing consumers' purchasing decisions. Because subscription services allow people to listen to music before deciding to buy, they are tools that enable consumers to spend money more efficiently—and probably spend less money in general. Finally, some consumers may want to purchase titles by their favorite artists and stream music by all other artists.

I don't think the download will outright die within the next 10 years, however. Just as some consumers continue to prefer and buy CDs 15 years after Napster launched a digital download revolution, some music fans will continue to enjoy downloads for many years. And there could very well be an incentive for artists to release and/or sell downloads. If consumers will pay for them, why not offer downloads in order to acquire a lump sum of royalties immediately rather than wait for streaming revenues to slowly accrue?

Will Streaming Save the Record Business?

SG: Can streaming save the record business? At the time I am writing this question, Spotify only has 1 million paying subscribers in the US. To date, advertising on the free services plus subscriptions have not yet yielded a profit for Spotify. With these facts in mind, can Spotify and other streaming services revive a recording business that has declined in overall income from approximately $14.5 billion in 1999 to approximately $7 billion in 2013? Will streaming save the record business?

GP: In general, I think it's safe to say there is no single silver bullet that will solve the record business's woes. I'm not the first person to phrase it that way. This is a common, long-held belief within the music business.

But what does it mean to save the record business? Will streaming return the record business to its revenues at the peak of CD sales in 2000/2001? No, I don't see that happening within the next 10 years (especially after adjusting for inflation) and I think that particular (and often used) benchmark is unnecessary. The peak of the CD era was unique in many ways based on the absence of an à la carte offering of songs (you had to buy the CD to get a particular song). Now you can buy only the songs you really like as singles from download stores. Also mass merchants are paying less at wholesale because CDs have become a loss-leader (lure consumers with inexpensive, heavily advertised CDs, sell more TVs and refrigerators.)

Will streaming produce enough revenue to offset the inevitable loss in download revenue? This could happen within 10 years if (a) subscription services become a mainstream product and (b) listening to advertising-supported streaming in the automobile becomes as common as listening to broadcast radio. Will streaming produce enough revenue to sustain record labels and encourage investment in new artists? New artists have a more difficult time in the streaming world because catalogue represents a higher share of streaming activity than download activity. Nevertheless, I believe the structure of the record business will change to whatever the current business models support. If you can't affordably dig a ditch with the tools available, find cheaper or more efficient tools, or find an entirely new process for digging ditches (which was the impetus for the 360 model).

The question of streaming services' profitability is a different matter. Any licensed service will never have Google- or Facebook-like margins, but they will be able to operate profitably while paying royalties to rights holders. I'm more optimistic than the critics, who don't seem to appreciate two important factors about today's streaming services. First, these services are in their infancy and are in growth mode, not profit-maximizing mode. We're seeing a land war, and the services—and there may only be one or two or three—with the most subscribers will become sustainable over the long term. Second, both subscription and Internet radio services will achieve much greater scale in the coming years. Not only will they operate in more countries, they will obtain more users and paying customers and will increase their average revenue per user. There is also opportunity to change listening behavior. Imagine how much royalties will grow if subscription services and Internet radio replace much of broadcast radio's listening share. The revenue opportunity is massive over the long term. The largest services (e.g., Spotify, Pandora) will have enough funding to compete over the long term and chase a share of global revenue.

The Significance of Beats Music's Partnership with AT&T

SG: As you know, Beats Music, which is led by Dr. Dre and Jimmy Iovine, recently announced a partnership with AT&T. As you have reported in *Billboard*, the "holy grail" in reviving the record industry has been monetizing digital music without making people think that they are actually they are paying for it. For instance, I pay Time Warner Cable about $100 a month for hundreds of different basic cable stations. Each of these services receives a piece of my monthly subscription, although I don't feel like I am paying for any particular channel . . . although I do pay a few bucks extra for HBO because it has terrific shows I can't otherwise access. Is Beats Music's deal with AT&T the "holy grail"?

GP: No single deal with a single carrier is a "holy grail" or "silver bullet," but partnerships with telecommunications companies are important for a number of reasons. First, they give subscription services access to a large number of consumers. There is no guarantee that AT&T subscribers will buy into Beats, but AT&T provides direct access—through integrated billing—to 110 million subscribers (as of December 31, 2013). Second, subscription services don't have the marketing resources of an AT&T. A partnership with a major carrier allows subscription service to piggyback on the advertising and marketing budget of an enormous company. To put it in perspective, in 2013 AT&T Wireless had revenue of $69.9 billion—about four times greater than global recorded music revenues by a single company in a single market. A company that big is able to harness ample resources to promote and market a subscription music service. Third, partnerships allow for integrated billing. In other words, a person can subscribe to a service through the carrier and the cost is tacked onto the monthly mobile bill.

The most important aspect of the Beats Music/AT&T deal is what it represents: the first partnership between a music subscription service and a major mobile carrier in the United States. Prior to that deal, Rhapsody offered a discounted price to prepaid mobile provider MetroPCS. And although it doesn't represent a partnership, Cricket Wireless offered its proprietary Muve Music service to its subscribers as a free feature with unlimited plans for Android devices.

Deals like the Beats Music/AT&T partnership have been more commonplace in other markets. Spotify has used telecommunications partnerships to great effect in Europe. Deezer has used partnerships to help launch in countries around the world. Rdio was the first subscription service to partner with a mobile carrier—called Oi—in Brazil. WiMP, a service that operates in five Northern European markets, has partnerships with Telenor, Canal Digital, and Polish mobile operator Play, among others.

There's a potential downside here, however. Partnerships are short-term and relatively shallow relationships. A deeper relationship would be an equity investment—by the mobile carrier in the subscription service—that aligns both companies' interests. The deepest relationship would be an acquisition of the subscription service. As long as these relationships are mere partnerships, a possibility exists that mobile carriers will refuse to renew the partnership and seek other content plays to attract and retain subscribers. (This is not uncommon in business. Retail partners are valuable only as long as they are committed to your product. Once they lose interest, you've lost that distribution channel. This is why labels have bent over backwards to appease mass merchants who have cooled on selling CDs in their stores.) Thus, it's imperative that subscription services display good timing and strike partnerships when their products are likely to connect with consumers in a given market. There may not be any second chances. That said, telecommunications companies like Telenor have renewed many of their partnerships in Europe. The model can work.

The continued availability of Pandora and other free Internet radio services is a problem that could be overcome. Subscription services will need to communicate to potential customers how their services are both different and superior to Internet radio. If people simply want a radio service, they are going to be unlikely to pay for a premium service. But if they want a virtual music collection, recommendations, and additional content not available from Internet radio, they may make the switch. It wouldn't surprise me in the least that some people use both Internet radio and subscription services. I don't think subscription services can offer radio services to compete with the product offered by companies that specialize in radio.

Who Does BitTorrent Piracy Hurt Most: Music, Movies, TV, Games, or Porn?

SG: In an article for *Billboard* in 2013, you wrote, "Digital piracy remains a problem for the entertainment business, but it's disproportionately hurting film and TV industries more than music." In a graph accompanying the article, which I have included, you tried to demonstrate that illegitimate content is dominated by video, not music. The grid shows that over 80 percent of bandwidth consumed by unauthorized BitTorrent content was for film, TV, pornography, and video games. Only 7.6 percent was used for music. However, since you can download so many more songs than a motion picture, for example, it seems to me that that 7.6 percent of bandwidth could add up, in terms of the number of songs, to the equivalent of all the movies, TV shows, and games. So is it really such good news that illicit music content consumes so much less bandwidth than movies, TV, and games?

GP: What matters here is the trend, not each segment of the entertainment industry's relative amount of file-sharing traffic. Market research suggests music piracy has declined in recent years. A 2012 report by NPD claimed the percentage of US Internet users who illegally Ofcom [Author's note: the Office of Communications, a UK regulatory authority] said the downloaded music dropped to 11 percent in 2012 from 20 percent in 2005. A 2013 report by the number of pirated tracks in the UK fell to 199 million in 2013 from 301 million in 2012. A study in Norway, where streaming services have led to a rebound in total recorded music revenues, showed that music piracy fell about 83 percent from 2008 to 2012 while movie and TV piracy fell by roughly half. Those are just three examples of many.

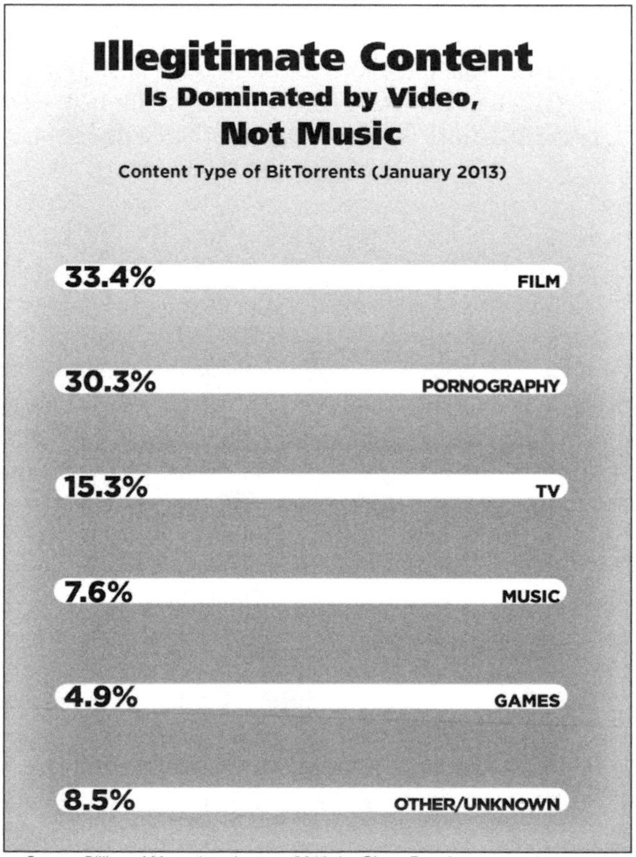

Source: Billboard Magazine, January 2013, by Glenn Peoples.

Consider the change in mood and discourse over the last 10 years. In the mid-2000s, before and for years after the Supreme Court's decision in *MGM Studios, Inc. v. Grokster, Ltd.* spelled the end of traditional peer-to-peer services, the music industry was scared to death it would be destroyed by piracy. It wasn't difficult to find people—on the music business group Pho, for example—who suggested the music industry acquiesce to piracy and find ways to survive on free music. Fortunately, few people took that path, although some artists and labels have embraced file-sharing for purposes of fan engagement and promotion. Legal alternatives and enforcement have reduced, although not eliminated, music piracy.

Today, the biggest concern is not piracy but the royalties of services that have, to a large extent, replaced the activity that used to go, or would otherwise have gone, to piracy. Regardless of your thoughts on these services' payouts, it's hard to argue that that's not an improvement over the piracy madness that captivated the industry fewer than 10 years ago. And one must go back nearly a decade to appreciate the improvement. Changes in consumer behaviors and business models don't happen quickly. It took years for the entertainment industry to shut down, either directly or indirectly, peer-to-peer services, illegal download sites, and cyberlockers.

These are positive developments. It's not that music has become less popular. Given the ease with which people can share, discover, and listen to music, it's possible that music has never been more popular. And music piracy hasn't gone away. But it's far less common than the pre-Grokster days when the Internet was awash in pop-up ads that promised free, unlimited music downloads that, unknowing to the average consumer, were not licensed and did not pay royalties.

Chapter 19

CURRENT STATE OF THE MUSIC BUSINESS IN THE LARGEST POTENTIAL MARKET ON EARTH—THE PEOPLE'S REPUBLIC OF CHINA

Q&A with Eric de Fontenay, Founder and President of China.Musicdish.com

China represents the world's largest population, and as such the greatest potential audience for both live and recorded music on earth. But for years live concerts have been limited by political conflicts and governmental restraint, and the market for recorded music has been dominated by piracy. However, things are changing. According to the IFPI *Digital Music Report 2014*,

> China is a market of enormous potential, long stifled by piracy. Ranked just 21st in the world, 2013 revenues were estimated at US$82.6 million. Yet the landscape for the music industry in China is changing. Over the last two years, major record companies and some independents have licensed eight of China's major online music services, most of them previously copyright infringing. The deals trace back to a landmark agreement struck in 2011 between three international record companies and Internet giant Baidu, that involved the settlement of antipiracy litigation and a commitment by Baidu to close its infringing "deep links" service. The opportunity for the music industry lies in China's vast Internet population, with 618 million users in 2013, with 81 percent connected to mobile.[347]

What is the music scene like in China now? Can artists make money from live shows and touring? And can the record business finally start making money from distributing physical records and use the Internet and smartphones to distribute recorded music? I asked Eric de Fontenay these and other questions in the following interview.

Eric founded the digital media firm MusicDish in 1997, subsequently launching the largest music newswire, Mi2N (www.mi2n.com). MusicDish has a long history of working with major conferences and festivals, starting with the MP3 Summit 1999, as well as long relationships with Canadian Music Week, Midem, and Music Matters. In 2009, he turned his focus on China's music industry, culminating in the MusicDish*China brand (http://china.musicdish.com). He has been active with key events in China, from Midi and Zebra festivals to Sound of the Xity conference. Eric has worked on showcases featuring award-winning Taiwanese acts since 2011 at Midem, CMJ, and Canadian Music Week, and recently signed Asian acts such as DJ Code and RED for international development and management. He develops Western acts in China through marketing, social media, and touring. He's been quoted in media as diverse as *FT China* and Portugal's *DIF* magazine, and was featured in *The Beijinger*'s 2012 Music Issue.

SG: What are the most popular kinds of music in mainland China? What are people listening to?

EF: Chinese pop music is most popular and listened to in China. This includes mainland and Taiwanese pop music (known as C-pop or Mandopop) as well as Hong Kong pop music (known as Cantopop). An online survey conducted of 314 individuals between September 21, 2012, and April 28, 2013, found pop music leading, followed by classical music and independent music. International genres that have also had an impact on the Chinese music market are Korean Pop (K-pop) which has grown considerably in recent years, followed by Japanese Pop (J-pop).

Music and Traditional Media in China

In the US, normal broadcast or "terrestrial" radio is still one of the major ways people listen to music, although it is now competing with many other forms of music delivery, including Internet radio and streaming services. In fact, even in their cars, one of the few places people still listen to music on terrestrial radio, many people are now listening to satellite and Internet radio services.

SG: Is terrestrial radio more important in China than in the US? If anyone is still listening to music via terrestrial broadcast in China, what are they listening to?

EF: According to CSM Media Research, comprehensive nationwide broadcast coverage of the population reached 96.78 percent in 2010. The home remains by far the primary location for listening to radio, followed by the automobile—that, though, has been increasing in recent years, probably reflecting growing car ownership. Lagging far behind is listening to radio at work and school. In terms of programming, the three most listened-to categories in order are news, talk radio, and music entertainment.

Internet radio has really taken off in China. According to research conducted by Beijing University, 58 percent of respondents listened to it out of a sample of 110 surveyed. Among those listening to Internet radio, 11 percent listened daily while 30 percent listened three to five times a week. The major Internet and social media platforms are the primary sources for online radio listenership, including RenRen, Sina, Xiami, and Baidu.

SG: Another question about traditional forms of music delivery before we get into digital methods: What about music on Chinese TV? What do they watch and listen to in China and how popular is it?

EF: *Super Girls*, a TV show produced by HNTV (Hunan Satellite TV) between 2004 and 2006, launched the music competition craze in China. As the show's popularity grew, HNTV's audience rating jumped to number two nationwide, right behind national broadcaster CCTV. Today's most popular Chinese music TV show is *The Voice of China*, which has kept HNTV at the top of the ratings heap.

SG: Final question on traditional music distribution in the PRC: We have all heard about rampant physical piracy in China throughout the years, even government-run factories that pirates use at night to make unauthorized CDs. Is there a legal physical record business in China, or are you considered a fool if you buy an authorized CD?

EF: The rampant state of piracy in China has of course been well documented. For years, there was an interesting cat-and-mouse game between the labels and pirates to try to be first to market with new releases. Worst of all, this piracy quickly migrated to the digital marketplace, much as it had done in the West, though more thoroughly. But the situation has been changing in recent years. Leading the charge has been the government that increasingly sees the value of protecting intellectual property (China and the US now lead the world in patent filings according to WIPO) and having a healthy cultural market.[348] Pirate sites have been shut down and major online platforms such as Baidu have to some extent cleaned up their acts. This is perhaps most evident in the online video market where online video portals have banded together to fight video piracy.[349]

Ironically, independent artists and labels, including the two largest ones, Modern Sky and Maybe Mars, continue to release physical CDs in China. These in part serve as promotional tools as well as being sold at live shows.

Music and New Media in China

SG: Do the Chinese listen to music on their desktops or laptops? For instance, I listen to Spotify on my desktop throughout a typical day. If they do listen to music on their home computers, what are they listening to? And is it licensed?

EF: While the Chinese listen overwhelmingly to music from online sources (a study found that 79 percent of Chinese people listened to music online), there is little data on the breakdown between PC (desktop/laptop) and mobile. According to Youku, the largest video platform, the split is 50/50. Nearly all the major music streaming services as well as video platforms have mobile apps that appear to be ubiquitously utilized. These services have begun licensing music and video content, though these are usually upfront deals with no revenue-share.

SG: We have heard that the leading Internet search engine in China, that is, Baidu, cooperates with and profits from online piracy, true? Or have things changed?

EF: Baidu actually used to have a page dedicated to searching MP3 files. But they have since launched a music service called Ting (which means "listen" in Chinese) subsequent to a licensing deal with the major labels.[350] This came in part as a consequence of pressure from their joining the WTO and from USTR (the Office of the United States Trade Representative). Generally, things are changing, and there is even greater awareness among consumers of copyright issues and respect for intellectual property.

SG: Does YouTube operate in China? If not, is there a service like it, how popular is it, and what's the most popular content?

EF: YouTube is blocked in China, as are most Western social media sites such as Facebook and Twitter. I was recently surprised to find Soundcloud being blocked on my last trip. The one notable exception is Linkedin, which recently launched a Chinese version of their site.

One consequence of this has been the growth of a healthy domestic Internet market, something somewhat unique in the world. Sites like Renren (Facebook), Sina's Weibo (Twitter), and Youku (YouTube) have hundreds of millions of users with their parent companies traded on Wall Street. This success has extended to mobile apps, where WeChat has grown overnight to over 300 million members.

Speaking specifically of video, a China Internet Watch report from February/March 2013 found that the top three video networks were Youku, Tencent, and Letv. The most popular content are TV series (typically dramas), followed by variety shows (mostly singing competitions such as the *Voice of China*).

SG: In the US, YouTube has negotiated licenses with music copyright owners and pays them a portion of ad revenues when their music is played. Is that how it works in China?

EF: As I mentioned, both video platforms and streaming services are licensing content from copyright holders, though these are typically up-front payments with little to no ad-revenue sharing. In part, this is due to the inability and/or unreliability of data reporting.

SG: China is now the second leading market for smartphones. Do they listen to music on their phones, and has that become the primary source of listening to prerecorded music in China? If so, what kind of music are they listening to on their smartphones?

EF: All the major streaming services have apps that are widely used and have become one of the leading sources for listeners. These include QQMusic, Xiami, Douban, and Baidu, to name just a few. In 2013, Tencent partnered with Guangdong Telecom to offer a data package for QQMusic music service.[351]

State of Live Music in China and the US

SG: Do the Chinese like to see live music? Where do they go and what do they listen to?

EF: Live music has gone from practically nonexistent to around 300 festivals per year. The biggest festivals are Midi Fest (oldest and longest-running rock fest), Strawberry Festival (run by the top indie label Modern Sky), and Zebra Festival, which features more pop artists. But beyond that there are festivals covering nearly every genre, such as JZ Shanghai (jazz) or Hanggai (folk). In the last few years, festivals have been branching outside of first-tier cities and spreading across the country.

Live houses are also quite popular, particularly in first-tier cities, with Beijing having over a dozen playing primarily independent Chinese bands. Some of the more popular ones are Yugong Yishan, Mao Livehouse, and Temple Bar. Shanghai, on the other hand, has a thriving club scene featuring every form of EDM and attracting world-class DJs.

SG: Do Western artists tour? How do they do?

EF: AEG and Live Nation have become quite active in China, bringing big-name Western artists ranging from Metallica to Justin Bieber. One factor that had limited Western artists touring China was the lack of infrastructure, particularly the quality venues required by major label acts. But that has changed with the new world-class venues such as Mercedes Benz Arena in Shanghai and Mastercard Center in Beijing. A more recent problem for major Western acts has been sticker shock, with ticket pricing rivaling what one would find in major Western markets, despite the income disparity. Beyond major acts, a growing number of independent acts have been touring China, usually in conjunction with festival bookings. Despite the challenges I mentioned, Western acts have generally found an enthusiastic audience in China.

SG: Tell us about Chinese music in the US. I know you're active in this area. Tell us about what you are up to!

EF: Chinese music, like any foreign-language music, has an incredibly hard time penetrating the US market. For independent Chinese bands, this is compounded by travel costs and onerous costs for performance visas. I've been involved in Taiwan Music showcases at CMJ for the past three years, which have been funded by the Taiwan government. One bright spot we've capitalized on is the significant Chinese immigrant and foreign student population in NYC that have shown a real enthusiasm for supporting their artists. In fact, Live Nation recently launched in Taiwan, resulting in their bringing the biggest Mandarin rock band, Mayday, to Madison Square Garden. But it will still take many years of effort to break through to an English-speaking audience.

In my own case, I've signed several acts from Taiwan and China (DJ Code, for example) that I believe have a real opportunity to cross over to a broader audience.

PART IV
WINNING STRATEGIES AND COMPELLING IDEAS

This section provides practical "how-to" advice regarding success in the digital era for both artists and entrepreneurs. It's intended to inspire those who seek to thrive in the new world of music business with examples of people who have taken advantage of emerging technologies in the digital era.

Chapter 20

HOW TO WRITE HIT SONGS IN THE DIGITAL AGE

An Interview with Jay Frank, Author of *FutureHit.DNA*

In *FutureHit.DNA: How the Digital Revolution Is Changing the Top 10 Songs*, Jay Frank details the ingredients of successful songs in the digital age. Jay also recently launched his own record company, called DigSin (see the interview with Jay about DigSin, which incorporates a unique business model, in Chapter 1).

SG: Tell us a little bit about your background and what inspired you to write your book.

JF: With regard to the book, I have been involved in digital music since its dawn in around 1995. I have constantly been watching from interesting vantage points on how people use music. I wrote my book *FutureHit.DNA* because people were paying attention to the technologies, but nobody was paying attention to exactly what that was doing to the music fan or the consumer on the other end.

Through various jobs I have had in the business, including senior vice president of music at Country Music Television and as vice president of label relations and music programming at Yahoo Music, I got to see the consumer perspective, what made them connect with songs and what did not. That was the inspiration for the book.

SG: The principal thesis of your book is that due to digital distribution, the elements that made hit songs yesterday are losing ground and new techniques must be implemented for number one songs today. Did you write *FutureHit.DNA* primarily for songwriters and artists?

JF: I wrote it primarily for songwriters, artists, and producers. Because I certainly have felt, to some degree, that the business model conversation that dominated the bulk of the last decade was somewhat of a red herring. I wanted to see, if there was music or artists that really played well, whether they would sell at levels that were pretty close to some of the peak years of the music business, Taylor Swift being the prime example.

When you look at how well her records sell, both physical and digital, you say, well, geez, there must be a reason for this. When I was at Yahoo, I would notice patterns of what songs were really driving user interaction online. I was really seeing some similarities, and through that was somewhat able to predict which songs had a higher likelihood of becoming hits, versus some other songs. And, you know, I just started writing it down, and before you knew it, it was an outline for a book, and I just kept going.

SG: So what are the elements that you need in order to have a hit song today?

JF: Well, a lot of what I talk about is really focusing on three major points of the song: the beginning, the middle, and the end. Which sounds pretty obvious but is pretty consistent. The beginning is what I tell artists to focus on the most. And that's because the major change in the last several years has been in the platform of music discovery: the new song you used to stumble upon on the radio has become something that you get on demand through online streaming. The difference there is that, with the radio, you might happen to come in at a song's hook and say, "Ooh, this is fairly good," and stay to hear the whole song. Now, when you're discovering online, all discovery is happening at the same point, which is the very beginning of the song, at the zero-second mark. So now you have to say, "Okay, now the beginning of my song is more crucial than ever." On top of that, you don't have a DJ to help guide you into the song, talking over the introduction. So you have to make the beginning of the song that much more compelling. And the one thing that I've seen, and I saw this all the time, is that consumers give a song about 10 seconds to impress them. So, if you have an introduction to a song that goes 16 seconds and just kind of meanders along, the listener is going to lose interest. You pretty much have about seven seconds before something triggers in the listener's mind to say, "Eh, this song is not interesting to me, I need to go to the next song." So, more and more, the popular songs are songs that have shorter introductions. As a matter of fact, so far in the first half of this year, the top 25 selling downloads have an average introduction length of just over six seconds.

SG: So a major change is that there's no DJ describing what's coming up on most digital services such as Pandora, Last.fm, iRadio, or Spotify, so you as the writer have to introduce the song well yourself.

JF: Right, and on top of that, you then also have a much higher level of volume of discovery at your fingertips. You know, a radio station might add two or three new songs a week, and you're going to discover from that pool. Meanwhile, now any day that you go online, there's thousands of songs that are released every week. It's physically possible, if you were to listen to all the music 24 hours a day, seven days a week, it's physically possible for you to hear only five percent of what's released in any given week. So that volume of music is always calling out to the people who are trying to discover music. So, when they go and hear something and immediately make a split-second decision to say, "Eh, I'm not that interested in it," there's another song that's calling them. So they will go to a different website, they'll skip ahead to the next song.

And the thing is that when you press the skip button or go to a different website, in your brain you are making a negative association with that artist. So even if that song might actually be good, after the listener has dismissed it, maybe after only seven seconds, you now have a bigger hurdle to convince that person to like that song, and/or that artist. Now there's a negative association, and who's got the time to go back; I've got to go listen to the other 95 percent of the songs that it's impossible for me to hear. So you have to really impress someone quickly, you have to engage them fast, because if you don't, there's just a very high likelihood that they'll never come back.

SG: *Future Hit* focuses on the end of a song a great deal. Why is that so important?

JF: I write a lot in the book about how at the end of the song, an artist should actually put something that makes the ending seem somewhat incomplete, or a false ending. And the reason for that is, with so many songs out there, how do you make a song sticky once someone gets to the end? How can you actually make it memorable? And it's a somewhat obvious trick, but what you can do is, you actually fail to provide a chord resolution, therefore making the end of the song seem incomplete, especially if it happens somewhat abruptly. Then the consumers, the listeners, in their minds, are trying to build that song. It's similar to when you go walking around, and you say, why is that song stuck in my head? Chances are, that song is stuck in your head because you were somewhere—maybe it was a store, maybe it was in your car—and you left that area before the song was completed. And your brain tries to complete that song in your head. There's a great book called *This Is Your Brain on Music* that really dives into the phenomenon of how that happens. And one way that you can trick the listener is to actually create those intentionally. So that if a song actually ends where there's not that chord resolution, then the listener's brain will likely keep humming that song or thinking about that song. To the point where if you do it right, it becomes the itch that you can't scratch, which means that you have to listen to the song again in order to be able to feel satiated by that song. But of course, the song always has a false ending, so you're just going to create an endless loop. But through that endless loop you'll actually create a song that people will want to listen to again and again.

SG: Can you give us an example of a song with a great ending?

JF: One of the best examples, I think recently, is the Ke$ha song "Tick Tock." I think it's a perfectly constructed song for the new digital ag. It's got a zero-second intro; it just dives right into the first verse the minute that it starts. There's a lot of other details throughout the song, but then when it gets to the end of the song it actually plays the first note of the chorus. It's the very ending of the song, and it's a short ending, and a very cold ending, but that first note of the chorus is not actually the chord resolution. The chord resolution actually happens at about the seventh beat into the chorus. So it feels like it's not resolved, even when, to some degree, it is, and it's starting the chorus, just a little bit, so that your brain will want to start singing that chorus again once you leave that song. Very, very tricky but very, very effective. One of the reasons why, in less than a year, that song became one of the top 10 selling downloads of all time.

SG: You also write about how making a song longer can result in more financial success when it comes to digital services. Can you elaborate on this?

JF: That's the notion that every one of these new companies, whether it's going to be iTunes on the sale side; Spotify, Rhapsody, or Rdio on the subscription services; or even Internet radio stations such as Pandora or Last.fm, they all have to do one thing, which is manage their costs. And the best thing that they can do is keep people on as long as possible while paying out as little as possible. Let's make no bones about it. Much as they're glad that artists are making money from their service, they want to pay out as little as they can. They're a business. So one way they're able to do that is by monitoring which songs are most popular and then figuring out which songs actually cost them the least. So, you know, one of the examples I use is that, if somebody has a two-minute punk rock song, and that punk rock song is not that exciting, somebody in one of these services might take notice and say, "Hey, you know what, it costs us three times as much to stream three two-minute punk rock songs as it costs us to stream 'Stairway to Heaven' or 'Hotel California' once." So what is their incentive to stream those songs? It's three times as much to stream those punk rock songs as it is a proven favorite like "Stairway to Heaven" or "Hotel California." If you were a business, who would you side with? You'd side with "Hotel California." A lot of these songs that are short that don't necessarily have a great user interaction are going to have difficulty gaining traction.

Figure out ways to subtly lengthen the song a little bit more, just so that song becomes that much cheaper than something else. If a company like, say, Pandora, can figure out how to reduce their average from 15 songs played on the radio per hour to 12 songs, if Pandora can do this, with their millions of listeners, we're talking millions of dollars in cost savings per year. So it's in their best interests to do that. So if you as an artist are able to create all these things, make them happen, and then just subtly, somehow, without really making the song overstay its welcome, extend the song by a good 20 to 30 seconds, then you have a higher likelihood of making it more cost effective to that service.

SG: So you're saying that Pandora, which pays SoundExchange based on the number of times a user listens to each song, would prefer longer songs to decrease its payout?

JF: Yes, SoundExchange is most directly affected because the law reads that you are paying per stream. Similarly, though, what I believe is going to be happening is that, as you get more and more personalized services and personalized streams, it's important for the artist to own the listening experience. Say the listener, the person on the other end, let's call it, has an hour to listen to music. Listeners have other things going on in their lives, and they have a finite period of time to listen to music. If with a longer song you are able to own more of that time, more of that listening experience, then you are blocking out your competition, you're preventing them from hearing another person's song, and then therefore you're going to get a larger percentage of that listener's royalty perspective coming towards you. So the more that you're actually able to own that experience—and I think that this will also play out in your performance rights obligations, because if you're able to do that, then you can actually create a bigger share of the plays, and ultimately, when all the figures are reported back to you, whether it's SoundExchange or an ASCAP or a SESAC, you are actually going to get a larger percentage of the royalties. Now, that larger percentage may not be super huge, but at the end of the day, these things will start to add up as more and more of these services really start to generate meaningful revenue.

SG: I'm going to play devil's advocate: Many critics and music fans complain that when it comes to certain genres, pop and R & B in particular, there's a deep similarity between all the songs and especially the hits. If everyone followed your advice, wouldn't we get even more same-sounding songs?

JF: The answer is yes. Guilty as charged! And I don't necessarily think that's a bad thing. As much grief as the record companies get, the one thing you have to remember is that, for the most part, they're music fans. They really, really enjoy music. And when you have pop hits that spin off tons and tons of cash, these people usually go and make investments, it could be half a million dollars, it could be 2 million dollars, and they go and find things that they just feel artistically are good and deserve a chance. One of the biggest problems over the last several years is that they didn't have that cash on hand to develop those other artists. I can't point to one specifically off the top of my head, but there have been plenty of studies that say that when a media or entertainment business gets into a period of significant homogenization it actually also becomes the period of biggest creativity, because there's more money flowing to fund that creativity. So what I actually think will happen is that, as some of these pop hits become bigger and bigger, and become more monetizable, it will create more cash flow in the business, these record companies will actually start experimenting more, and quite frankly, like you're doing a new edition of your book, probably in three or four years I'll have to do a new edition of mine because there will be all new techniques that define what the future hits are.

SG: A lot of people also complain about Auto-Tune, which is, as you know, software that music producers use to correct pitch in vocal and instrumental performances, to disguise off-key inaccuracies and mistakes, and that has allowed singers to perform perfectly tuned vocal tracks without actually singing in tune. The backlash is that performances are kind of phony—you're not hearing human voices, you're hearing machine-generated music—and it's also resulted in many songs sounding more or less alike. What's your opinion on Auto-Tune?

JF: I probably have two opinions. One is that, just like any other technology, you can have people who can take that technology to a place of creativity. T-Pain was the first person who really did that with Auto-Tune by taking it to its extreme and coming up with a unique sound that worked for him. And I think Will.I.Am is actually doing the same thing right now with his music. On the other side of it, one of the biggest problems I have with Auto-Tune is not the homogenization of the song, but the fact that people spend way more time making their sounds perfect versus getting more songs out into the marketplace. I talk a lot in my book about how people need to release more songs more often. Nowadays, when you have two years in between people's albums, and in some cases you might even have a year to a year and a half between singles, people are forgetting about artists. They're moving at the speed of light. And so, all of a sudden, artists will find with their second album that they might as well be new artists, because they've lost their fan base in that intervening time. It's much more effective for artists to release more singles more often, because then they can keep fans excited, keep them engaged. Then the artist can experiment more. Because, if fans know a new song's going to come two or three months later, then they know that if the song is a dud, that's okay, we might get a good one coming up in a couple of weeks. I don't think there's nearly enough of that right now, and one of the biggest problems with Auto-Tune is that rather than just accepting something for being really good and enjoying the spontaneity of the performance, people are spending that much extra time trying to make the song perfect. And I don't think that that necessarily helps it, because, as I think you know all too well, if the underlying song itself isn't good, all the Auto-Tuning in the world isn't going to save it, and all the Auto-Tuning in the world isn't necessarily going to make it that much more saleable. I think it's much more productive for an artist to release more songs more often and grow their fan base that way.

SG: You're what you are saying is the problem isn't really the technology itself, it's the way you use it?

JF: That's correct. It's totally in the way you use it. And, you know, on that point, there are plenty of people who use it to homogenize the sound of the song, and I agree with you. I don't think in the long term that helps anybody.

Chapter 21
HOW TO MARKET A RECORD IN THE DIGITAL AGE

Twenty by Boyz II Men

Mark Offenbach is a former senior vice president of Sony Music, and currently serves as an associate professor of music marketing at Drexel University. He recently worked on the production and distribution of the 10th studio album of the great American R & B group Boyz II Men. The album is called *Twenty* in recognition of Boyz II Men's 20 years in the music business and includes 13 original songs and 8 rerecorded Boyz II Men classics. Boyz II Men are no longer on a label and this was a complete indie project. In this interview we discuss how the record was produced and distributed without the help of a major label, the strategies that Mark and his partners implemented, and the challenges that they faced.

SG: How did you break into the music business?

MO: I graduated from Brooklyn College with a degree in music. Although I studied classical music, I love all kinds of music, including jazz, pop, R & B, hip-hop, everything. After graduating I tried to get a job in the music business, but the best I could do was a job working at the great, but now defunct, music retail chain Sam Goody. That is kind of where I started cutting my teeth working music retail. Then I got a job at a small classical label. Although I love classical music, I wanted to really get into the pop/rock world. So I went to work with an independent distributor of alternative rock music. After that I landed a job at Universal Records, but soon secured an executive position at Sony Music, where I spent the majority of my career as a senior marketing executive.

SG: Boyz II Men are no longer signed to a label, so who came up with the idea of making *Twenty*, and how did they convince the other members of the team to go ahead with this project?

MO: Well, first of all, the music business is about art. But it's also about commerce. The reason why I'm in the music business, and I would imagine the reason why most people are in the music business, is that they love music. But, as I said, there is commerce involved, because everybody's got to live and eat and pay rent and all that. With *Twenty*, I had left Sony Music and I was getting consulting jobs here and there, which were great. Through my connections of managers and artists, I heard that Boyz II Men were unhappy with their major label connection and wanted to possibly do something new.

So, just from a friend of a friend of a friend, I got to speak to their manager and then eventually spoke to the band with some other people I had done business with before. Then we said, "Hey, why don't we try to do this on our own? Let us do a joint venture, 50/50 profit split with the artist." Because of the way the business is today, and because of the way you can reach people online, you don't need a huge staff. The way I look at it today, and the way a lot of artists are looking at it today, if you have a small team (three to four people) who really have a lot of experience in the business and really understand the business and know the business (all aspects of marketing, sales, promotion, A&R, packaging, digital marketing), you do not need that many people if you have the right little core. You can really make something happen. So we felt Boyz II Men, their management, and myself and my partners (only two other people), could be successful.

SG: *Twenty* includes 21 new tracks—that's really two albums. Was it expensive to produce?

MO: The recording budget was . . . I think we ended up close to $300,000.

SG: So, in terms of major artist releases these days, is $300,000 a lot of money, a little money, or in-between?

MO: No, that is a lot of money. The reason why it ended up being a lot of money is that Boyz II Men don't write all of their material. They write some of their material, and in the R & B hip-hop world, that's kind of the case out there. A lot of people have to go out and get other people to write and help produce the albums. And we used some of the best in the business, including Babyface, Dallas Austin, and Jimmy Jam and Terry Lewis and Teddy Riley. So a lot of the costs involved were getting all these great, great writer/producers out there who definitely deserve to get paid. They write great music and that's how they make a living. I think all the producers and writers involved on the Boyz II Men record delivered great, great songs.

SG: What were these legendary artists and producers like to work with?

MO: Unfortunately, the only aspect I worked on was getting contracts done with the band and with the writer/producers. It was really due to the fact that it was a joint venture. Boyz II Men wanted to make the record themselves. This is the first time they really themselves put a record together. But my partners and I did have a creative vision. We brought in Charlie Wilson, which was the first single off the record. That was kind of our input, because Charlie is a great R & B singer and big in the urban-adult radio arena, and we thought if we put Charlie Wilson and Boyz II Men together to do an urban-AC record it could become a pretty big hit, which it was. The first single was "More than You'll Ever Know," featuring Charlie Wilson. It was one of the biggest R & B, urban-AC debuts of the year. It did very, very, very well. And one of my partners was involved in the creative process, but mostly it was the band working with the producers. I did the marketing of the record.

SG: I understand that the key to your distribution strategy was setting up an exclusive deal for distribution of the CD through Walmart.

MO: Right, Walmart was a great way of getting the record out there. I knew that Walmart sold a lot of Boyz II Men records, physical product. So, with Walmart having over 3,000 stores and 150 million people a week walking into those stores, it is a nice partner to be involved with.

Plus, I had done other exclusive deals with Walmart through my career, so I kind of looked at that as, "Hey, that might possibly be an avenue." When it was introduced to them, they were 100 percent into it. They really, really wanted to do it, so that is kind of why we went that route.

SG: What were the benefits of the Walmart deal?

MO: Tremendous amount of marketing back from Walmart. Having stacks of Boyz II Men records all around and having signage all over the Walmart stores. And doing a special Walmart Soundcheck, which is an in-store video promotion where we record the band live. Yes, so a tremendous amount of giveback from Walmart.

SG: Were you happy the way the exclusive CD deal with Walmart turned out?

MO: We had a certain sales goal to hit for the record, which we hit, which was great. The fact of the matter is, when *Twenty* came out it debuted (funnily enough) at #20 on the *Billboard* album chart, which for an independent small little rinky-dink bunch of guys running around, to have an album debut at #20 is pretty . . . very, very fulfilling and it was like, "Wow. We did it."

SG: Did Walmart make available older Boyz II Men albums with *Twenty*? If so, did catalogue sales get a boost?

MO: They did, and there was a definitely a tremendous boost in sales from catalogue, but my concept of the new Boyz II Men record was that they rerecord eight of their biggest, their greatest hits for the new record. So my whole plan was, "Okay, if I am a Boyz II Men fan, here is the brand new record plus, oh my god, here is 'Mama,' and 'End of the Road,' and 'I Will Make Love to You,'" which are their classic, classic, huge hits. So I kind of used that as a big value statement for people to buy the new record.

SG: I understand that even though you had an exclusive CD deal with Walmart you kept the digital rights. How did you get Walmart to agree to this? Didn't they fear that downloads would cannibalize the physical sales?

MO: No, they did not. If you look at past history of Boyz II Men, it's 75 percent physical, 25 percent digital. Plus, the real reason was . . . I was very, very honest with the Walmart people. It is the fact of the matter that nobody is going to Walmart.com to download digital music. If they had a platform that enabled, that was viable, out there to consumers I would have suggested that. But I kind of laid it out on the table, and they agreed and they were great about it. I said, "Look, obviously the business is going towards digital. Obviously digital is growing, physical is shrinking. So it would be unfair to the artist." I mean, I am representing the band. I said, "It would be unfair in my representation of my artist and my partners on this project not to give them a fair shake out there in the world of selling digital music. You cannot offer that, so you really have to be understanding about this and allow us to go elsewhere on the digital." They were very understanding. It was also helpful that at that time they were just about closing down their digital store.

SG: Did they at least insist on a holdback before you went digital? Allow them to sell CDs for at least a period of time before the digital release?

MO: No, they did not.

SG: You must have been very persuasive. So, how did you do with digital sales? Did you sell a lot of units compared to the CD?

MO: Yeah, we are at a little less than 40 percent digital compared to CD.

SG: Where are most of these sales occurring, on iTunes?

MO: Yeah, iTunes. But Amazon's been great. eMusic has been really, really good. But obviously iTunes was the bulk of it.

SG: And did you make a direct deal with the digital stores or use an aggregator?

MO: Our digital distributor in the US for the record was The Orchard. They put the record in all the digital stores here. I worked with them on the digital side and on the physical side. Outside the US, I did a distribution deal for both CD and digital with Universal. So sales outside the US are all run by Universal out of London.

SG: How are you doing with foreign sales?

MO: Fine. That was a really big part of the whole deal, that I have relationships internationally. So when doing the pitch to Boyz II Men I had already spoken to Universal for ex-US and they were very, very excited because they had all the past Boyz II Men albums. So part of the pitch to Boyz II Men was, "Hey, by the way, we have the US, but we can also get a great partner with Universal ex-US." Japan was carved out of that, because Boyz II Men have a separate direct deal with Japan. But they were very happy with the results.

SG: Okay. Now, are you selling singles digitally, or just the album?

MO: No, absolutely singles digitally. That is how it's done . . . it's almost like the olden days, when you had to sell a bunch of singles and you did not sell many albums a lot of times.

SG: Are you selling more singles than albums?

MO: Quantitatively, we have sold more digital singles than albums, yes.

SG: The *Twenty* album is available on Spotify. A lot of critics complain they don't pay enough money to labels and artists. What was your experience?

MO: We haven't received much money from Spotify. But I believe it's just starting to grow in this country. It is at a very early stage. I was in a very interesting Spotify presentation last week, as a matter of fact. Subscription music services I think are going to be a big part of the business. Whether or not those subscription music services are paying enough now, that could be up for question and discussion. But it's definitely, I think, going to be a huge part of the music business in the future.

SG: We can agree that you did not make a lot of money from Spotify, so the next question is, is Spotify helping promote the album or is it just like another pirate site where people can get it for free and don't have to pay?

MO: It is a combination of the two. Look, obviously if I'm a 20- . . . a 15-, 16-, 17-, 18-year-old kid, and I have the ability to go to Spotify and listen to something for free, I might not buy it. But, if you are an artist like Boyz II Men, who have a very vast catalogue, a lot of titles out there, or any artist that has a pretty decent catalogue, that is the big question that is up for discussion: "Okay, if you have a dozen albums up there and the Spotify users can sample all the albums, are they eventually going to move to purchase?" I mean, Spotify obviously tells you that, yes, they do. But I have not seen that proven yet. I would like to believe that somebody would do that, but back in the day when you and I were buying records, you wanted to own it. Now you don't have to. You can listen to it any time you want. But hopefully as they get more subscribers and/or advertising money the payouts will increase.

SG: You said that Walmart's really helped with marketing, especially in-store. But did you have to promote the project independently, and was it expensive?

MO: Definitely you always have to promote independently. If you have units available in-store or if you have it up digitally on whatever digital service provider there is, you still have to do marketing. You still have to let people know that the record's out and that the music is out. So, yeah, we did a ton of TV shows. *The Today Show*, *The Rosie O'Donnell Show*, *Entertainment Tonight*, and more. You do all those shows and that costs money. You have to get the guys around and move them around and fly them around. So it definitely is not cheap.

SG: Those shows never pay travel costs and only pay a few dollars as "scale" required by the unions, correct?

MO: That's right; you do not make any money from being on TV shows. The point is . . . you eventually make money from being on a TV show because of exposure.

SG: Right. And you were able to get that kind of exposure because Boyz II Men was the most famous and bestselling R & B act of all time.

MO: Yes. But it still was not easy. In fact, we had a great publicity partner and I have a lot of connections in that world as well, so if you have the right team, it's doable. The fact that Boyz used to be the most successful R & B act does not make getting great exposure a slam dunk.

SG: Let's go to the magical place they call the bottom line. At the end of the day, did this project make a lot of money for you, your partners, and the band? Some money? Or did you lose money?

MO: Definitely no one lost money. On the other hand no one made millions of dollars, either. I was not like, "Oh my god, look how much money we are making!" That did not happen, but it was all very satisfying for all parties financially as well as artistically. And we would love to try and do it again.

SG: What did you learn from this project about making and selling records in today's very challenging record business?

MO: What I learned was that although Boyz II Men are an iconic group it's still not easy to sell records today. It is very difficult. The market is bombarded with hundreds if not thousands of new records every day. So it was a lot of work to get attention. It was a lot of fun but a lot of work, too. What I learned is you just have to really dot all your i's and cross all your t's. If you are launching new music out there, you have to really be very intelligent about it and smart about it and really be ready to spend a lot of energy. But it's very fulfilling at the end of the day.

SG: Any last words of advice?

MO: I guess the parting shot is from one of my mentors, Henry Droz, who ran WEA (Warner Elektra Atlantic) back in the day when the business was incredibly profitable and selling tons of tons of units and everybody paid for music. Henry said to me, "Marc, the most important thing is that you are having fun." And he said, "Because if you cannot have fun in the record business, in the music business, something is wrong." And that is my parting shot. It's still possible having financial success selling records, but it isn't worth doing unless you are having fun.

Chapter 22

HOW TO USE SPOTIFY TO EXPAND YOUR FAN BASE AND MAKE MONEY

Spotify has often been criticized for not fairly compensating artists, particularly indie artists, for their music. But in this article, New York City–based independent artist Ron Pope reports that not only is it possible to make some money from Spotify, but Spotify can also be a useful marketing tool.

The following piece was originally published in the *Huffington Post* and is reprinted with permission.

"No One Wants to Talk Numbers When It Comes to Streaming Revenue. Well, Here Are Mine"

My name is Ron Pope. I'm an independent musician, producer, songwriter, and label owner. I read the recent post on the *Guardian* "Plugged In" which questioned why no independent artists are standing up and cheering for Spotify. It seemed as if they were beseeching someone like me to respond.

I want to be clear that no one from Spotify has asked me to write this article and I'm not being paid for sharing my opinion. In the past, I've heard many people complain that no one wants to talk numbers when it comes to streaming revenue; well, here are mine. My music was added to Spotify in September of 2010; through the most recent report, which runs through November 2013, I've had over 57 million plays and they've paid me out $334,636 with over $200,000 of that coming in 2013. I'm getting over a million streams in Sweden alone most months. As a result of this, I was offered a very respectable guarantee to play at the Bråvalla festival there last summer.

I have an extensive catalogue; Spotify allows fans to take in all of my music so that they can become fans of me as an artist, rather than directing them to one particular single. That's why my Swedish fans are able to sing along to songs that are eight years old the same way they sing along to songs that are eight months old. With Spotify, it's not about a single; the fans can pore over my entire catalogue and follow my journey from my first album all the way through to today.

When I played in Norway in early 2012, I sold around 100 tickets; since then, my music has exploded on Spotify there. My upcoming show sold out at 450 tickets more than three months in advance. I'm seeing tangible effects from Spotify every day in my career. I can now sell hundreds of tickets in cities I'd never heard of just a few years ago. Last year, in countries where Spotify is popular, such as Norway and Sweden, I made eight times more per capital than I did in the United States. My three top countries in earnings for 2013 were the US, where there are about 317 million people, Sweden, where there are about 10 million people, and then Norway, where there are about 5 million people. Almost no one in Sweden and Norway is buying music; more than 97 percent of the revenue I'm generating in those countries comes from streaming.

I'm not going to argue about whether or not streaming cannibalizes sales; of course it does, and anyone who tries to convince you differently is selling snake oil and magic beans. Regardless of that fact, what I'm seeing is a marked increase in revenue because so much of my music is now being consumed by so many people. I'd argue that many of these people wouldn't have taken the opportunity to listen to me in the first place if they didn't have the option to check me out on Spotify without any initial monetary commitment.

Until a few years ago, I was deriving 95 percent of my income from selling digital singles; if there's anyone who should be afraid of streaming, it's me. Instead, I'm watching my fan base grow exponentially. My fans utilize social networking and streaming sites like Spotify to create an honest-to-goodness grassroots movement. These fans are consuming my entire catalogue rather than one specific single.

At this point, standing at the gates of Spotify with an angry lynch mob waving pitchforks and torches is like people who threw up their hands eight years ago bemoaning the death of the CD. At this juncture in history, the music industry is like the Wild West; we're all trying to figure out how to exist in a volatile new place that is constantly changing. Artists, label owners, producers, all of us have to look forward, not backward, and try to learn how to exist in a streaming world. I don't know that Spotify will be the savior of the music industry and bring back the boom time '90s bonanza that this business once enjoyed, but it has certainly worked wonders for my career. I felt it was only right for me to stand up and say so.

Chapter 23
HOW TO USE YouTube TO GET DISCOVERED:
(And How to Use MCNs to Expand Your YouTube Audience and Make Money)

Using YouTube to Get Discovered

We all know about videos going viral on YouTube, from Psy's "Gangnam Style" to "Harlem Shake." But new artists should be aware that they can use YouTube to get discovered even if their videos don't go viral. In fact, if only one person sees a video, that could be all that's needed, if that viewer is the "right" person.

Everyone knows or should know that if Justin Bieber's mom hadn't posted his second-place finish in a local talent show in Canada, he might have wound up flipping burgers in Ontario instead of becoming a superstar. YouTube is how Scooter Braun discovered him. In fact, as I am writing this in early spring 2014, Justin may wind up back in Ontario if he doesn't check into rehab, but that's not the Internet's fault. Others besides Justin's mom can take advantage of the Internet as well.

Bilingual singer/songwriter Lisenny Rodriguez was studying to become a music teacher when she realized, through singing before live audiences at school and church, that performing was her true calling. After graduating college, she used YouTube, Soundcloud, and Facebook to jump-start her journey into the music world. She began by recording covers of songs originally recorded by artists such as Leslie Grace, Beyoncé, and Prince Royce. A few months later, the girlfriend of a piano player in Henry Santos's band saw the videos. Santos is the cousin of one of the most successful Latin artists in the world, Romeo Santos, and both are former members of world renowned bachata band Aventura. Then the piano player messaged her through Facebook: "So I ran across ya youtube page the other day. Ma girl showed me. I'm like yeah diggin this girls talent. I play with Henry from Aventura. Ma brother is also one of the managers."

Within a week a meeting was arranged with the piano player and his brother, Henry's manager. They spoke with Lisenny about her musical interests and their plans for the band, and asked her to learn as much as she could of the vocal background parts of their songs for a rehearsal the following week. Impressed with her grasp of the material and her harmonizing skills, they immediately invited her to join them for their next show in Washington, DC.

How to Use MCNs to Expand Your YouTube Audience and Make Money: Interview with Fiona Bloom, Founder of the "Efficacy Channel"

YouTube is by far the world's leading video-sharing website. Launched in 2005, and owned by Google since 2006, YouTube is dizzyingly popular, and the stats are mind boggling:

More than 1 billion unique users visit YouTube each month.
Over 6 billion hours of video are watched each month on YouTube—that's almost an hour for every person on Earth.
100 hours of video are uploaded to YouTube every minute.

According to comScore, a company that provides analytics for the Internet, YouTube's 159 million active monthly US users watched 13 billion videos in December 2013, and YouTube reports that nearly 40 percent of all videos were music-related.[352] YouTube can give incredible exposure to new artists and even work with them to monetize their videos.

This interview helps explains how artists can harness the power of YouTube to make money and build an audience. Fiona Bloom is a well-known music publicist, promoter, and social media expert. She runs a one-stop music company for artists, the Bloom Effect, which focuses on publicity and PR but also organizes high-profile events and showcases on behalf of her clientele. She also operates a YouTube channel called Efficacy, which features interviews with new and emerging artists. Last year she decided to partner with IND Music, a leading Multi-Channel Network or "MCN." MCNs are companies that try to help people who produce content for YouTube, such as Fiona, reach a wider audience in exchange for a percentage of ad revenue generated by that content. MCNs try to extend a client's audience by promoting the client's content to the MCN's subscribers, who may be far more numerous than a client's original number of followers. IND, for instance, has over 4 million subscribers. MCNs also have relationships with advertisers who may offer the MCN's clients money in exchange for product placements and sponsorships.

SG: What is Efficacy and what inspired you to launch it?

FB: It's a channel that offers weekly interviews with super talented but undiscovered music artists from around the world. We focus on the personality of the artist by asking about the stuff behind the art—what excites them, and fun stuff like "How spicy do you like your food?" I launched it in 2008, when YouTube was still a fairly new platform. Obviously, many people were already using it to upload their favorite pet videos, but few realized the effect it would have on social engagement, and its power to reach a mass audience.

The Efficacy channel basically was inspired by all of the thousands of artists that I come across on my journey. I am out almost every night. I'm always discovering someone new, some new artist that blows me away, or an artist that has a passion or a flair for something. I also travel around the world, whether it's a festival that they have flown me out to speak at, or an event that I am producing overseas.

I meet tons and tons of artists. Most of these artists are unsigned. You might have heard of them, because they might be quite big in their local market, making quite a bit of noise, doing open mic or doing festivals, in small secondary markets in Holland, for example, or a tiny place in Malaysia. Nobody else has heard of them. So here I am, coming across them; I think they are pretty damn amazing, and I am thinking, "These artists need a platform. They need an outlet. They need a place to become discovered, express themselves, and get their message across to American audiences, or at least to people in the US, that they would not ordinarily have access to otherwise."

I started Efficacy as a platform for talented artists who deserved more exposure.

SG: Why the name, Efficacy?

FB: I came across the name as sort of play on words relating to my primary company, The Bloom Effect. Efficacy means "to create a desired effect." That's the literal definition. I thought, "Hmm, that's an unusual word; half the people aren't going to know what the hell it means, but it's intriguing . . ."

SG: You have almost 200 interviews up. I noticed they are approximately 5 to 10 minutes each. Do you produce them yourself, or do you hire a team to produce and edit them?

FB: No and no. This is what is so unique. What I do is send each artist an outline, just a general outline of really fun questions, and then the artists take it upon themselves to get the shooter, or do it themselves, and edit it. So what is beautiful about this is artists get their feet wet in learning editing and learning about shooting five- to seven- minute videos that they might not have ordinarily done otherwise. Or they become a professional about it and say, "I'm going to get a shooter to do this, and then we're going to go into edit, and I'm going to deliver you something great." So, if you look at the 121 episodes that are up right now, some of them are really excellent, some are average, some are, you know, some are so-so. It depends on the artist, it depends on how seriously they took it, and it depends on how savvy they were with creating video.

SG: In terms of popularity, some of your channel's videos don't have many views, but an artist like Allyssa Chic got more than 70,000.

FB: Yeah, basically over four days, there was a huge spike. I looked at my dashboard and I had over 21,000 engagement (retention), like you know you can see on the dashboard how many minutes people are listening. It was mind blowing to see "21,000 minutes viewed on Allyssa Chic," I was like, "Holy cow, that's a big number."

SG: Her video basically shows her driving around in her car talking into a camera. How did she get so many views?

FB: She has a large following. She is out of Miami and she also travels and has a lot of following overseas. She is a pretty girl, she is young, she is intelligent, and she is well spoken. Her music is great—I have seen her perform and she is fun, she is amazing. I do not know why a major label would not have scooped her up already and put her out.

SG: I understand that YouTube gives good analytics. How does that work?

FB: Absolutely! If you set up your own channel, when you go into your "dashboard" YouTube breaks down everything from the number of views of any particular video, for any particular time period, to the age of each person watching, to what county they watched the video from, to how long they watched, and much more. There is so much information there. The analytics are huge.

SG: I understand you recently partnered with a network. Which one, and why?

FB: For the first few years, Efficacy was really just kind of a side project, a fun thing that I was doing to give artists some exposure. Last year, though, I signed a deal with the largest music network on YouTube, called the IND Music Network. They believe in my content and they are helping me with audience outreach and promotion. So that relationship has really put YouTube at the forefront in everything that I am doing.

IND is promoting Efficacy in their online social pages. I put out a new video each week. When one comes out I will tweet it to them on Twitter or send it via Facebook, and then they retweet to their network . They post up new content video from their channel partners on their social web pages. They post me on the page of their channel on YouTube.

They also do a lot of events themselves, so whether they're at CMJ or New Music Seminary, they have signage up that will mention all their partners. Slowly but surely, they are starting to put me into more of their promotional packaging. Because, if you look at their channel feed, they have huge partners, I mean, partners who are doing way more business than me. But, at the same time, I'm new, they believe in me, and I am doing something really unique. Unique in the sense that these were all unheard-of artists that I'm giving spotlight to that have potential to really shine.

SG: Are you making a lot of money?

FB: No, not making a lot of money yet, but I am starting to see some checks. And, even though they are small at this stage, I do believe that in a year if you ask me that same question I will be able to say, "Not a lot of money, but it's a significant amount of money." And their share of the revenue that Efficacy generates is a very small percentage, considering what they're doing and what they bring to the table. But the partnership is definitely more me than them.

SG: How does IND monetize Efficacy?

FB: The same way as anyone can do it themselves: advertising. But IND puts select ads and strategically places the ads in the beginning and some at the end, and I have a lot of control over how often I want the ads to run, whether it is just a banner ad on the channel or a pre-roll in a video, etc.

SG: You get these options from IND, or directly from YouTube, or does IND work with YouTube on that?

FB: IND works with YouTube on that.

SG: Are you getting any kind of accounting statements?

FB: Yes. I get them from IND every month. IND keeps a small percentage and pays me the balance.

SG: What kind of information can you give us about how YouTube calculates what your share revenues are? Do you have any idea?

FB: Well, that is little gray for me, Steve. I can't really comment on that.

SG: Well, what we know is that YouTube pays primarily in accordance with the number of views that your videos receive. Those who have discussed how much they are making publicly are generally reporting that they receive around 3 to 4 one-hundredths of a penny per view—so that 10,000 views will generate $30 to $40. However, the amount may change depending on a number of factors, including how much ad revenue YouTube collects, if viewers are only seeing a banner versus a pre-roll, and whether they watch the pre-roll or skip it as soon as they can. However, the precise formula YouTube uses and what percentage of ad revenues they actually pay out are still pretty mysterious.

FB: I think as monetization becomes more popular, then it will come more to light. It will be less gray, and more black-and-white, absolutely.

SG: I hope so! What would you recommend to artists about YouTube?

FB: Well, to be honest, I would recommend every artist try to do this themselves. YouTube offers free access to millions of potential fans. Everybody has that at their fingertips. It is just a matter of the artists not being lazy and getting off their asses and creating more opportunity for themselves. I mean, I think all artists should take advantage of what YouTube has to offer.

SG: Should they do it themselves, or partner with a network as you have done with IND?

FB: As far as going into partnership, I mean, it is really up to you. I think initially the artist has to make some noise first. The artist has to at least come with, maybe not 100,000 channel views, but at least have enough content up there that they can then go to a partner and say, "Look, I have 50 shows up, I'm getting between 500 and 750 views over 2 to 3 days. I'm getting queries from Germany, queries from Japan." When it gets to that level, that's definitely when it's time to seek out a partner to help you take it to the next level. But I think every artist should be able to take advantage of this. Absolutely.

SG: So what's next for Efficacy? Any plans to enhance the service, or . . .

FB: Yes. What I would like to do with the Efficacy series is start to do some showcases. Maybe have fans choose their favorite Efficacy artist, then produce a showcase for the top three. Maybe I'd partner with ReverbNation—we'll see, I mean ReverbNation wants to work with me, so we'll see—but I will tabulate them and those top three, those winners so to speak, will get selected to play a showcase, whether it's Le Poisson Rouge, Drom, you know, anywhere. We can take it to New York, maybe we'll do it in DC, maybe we'll even do it in LA. What I'd eventually like to do in 2014 and 2015 is partner with SXSW or with CMJ and do an actual Efficacy showcase with one of those conferences. Then I want to get to the level where I have my own video production team that can go out on the field and shoot and edit as well.

SG: It seems like the opportunities are almost limitless and they exist for both for both artists and entrepreneurs like you. I think you've captured the spirit of this climate really well. Do you have any other advice to offer about using YouTube?

FB: My best advice to artists out there is to really believe in the brand that you have. Find your voice, make sure that it's unique and authentic, and just shoot. Get out there and shoot. You have got all kinds of opportunities with your smartphone, you can use a video camera. It isn't expensive anymore. Just go out and create content, capture content. Do it on the way to a nail salon. Shoot footage backstage or coming out with another musician. Let fans see a personality.

When they see your personality, you gain traction and you make new fans. Make sure they are not too long, because the attention span for most fans out there, they say, is about two minutes. If it's a music video, that's different, but if it's not a full song it's usually 2 to 3 minutes. Well, yes, you might say, "Fiona, your Efficacy videos are 7 minutes long." Yes, you are absolutely right, so part of me is also thinking to cut down some of the questions and make them a little shorter, absolutely. Because people don't watch all seven minutes. They're going to watch about 2 to 3 minutes on average, unless they are absolutely a huge, huge, huge fan, and then they will watch from beginning to end. Nine times out of 10, nobody is going to watch your clip from beginning to end. So, as far as that advice, just shoot, get out there, create that content, upload your content, and start having fun.

Chapter 24
HOW TO USE OTHER DIGITAL TOOLS TO SUCCEED
(And Why There Is No Guarantee That They Will Work)

- **Music blogs—how to use them to get a deal**
- **Your website—why it is still important and how to make it great**
- **Twitter and Facebook—how to use them to promote your music and make some money**

In 2011, when I wrote the third edition of this book, new digital resources and tools seemed to provide, if not a guarantee of success, at least the opportunity of tremendously improving its likelihood. Although the major labels were signing fewer and fewer artists, it seemed as though bands could use digital tools to replace them. For instance, services such as TuneCore and CD Baby offered any artist the opportunity to sell records on iTunes and other digital platforms throughout the world. This was never possible before. However, just after the third edition was published a study by Will Page, chief economist of the MCPS-PRS Alliance, found there were at least 10 million tracks available for sale by download on the Internet that had not been downloaded—even once! Although the web has made worldwide distribution possible, it does not guarantee that anyone will listen, let alone buy, new music. Marketing and promotion are still crucial to success in the music business, and the loss of the money and the small army of staffers that the labels used to provide has hurt new artists' chances for success. As Amanda Palmer pointed out in the foreword to this book, artists "still need HELP" to help promote their records, their tour, their merch, and, yes, even their crowdfunding campaigns, but without funding from the labels, how is a new artist supposed to pay for that "help"?

On the other hand, as discussed in the prior chapter, artists can easily take advantage of YouTube by themselves and for little or no cost, to give themselves a realistic chance of being discovered. There are other basic digital tools that are free or nearly free and that are easy to use. This chapter explores those opportunities. It is not meant to substitute for other sources or books that provide comprehensive overviews of different DIY online marketing techniques. For instance, one such resource is Ariel Hyatt's *Cyber PR for Musicians: Tools, Tricks, and Tactics for Building Your Social Media House.* Instead, this chapter discusses the most popular vehicles for online marketing as of 2014, and how musicians, even without financial resources or a professional team, can use them to improve their chances of getting noticed, building a buzz, and eventually finding the right person, or a deal, that will get them to the next level.

Music Blogs: How to Use Them to Get a Deal

As I was writing the third edition, I had an assistant who was also a talented musician. She was extremely bright, and always did a great job. When she wasn't working for me, she spent a great deal of time online. She corresponded often with blogs that specialized in her genre of music, progressive electronic. At first she would write about artists and songs that each of these bloggers was interested in. After she built up a strong rapport with them, she presented some of her own music. Because they already knew her as someone interested in the same music as they were interested in, and because she is extremely talented and her music was extremely polished, they gave her rave reviews. Eventually she appeared on the radar of major music blogs, particularly Pitchfork and Hype Machine. These blogs often follow smaller ones, including the ones that were singing her praises. They also reported positively on her music. She soon received an offer by a small label specializing in electronic music that was owned by one of the three major record companies. That label funded her first European tour, and manufactured and distributed her first album. She is now a very successful artist in her genre of music. Her name is Laurel Halo.

I asked Laurel if she thought blogs were still important and she said, "Music blogs aren't as popular as they used to be . . . [it's] mostly just big websites now. Social media is still valuable, but even that is questionable . . . [it's] generally best to create community in real life first." Although blogs may be less important than they used to be, a good review on *Pitchfork* or *Brooklyn Vegan*, which started as blogs and are now full-blown music websites, can exponentially expand an artist's potential fan base. In addition, for niche artists, such as progressive electronic music, getting the attention of lesser-known blogs can still be very important in getting a deal just as Laurel Halo did. Here are some suggestions for getting that attention.

Who Are Bloggers?

As of February 2014, there were around 172 million Tumblr and 75.8 million WordPress blogs in existence worldwide. Google's Blogger is probably the most popular blogging service used today, though Blogger does not offer public statistics. Of these tens of millions of blogs, there are probably millions dedicated to just music. No one has the precise number. As we suggested previously, the most read blogs, such as *Brooklyn Vegan*, *Pitchfork*, *Stereogum*, NPR's music blogs, and the hip-hop-oriented *WorldStar*, can deeply influence trends and give major boosts to particular musicians. However, a new artist can gain traction by approaching small blogs before they appear on the radar of these sites.

The individuals who maintain their own blogs tend to be literate, nerdy, and very enthusiastic about what they feature or discuss. Music bloggers are no exception—they are fierce music fans, often obsessively so. Some music bloggers love to write about new and undiscovered acts; some choose to feature what larger sites have already featured (artists that have the cultural "stamp of approval"); some write only about death metal, some only about Gregorian chants, others about very obscure types of dance music. Music bloggers' tastes vary widely, but one thread remains the same: They are devoted music fans who frequently write articles on the musicians and artists that they enjoy.

Which Blogs Should I Approach?

The most important factor in getting blog write-ups is to do your research. Be absolutely meticulous in finding blogs that write about the kind of music you make. Find blogs that feature the style or genre you are working in, as many blogs are genre-specific and will not post MP3s of artists who fall outside their preferred genres (remember, bloggers are mostly intense music nerds who tend to obsess over a few different genres and feature only artists that fall within their taste spectrum). Also, be sure to seek out blogs that feature artists at your level of visibility. There are plenty of music blogs on the Internet devoted to exposing new artists—seek these blogs out. There's not much point in sending e-mails to blogs that feature more established artists—many bloggers lament receiving hundreds of e-mails a day from aspiring musicians and simply have to delete whatever they don't instantly recognize by name. With a little research you can find many blogs well suited to your type of music and your level of success.

How to Attract Bloggers to Your Music

Let's discuss appropriate ways to contact bloggers. Remember that (1) they receive many e-mails a day from artists just like you, and (2) they are human—though many music bloggers make a career simply from writing, the vast majority are either working or in school and take time out of their already busy schedules to maintain a blog. You need to consider ways in which you can get an edge on other artists in actually establishing a rapport with potential writers:

1. Actually read the blogs: Following the blogs you'd like to be featured on, and leaving comments about their posts (not spam posts like "You're awesome—check out my band") on a regular basis can help you establish a relationship you can later draw upon when contacting for a write-up. Plus, you'll get a better sense of whether the blog would feature your kind of music at your level of accomplishment.
2. What to write: When sending e-mails to bloggers, try to at least find out their first names (located usually in the "about" or "contact" sections of their sites) and send a personal e-mail to each blogger. Never send a mass e-mail to 200 bloggers—they will get turned off and feel slighted. Send a personal e-mail with an individual comment directed toward the blog (i.e., "I read that article about this band, I like your writing," etc.), and then keep your e-mail short and sweet. Come up with a clever one-sentence description of your music, include no more than three tracks to listen to, and then describe your upcoming projects (a forthcoming EP, a remix, a show at this venue). Bloggers tend to love music videos, because they are stimulating for their readers both musically and visually; try to make a video for one of the tracks you send, even if it is a budget, DIY kind of video.
3. Be sure to include links to other instances of your music online: Your Myspace, Facebook, and Twitter pages are a good place to start. Your SoundCloud, Last.fm, and Bandcamp pages are also good sites to direct to. However, be sure to again not overload your e-mail request—include a maximum of three links.
4. Don't follow up: As stated before, bloggers are people with lives, just like you. If a blogger likes your music and wants to post it, he or she will let you know. There is no quicker way to turn off a blogger than to write again asking whether he or she received your e-mail.

Aggregators

The beauty of blogs is that they are often aggregated, meaning that posts from hundreds of different blogs are gathered onto large sites and displayed under various genres of music in one all-inclusive RSS feed. Examples include Hype Machine (Hypem.com), Music Blogtrotter (www.musicaggregator.blogspot.com), and We Are Hunted (http://wearehunted.tumblr.com/). Try to seek out blogs that are aggregated on larger sites, because these posts will be visible for a larger audience. All of these aggregators list the blogs that they follow. Users of aggregate services, including writers at the most successful blogs such as Pitchfork, are often on the lookout for the next big thing and will scour through MP3s on a daily basis.

Your Website: How to Make It Great and Why It Is Still Important

Why Your Own Website Is Essential in Crafting an Online Presence

Perhaps the most important part of your digital arsenal is your website. The primary reason for artists, particularly up-and-coming acts, to invest time, energy, and a modest amount of money in a quality website is that the Internet provides a worldwide audience for your music. Your website can be your press kit, making any physical press kit almost irrelevant in today's world. You can use your website as a vehicle to create a strong and credible web presence. Through your website, you can promote, sell, and distribute your own music as either physical albums or downloads, sell merchandise, and promote live performances and tours.

Some argue that an artist's website is irrelevant in the age of social networks, asking, "Why would I need a website when I already have a Facebook page and a Twitter account?" While these pages do offer platforms for content once available only on a dedicated website (including a music player, the ability to link to shopping carts, and mailing lists), it is still nevertheless essential to have a website for the following reasons:

- A well-developed website will make your project look professional and easily searchable on engines like Google and Yahoo.
- It allows you to have full control over essential aspects of your online presence, e-commerce, and mailing lists, and it lessens reliance on third-party providers' platforms, rules, and business models. Control and stability in the rocky terrain of the Internet is invaluable, though it does involve some care and maintenance.
- Your website can serve as a highly connected hub, linking to all your other social-networking accounts—this cohesive element will add further credibility to your Internet presence.

Methods to Easily Create Your Own Website

What you need to bring to the table: There are three essential forms of content that you, as the artist, need to furnish to create a website: a bio, high-quality photos, and at least several high-quality samples of your music. These items have traditionally constituted a basic press package that managers and agents use for radio promotion and to get club gigs and record deals. They are also the core of any good website. Other essential items are tour schedules and a mailing list, so that fans can keep up to date with upcoming shows and announcements. Additional materials like videos and links to press write-ups are helpful, as well. Finally, it is necessary to consider a visual layout of the site, or how you want to project your music aesthetically. But before we go any further, let's cover all the bases and outline three elements common to all websites:

1. *Domain name:* The unique ID that points to your website, such as www.stevegordonlaw.com. Domain names include a suffix such as .com, .org, .gov, or .tv. You can purchase

domain names from sites called "registrars." For more information on securing and protecting your domain name, see Chapter 2.

2. *Web hosting:* No matter what you have on your website, you'll need a "web host" to make your site available over the Internet. The physical computer where your website exists is called the *server.* A server is a computer or device on a network that manages network resources. GoDaddy.com is an example of a good web hosting service, as they offer domain name registration along with their hosting services in a single, inexpensive package.
3. *Web design:* What shows up when people type in your domain name and are transported to your site.

The cost can range from nothing—if you do it yourself or a friend does it for you for for free—to a few hundred bucks for a bare-bones site created by a professional (such as my site, www.stevegordonlaw.com, which cost me $500) or into the thousands for a site designed by a respected commercial service. Web designers with rudimentary skills are currently "a dime a dozen." If you don't know someone who does it, they can be easily solicited at sites such as www.craigslist.org. Freelance web designers are always looking to build their résumés by working with highly visible, highly creative people such as artists, and some will even do the work pro bono in exchange for a prominent credit on the site.

On the other hand, both Bandzoogle and WordPress offer musicians free website templates. Bandzoogle, for example, gives you the option to design your website or choose from many layouts, sell music while keeping all of your profits, and manage your social networking sites from the website. Unlike creating the website from scratch, using a premade template could generate a fully functional, professional-looking website in a very brief period of time. A huge advantage of these services is that you can update the sites without knowing HTML, which can be very difficult to use, or depending on a web designer who may outgrow you and not have time to tweak your site.

Bottom line: The competition for your website design and hosting dollars is fierce, with many competitors, so it is really a buyer's market and you can find great deals.

What to Include on Your Website and Why

You should conceptualize what you want your site to look like and what you want to accomplish before designing the actual web page. What is the first thing you want people to see when they log on to the site: flash animation, or an ad for a new release, or an e-mail list sign-up? What kind of color scheme do you want for the site? What visual elements will you use to make the site easy to navigate? These questions are very important if you are building your site yourself. If a site has a good "flow" or aesthetic, it can draw a great deal of attention and enhance your image. Bear in mind that you want to make sure that information (photos, MP3s, bio, tour dates) is quickly and easily accessible, that the layout is simple and easy to navigate, and that it offers links to other social networks that you use.

Twitter vs. Facebook: How They Compare in Popularity

According to reports published by Facebook, there were over 1.3 billion monthly active Facebook users as of the beginning of 2014. Interestingly, roughly 84 percent of Facebook's users are outside the United States.[353] This makes it the most popular social network in the world. YouTube is close behind, with over 1 billion monthly active users or "MAU."[354] At the beginning of 2014, Twitter surpassed 255 MAU.[355]

In early 2014 Facebook purchased the world's leading text messaging service, WhatsApp (WhatsApp has more than 450 million active users), for a whopping 19 billion dollars in cash and stock. One theory as to why Facebook paid so much money for a service that does not make much money itself is that Facebook is becoming a social media conglomerate. It may not be able to own every popular service, but it can become the dominant player with different tools like Instagram (which it purchased in 2012) and WhatsApp in its arsenal. Each one does things that the other property can't.

Obviously, neither Facebook nor Twitter can be ignored by anyone wishing to use social networks to enhance his or her career in any field. The following graph provides a visual comparison of all the leading social networks as of late 2013:

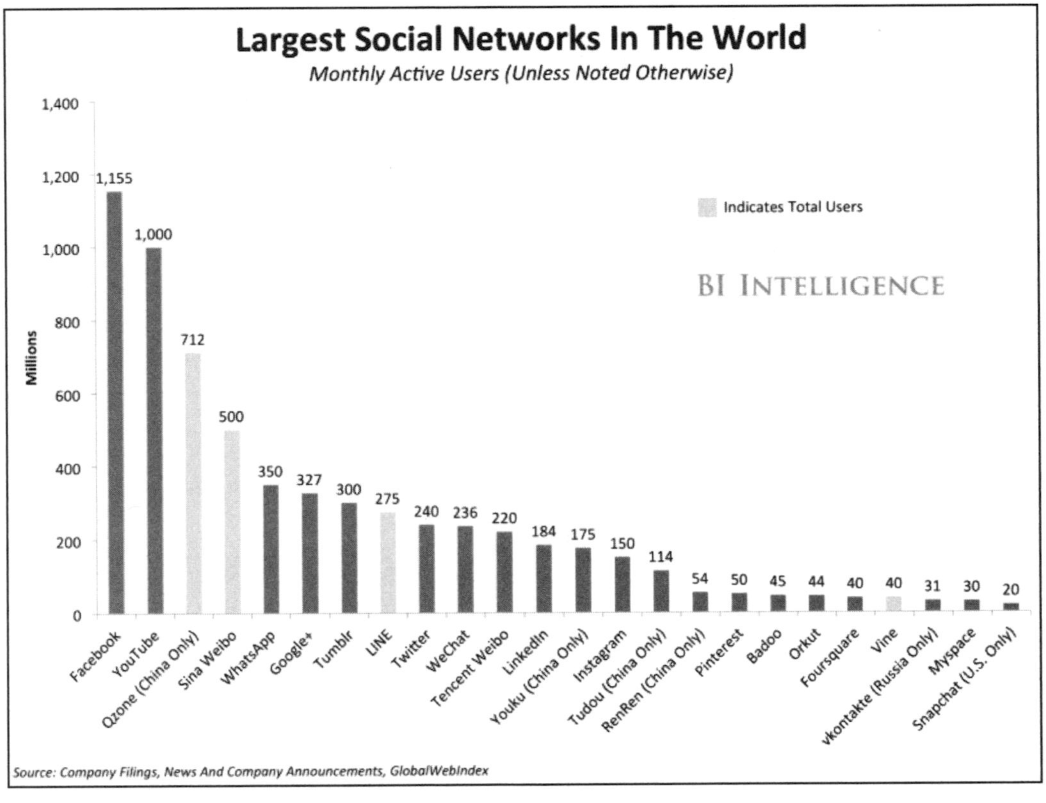

Twitter: How to Market Your Music and Make Some Money

Since its creation in 2006, Twitter has become the second most active social network on the Internet, with over 100 million users worldwide. As we all know by now, Twitter enables its users to send and read text-based posts of up to 140 characters. Users can subscribe to (or "follow," in Twitter-speak) other users' feeds, whereby the user will receive their tweets in reverse chronological stream on their main Twitter homepage. Users can easily cross-pollinate tweets by directing them to the attention of certain users (through the use of the @ symbol, followed by the user's name—for example, "Can't wait for the @brahmsband show tonight!"). You can also create a hashtag, which is a pound or hash symbol before a word that will be the subject of a search by others on Twitter (for example, "Can't wait for the @brahmsband show tonight! #brahmsband" allows users searching for tweets about Brahms to see this one). Users can also retweet the tweets of other users (for example, "RT @brahmsband Come see us play tonight @mercurylounge!").

As a social network, Twitter is based on two principles—subscription ("following") and cross-pollination. Following creates the foundation for communication on Twitter, and cross-pollination enriches the content and searchability of your tweets. As an aspiring artist, band, or record label, it's essential to know the subtleties of Twitter and how to best optimize it for promotion of your online identity and brand. Outlined here are successful methods for the optimization of following and cross-pollination:

1. **Subscription Strategies**
   As always, your goal should be to have high online visibility with those who would be interested in your music and brand. Therefore, your goal with Twitter should be to secure a high number of followers who are interested in staying in touch with you and up to date on what's going on with your project. What are the best ways to secure a high number of followers?
   a. *Less is more*—There's a temptation to start mass-following others on Twitter, in the hopes that others will follow you back. Resist this temptation. Twitter does not penalize users for mass following, but it simply does not look good to start mass following on Twitter. There's no guarantee that others will follow you back, and there's no way that others will be able to read your tweets unless they follow you back or visit your profile page. The best thing to do is to selectively and slowly create a list of those you follow, and develop relationships with those few that follow you back. Allow others to follow you first, as well. A smaller, tighter network is vastly stronger than a wide, empty one.
   b. *What to say*—Once you have secured followers, be sure to stay in touch with them and engage with them in a meaningful way. Resist the urge to post about mundane minutiae (for example, "Wow Frosted Flakes taste ggrrrrrreatt!"), but also resist the urge to endlessly self-promote. Strike a balance between promoting your own project, supporting the projects of others in your network or scene, and posting about relevant and interesting content. For example, if you are a hip-hop artist, post links to articles or interviews about MCs who have inspired you, in addition to any upcoming shows you have or recent press you've received. If you're a folk musician, post a link to a story about music and activism, in addition to posting about fellow folk artists and your upcoming releases. The more interesting the content you post, the more likely it is that followers will respond to or retweet your tweets, which will help you gain more followers.
2. **Cross-Pollination Strategies**
   Equally as important as tastefully following and being followed is the successful use of cross-pollinating tactics. The correct use of replies, retweets, and hashtags can go a long way in enriching the relevance and searchability of your tweets. Let's explain:

a. *Replies*—Replying to others' tweets is a great way to start dialogue with other users, especially if they haven't started following you yet. If you use the @ symbol with someone's username directly proceeding (i.e., @brahmsband), your Tweet will be sent to that person's @brahmsband list and later show up in search results for that user's account. In addition to starting a dialogue and potentially gaining a new follower, you also show that you are interested in using Twitter to actually communicate with others, as opposed to endless self-promotion. Moreover, other users who reply to you will increase the visibility of your name on Twitter and entice other followers of theirs to start following you.

b. *Retweets*—If you find another user's tweet interesting, you can retweet the post to your own feed, so that your followers can read that user's tweet. It may seem like a redundant practice to quote other users in this way, but it's actually an incredibly useful means to increase your own visibility—if you retweet another user's post, he or she will see the post later as being retweeted by you, and your name will also show up in search results in connection with this other user, through your retweet. Furthermore, those who retweet your posts will increase the visibility of your username on Twitter and entice other users to start following you.

c. *Hashtags, or #increasingyourvisibility*—Hashtags are also a key way to stay in touch on Twitter. Hashtags start with the # symbol, followed by a word or phrase with no spaces, and increase the searchability of your tweet, if you use hashtags that other users might also use. For example, #nowplaying is a very common hashtag that users include with tweets about bands or artists, and its popularity makes it easy to find out about new bands and artists through Twitter.

3. **Make Some Money**

Twitter can be used to do any number of things, including communicate ideas, promote your brand, or get feedback, but it can also be used to make some money. According to Amanda Palmer, who wrote the foreword to this book, "the great thing about Twitter is that the minute I started using it, I realized the possibilities are endless."

In 2012, Amanda used Chipify, Twitter's e-commerce tool, to sell T-shirts stating "Stop Pretending Art is Hard" for $20 each. Two hours after launch, she was logging a sale every 30 seconds. This wasn't the first time that Palmer has profited from a flash sale on Twitter. In 2009, she used Twitter to sell "Friday Night Losers" T-shirts in just 10 hours. "I hereby call THE LOSERS OF FRIDAY NIGHT ON THEIR COMPUTERS to ORDER, motherfucker," Palmer tweeted her fans to launch that campaign. Ten hours later she reported total income from the shirts as $19,000. These stories illustrate that when you have a loyal following on Twitter, it becomes an incredibly powerful tool to accomplish your goals.

Facebook: Still a Major Force in the Social Media World

A savvy critic recently announced, "Facebook isn't cool anymore. People obviously still use it. But it's to feed their addiction."[356] Nonetheless, according to Alexa Internet rankings, Facebook is the second-most visited site on the Internet, after Google and before YouTube. As was just mentioned, Facebook reports that it has over 1.3 billion monthly active users. So, although it may not be as "cool" as it once was, it cannot be ignored. Also, according to Facebook, its monthly active users actually increased 22 percent from 2012 to 2013. Even Mr. Herstand admits, "Musician pages are . . . a quick legitimacy checkpoint. And to see how 'popular' you are. Or, rather, if I should pay attention." If Facebook were no more than a measure of an artist's popularity, that would still be important. But beyond that, it can be useful to an artist in other ways. This section explains how.

Facebook for Artists: Do's and Don'ts

Artists can use Facebook in two ways—by utilizing their basic Facebook profile, and by creating an official Facebook "fan page."

Do's:

- Keep existing friends and fans informed of what's going on with your music, without being excessively self-promoting.
- "Friend" contacts that you meet through attending events and playing gigs.
- "Friend" contacts that you meet online through other social networks—these could be bloggers, label owners, and/or other musicians in your scene.
- Cross-pollinate! Promote the work of others in your scene—invite your friends to events held by other artists and labels, and create status updates with links to press and websites of other artists and labels.

Don'ts:

- Don't excessively self-promote—your friends will think that you are interested only in yourself!
- Don't be too serious about your own project—you want to keep the tone on your own profile informal.
- Don't "friend" people whom you haven't met in person or online before—this is an obnoxious practice and will make you come off as aggressive or overly eager.

The Fan Page

Perhaps the most powerful tool that Facebook offers to artists and bands is the "fan page." This page is intended for organizations or people who would like to communicate with a group of people and is also used by public figures and companies to communicate with their fans and customers. It is obvious that artists and record labels are candidates for using this important tool, and they do. The difference between a normal Facebook account and a fan page is that you must have a basic Facebook profile for yourself before you can create a fan page. Also, you cannot "friend" other users on Facebook through your fan page—you can add contacts only through your basic Facebook account. The beauty of the fan page is that anyone—any artist, band, or label—can create and maintain one from the personal account.

How to Set Up Your Fan Page

To set up a page, you must already have a basic Facebook profile. Then simply visit any page on Facebook, and in the bottom left-hand corner you'll see a link that says "Create a Page." Then you will be directed to set up your own page.

The Benefits of Having a Facebook Fan Page

To put it into perspective, one-third of Facebook users—that is, one-third of 1.3 billion people—are fans of at least one music artist or band page, and the average user becomes a fan of four pages each month. This means that it's absolutely essential to have a page for your solo project, band, or label. Fan pages can include pictures, a bio, links to press, and other related stories about your project. You can create official events through your page identity. You can also keep your fans up to date with status updates—each time you create an update, it will be displayed in your fans' respective news feeds. The status updates can feature new tracks you've made, upcoming shows, recent press, new photos, links to new music videos, and more. Furthermore, you can upload and display MP3s using the Facebook Music Player application.

The fan page is the best way to utilize Facebook for promotional purposes. You can invite your existing friends on Facebook to become fans of your page, and they can in turn suggest your page to other friends of theirs. Your fans can then stay easily up to date with what's going on with your project, simply because your updates will show in their news feeds along with the endless other updates from their friends and other pages.

How to Use the Facebook Fan Page

Do's:

- Use a first-person voice to show fans you are active on the page, and encourage them to post feedback and comments.
- Share everyday stories to bring fans closer to you—share behind-the-scenes updates and content, such as candid photos of you at rehearsal, on the road, or just relaxing.
- Ask fans a question now and then in your status updates to generate conversation, and show that you're listening by responding with comments to fan replies.

Don'ts:

- Don't post more than a couple of status updates each day—you do not want to inundate your fans with unnecessary content and perhaps turn them off from wanting to stay in touch with you.
- Don't send excessive mass messages to your entire page membership—send mass messages only when you have an announcement like an album release or a very important gig.
- Don't aggressively invite your friends to become fans of your page—invite them once, but don't persistently remind them again and again. Remember that Facebook is a community of friends, not consumers.

Criticism of Facebook

I asked a client who manages a prominent EDM artist for his opinion of recent changes on Facebook. These were his comments:

"Overall I'm not a big fan of Facebook lately. They have made it extremely difficult for pages to reach their fans if you don't advertise. For instance, my artist has 190,000 Facebook fans, but when he makes a Facebook post the post only reaches 20,000 of those fans. The only way to reach the other 170,000 fans is by advertising. Based on research, Facebook is limiting pages to only be able to reach 2 percent of their fans unless they advertise.

Facebook is still a leader in social media based on active users. However, I just wanted to point out to you the difficulties of using Facebook."

The prominent advocacy group Future of Music Coalition agreed:

Why Musicians Don't "Like" Facebook Changes

> . . . in spite of its popularity, Facebook hasn't managed to become the ultimate Swiss army knife for musicians. Part of this is because the company keeps changing its functionality. Now that Facebook is publicly traded, it faces more pressure to monetize user activity. Unsurprisingly, some of the recent changes don't seem to favor independent musicians or indie labels.
>
> . . . What once was a level playing field is now skewed by algorithms that favor the "haves" over the "have nots." While it makes good business sense for Facebook, making artists, businesses, and brands pay to "promote" content has taken some of the sheen off the Facebook experience. Facebook claimed in 2012 that about 16 percent of fans see content posted by a page without paid promotion. But now that number has declined even further.
>
> . . . For bands and artists who have spent years building a fan base online, and who don't have the deep pockets of a major label to help boost their posts, these algorithm tweaks are a large blow. As news feeds are filled with superficial memes and viral videos and promoted advertisement, musicians simply trying to reach their fans are crowded out. When artists can't simply get their music, updates, and show information into news feeds because of an inability to fork over cash to a multibillion-dollar website that built its user base on the promise of connecting individuals across the globe for "free," many start wondering if it makes sense to continue using the platform.

These complaints by Mary Wilson, an intern at the coalition, reinforce two points:

1. Facebook and Twitter operate differently. When a user tweets, it becomes part of a giant stream of billions of messages that are (theoretically at least) available to anyone. That may seem noisy—and Twitter gets regular complaints about how hard it is to filter the stream effectively—but to many it is the way that an open social platform should work. On Facebook, however, users are at the mercy of the company's algorithm, which determines what is signal and what is noise.
2. You need your own website free of the vagaries of third-party social platforms that may change the rules on you at any time.

Chapter 25
HOW TO USE CROWDFUNDING

Create a Successful Crowdfunding Campaign: Interview with Brian Meece, Cofounder of RocketHub

RocketHub, launched in 2010, is an online crowdfunding platform. Users from around the world—including musicians, entrepreneurs, scientists, game developers, filmmakers, photographers, theater producers/directors, fashion designers, etc. use RocketHub to raise funds and awareness for their projects. The site was founded by Brian Meece, Jed Cohen, and Vladimir Vukicevic. In January 2011, Alon Hillel-Tuch joined the team as the fourth founder. The founders each have creative backgrounds: Brian Meece as a singer-songwriter; Jed Cohen as an actor/producer; Vladimir Vukicevic as a tech-thinker/writer; and Alon Hillel-Tuch as a musician/linguist.

SG: What does RocketHub offer?

BM: RocketHub is a grassroots crowdfunding platform. And what we mean by that is that projects looking for funding and awareness come to RocketHub, upload their projects, set a campaign goal and a time frame, and then reach out to their audience and fan base to engage them with support for their campaigns. We've been open for a relatively brief period but have had thousands of artists come through our doors and successfully crowdfund their projects, which is super exciting.

SG: Tell us how crowdfunding on RocketHub works.

BM: Think of crowdfunding as an online event. It's got a beginning, a middle, and an end with a deadline. It's different from other forms of e-commerce. These campaigns are really events that happen online. Because they are an event, with a kind of beginning, middle, and end, we see patterns in how people participate with the campaign. Oftentimes they look like a U. They start off strong when they come onto the site, they dip down a little bit as the campaign heads into the middle, and then with the deadline looming we'll see a big pickup in traffic and contributions. Nothing gets people motivated like a deadline. I mean, I'm guilty of it myself, waiting until the last minute to write my college papers and waiting until April 14 to do my taxes. Part of that is human nature, to kind of wait until the last minute. So because of the deadline we found crowdfunding to be a really, really nice kind of reason for people to participate in projects in a very new and different kind of way.

SG: You work on all kinds of campaigns. What proportion of your projects are music based, and how many are going at the same time?

BM: About 20 percent at this point of our campaigns are music. Music happens to be very near and dear to my heart, because I'm a musician. I still perform regularly in the New York City scene. I'll do a shameless plug for my band, Brian & Silbin and Friends, if that's okay. I'm a third-generation musician, singer, and songwriter, and I found that crowdfunding and musicians go together like chocolate and peanut butter. A lot of the costs for production have come down from where they were 10, 15, 20 years ago, but they still cost something to make. So we've kind of hit this point where, "All right, I need two, five, ten thousand dollars to make my record, produce my video or finance my tour." And we found that those are the budgets that really work well for crowdfunding, and musicians really got the concept of crowdfunding because a lot of us musicians are already having authentic conversations with our fan base and with our audience and with our community. So musicians and crowdfunding are a really great fit. I'm excited at all the projects that have come through our gates, mine included; I did my own crowdfunding project.

SG: Tell us about your personal crowdfunding project.

BM: My partner in musical crime is Silbin Sandovar. We have a band, as I mentioned, called Brian & Silbin and Friends. We wanted to raise funds to make a record. I'm lucky enough to have some really talented musical super friends here in the New York City scene, and we wanted to make a record to really represent what we do here in New York. We figured it would cost us around $6,000 to work with Mike West, a producer out of Lawrence, Kansas; he's originally from New Orleans. I used to work with him back when I was on the Gulf Coast. But we basically uploaded a project, said we're looking to raise five grand to make this record happen, and here's how you can contribute and here's what you get. So for 20 bucks we would give you a copy of our CD with your own haiku poem. For 50 bucks we would Sgt. Pepper your ass. We would actually put your face on our record, and we have all these pretty little faces on our record, which is just such a cool thing. Every time I see the record I just get excited that all these people kind of came together to make it happen.

SG: What kinds of incentives did you offer?

BM: For $100 we would either give you a ukulele lesson or Silbin would give a songwriting lesson. For $250 I would take you surfing for an afternoon in Long Beach, New York. I told them I'm not responsible for the wave conditions, but we will get you out there and have some fun for the afternoon. So we did that. For $600 I'd write you your own custom song. I've got a lot of friends with kids, and I write songs for my brother's kids, so a lot of my community and my fan base said, "You know what, I really want a song for my kid." So we did a couple songs for some of my friends' and fans' kids, and that was really fun. For $1,000 we'd have you come into the studio with us. For $5,000 we would have you be in the music video. Nobody put those rewards for our campaign, but we did move a few of the $600 rewards, and we raised more than we were looking to raise, about $6,000, to make our record.

SG: Tell us about another success story. I think you mentioned somebody who crowdsourced for money to make an album and ended up touring with the late, great Lou Reed?

BM: Yeah. So, you know, Aram Bajakian is a very, very talented guitar player here in the New York scene. He was looking to crowdfund his record. He raised, I think, around $4,000 to make a record that was ultimately picked up by John Zorn's Tzadik record label. From that connection, directly, he was hand cast by Lou Reed to go on tour as Lou's guitar player for the European summer tour. Aram just got back, so I was really excited about that success story. You know, first thing that Aram said when he came back from his tour was, "Thanks so much to you and RocketHub for making this happen." I said, "Hey, you made this happen, we were the platform. We were the platform that you used to make this happen for yourself." But we were really, really excited to see Aram, through this partnership, go from relative obscurity to a pretty cherry gig there touring with Lou Reed.

SG: Yeah, that does sound fabulous. Now tell us a case that didn't work out so well.

BM: Well, projects that don't work out too well typically lack one of three things. Sometimes they're just not an engaging project; people don't bring the right kind of oomph or passion to them. Sometimes they don't have a big enough fan base, or any fan base at all. Or they'll have kind of lackluster rewards; they won't be creative with their rewards. We found that those three things really make projects happen: cool projects, great network, and killer rewards. And if a project doesn't have those then they're kind of behind the eight-ball from the get-go and some of them don't get traction.

SG: I understand one of the things that makes RocketHub unique is that you do give guidance to people who launch projects.

BM: That's right. So our team has been very accessible. We're available for feedback on campaign elements, such as your video or rewards or description. Shoot us an e-mail at support@rocket-hub.com and we'll respond typically within a handful of hours with some nice feedback on your project. We're also big on just educating folks in general on how to use this crowdfunding stuff. We have a little sister site, RocketHub.org, for the musicians and artists to hang out and learn. I took that from the playbook of one of my mentors, Derek Sivers, when he had CDBaby. He had CDBaby.org, which was kind of the back door for the musicians to hang out in. So we did something similar with RocketHub and RocketHub.org—lots of good information there, just how to use the phenomenon of crowdfunding.

SG: Many people associate crowdfunding with Kickstarter. How are you different?

BM: We're different in a few key ways. I think the first one is that we're a creatives-by-creatives company. My background really is as a creative person, and I know it may seem like a moot point, but that really guides virtually every decision we make as a company: How can we be more artist friendly, how can we provide more value to the creative class than ever before? That's kind of the intangible difference. Tangible difference is, for starters, you don't have to hit your full goal amount to unlock your funds. On some of our competitors you have to hit the full goal amount, otherwise you don't get anything. We've had projects, musical projects, setting a goal amount for $10,000, they raise $6,000 or $7,000 of it, and they walk away with their funds and say, "Thank you so much for having this platform. On the other platforms I would have done this work and I would have lost $6,000, $7,000, $8,000."

SG: How do you avoid fan disappointment? For instance, you told me, I think, for 50 bucks you get your picture on your CD cover. But if they don't reach their funding then there ain't no CD cover. So what do you tell the fans who contributed 50 bucks?

BM: So, first of all we talk to the creatives using the platform and say, "If you've got a chance at making your project happen, this is your platform." And I've found, especially with musicians, we just make stuff. We're constantly making records, we're going to do it one way or the other, and we're committed to making the project happen. So sometimes the scale can adjust. If you're looking to do a bigger record with a string section, a full-length album, and maybe you don't raise as much as you were intending to do, you can still make something; more of an acoustic, kind of EP kind of album. Just let your fans and your audience know what's going on with the project, and we've found 99.999 percent of the time that the fans are thrilled. As long as the lines of communication are open, and you're following through on what you promised with managed expectations, the fans love it, the musicians love it, and the artists love it. And again, most of these artists are committed to making something happen, with or without these funds, so we see ourselves as just a friend in that fight of getting more funds and awareness.

SG: Kickstarter takes five percent; what's the deal with RocketHub?

BM: We take four percent. For projects that hit their goal amount it's a four percent fee to RocketHub. It's also worth noting that there's a four percent credit card fee. That's actually for all the platforms; some of them don't necessarily disclose the full amounts, but on RocketHub it's four percent, and it's kind of all built into the back end of your project. Our interests are completely aligned with the artists and creatives who use our site, which means that we only make money when they make money, which is how it should be. We feel like our pricing is the most competitive out there, very fair in exchange for access to one of the top crowdfunding platforms in the world for creative projects.

SG: Anyone can set up a project on RocketHub, although you may have some parameters, which you should tell us about.

BM: Sure. Legal, and in good taste; that's it. As long as it's legal and in good taste.

SG: You have a unique program called Launchpad. Tell us about it.

BM: Launchpad came again from feedback I was getting from artists, from people who were saying, "Hey, Brian, I raised $5,000 to make a record, but I really want to showcase in front of labels, in front of music attorneys, in front of music supervisors; get my career to the next level." And meanwhile, record companies in the industry were coming to RocketHub and saying, "Hey, what's going on? Where are the artists that are raising the most? Where are the ones that are driving the most traffic and funds?" So we had it really from two points; the artists wanted to have access to media, and media wanted to have access to artists. So we said, "Let's put together a brand new product called Launchpad." And our first Launchpad was with Gibson Guitars, the iconic guitar brand. They have a beautiful showroom in midtown Manhattan, used to be the old

Hit Factory recording studio. Bruce Springsteen cut hits there, Michael Jackson cut hits there, FogHat cut hits there, all the biggies. So Gibson gave the artists a week to come rehearse and play in their beautiful showroom, with all the Gibson gear you could handle. So a band came in called Non-Violence that was selected for the Launchpad. They had all the Gibson gear they could handle for a week, and we arranged to have all the top record labels, all the majors, come in and give portfolio reviews, listen to a set, talk about the songs, and make relationships. So now this band, Non-Violence, is in talks with major record labels. We also had music supervisors come in who do stuff for film, television, and they also play stuff in theater projects on Broadway. We also had music attorneys, publicists, and press folks at the showroom for the week. So the chance for an artist, this band Non-Violence, to really have accelerated, rapid growth for their career . . . it's already proving to be quite fruitful. But that's really what our Launchpad product is about: finding a next-step opportunity that's clear, that's real, and that's transparent. That if you crowdfunded on RocketHub you don't have to pay for this stuff; it just comes with the package. That's really exciting for us. We have another one coming up, should be kicking off next week, where we're going to give a successful RocketHubber their own publicist for a month. One of the top publicity firms will give a month's worth of work, because again they came to us saying, "Wow, there's a lot of cool stories coming out of the RocketHub camp. We heard about Aram Bajakian and Lou Reed, and there's just so much happening. Let's do a publicity campaign with one of the RocketHubbers." So we're going to have a month-long campaign free for one RocketHub artist or creative out of our Launchpad product. It's really exciting.

SG: How do you select people for the Launchpad program?

BM: First of all, you have to have hit your goal successfully. So, if you set a goal of two to ten thousand dollars (which is kind of the bread and butter for music projects on RocketHub—more on that in a bit) and you hit it, you can submit an application to us at no cost. We will evaluate it based on the clarity of your vision and the possibility of greater success if we select you for Launchpad.

SG: RocketHub also has strategic partnerships with sponsorships and brands. How does that work?

BM: So, again, happening very organically, another thing that artists are coming to me and saying is, "How do I get picked up in an ad campaign? How do I get picked up to get my voice heard in a bigger way through traditional media?" Meanwhile, we have brands on the other side of things saying, "Hey, we want cool content. We want artists talking about us in a cool and authentic way. We have scarce resources (i.e., very powerful promo arms and cash) to give to artists to help them get stuff heard." So we're basically in talks now with a few top-end ad agencies here in New York City that are going to be tapping top RocketHub projects to work into different campaigns that are powered by brand.

SG: Do you work in the space between the artists and the sponsors, or just let the artists go and deal with the sponsor directly?

BM: We basically do some light managing, connecting the dots, more or less. Everything's handled through us here at RocketHub, but it's very straightforward. It's not tricky in terms of the deal structure.

SG: Are there any other dimensions or aspects of RocketHub that we didn't cover that you'd like to talk about?

BM: I think there are some metrics that are kind of fun for music projects. As I mentioned, I think musicians and crowdfunding go together like chocolate and peanut butter, because of the price point and the budgets that are involved. The average contribution for music projects on RocketHub is $60. The mode—the single most popular price point, from statistics class—the mode is $20. So we can back into budget amounts and say that if you're looking to raise $2,000 to $3,000 it's about 40 to 50 people. If you're looking to raise $5,000, about 80 to 100 people. If you're looking to raise $10,000, it's about 150 to 200 people. Not a whole heck of a lot of people that need to come together to make something cool happen for musicians. We had Anthony Cekay come through—he was basically doing a residency in webcasting, doing a live webcast for a jazz show. He raised $2,000, but NPR picked up the story. And that did a lot for his career and for the awareness factor to get him to the next level in terms of just getting his name out there. So, the funding is a really exciting component, but just as important can be that awareness the story, the momentum that comes out of the campaign. When I was done with my record, some really cool things started to happen. First of all, remember how I told you that we would Sgt Pepper you if you paid us $50 and we put your name on the cover? An editor for Nickelodeon is a friend of ours and he brought the CD in to work, because he was on the front. He thought, "This is really cool; I'm going to show my friends." So he had it lying at his edit bay and next to him is another edit bay for another channel, and somebody was putting together a show, and said, "Hey, can we use . . . Hey, I see that this is a cool CD. You're on it. How's the band?" He said, "They're okay, they're pretty darn good. Check it out." So he pops it in, he goes, "You know what, this would be perfect for this bar scene that I have to edit to. Do you think I could call these guys and get . . . clear the music real quick. Get them paid, get their music in a TV show." Jeremy's like, "Yeah, let me call Brian up real quick." So Jeremy calls me says, "Brian, the guy next to me wants to use your music in a show. It pays *x* amount, you're going to be on national TV. Are you cool with that?" And I said, "Uh, yeah." So, that was really exciting to have my songs in a TV show. And then, with the fan awareness, the support and the trust, you're getting paid before you actually make the record, so there's this tremendous good will that comes from a creative perspective. When I was in the studio, I was working so hard to make an awesome record. I ended up making the best album I've ever made in my life, and I think it's because I had the support and trust of the people to give me the $6,000 to make it happen.

SG: There is a mantra that "a thousand true fans" can support an artist. It sounds like you could do pretty well with even a hundred true fans.

BM: Yeah, 100 true fans is $5,000 to $6,000 on RocketHub.

SG: Do people have success marshaling their fans on Facebook or their Twitter following in crowdfunding?

BM: That's exactly right. This is less about the transaction and more about the relationship that you as an artist have with your fan base, with your audience, with your community, and also that that community can have with each other. When I was playing the show at the Living Room I was looking out, very grateful, at a packed house on a Saturday night, and I was seeing a lot of people who were saying hi to each other. People who were different ages, different demographics; we have all sorts of folks who come to our shows. I was thinking, "Wow, these guys come out to see our band, but they also come to see each other." That was very apparent in our crowdfunding campaign as well, because the Fuelers (as they're called on RocketHub) communicate with each other as well. This is very much about their relationship, about the ability for a funder, for a Fueler, to have an impact on if something happens and how something happens. And it's also about the relationship that they have with the person spearheading the project, with the artist.

SG: Look into your crystal ball and make some predictions for RocketHub and the next two years. Where do you intend to be?

BM: Well, I really see RocketHub as a new media incubator, where projects come in, they get funding, they find support with their community and beyond through RocketHub. Then they have places to go. Maybe they have a song or a project that's already shown traction through a bottom-up means, which is grassroots level, and we can connect that musical product, if you will, to the next step. Whether it's placing it in media or connecting the dots the way we're doing with the Aram Bajakian and Lou Reed story, we want to do more and more and more of that, formalize it and really provide value further up the vertical beyond just the crowdfunding. So think of RocketHub as crowdfunding plus, where you come in, you crowdfund, but then there are other places to go.

SG: And what's the first step in approaching RocketHub, besides going to the website.?What do I have to be thinking when I go there and start to imagine my project with you folks?

BM: Well, I would say take a look at RocketHub and look at the successful projects. Look at the successful projects in music, but also look at them beyond just the music, too, in terms of being what people resonate with in terms of the rewards. Then be thinking about ways you can model successful projects that are unique to you. If you have any questions, reach out to support@ RocketHub or reach out to me personally, brian@RocketHub.com. We're happy to provide any feedback there as well.

How to Maximize Your Crowdfunding Campaign and How One Indie Rock Club Used Crowdfunding to Survive: Interview with Nick Bodor, Cofounder of Cake Shop

Located at 152 Ludlow Street, Manhattan, Lower East Side, Cake Shop does, as its name suggests, sell cakes, but the club is better known for the live music it presents almost every night. In fact, since opening in 2005, Cake Shop has earned a reputation for showcasing up-and-coming bands, including now famous ones such as Vampire Weekend, Surfer Blood, MGMT, and Dirty Projectors. It is also one of the few remaining music clubs left in Lower Manhattan. Rising rents and property taxes have pushed many of the scruffy bars that nurtured indie music across the East River into Brooklyn. In this interview we focus on how the club used crowdfunding to survive.

SG: What inspired you to start Cake Shop?

NB: I have always had an entrepreneurial spirit. I grew up working in restaurants since I was 13. So when I got out of college and moved to New York, I quickly decided to start a coffee shop business. A coffee shop is much easier to run than a restaurant, and it was something I felt like I could do on my own. When I got to this neighborhood in 1993, Avenue A was still pretty shady. I walked out of a bar one night and there was a handwritten "For Rent" note taped to a door. Turned out the place had been vacant for 14 months. That was 1994. It's amazing now that places on Avenue A would be shuttered because the Lower East Side has become such a hot neighborhood.

After four years running the coffee shop, it was a logical progression to get into the nightlife and bar business, which I opened in '98. It was a straightforward East Village dive bar also on Avenue A, called the Library Bar, and the big deal there was that there was a jukebox. For me, being able to program my own jukebox was a sort of dream of a lifetime. The Library Bar was very rock-centric and the jukebox was a big part of the draw. I chose very interesting stuff that you didn't hear on other jukeboxes. The jukebox is kind of a dying art form in a weird way. It is a curatorial process because I choose the 100 CDs in it. So at the Library I got my feet wet in the bar business and it made sense to combine the coffee, the bar, and the music. My brother Andy and our partner Greg Curley and I always wanted to do a live music venue. That was the genesis of Cake Shop. We started getting financing together and shopping for spaces. We found a brand new building and became the first tenant, renting the ground floor and the cellar.

SG: Tell us how you think Cake Shop has contributed to the music scene in New York and what you are most proud of.

NB: We've been open now for eight years and it's just so great to look at past bands and see their success and how much they have grown. Pains of Being Pure at Heart, for example, their very first show ever was on our stage. We call them friends of Cake Shop, same as Surfer Blood. They are from Florida, but one of the guys told me it is their favorite venue. They were like, "We have traveled the whole world now, we are big enough where we are touring the globe, and we think Cake Shop is the best bar." Having bands say that to us really makes all our hard work pay off. Me and my brother Andy book really solid bands, and that is the thing that separates us from other places. Other places are like, "Can you bring 20 people? We'll book your band." We do not operate that way.

We craft bills. We'll take a touring band from Australia and put them together with a band from Brooklyn that complements them. We want people to come out for the whole night, not just to see their friend's band. We book bands that we think people should hear. Obviously it is not going to be everybody's cup of tea, but we want your experience at Cake Shop to be like, "I went to Cake Shop and saw three bands I would never have heard of, and they were all very good." Or blew you away. That is a great kind of feeling for us. So all these bands, including Vampire Weekend, MGMT, Dirt Projectors—it was great to catch them early. And it is interesting to watch them as their sound progresses and matures.

SG: What gives you the most satisfaction?

NB: Historically in New York there were times when nobody would go see live music, and if there was a band you knew maybe you'd go. But I feel like the rock climate is great in New York now. People want to check out new bands, and they do. Now with social media they want to catch the new band that hits before they blow up. They want to be able to say, "Oh, we saw this band. We saw MGMT with 100 people." People are here to see a good band and they will dance around and have fun. Because our stage is only 8 inches high, people congregate all the way around the stage, and it has a very intimate feeling. You're right there with the band.

SG: In August 2012, the *New York Times* reported that "after months of financial uncertainty, the indie-rock club Cake Shop has collected enough money through a novel Internet fund-raising site to avoid closing down." How did you run into financial difficulty, and how did you use the Internet to rise above it?

Basically, we had to pay a percentage of the real estate tax for the building to the landlord. I mentioned before that we were the first tenants here. We got an abatement for 5 years, meaning we did not have to pay our share of the real estate tax. So we knew it was coming up, but when you sign the lease five years seems like a long time. And then the landlord waited until year six and they billed us late. And while we were trying to negotiate, the second year came in. So all of a sudden we owed $50,000 in back real estate taxes. We just did not have that kind of deep pockets. The landlord's very fair, we really like them, but they basically said flat out, "We are not your bank. You need to get this money."

They took us to court and the judge imposed a very aggressive payment structure where we had to pay $16,000 for three consecutive months. We knew we would not be able to get that from our sales. We were able to borrow some money from friends and family, but not enough, and so we were getting fairly desperate.

We were familiar with Kickstarter, which is definitely a very popular crowdfunding source, but I felt like we might get buried on that. Then I found PledgeMusic. I think their platform is more unique. They are basically known for their focus on music. Ben Folds Five did fundraising there—they are a great band—they had their fans pay for their recording time and their studio time and basically used PledgeMusic to pay for an entire album. Also PledgeMusic has a philanthropic program. If you go over the goal, as ours actually did, five percent goes to charity. [Author's note: The charity tied to Cake Shop's campaign is Musicians On Call, a nonprofit organization that brings live and recorded music to the bedsides of patients in healthcare facilities.] We liked that aspect of it, too. That you are not just helping Cake Shop out, but the funders are helping other people.

SG: Did you use your pre-existing contacts in your campaign?

NB: Yes, we used our social media and our personal contacts as well.

SG: *The New York Times* wrote an article on your campaign that got you a lot of attention. How did you get the Times to cover the story?

NB: To be honest, I had tried a contact and I was not able to get through to them. They called us. PledgeMusic really did a good job of getting the word out about our situation as well. Pledge did a press blast and the Times picked up on it, and then they just reached out to us. The author, I think, was in the arts section and already knew about us.

SG: Crowdfunding platforms don't do special media blasts for all their projects. Why did Pledge-Music choose yours?

NB: I think they realized that there was an opportunity to get their name out there as well. When people started rolling in with donations we recognized some of the names, but a lot of the names we did not. I would say maybe 30 percent we knew, 70 percent we did not. We had pledges from Scandinavia and Germany and Australia and Japan. It was really neat that people would have great comments, like, "Oh, I came across Cake Shop when I was in New York. Saw a great band." It was really nice to hear everybody's comments about it and PledgeMusic apparently took notice.

SG: What did you offer the fans, in terms of incentives? I understand that for $20,000 you offered fans free drinks for life.

NB: Yep, basically free drinks for life. Nobody took us up on that one. We tried to have it so people who weren't in New York could enjoy some of the perks. There were limited edition T-shirts, only 20, hand silk-screened by one of our friends who is a famous cartoonist (pretty famous, at least in the cartoon world). What people seemed to respond to best was pre-pay discounts for drinks. Our drinks are $6 or $7. For $50, you got a 10-drink card, and you would save a couple of bucks. Other ones that worked was prepaid admission to shows plus drink tickets; those were pretty popular as well. Get on the guest list, plus two, and eight drinks for you and your friends. "Come out and have a night on Cake Shop" kind of a thing. We also had one we called "Keep Your Stuff, I Believe in Cake Shop," and that was a $2,000 pledge. That worked with one person and we didn't even know the person at all. It was really amazing. We also had a company who threw a party at the club for their employees for a pledge of $5,000. The other strangely successful one was for $300 you could name a drink special or a beer or shot special. I think we did 12 or 15 of those.

SG: Before we finish I would like to ask a couple of questions about music. You see new bands every night. What advice would you give them?

NB: There is nothing better than seeing a live band that just really sounds great and just looks like they are having fun on stage. And there's nothing worse in a small venue when somebody is just a little moody . . . we want to see bands that rock, we want to be entertained. So I think the stage show and the stage sound are really important. Some of these bands are a little bit too fussy, getting the sound guy to do this or that. Other bands just know how to set their instruments and sound great and go. I understand, we are Manhattan, so I think that sometimes bands can be nervous, even though we are small. If it is an industry show it's true that you never know who is going to be in our crowd. But I think you have got to be able to perform consistently, and just really be a good live band.

Sometimes a band that played great live gives me a copy of their CD, and it's like some of the songs are there, and they are okay, but they are better live. I think that happens because bands are making money from live touring. They are paying less attention to making their records. That's different from the past, when bands who played live sounded very similar to their records. With these less well-known, younger bands, I am seeing a big difference in their live show versus their recorded material. They have to even each other out. They both have to be great.

Also, you have to work hard; it is a job. If you act like it's a hobby, you're always just going to be a hobby musician. If you want to be in a band, and you relocate to New York, you have to work. You have to get out there, you have to hustle. Some bands get that; some bands do not. I think it is important that you have a good work ethic. That you show up on time. If you want to do a sound check, you do not flake out. When bands flake out it screws our whole business up. So, even just starting out, you should be professional and you should think of it as a job.

SG: For new bands interested in playing at Cake Shop, what suggestions do you have in terms of how they approach you?

NB: There is a fine line between reminding us who you are and being pushy. I do not have an easy answer for that. I would say that if you do not hear from us in a month, it's okay to check back in. We also fill up two or three months in advance sometimes. So you need to be persistent, and it helps if you are flexible. If we haven't given you a call and you follow us on Twitter and we are like, "Hey, we have an opening next Thursday," then you jump on it, like, "Here's my MP3, we can play this Thursday," then you can get in. And we are thankful when somebody can do that, so we will give you maybe another show two months down the road because you helped us out on short notice. We know it is hard to get people out, especially on short notice, so we will try to give you another show down the road, and you can promote it more. But being flexible is a good way to get a gig at Cake Shop.

Of course we take submissions on our website, Cake-Shop.com. But when you send us a link to your website, or Facebook, you have to make sure it's easy to find your music. If we can't find the songs, we are not going to surf around your website. You need to have the songs right up front, so we can find them easily.

Also, if we have musicians who have proven themselves, we will give them a night occasionally. We will be like, "You can book some of your friends." That works out really well because it's a whole party where, like I said, you are not just here to see one band; you are there for the whole night. They have to run it by us, but we will be like, "Look, you guys have proven yourselves here. You have a good draw. You are a good band. You can have the night. You can put a bill together."

Chapter 26

HOW TO DEVELOP A SUCCESSFUL INTERNET RADIO STATION

Interview with Elias Roman, CEO of Songza

In July 2014, a few months after we conducted this interview, Google purchased Songza. The purchase price was reported to be in excess of 39 million dollars.[357] As of the time this manuscript was submitted for publication in January 2015, Google had not changed any of the elements discussed in this interview.

Songza is still an Internet radio service supported by advertising with playlists made by music experts. What makes it unique is that Songza recommends playlists based on time of day and mood or activity. For instance, it offers playlists for activities such as waking up, working out, commuting, concentrating, unwinding, entertaining, and sleeping. Users can also find playlists based on themes, interests, and eras, such as "Songs in Apple Commercials," "'90s One-Hit Wonders," and "Music of Fashion Week."

The founders of Songza, including Elias Roman, started their digital careers as students at Brown University, where they created another streaming service, called Amie Street. After selling the business to Amazon for an undisclosed amount, they launched Songza in 2012. In its first year, Songza became the top free app on iTunes for the iPad and the number two free app for the iPhone.

SG: What makes Songza unique?

ER: Songza's unique because it makes the things that you do every day better. Now we do that in a very specific way. We match what you are doing at that instant with an expertly curated soundtrack made specifically to enhance it. So, whether you are waking up, working out, commuting, entertaining, or going to sleep, we are improving your everyday moment.

SG: In doing research for this interview I found the following comment about Songza from a fan of the service:

> I prefer songza vs spotify at times because i can simply choose the kind of music for the mood i'm in—it's very "brainless" and is nice when i'm not in a discovery mode (but even then, i run into new music in the genre that i like and i still "discover" new songs) . . .[358]

ER: Yeah, I am thrilled to hear the quote. People do discover new music with Songza. Instead of asking people to start their experience by typing in an artist they know of, we find out what they are doing, and effectively DJ for them based on their situation. It's not the subset of music they have already heard of. This really ends up enhancing the discovery experience. And so we have people coming to Songza and spending hours listening to playlists like epic film scores, or American primitivism, which are two of our most popular playlists, because they are phenomenally conducive to working without being distracted by music. No one would have ever found that, left to their own.

SG: Well, I see on the home page of the app, "a relaxing weekend, working out, creating a cool atmosphere, eating dinner, studying (no lyrics), cooking . . ." I think you have even got one called "If you get lucky."

ER: We do indeed; that's later in the evening.

SG: What is the most popular button that people click on?

ER: Actually the most popular situations everyday are waking up and going to sleep. Those are some of the most popular, followed pretty closely by working out and working.

SG: Tell us about your history in the digital music business. I know you had a prior start-up called Amie Street.

ER: Amie Street started out as a conversation around a keg at Brown, second semester senior year, back in 2006. The question was, "After 10 years of stealing music, is there any way we would ever pay for it again? What would that take?" And so this laundry list of features that we came up with sort of sounded like it might be a business. So, on a whim we incorporated, we put together a business plan, we built a prototype. All of a sudden, we were covered by TechCrunch, and then it was on—a ton of people immediately started using Amie Street. It became a company.

What made Amie Street so different was it did not make sense to us that all songs were worth exactly the same thing. So we built a dynamic pricing algorithm that said a song should be worth what the community thinks it is worth. Then, when people see the price tag, it is not just a price tag, it is what the community has said the song is worth. We had this very different purchase and discovery experience based on community participation.

SG: What happened to Amie Street?

ER: We eventually sold Amie Street, really the brand and customer base, to Amazon, who had been an early investor, in September of 2010. The reason we sold it was the fundamental method of consumption, i.e., downloading, was clearly giving way to streaming. We wanted to skate to where the puck was going.

SG: I think the so-called celestial jukebox is finally really here, because you've got over a billion smartphones in the world today, each one capable of playing any music you want at any time.

Each connected to the cloud. So, you know, there's really no need for CDs or downloading. I guess maybe that's one of the reasons Apple started iRadio. Are you apprehensive about Apple starting a streaming service?

ER: You know, it makes all the sense in the world for them. You can hike up the slope of their stock price since they embraced music really fundamentally with the iPod and the iTunes store. As I said before, the fundamental method of consumption that they initially embraced, downloading, is absolutely giving way to streaming, so it makes sense to embrace that. In terms of will their service be a threat, it all comes down to the details and the differentiation. I think we have forged a very, very clear, unique, different, and invaluable path for Songza that sort of set us apart from all of the other services we will face.

SG: In what formats is Songza available?

ER: iPhone, Android, desktop, laptop, BlackBerry 10, Chromecast, Windows 8, Windows 8 Phone, and Sonos.

SG: What percentage of your listeners listen to Songza on a laptop or desktop, and what percentage listen to it on their mobile phones?

ER: You know, laptop and desktop are the minority; they are about 25 percent. About 75 percent is mobile, and in mobile I am bundling tablet as well.

SG: Pandora, your main competition, boasts of 80 million active users. Give me an idea of your success and whether it is growing.

ER: Absolutely growing; we have millions of active monthly listeners.

SG: What is Songza's business model? How do you make money?

ER: There are two ways that we make money right now. Advertising on web and mobile, of course. That is where you start with a free streaming service. But instead of serving audio ads in the middle of your playlist (which is actually the middle of your workout, cocktail party, nap, etc.), our native advertising solution allows brands to own (and improve!) a moment from start to finish (think "Working Out" becomes "Working Out with Nike," complete with branded workout playlists brought to you by Nike). The idea here is that we can do better than serving ads that upset users. It's been said that there is something better than an ad: an experience. That's what our native platform allows brands to bring to their users: a unique, lifestyle-enhancing experience.

So in that hypothetical Nike example, let's say that the brand is targeting someone who is running with an iPhone. There are really two ways to interact with that listener. One way is to say, "I gotcha. You are captive. Because you are listening I am going to serve an audio ad and I am going to tell you my message in 30 seconds and you are going to have to listen to it." That is not the best way in our mind of interacting with a consumer who probably is interested in learning about your product, but probably not that way. We would pick the direction of saying, "How can we create content (in this case a "Working Out" playlist) that will make that run the user's best run ever?" How can we make sure the user knows about the sponsor, make sure the user's friends know about it when he or she shares the playlist—but most importantly, how can we make this user's run a better one, and not how can we ambush customers while they are on their run.

We also have a B-to-B platform that brands can build on top of and offer a co-branded version of Songza. So imagine Songza Concierge, which is more generally geared towards your lifestyle under the direction of a brand that is more focused on something particular. Maybe it is working out, or health and wellness, or entertaining, or whatever it might be. That is the other way that we make money. There are other revenue streams that we are really excited about. There are doors that are open to us because at the core we're not a music product. We are a lifestyle enhancer. When you are a lifestyle enhancer, you have more doors open to you than just either subscription or ad support as your business model.

SG: How are you doing financially?

ER: You know, we are happy with our progress. It is still very, very early. But we are very happy with the traction, both usage and on the revenue side.

SG: But tell us how you are dealing with that challenge of advertisers being hesitant to pay much for ads on tiny screens.

ER: So there are two primary challenges with mobile monetization when you are talking about advertising. One, the real estate, i.e., the screen, is tiny. Two, when you are talking about music, for the vast majority of the time the device is in someone's pocket, so it does not even matter how big the screen is. I think there is a lot of momentum behind branded content and native advertising, which is basically saying, instead of slapping ads around the content, how can we make content compelling enough that it is both content and advertising? So that is something that we are really excited about doing in our way, and the traction on our native advertising platform has been fantastic. Forbes recently named us "One of Five Companies That Transformed Advertising in 2013."

SG: One of the most important and controversial issues in the music business today, as you know, is the cost of using recorded music in streaming services such as Pandora as well as Songza. Noninteractive Internet radio stations can play any recording you want so long as you pay the compulsory-license rate negotiated by SoundExchange. But Pandora complains that that rate is so high, they can hardly make a profit. They complain that SoundExchange eats up approximately half their income.

Does Songza pay the same rates as Pandora? If so, what percentage of your revenue are you paying SoundExchange, and do you agree with Pandora that the rates are just too high?

ER: We do fall under the same license as Pandora. All you have to do is look at Pandora's financials to understand the full story about the rates. They can be challenging. And can be very challenging for some of the reasons we have discussed around mobile advertising, now that the vast majority of Internet radio consumption is in fact mobile. And then of course you have this element of a fixed fee per song [Author's note: The rate is currently *the greater of* **25** percent of gross revenues or $0.00130 per stream], even though the incremental revenue you can earn per song, when you are an ad-supported business, goes down and down and down with each incremental song during a given session. Those are indeed real challenges.

SG: Let me play devil's advocate: It seems egregious that you are paying, or Pandora at least is paying, more than half of its revenue for records, when normal broadcast radio pays nothing at all. Nada. Which is largely because Congress needs broadcast radio to run for election every campaign cycle, so terrestrial broadcasters still have tremendous influence in Washington and on copyright law.

However, for decades record companies have been distributing their records by selling wholesale to accounts, including record chains and big-box stores like Walmart. They usually receive more than half of the retail selling price. And in the case of iTunes, they actually get $0.70 for every $0.99 download, which is better than 70 percent. So, why should Internet radio pay less for recorded music than the chains and Walmarts?

ER: That is a fair question. I think part of the answer that this is the Internet we are talking about. The cat, that is, free music, is totally out of the bag. If you look at the brief history of the Internet, there really are very few things that consumers want and have gotten for free that they end up being willing to pay for. That is not how the Internet tends to work. I think the relevant question for all the parties here is how do we make free streaming, advertiser-supported work?

SG: What do you think you as well as Pandora should be paying?

ER: I'll withhold comment here, but I think it's fair to say we could certainly benefit from an adjustment being made, but I think it is also fair to say, "We need to be paying artists fairly."

SG: To me 25 percent seems right, because if Songza and Pandora, and interactive services like Spotify, which also pays a steep rate to big labels, were allowed to keep more money, they could innovate, grow, and create more value for the rights holders. And then you would have even bigger and better rivals to BitTorrent and even more people would migrate to the legal services, creating more money for the record labels and the artists. I would imagine you would agree with that.

ER: Absolutely. And not just sort of increasing the level of legal consumption in the United States, but you have got a lot of other countries, a lot of other people out there that companies like Pandora are not even trying to enter because it is so expensive to acquire the music rights. The challenge in the United States is difficult enough without thinking about the other countries. But, if there were a fairer rate structure, but also a global licensing structure that made international expansion easier, then I think you're talking about bringing a lot more people into the legal, monetizable fold. And that is a win for everybody.

SG: Yes, because now if you want to operate outside the US you have to deal with every record company individually and they ask, I understand, for even more money than SoundExchange. In addition, in the US, when it comes to licensing the songs at this point you only have to deal with ASCAP, BMI, and SESAC instead of all the individual publishers. Although the big publishers are now trying to change the game and make direct deals. What is your position on "direct licensing"?

ER: You know, the first business we had, Amie Street, was a business that required direct licensing. Not on the publishing side, but we went label by label, artist by artist, distributor by distributor, and an incredible amount of our resources, our time, our thinking, our energy, our capital went to that process as opposed to, let us say, innovating on the product itself, marketing, expanding, etc. One of the things we love about the new space we found ourselves in with Songza was how efficient the licensing process is. We are thrilled with our interactions with SoundExchange and with the PROs. So, anything that adds more moving parts, more time spent negotiating, more difference within rates, and certainly any less efficient use of capital to us can only be perceived as a regression. A significant step backwards. So I cannot emphasize enough how great a structure SoundExchange and the three PROs is for us on the licensing side. I am sad to see changes there.

SG: Let's focus on foreign expansion. I know you launched in Canada. Congratulations, but what is the lay of the land with respect to licensing recorded music outside of the US? Is it as expensive, less expensive, more expensive? What does it look like out there?

ER: The defining attribute, from our perspective, is how fragmented it is. It is incredibly fragmented, and so that, by itself, means it is expensive. Because it is time consuming and it is different in every place. That requires new research, new licensing, new contracts to be made, new negotiations, and new rates. So it is very, very challenging. We spent a while working with the folks in Canada at Re:Sound and SOCAN, really thrilled with those guys. They are willing to work with anyone who is bringing in awesome music service to Canadians. We could not be happier with our launch. In the first 70 days we had over 1 million registrations and so we will continue to evaluate countries on a case-by-case basis, but I wish we did not have to. I wish there were more of a global licensing framework that we could fall under.

SG: Well, how does it work in Canada? Do you have one central body, like SoundExchange, representing all the record companies?

ER: It's not exactly apples to apples, but I think they have taken a very simple approach. You have Re:Sound, which is the Candian version of Sound Exchange, and you have SOCAN instead of ASCAP, BMI, and SESAC.

SG: Okay, so what is next for Songza? Are you planning on any enhancements, changes; or are you just going to go in the same direction that you have already had a lot of success with?

ER: When your direction is making the things your users do every day better, I think the sky is really the limit. There is so much more for us to do.

There is almost no limit to the things you can bring to bear on that experience. As I mentioned, we opened our doors in Canada. You will see a lot more expansion from Songza, too, whether it is new countries or new platforms. There are a few projects we are working on now that I am really excited about, and they will all go live soon and make the Songza experience strong. Whether it is improved quality of the audio experience, or it is different and more moments of your day, or more data that we are bringing to bear to predict exactly what you are doing and how we can make it better, there's a lot of new stuff that we're working on that we are really excited about.

SG: Are there any other thoughts that you would like to share?

ER: When we started Songza, one of the things we wanted to do was create a service that instead of trying to change consumer behavior just reinforced it, took the things that you already do and made them better. If I had to pick the most pleasant surprise that we have come upon it is that we are actually changing off-line behavior. There are very few apps that are doing that. We hear consistently that more people go to the gym more often since they discovered Songza. That is number one. The second thing that we hear that we love is, "Monday morning is not as difficult, because of Songza." We are getting people out of bed more easily. We are getting them through their Monday morning commute more easily. I was sitting down with someone the other week and he said, "You know what my dad told me? Since he found Songza he entertains more often." So those are some of the most exciting pieces of feedback we get. Again, changing off-line behavior is very, very rare. So we are helping enhance people's lives as well as their music experience. And that is something we're super proud of.

Chapter 27

HOW A JAZZ CLUB IS USING THE INTERNET TO REACH A WORLDWIDE AUDIENCE AND CREATE NEW REVENUE STREAMS FOR THE ARTISTS WHO PLAY THERE

Interview with Spike Wilner, Jazz Pianist and Co-Owner of Smalls Jazz Club in NYC

Spike Wilner is an accomplished jazz pianist and the co-owner of Smalls Jazz Club in New York City's Greenwich Village. He also has been using the Internet to expose the artists who play at Smalls and their music to a worldwide audience by simulcasting live shows every night (click on "live video" at http://www.smallsjazzclub.com/). In addition, over seven years ago he started creating an archive of recordings of the live music performed at the club, and plans to offer fans the opportunity to listen to any show on demand in exchange for a small monthly subscription fee which he will share with the artists. In this interview we discuss Spike's experience with expanding Smalls' audience by using the Internet, what he plans to do next, and his vision of the future.

SG: Please give a thumbnail sketch of your career as a jazz pianist and entrepreneur.

SW: I went to the New School for Social Research and was part of an experimental music program led by the legendary Arnie Lawrence. In this small, exclusive school I met many of my peers who, to this day, are at the top of our field. Many great musicians were in my class, including Brad Mehldau and John Popper from the Blues Travelers (who started the band at our school). After graduating I made my living playing any little gig I could—restaurants and bars, solo piano and private parties. In the early 1990s, New York still had quite a few nice places to play and dozens of dives where you could play (and not make too much dough, but it was a great vibe). I did some touring, notably with Maynard Ferguson and also Artie Shaw's big band, which was led at that time by clarinet great Dick Johnson. It was during this time that I also began to put pianos into bars that didn't have one. My deal was this: I bought a cheap piano and, at my expense, put it into the bar. In exchange I got two or three nights to do a gig there with my band. We agreed on some regular amount of pay and dinner included. The other nights of the week the bar had the right to use the piano in any way they wanted. I did this successfully in about four different spots that all became jazz hangs. I guess in this way I planted the seeds for my future as a club owner.

In 1994 Smalls Jazz Club was opened by Mitchell Borden. I began to play there within the first few weeks of the club's opening. Mitch booked and ran the club nearly on his own. I became embroiled in the fabric of the club, which was a simmering pot of young musicians, staying up all night and morning, playing and practicing jazz and also indulging in licentious behavior, as is normal for musicians. This lasted until 2002, when the club finally closed and Mitchell went bankrupt. Rents in post 9/11 New Yorkhad gone through the roof. The original Smalls had an $800/month rent. Now it went to $8,000, so Smalls closed down. Afterwards, the space was bought and converted into a Brazilian bar. After Smalls closed I was so distraught that I left the US. I worked in Paris and started spending a lot of time in Europe.

In 2006 I decided to go back to school and went to SUNY for my master's degree. I was the oldest student there, but my idea was to get a teaching job. At the end of the year I got word from Mitch that the Brazilian guy wanted to sell the bar. I knew it was a great chance and so I mortgaged my apartment and bought Smalls. Originally I had a partner with me, an old college friend. But things got difficult and we decided to split. I made Mitch honorary partner and we dedicated ourselves to resurrecting Smalls with the same spirit of musician community and musical growth as the original. We also wanted it to be a listening room where people could really listen and participate in this great art form. It's now seven years since I became partner and manager of Smalls.

SG: Give us a brief description of what happens at Smalls, that is, the music and the artists featured there and what folks can expect if they visit the club.

SW: Smalls Jazz Club is generally open from 4:00 p.m. to 4:00 a.m., with some exceptions. Normally we have three bands per night. We do two two-set shows and then an "after hours" set, and then a jam session at the very end. Jam sessions are an important part of Smalls and there's traditionally a jam every night of the week quite late (sometimes not even starting until 2:00 a.m.). We also have afternoon jam sessions on Friday and Saturday. On Wednesday in the afternoon we host a tap dance jam session and the tap community comes out for that. On Wednesday and Thursdays we do a 9:30 p.m. "main show" that usually features an important or famous musician or band. The same on the weekend, but it starts at 10:30 p.m. Our "after hours" shows start either around midnight or 1 a.m. and are all seasoned veteran players hosting. Sundays we are open all day with a vocal workshop at 1 p.m., a showcase show at 4 p.m., a duet show at 7:30 p.m., and then at 10 p.m. we have the legendary Johnny O'Neal, who is in a permanent residence with his trio.

Smalls has a "no reservation" policy, first come first served. Our cover is $20 until after hours, and then it's $10. We have a one-drink minimum for those seated or at the bar, but standers in the back don't have to buy a drink. It gets crowded and the vibe changes as it gets later. After hours has the coolest vibe and is not for everyone. But the music is always great at Smalls, from the beginning of the day to the end.

SG: You have been experimenting for some time now with harnessing the power of the Internet to create a broader audience for the music and artists who play at Smalls. You are now simulcasting every show at Smalls on the web. Tell us more about your live simulcast, including how you implement it, how many people are tuning in, and the feedback you have been getting from fans and the artists themselves.

SW: I remember in my jazz history that John Hammond, the great record producer, was driving to Chicago when he picked up a radio broadcast live from a jazz club in Kansas City. The music blew his mind and he turned his car around and drove to Kansas City to sign whomever the artist was. It turned out to be Count Basie and the rest is history. What fascinates me about that story is the idea of a club using a radio wire to transmit to the world. I wanted to do this and used the Internet. We started live streaming about seven years ago with a very simple system. As the years progressed, the technology for live streaming has grown in leaps and bounds. Now it's possible for anyone to very inexpensively create his or her own "television studio." We began to generate an enormous audience world wide, with jazz fans checking in from literally all parts of the globe. I was in Italy last year and it shocked me how famous Smalls has become internationally. I attribute this to the Internet and doing a live broadcast every night of the week. The other thing is, I'm an archivist and firmly believe that the music being played nightly at Smalls will be of historic importance to future generations. Therefore my mission has been to record every single show and have it organized by date, who the leader was, and who was on the date. The first thing I did was to install a recording device and began recording. This has evolved over the last seven years but we are currently up to about 8,000 recordings in our library, which now includes our HD video.

SG: Recently you had a crowdfunding campaign. What were your goals, did you succeed and what challenges did you face?

SW: Our goal with the crowdfunding campaign was to raise money for new equipment for our live streaming (i.e., computers and cameras) as well as to buy a new piano. We were successful in this and hit our goal. We did buy a new Steinway for the club and installed an entirely new and up-to-date streaming system and in-house recording studio.

As far as the crowdfunding experience—my thoughts are that it is a terrible way to fund a business. For one thing, you tap the good will of everyone who likes or supports you. Secondly, you can't do it again—it's a one-time shot. The other thing that nobody talks about is that if you do get your money there's this huge tax liability at the end of the year in the form of a 1099. If you don't properly prepare for that, and spend all the money, then you're going to get hit. Furthermore, Indiegogo took a big chunk in "fees." I don't like crowdfunding and hope it's just a passing fad.

SG: I understand that you would like to use the Internet to monetize your archive of recordings of the shows performed at the club in the last seven years and share revenues with the artists.

SW: My idea is to build a website platform where we can disseminate our huge library of recordings and videos. This has proved more complex and expensive than I had planned. The plan is to do a full revenue share with all of the artists that are in our archive. We want to charge a small subscription rate for fans to access our ever-growing library. The revenue from the subscriptions is pooled and distributed to artists based on how much their work gets listened to. The more popular an artist is, the more they make—law-of-the-jungle economics. This is a big system, and what I realized I had to do and have since done is taken on partners to make SmallsLIVE LLC real. I've partnered with two guys; one is a programmer and has his own successful website development company. The other partner is an investor to finance the building of this site. Once the site is up and launched we will be able to use it to accommodate an entire range of related media projects, including our live stream and video library as well as educational videos, downloads, and merchandise.

SG: You now have over 4,000 subscribers on your YouTube channel, and over 34,000 Facebook fans. What other social networks do you use? How much work does it take to maintain engagement with your fans through them, and is it worth it?

SW: We were, at first, excited about YouTube. It seemed amazing that you could have a CDN [Content Delivery Network] host your live stream for free. Well, it's not really free in the sense that you don't have real control over the content that you stream. YouTube screens your video and scans for illicit use of copyrighted material. In our case, when we play our iPod on breaks, we get flagged even though we are paying for the right to publicly perform that music to the appropriate music collection societies. But if you get flagged, YouTube will not allow you to stream any music, including our live performances. It was a headache. On the other hand, it's very affordable to rent time on a good CDN such as Bit Gravity. Then you have full control of your stream and the content that you're creating.

We have a large fan base on Facebook and also Twitter. We also have a rapidly growing e-mail list and regularly do a newsletter and post to our social media. Facebook is great because it's very affordable to use and reaches a lot of people who you know are already interested in what you're doing.

SG: What are your next goals?

SW: Our next goal is to get our new website built with the revenue sharing system. The new company is now formed and work will begin soon. Smalls Jazz Club is wonderful and more and more popular. The music is always great. As far as myself, I am also focusing more on my trio and concertizing much more. I had a great two-week European tour last year with the trio and plan to do more of that. [Author's note: In fall 2014, Wilner opened a new jazz piano club, Mezzrow, in Greenwich Village across the street from Smalls.]

Chapter 28
HOW TO USE A MUSIC COLLEGE EDUCATION

Is It Worth the Time and Money?

Recently I came across an article containing a list of music colleges and universities with music business and music performance programs. The article included the yearly cost of studying at each institution. When I attended State University of New York at Binghamton the tuition was around $1,800 per semester for in-state students. Now tuition is approximately $12,000 per year, which is still pretty reasonable. But I was amazed how expensive the private music conservatories, colleges, and universities with music performance programs were—generally $50,000 and up. Of course, this mirrors the rise in costs of attending virtually any private college or university in the US, and practically all of them offer a variety of scholarships and/or financial aid. But I could not help but stop and wonder if the investment of time as well as money was worth it for those who want to become the next Bob Dylan, Bono, Eminem, Katy Perry, Rihanna, Jay-Z or Beyoncé, none of whom attended, let alone graduated from a college-level music program.

For those students seeking a career as music industry executives, I think it's a relatively easy call to major in music business studies at colleges such as NYU's Steinhardt School. First and foremost, college grads always have a huge edge in almost any sector of the job market. The music recording, publishing, and touring businesses are no exceptions. Additionally, the internships that are made available during any given institution's course of study offer students in those programs a tremendous advantage.

But what about performance? Is it worth the investment of time and money any more to study at a conservatory or music college? Does it depend on what kind of artist you are and what kind of music you want to perform or create? Does it depend on the college or university that you attend?

In this section I include two interviews. The subjects are graduates of two of the leading music colleges in this country or indeed the world, Berklee College of Music in Boston and the Juilliard School in New York. In 2013 the *Hollywood Reporter* included both Berklee and Juilliard as among the top 10 music schools based on a survey of academic and entertainment professionals.[359]

The Juilliard School is world famous for training some of the great classical musicians of all time, such as Leontyne Price, Itzhak Perlman, and Yo-Yo Ma, but it has also educated some of the greatest names in jazz, including Miles Davis, Tito Puente, Chick Corea, Nina Simone, and Wynton Marsalis.

Berklee is renowned for turning out successful musicians, even though not all have graduated. The most famous include Quincy Jones, Esperanza Spalding, John Mayer, Melissa Etheridge, Branford Marsalis, Al Di Meola, Bruce Hornsby, Will Calhoun, Jeff Tain Watts, and many other successful artists, producers, and songwriters.

Another artist who attended Berklee for three years before dropping out is St. Vincent. She was recently quoted on her education there:

> I think that with music school and art school, or school in any form, there has to be some system of grading and measurement. The things they can teach you are quantifiable. While all that is good and has its place, at some point you have to learn all you can and then forget everything that you learned in order to actually start making music.

Just one year's tuition at Berklee is over $38,000. That's a lot of money for forgetting everything you learned. So the question is whether music school is worth the time and expense.

The first interview is with a young but already fabulously successful musician, songwriter, and band leader, Jonathan Batiste, who earned a master's from Juilliard. At only 28, Jonathan has toured the world, headlined at Carnegie Hall, and released two albums. He's also collaborated with many acclaimed musicians in various genres of music, including Wynton Marsalis, and was featured in *Red Hook Summer*, a film by Spike Lee. Most recently he was appointed as the associate artistic director of the National Jazz Museum in Harlem.

The second interview is with Linda Lorence Critelli, vice president of writer/publisher relations for the performing-rights organization SESAC, and president of the New York Chapter of the National Academy of Recording Arts and Sciences (NARAS). Linda is a graduate of Berklee. She tells an inspiring story about a girl who dreamed of being a professional singer, but used her education in music to build a fabulous career as a leading music business executive.

Interview with Jonathon Batiste

SG: I know you received your master's from Juilliard; did you go there for your BA as well?

JB: Yes. I took a professional leave of absence to tour the world, so it took one extra year to graduate. Seven years total.

SG: Why did you want to attend Juilliard?

JB: To be in New York City and to be amongst artists from all of the performing arts. I wanted to be a part of a community of the best artists that I could find and be in a city where I could make something epic happen.

SG: Was it expensive or did you have a scholarship?

JB: I had a scholarship. Living in New York is expensive, though.

SG: What did you study at Juilliard and what was your focus?

JB: Jazz studies on piano officially, though I took some classes in every division, even dance and drama.

SG: Were you inspired by any of your teachers and what did you learn from them?

JB: The teachers were all very accomplished, but I was inspired most by my peers. The community of artists and our potential to change the world was inspiring. We shared a lot with each other. I learned many lessons by spending time talking to and playing with the other students at the school.

SG: Did attending change your style or perception of music?

JB: It did not change my style or my concept. It added another dimension to it that I gained from the experience of going there. Any life experience will add a dimension to your playing. It wasn't so much about what I actually learned there.

SG: Did the contacts you made at Juilliard help launch your career?

JB: No. School for me was almost a hindrance in that regard because I had to turn down some work in order to graduate. School is not about the career move; it's about cultivating your talent in an amenable environment.

SG: Are you involved in any other endeavors as an educator?

JB: The National Jazz Museum in Harlem is the main educational endeavor that I'm involved in, although I still collaborate with Music Unites and many other education institutions frequently. We are all in this together, so I think helping each other out is a necessity.

Interview with Linda Lorence Critelli

SG: Can you tell us what your job is now, and what your role in the music business is?

LL: I am vice president of writer/publisher relations for SESAC, the performing-rights organization. I represent our organization all over the country at different music events and conferences, and my main responsibility is to sign up new as well as established songwriters to SESAC. [Author's note: SESAC's writers include Bob Dylan and Neil Diamond.] And once they are signed, I'm basically their client rep. I help manage their accounts and make sure they get the top service that they deserve. "Writer/publisher relations" means handling our songwriters, handling our publishers, and making sure they are as successful as possible, both creatively as well as financially.

I'll tell you a big success story that is happening right now. We signed a small band out of Boston about eight years ago and now they have become the American Authors, and they have a number one hit on the radio, "Best Day of My Life." It turns out, by the way, that a couple of the kids in the band went to Berklee.

I am also the president of the New York chapter of the Recording Academy, known as NARAS, the organization that produces the Grammys. In that position I oversee all of the initiatives that the New York chapter takes on. We have about 3600 members in the Northeast, including New York and Boston, and we put on programs including panel discussions and networking events.

SG: How long have you been at SESAC?

LL: Twenty-five years, thank you (laughs). I was hired as an affiliations representative; that was my title.

SG: I know you graduated from Berklee. Was SESAC your first job? And how long after graduating Berklee did you get your job at SESAC?

LL: Actually, it wasn't my first job out of school. You know, I've been working since I was a kid. At 13 I ran a babysitting business out of my house. I've always had a very strong work ethic, and that came from my family. In fact, I was making money from singing at weddings and clubs before starting at Berklee. After I got in, I continued earning money from singing. We call them GB gigs in Boston; in New York you call them club dates—weddings and fancy events where they hire a big orchestra or a band, and I was the singer for a number of different orchestras. After graduating Berklee, I continued working as a freelance singer, but about 6 months after graduating, I took a "real" job.

I was still getting gigs, but it was hard to pay the rent. I ran into somebody I knew from Berklee on the street, right in front of the school, and during our conversation I mentioned I might be looking for a steady job. I was just gonna pick up any job I could get, just to tide me over until the spring singing market opened up. And this guy I knew from school said, "Why don't you come work for me, I'm looking for someone to be my assistant in the career resource center at Berklee." And I was thinking, "Wow, you know, I don't know if I could work full time, this is gonna be weird, but I need to try it." So I took the job. And it turned out to be right up my alley, because it was about mentoring people, Berklee kids, and I didn't know a whole lot, I had just graduated, but I knew how to find the answers. I also helped the center build their library. They had a budget, and I ordered the best music business magazines . I also kept up on the business side of things, and the job for SESAC actually came through that office.

SG: How did you get the job at SESAC?

LL: The person who ended up hiring me at SESAC, Tom Casey, called the resource center one day, and I answered the phone. It turned out that he knew who I was. Tom, who is also a Berklee grad, had come on campus the year before as a SESAC rep, and at that time he had seen me perform when I was student, and he remembered me. He said he was calling to post an ad for a position at SESAC. So we started a dialogue on the phone, and I told him I had thought about moving to New York to pursue my singing career, and he said he really wanted to hire a Berklee graduate, and he wanted someone who could work effectively with new songwriters, but that person should also have some administration experience. I said, well, you're describing me! And he hired me on the phone. We talked a few times after that, but he hired me on the phone, and I came down here to New York City. I remember I walked into that SESAC office and it was like something out of the movie *Working Girl*. Here I was in this beautiful high-rise office building around the corner from Carnegie Hall in Manhattan. I was 26 years old and I didn't know where I was, or what I was doing, but here I was on the 26th floor overlooking Manhattan in this nice little cubby with a window.

SG: Were you still thinking about becoming a professional singer?

LL: Yes. I remember crying a few times and being like, "What have I done?! I've left all my friends and a secure job that I knew I could do well." But I had come to New York to follow my dreams, and I was still determined to pursue my singing career. At that time all I really wanted was to be a backup singer for a band like Pink Floyd or to sing jingles, but be a really serious singer. I had just graduated from Berklee and I had studied and I could read music. I was really at the top of my game. So I took the SESAC job and moved to New York really to pursue my career as a singer.

SG: And what happened to your aspiration to make it as a singer?

LL: I tried very hard to make it as a singer, but it was really challenging to break in. I learned very quickly that the opportunities for singers were really slim. I learned that the whole jingle business was unavailable to me. Except for the lead singer, the only singers they used were already working for the jingle houses. That was the payoff for the houses for spending hours creating demos: If someone in their office landed the gig, the commercial, they would all go on the contract as the background singers, so there was no work for background singers who didn't work for their company.

And that was a real rude awakening because that's what I had studied in school. And I started with some orchestras here in New York, including a swing band, and I did gigs on the weekends, but it soon became very exhausting, working five days a week and then doing weekend warrior work singing out at these weddings in Connecticut or Long Island. So I started focusing on the other end of my career, which was on the other side of the desk.

I never dreamed I would be working in an office. I can remember my first week working in the career resource center at Berklee. I had never sat down for that long in my life. I remember getting up and walking around and just thinking, "Golly, how do people sit down for 40 hours?" During the first year or two at SESAC, I wasn't even considering it as a career. It was really kind of a day job, but I had this crazy work ethic so I wanted to do a good job at it regardless, so I did.

When I started meeting other people in New York, I would see these girls writing their own music and they had their own bands and they were really pursuing their careers in the right way if you want to be discovered. That wasn't the track I was on. And I realized, thankfully quickly, that I didn't really have *that*. I didn't have the "it" thing. I was a great singer and I got work all the time, but I wasn't a phenomenal artist. I really became a student of these performers watching them and going, "Hmm, that's 'it.'" That's the one thing I failed to learn at Berklee—the idea of creating myself as an artist. I didn't know what I wanted to say. If you asked me what I wanted to say when I was 25 or 26, I would have said I didn't know. It was easier for people who knew what they wanted to say, how they wanted to make an audience feel—they were several steps ahead of the game.

SG: When you finally decided to try to make it in the business of music rather than as a musician, was it helpful that you had studied music in college?

LL: Yes, just the fact that I was immersed in music has helped me in my career in the music business immensely. Number one, I have a deep understanding of my clients, their talent, and their ambition. Being able to speak their language is totally key in what we do. It's also helpful when I am trying to sign up a promising writer or giving advice to writers who are already SESAC affiliates.

SG: The tuition at Berklee is $18,900 a semester, and total costs for a year are approximately $60,000. Do you remember exactly what you were paying and if you got a scholarship?

LL: I think my tuition back then was about $2,500 or $2,800 a semester. Because I remember it was around $5,000 or $6,000 a year, and yes, I did get scholarship; I had two scholarships. I won the Cleo Lane Jazz Masters, but I won it two years in a row, and that was like a $1,500 scholarship, which was about half my tuition, so it paid for half a semester . . .

SG: So it was definitely worth it for you?

LL: Absolutely.

SG: A lot of people who were very successful and went to Berklee actually dropped out. John Mayer, one year. St. Vincent, three years. We know about your success story in the business, but for people who never want to be in an office, as great as your job is, is it worth it for them?

LL: One of the great things about going to a music school is, if this is your passion, if you really have a deep desire to, and it's really what you really truly love, it's well worth the time and money and effort. You will eventually at the very least have something to do with music. And Berklee is one of the hottest music schools. I think it's number one; it's been number one for many years. They have been getting a lot of acclaim and they're marketing their brand like crazy. Perhaps that's why it costs so much to go there, because they advertise it everywhere. But they are turning out a lot of really talented people and it does matter, that degree does matter. People in the business look up when you say you've got your degree from Berklee. It means something.

It's one thing just to attend, and yes, many musicians have gone to Berklee and dropped out—Melissa Etheridge, in addition to the ones you mentioned. But other hugely successful musicians have graduated. Paula Cole was one of my colleagues in college and she went on to have a wonderful career, including winning a Grammy for best new artist. She is now teaching at the school.

I will say that going to an elite school like Berklee carries you on throughout your life. There is unstated fraternity. You immediately relate to someone who went there because you know they are very serious about music, and you know they were educated well. It's always helped me; it's always been a great thing to pull out of my back pocket if I have needed to. You know, to say that, "Oh, yeah, I did graduate from Berklee. And all of a sudden people think, you're one of us.

SG: Is there any other advice you would give aspiring musicians?

LL: The one thing I will say to anyone who is reading your book and is interested in music is that there is a lot of truth to following your heart. I know that sounds really corny, but if you do follow what your desires are in your heart, you will succeed, because you won't be forced into something that isn't you, so you will enjoy doing it, you will work harder at it, and you will be successful.

Note to readers: Berklee also offers a broad range of alternatives to the traditional four-year program, including online courses, certificate programs, and a 12-week full-credit summer program, which may be more suitable for certain students or people who have already launched their music careers. For more information, check their website, www.berklee.edu.

ACKNOWLEDGMENTS

I would like to express my appreciation to my assistants and interns who helped with the preparation of this manuscript, including Margot B, Emily Borich, Esq.; Markova Casseus; Mona Goodarzi; Kara Gooley; Michael Huseby; Seth Jones; Sarita Kataria; Alex Kovacs; Teronse Miller II; Anjana Puri, Esq.; Lisenny Rodriguez; Neda Shahram; Jennifer Sullivan and Brooke Weinberg.

I would like to also express my appreciation to those who helped me with their expertise, insights, and encouragement, including Ray Beckerman, Esq.; Corey D. Boddie, Esq.; Paul Brandes; Powell Burns; Wallace Collins, Esq.; Amy Dadow; Eric de Fontenay; Ricky Gordon (a.k.a. "Dirty Red"); Marty Novare, Esq.; John Paige, Esq.; Paul Resnikoff; Tetyana Todos; Kristin Thompson; Peter Thall, Esq.; Ashford Tucker, Esq.; and Jana Vejmelka, Esq.

Special thanks to Dan Coleman, the producer of many of my "futureofthemusicbusiness" podcasts available at Tunein Radio and my YouTube channel, Stevegordonlaw. Also special thanks to John Cerullo, my publisher, for taking on this edition; Bill Gibson and Zahra Brown, my editors; and my literary agent, Andrew Stuart.

Finally, I would like to acknowledge my great mentor and partner, Eric Kulberg of Universal Media.

ABOUT THE AUTHOR

Steve Gordon is an entertainment attorney, educator, and consultant based in New York City specializing in music, television, film, and digital entertainment projects. His clients include music artists, songwriters, managers, record companies, and music publishers as well as television and film producers, TV and Web networks, and digital start-ups. Steve also operates a music-clearance service for producers and filmmakers who wish to use music in documentaries, feature films, ad campaigns, stand-alone digital projects, and more. His clients include music artists, songwriters, and producers; TV and motion picture producers and distributors; and major entertainment companies and institutions. He is also a Fulbright Scholar, having taught courses under the auspices of the Fulbright on music business and law at Boconni University in Milan, Italy, and at Recanati, the graduate school of business at Tel Aviv University, Israel. Steve served as director of business affairs at Sony Music for over a decade, and previously worked as an attorney for Atlantic and Elektra Records as well as for the performing-rights organization SESAC and for Dino de Laurentiis, a Hollywood studio. He is a graduate of New York University Law School. For published articles, podcasts, videos, a client list, and contact information, see www.stevegordonlaw.com and www.futureofthemusibusiness.com.

NOTES

Preface

1. *Entertainment Law* by Melvin Simensky and Thomas Selz (Matthew Bender, 1984).

Introduction

2. The RIAA is a trade group representing the major labels (Universal, Warner, and Sony)and their wholly owned affiliates, including Epic, Columbia, and RCA (Sony); Atlantic, Warner Bros., and Rhino (Warner); Motown, Interscope, MCA, Def Jam, Capitol (Universal). But the RIAA's members also include many indies who distribute through the majors.
3. The RIAA's statistics for the recorded music industry represent their "estimate of the size of the US recorded music industry based on data collected directly from the major music companies (which create and/or distribute about 85 percent of the music sold in the US), and estimate where possible for the remaining parts of the market" (https://www.riaa.com/keystatistics.php?content_selector=research-about). According to the RIAA, "A frequent question we get is whether our data represents the whole US market, or just the RIAA member companies. Our aim is to describe the whole market, and we use independent estimates to account for the parts that are not created or distributed by the major record labels" (https://www.riaa.com/blog.php?content_selector=riaa-news-blog&blog_selector=So-What-Exactly-Is-A-Shipment&news_month_filter=7&news_year_filter=2009).
4. Per the data on the RIAA website, total revenue from recorded music in the US in 2013 was 6.996 billion (including sync income); in 1999 (in 2013 dollars) the total was 20.393 billion. 6.996 divided by 20.393 = 34.3 percent. Note the RIAA only started counting sync income in 2009, and as of 2014 it totaled $189.7 million. So the drop is actually greater than 34.3 percent.
5. Although over 9 percent accounting for inflation.
6. *News and Notes on 2014 Mid-Year RIAA Shipment and Revenue Statistics* by Joshua P. Friedlander, Vice President, Strategic Data Analysis, RIAA, http://riaa.com/media/1806D32F-B3DD-19D3-70A4-4C31C0217836.pdf.
7. http://www.ifpi.org/downloads/Digital-Music-Report-2014.pdf.
8. http://www.ifpi.org/content/library/worldsales2000.pdf. The IFPI report tries hard to put the best face on some disappointing stats by stating:

   > Overall, recorded music revenues grew in Europe and Latin America and continued to stabilize in the US, growing 0.8 per cent in trade terms. Music sales on a global scale, however, were sharply influenced by a steep 16.7 per cent fall in Japan, the world's second largest market. Outside Japan, global music revenues fell (0.1 per cent decrease); including Japan, they fell 3.9 per cent to an estimated US$15 billion.

   But the decline in Japan is shocking as it is the second biggest market in the world. The report glows about the increase in money from streaming services:

> New services with big global ambitions are launching, such as Beats and iTunes Radio—services that we hope will soon spread around the world. Meanwhile, the existing international services, such as Deezer, Google Play, iTunes, Spotify, and YouTube are generating income in many new markets following their global expansion. The competition is intense and consumer choice is ever-widening—these are very positive dynamics in the development of the digital music landscape.

However, a *Wall Street Journal* article pointed out that the decline in Japan could well be caused by the very media that the IPFI report is so optimistic about. *The Wall Street Journal* points to several reasons for the steep downturn in Japan, including a steep decline in sales of ringtones. The most telling remarks were about the damage created by YouTube's arrival in Japan:

> [S]ales of CDs at Tower Records Japan, the country's largest music chain, with 84 outlets, have been in decline. "People increasingly listen to music through free access sites like YouTube," said company spokesman Tatsuro Yagawa.
>
> Tatsuyoshi Kimura, a 22-year-old college student, used to spend 3,000 to 4,000 yen a month on CDs. But he rarely spends money on music any more, he says. "There are many sites like YouTube where I can listen to music free," he said. "That was not possible five years ago."

We discuss both the good and bad impacts in Part III of this book.

9. "Pandora's Revenue from 2006 to 2013, by Source (in Million U.S. Dollars)" by Statista, 2014, http://www.statista.com/statistics/190918/revenue-sources-of-pandora-since-2007/.
10. "Are there any music streaming standouts?" by Kapitall, May 28, 2014, http://www.nasdaq.com/article/are-there-any-music-streaming-standouts-cm356928.
11. https://press.spotify.com/us/information/.
12. They also tend to lock their customers into contracts that make it pricey to switch to another cell phone provider, thus reducing churn that might otherwise be controlled by offering a more attractive set of features (including ad-free music streaming).
13. "iTunes Store Sets New Record with 25 Billion Songs Sold." Apple Press Info. Apple, Inc. February 6, 2013. Retrieved April 18, 2013.
14. "Apple Reports First Quarter Results." Apple Press Info. January 17, 2007.
15. "Apple's iPhone Is Now the Most Profitable Business in the World" by Henry Blodget, April 25, 2012.
16. "Apple Breaks Revenue, iPhone, and iPad Records in Q1 of 2014" by Andrew Cunningham, January 27, 2014, http://arstechnica.com/apple/2014/01/apple-breaks-revenue-iphone-and-ipad-records-in-q1-of-2014/.
17. Id.
18. Id.
19. We talk about all these revenue streams in greater detail in Part I, and explain how to clear songs for use in records and audiovisual works in Part II.
20. http://www.nmpa.org/media/surveys/twelvth/NMPA_International_Survey_12th_Edition.pdf.
21. http://rhmusicroyaltypartners.com/resources/music-publishing-market-overview.
22. https://www.nmpa.org/media/showwhatsnew.asp?id=112.
23. Id.
24. http://www.pollstar.com/news_article.aspx?ID=808976, January 10, 2014.
25. http://www.pollstarpro.com/files/charts2013/2013YearEndTop200NorthAmericanTours.pdf.
26. "What the Top DJs Are Paid Per Gig" by Ray Waddell, *Billboard*, July 5, 2014, p. 47. Those DJs are Deadmau5, Calvin Harris, Tiesto, Skrillex, David Guette, Avicii, Steve Aoki, Pretty Lights, Kaskade, Steve Angello, Martin Garrix, Bassnectar, Hardwell, Nicky Romero, Zedd, Disclosure, Afrojack, Paul Van Dyke, Diplo, and Eric Prydz.
27. http://money.futureofmusic.org/jazz-musicians/4/.

28. "Jennifer Lopez Lands $17.5m Deal to Return to American Idol" by Heidi Parker, *Daily Mail*, August 30, 2013, http://www.dailymail.co.uk/tvshowbiz/article-2406911/Jennifer-Lopez-lands-17-5m-deal-return-American-Idol-securing-bumper-pay-rise.html.
29. See e.g., " How Taylor Swift's 'Red' Is Getting a Boost from Branding Mega-Deals" by Andrew Hampp, October 22, 2012, http://www.billboard.com/biz/articles/news/branding/1083319/from-this-weeks-billboard-how-taylor-swifts-red-is-getting-a
30. "Musicians' Income Can Still Be Huge—With the Right Brand, Team" by Joe Satran, *The Huffington Post*, July 31, 2012, www.huffingtonpost.com/2012/07/30/musicians-income_n_1719908.html.
31. Id.
32. Id.
33. "Beyoncé Knowles Tops the FORBES Celebrity 100 List" by Dorothy Pomerantz, *Forbes*, June 30, 2014, http://www.forbes.com/sites/dorothypomerantz/2014/06/30/beyonce-knowles-tops-the-forbes-celebrity-100-list/.
34. "Meet the New Boss, Worse than the Old Boss? "April 15, 2012, http://thetrichordist.com/2012/04/15/meet-the-new-boss-worse-than-the-old-boss-full-post/.
35. "Are Musicians Making More or Less Money?" http://money.futureofmusic.org/are-musicians-making-more-or-less-money/.
36. "10 Million Digital Music Tracks Left Unsold" by Marc Chacksfield, December 22, 2008, http://www.techradar.com/us/news/world-of-tech/broadband/web/internet/10-million-digital-music-tracks-left-unsold-496820.

Chapter 1

37. Section 102 of the Copyright Act.
38. *United States Copyright Office: A Brief Introduction and History*, Circular 1a, http://www.copyright.gov/circs/circ1a.html.
39. Id.
40. Copyright standing is governed by Section 411(a) of the Copyright Act of 1976, which states that "no civil action for infringement of the copyright in any United States work shall be instituted until preregistration or registration of the copyright claim has been made in accordance with this title."
41. It is also possible to register more than one song and/or sound recording at a time by carefully following the rules established by the Copyright Office. See Circular 1, Copyright Basics, p. 8, http://www.copyright.gov/circs/circ01.pdf. However, it is important to note that if a recording is contained in an album, which may be deemed to be "one work," statutory damages may be limited to one award per album. In 2010, the Second Circuit in *Bryant v. Media Rights Productions, Inc.*, 603 F.3d 135 (2d Cir 2010), held that the owner of multiple sound recordings contained in two albums was entitled only to one statutory damages award for each album and not for each recording. The court found it irrelevant that each recording was registered separately and that the distributor sold each recording as a single. "Based on a plain reading of the statute . . . infringement of an album should result in only one statutory damage award. The fact that each song may have received a separate copyright is irrelevant to this analysis." Id. at 141.
42. A resource that I find useful is https://copyright.cornell.edu/resources/publicdomain.cfm. This chart identifies the precise duration for a diverse variety of possible scenarios, including works first published outside the US and other special cases that are beyond the scope of this section, which lays out the basic applicable rules.
43. The 1976 Act also loosened formalities such as notice and registration. A work published without proper copyright notice would lose copyright protection under the old Act. This is not the case under the 1976 Act, although notice ("Copyright" or ©, year and author's name) is still advisable for several reasons, including identifying the owner of a work to potential licensees. Registration is not necessary, although for the reasons stated above it is extremely beneficial.

NOTES

44. Works originally created before January 1, 1978, but not published by that date (for instance, private letters) have been automatically brought under the statute and are now given federal copyright protection. The duration of copyright in these works is the same as post-'78 works, that is, life of the author plus 70 years. So, for instance, the unpublished correspondence of a famous author who died in 1965 will remain protected by copyright until 2035.
45. Any work published with notice and registered and renewed in 1923 or thereafter. Songs published prior to 1923 would have gone into the public domain prior to January 1, 1978, the effective date of the 1976 Copyright Act.
46. Two current lawsuits by the recording industry against Sirius XM and Pandora raise the issue of the scope of protection that state law affords to sound recordings. The major record labels have initiated lawsuits against both companies for not paying for public performance of their pre-'72 records. But the services are arguing that state law does not provide any public performance rights in sound recordings and are designed merely to prevent unauthorized copying. We will address these cases in greater detail in Chapter 6.
47. See *Capitol Records v. Naxos of America*, 4 NY3d 540 (NY April 5, 2005). State law protection is independent of whatever a foreign country might do. Naxos was putting out classical reissues of foreign recordings that had gone PD in their home country, and they were sued (successfully) by the US copyright owner of the recordings.
48. H.R. Rep. No. 94-1476, at p. 124, http://en.wikisource.org/wiki/Copyright_Law_Revision_(House_Report_No._94-1476).
49. See "Duration of Copyrights" for the language of the statute defining "publication."
50. The 1976 Act actually omitted such so-called "gap works," but the Copyright Office issued a regulation in 2010 correcting Congress' inadvertent omission. See "You're Terminated! Termination and Reversion of Copyright Grants and the Termination Gap Dilemma" by Pierre B. Pine, *Entertainment and Sports Lawyer*, Vol. 31, No. 1, May 2014.
51. Although Section 304(c) also exclude works for hire and applies to sound recordings made on or after February 15, 1972 (the effective date of the Sound Recording Act of 1971) and January 1, 1978 (the effective date of the Copyright Act of 1976), the earliest that termination could occur would be 56 years from 1972, that is, 2028.
52. http://www.statista.com/statistics/188926/current-versus-catalog-overall-album-sales-in-the-us-2010/.
53. 490 U.S. 730 (1989).
54. Id. at 752–3.
55. https://www.techdirt.com/articles/20110816/09574115549/dear-musicians-riaa-is-about-to-totally-screw-you-over-again.shtml.
56. "Record Industry Braces for Artists' Battles over Song Rights" by Larry Rohter, August 15, 2011, http://www.nytimes.com/2011/08/16/arts/music/springsteen-and-others-soon-eligible-to-recover-song-rights.html?pagewanted=all&_r=0.
57. *Campbell v. Acuff-Rose Music, Inc.*, 510 U.S. 569 (1994).
58. *U.S. v. ASCAP*, 607 F. Supp. 2d 562, (S.D.N.Y. 2009).
59. Id. at pp. 571–572.
60. *Lennon v. Premise Media Corp.*, 556 F. Supp. 2d 310 (S.D.N.Y., 2008).
61. https://wiki.creativecommons.org/Pt:FAQ.
62. https://www.nmpa.org/media/showwhatsnew.asp?id=112.
63. http://rhmusicroyaltypartners.com/resources/music-publishing-market-overview.
64. The largest music publisher is Sony ATV, which recently took over the administration of the EMI catalogue. Together these four publishers control approximately two-thirds of music publishing global market share (http://rhmusicroyaltypartners.com/resources/music-publishing-market-overview/). Each of these publishers, except for BMG, is associated with the three major labels, i.e., Sony, Universal, and Warner.

65. http://www.copyright.gov/circs/circ1a.html.
66. Note that movie theaters are an exception; the PROs do not license them in the US, because a federal court barred them from doing so. In *Alden-Rochelle, Inc. v. ASCAP*, 80 F. Supp. 888 (U.S.D.C. 1948), the court found that studios were using the PROs, in this case ASCAP, to make movie theaters pay them twice. The theaters paid the studios to show their movies. The studios also retained publishing rights in the music contained in those movies and then placed their publisher's share at ASCAP. So when the theaters paid ASCAP they were really paying the studios twice. The court found that this was an antitrust violation and barred the PROs from licensing movie theaters. Now when the studios hire a composer to score music for a movie, they usually allow him or her to retain the "writer's share" so that he or she can collect royalties from the PROs from performance of the movie on television; but the studios require that the composer transfer theatrical public-performance rights to them so they can license 100 percent of the public-performance rights directly to the theaters.
67. In every other country in the world there is generally only one performing-rights organization. Some of the most important PROs worldwide include PRS (England), GEMA (Germany), JASRAC (Japan), SACEM (France), Australia (APRA), RAO (Russia), MCSC (China), and ACUM (Israel). For a full list see http://www.bmi.com/international/entry/reciprocal_representation_agreements_foreign_performing_rights_societies.
68. "SESAC Facing New Anti-Trust Legal Challenge" by Ed Christman, *Billboard Biz*, March 14, 2014, http://www.billboard.com/biz/articles/news/publishing/5937426/sesac-facing-new-anti-trust-legal-challenge.
69. https://www.nmpa.org/media/showwhatsnew.asp?id=112.
70. http://www.bmi.com/press/entry/563077.
71. Id.
72. http://www.ascap.com/press/2014/0213-2013-financials.aspx. SESAC does not disclose its income.
73. For more information on how the PROs value each performance:
http://www.ascap.com/members/payment.aspx (ASCAP)
http://www.bmi.com/creators/royalty/how_we_pay_royalties/basic (BMI)
http://www.sesac.com/WritersPublishers/HowWePay/generalInfo.aspx (SESAC).
74. The Copyright Act reads in relevant part: ". . . the owner of copyright under this title has the exclusive rights to do and to authorize any of the following: (1) to reproduce the copyrighted work in copies or phonorecords."
75. Live performances of music such as you see on awards shows do not trigger sync rights, nor does the producer need a license from the copyright owner, because there is no synchronization, also referred to as a "fixation." However if the performance is taped and the show in which it appears (for instance MTV's *Video Music Awards*) is repeated, sync licenses are required.
76. Website of Edward R. Hearn, Esq., http://www.internetmedialaw.com/articles/music-publishing/.
77. Also see websites and apps that republish lyrics, discussed in Chapter 13.
78. "Love and Happiness—Hi Rhythm Memphis' Other Soul House Band Made Music into a Family Affair" by Andria Lisle, *Memphis Flyer*, July 2, 2004.
79. http://rhmusicroyaltypartners.com/resources/music-publishing-market-overview/.
80. Except in regard to sheet music, where the writer was and still is usually paid on a penny basis; see "Sheet Music" above.
81. Most states have unauthorized-duplication statutes that make it illegal to copy, reproduce, and distribute sound recordings without authorization. Those statutes apply to songs recorded before February 15, 1972. See "Duration of Copyright" above to learn how long that protection lasts.
82. As we discussed in "Special Rules for Sound Recordings," the Copyright Act of 2006 provided for continued protection of pre-'72 recordings under state law. Most pre-'72 recording will continue to be protected by state law until 2067. For limited exceptions for certain records released without proper notice see https://copyright.cornell.edu/resources/publicdomain.cfm.

83. See http://thetrichordist.com/2014/04/17/meet-the-new-boss-worse-than-the-old-boss-2-years-later for the entire blog and an update.

84. *Ripped: How the Wired Generation Revolutionized Music* by Greg Kot (Scribner, 2009). The blurb on Mr. Kot's website reads, "*Ripped* presents the first definitive account of the digital music revolution, which changed the way music fans have sought and acquired music and led to the end of the recording industry as we know it. In the mid-1990s, advances in Internet and digital technology made it easy for fans to store, play, and share music, and leveled the playing field between better-marketed major-label bands and smaller independent artists who communicated directly with their audience."

85. http://www.digitalmusicnews.com/permalink/2014/08/07/amanda-palmer-youre-asking-whats-youre-wrong-business.

86. See "Label's Blocking Rights" in Chapter 9.

87. As we discussed in the section on termination rights above, it is possible that the work-for-hire provision of the recording agreement is unenforceable. However, even if that turns out to be the case, the contract always states that if for any reason the recording is not a work for hire then the artist is deemed to transfer any copyrights interest in the recordings to the label. Either way the artist gives up any ownership interest in the copyrights in the recording to the label. It's just that if the works are not "works for hire" the artist may be able to terminate his or her transfer of rights after a given period of time.

88. George Michael Loses Lawsuit against Sony" by Richard W. Stevenson, *The New York Times*, June 22, 1994.

89. *Panayiotou and Others v. Sony Music Entertainment* (UK) Lrd [1994] EMLR 229.

90. "Music Biz Lawyers Wary of Labels' New Grab" by Susan Butler, Reuters, December 28, 2007, http://www.reuters.com/article/2007/12/29/industry-lawyers-dc-idUSN2849012220071229.

91. Indeed, soon after this interview took place, AT&T and Beats Music announced that they had concluded a deal. Per the AT&T website, the plan offered "unlimited downloads and streaming...access to over 20 million songs what you want, when you want across multiple devices: $14.99/mo Family. First 90 days free. Up to 5 users and 10 devices. $9.99/mo Individual. First 30 days free. 1 user and up to 3 devices." Although this plan did not catch on—as of May 2014, Beats Music only had approximately 200,000 paying subscribers—Iovine and Dre sold the service together with the their headphone business for more than 3 billion dollars, proving once again there is money in the music business, although it may not be going to artists and songwriters.

Chapter 2

92. *Bright Tunes Music v. Harrisongs Music,* 420 F. Supp. 177 (S.D.N.Y. 1976).

93. *Paramount Pictures Corp. v. Dorney Park Coaster Co.*, 698 F. Supp. 1274 (E.D. Pa. 1988). Owners of rights in the film *Top Gun* were able to shut down the operators of a TOP GUN amusement park ride where the ride invoked elements of the film.

94. 489 F. Supp. 827 (S.D.N.Y. 1980).

95. 895 F. Supp. 616 (S.D.N.Y. 1995).

96. The strongest trademarks are those that are arbitrary or fanciful in relationship (bear no relation) to the products or services with which they are used. On the other hand, marks that describe the products or services with which they are sold are weaker and may be registered only with a showing of "secondary meaning," or that consumers associate the mark with the goods or services. Generic marks are unprotectable. For example, the APPLE mark is a strong trademark when used to sell computers, because the mark bears no relation to the goods. By contrast, an APPLE mark cannot be protected as a trademark to sell actual apples, because in this context the mark is the generic term for the goods.

97. 236 F.3d 487 (9th Cir. 2000).

98. 213 U.S.P.Q. 991 (C.D. Cal. 1980).

99. 318 F.3d 900 (9th Cir. 2003), rev'd on other grounds, *KP Permanent Make-Up, Inc. v. Lasting Impression I, Inc.,* 543 U.S. 111 (U.S. 2004).

100. *Id.* at 908. By contrast, the doctrine of statutory or "classic" fair use allows a defendant to use a plaintiff's trademark to describe the defendant's goods where the defendant uses the plaintiff's trademark in a descriptive manner and thus the use is not fairly characterized as trademark use.

Chapter 4

101. "Apple iTunes Dominates Market but Amazon Gaining: NPD Group" by Michelle Maisto, *eWeek*, April 17, 2013, citing NPD Group reported April 16, 2013.
102. See http://www.diffen.com/difference/Amazon_MP3_vs_iTunes_Music_Store for a side-by-side comparison of the two services in terms of catalogue, file format and sound quality, openness, availability, pricing, and other factors.
103. As we stated in the introduction, the RIAA's statistics for the recorded music industry represent their "estimate of the size of the US recorded music industry . . . and estimates where possible for the remaining parts of the market" (https://www.riaa.com/keystatistics.php?content_selector=research-about). According to the RIAA, "Our aim is to describe the whole market, and we use independent estimates to account for the parts that are not created or distributed by the major record labels" (https://www.riaa.com/blog.php?content_selector=riaa-news-blog&blog_selector=So-What-Exactly-Is-A-shipment&news_month_filter=7&news_year_filter=2009). The RIAA's shipment statistics used in this chapter as well as Chapters 5 (Interactive Streaming) and 6 (Webcasting) represents their "estimate of the size of the US recorded music industry based on data collected directly from the major music companies . . . and estimates where possible for the remaining parts of the market."
104. All the numbers in this sentence are based on the RIAA Shipping Database (RIAA.com), except the amount from noninteractive streaming, which is from http://www.soundexchange.com/wp-content/uploads/2014/06/2013-SoundExchange-Fiscal-Report.pdf.
105. *News and Notes on 2014 Mid-Year RIAA Shipment and Revenue Statistics* by Joshua P. Friedlander, http://riaa.com/media/1806D32F-B3DD-19D3-70A4-4C31C0217836.pdf.
106. https://www.riaa.com/keystatistics.php?content_selector=research-about.
107. As we discuss below, this amount does not mean that the majors own all of the copyrights in the music that they distribute. In fact, the indie trade group AI2M points out that per 2013 year-end Nielsen Soundscan statistics independent labels had 34.6 percent of the overall recorded music market share based on master ownership (http://www.billboard.com/biz/articles/news/indies/6121566/rich-bengloff-on-a2im-indie-week-youtube-licensing-alleges-majors).
108. http://www.tunecore.com/index/sell_your_music_on_itunes.
109. "Warner Music to Buy Some EMI Assets from Universal," Ethan Smith, *The Wall Street Journal*, February 7, 2013, http://online.wsj.com/news/articles/SB10001424127887323951904578289961217066052.
110. http://a2im.org/mission/.
111. *F.B.T. Productions, LLC, et al. v. Aftermath Records, et al.* 621 F.3d 958 (9th Cir 2010).
112. Id.
113. In fact, Universal tried to appeal the case to the Supreme Court of the United States, but the Court declined to hear the case. US Supreme Court certiorari denied by *Aftermath Records v. F.B.T. Prod.*, 2011 U.S. Lexis 2255 (U.S., Mar. 21, 2011).
114. "10 Million Digital Music Tracks Left Unsold" by Marc Chacksfield, Tech Radar, February 22, 2008, http://www.techradar.com/us/news/world-of-tech/broadband/web/internet/10-million-digital-music-tracks-left-unsold-496820.
115. 627 F.3d 64 (2d Cir. 2010).
116. 627 F.3d at 73.
117. Id.
118. United States v. ASCAP (application of AT&T Wireless), 599 F. Supp. 2d 415 (S.D.N.Y. Jan. 30, 2009) (Conner, J.).

Chapter 5

119. This summer YouTube announced plans to launch a premium subscription service; see below.
120. However, registered users can download up to 100 free tracks. SoundCloud has been intended primarily as a platform for people to share their own musical creations and mixes, and charges a subscription fee to those who wish to upload more than two hours of music.
121. Although, as we discuss in "Update on Recording Industry's Battle with 'Free Music'" (Chapter 16), many people use third-party apps that allow them to "rip" and permanently download files from services such as YouTube.
122. iRadio is an anomaly—it is a noninteractive service that probably would qualify for a statutory license to play sound recordings, but Apple chose to make direct deals with the sound recordings' copyright owners instead, including all three major labels.
123. In early September 2014 Rdio announced that it planned to launch a free ad-supported service (http://www.nytimes.com/2014/09/04/business/media/rdio-moves-to-free-music-model-to-compete-with-spotify-and-others.html?ref=media&_r=0).
124. YouTube allows copyright owners to "monetize" their content. YouTube keeps 45 percent of ad revenues and pays the balance to copyright owners, but YouTube will pay 100 percent of ad revenue for ad inventory that exceeds YouTube's rate card. That means copyright owners receive 55 percent of ad revenue up to YouTube's CPM (cost per thousand impressions) threshold, with everything above that going to the content owner. "YouTube Standardizes Ad-Revenue Split for All Partners, But Offers Upside Potential" by Todd Spangler, *Variety,* November 1, 2013, http://variety.com/2013/digital/news/youtube-standardizes-ad-revenue-split-for-all-partners-but-offers-upside-potential-1200786223/.
125. Other interactive services with limited downloads include France-based Deezer, which is a leading digital music service in Europe and other parts of the world, but is not available in the US yet.
126. *News and Notes on 2013 RIAA Music Industry Shipment and Revenue Statistics* by Joshua P. Friedlander, Vice President, Strategic Data Analysis, RIAA, http://riaa.com/media/2463566A-FF96-E0CA-2766-72779A364D01.pdf.
127. Id.
128. Id. In 2014 Spotify announced that it had 10 million paying subscribers worldwide and more than 40 million active users across 56 countries (https://news.spotify.com/us/2014/05/21/10-million-subscribers/).
129. Id.
130. There was also controversy that consolidation by the major record companies had left indie labels squeezed in negotiations with YouTube and that YouTube was threatening to block their videos unless they signed licensing deals that were not as favorable as those offered to the majors ("Indie Music's Digital Drag, Small Music Labels See YouTube Battle as Part of War for Revenue" by Ben Sisario, *The New York Times*, June 24, 2014). See "How Much the labels Receive" for more details on the disparity of bargaining power between the majors, the indies, and unsigned artists.
131. As we pointed out in an earlier note in this chapter and discuss in more detail in Chapter 16, there are a myriad of software programs and apps that allow you to rip YouTube videos and create permanent playlists. It will be interesting to see if YouTube, or its corporate parent, Google, will take steps to ensure that these apps and software programs cannot be used to impede the potential success of Music Key.
132. "Spotify pays royalties for all of the listening that occurs on our service by distributing nearly 70 percent of all the revenues that we receive back to rights holders. By 'rights holders,' we are referring to the owners of the music that is on Spotify: labels, publishers, distributors, and, through certain digital distributors, independent artists themselves. . . . We retain approximately 30 percent . . . That 70 percent is split amongst the rights holders in accordance with the popularity of their music on the service. The label or publisher then divides these royalties and accounts to each artist depending on their individual deals. When we pay a rights holder, we provide all the information needed to attribute royalties to each of their artists" (http://www.spotifyartists.com/spotify-explained/).

133. According to the testimony of the Warner Music attorney before the Copyright Royalty Board, "In the US, WMG does not have a single agreement with an audio streaming service where the payment amount is based solely on a per-play rate, as is the case with the statutory license. In all of our negotiated agreements we view the per-play minimum payment as the absolute floor for our revenue, a minimum protection for the value of the recordings we provide. [The per-play royalties] represent the potential upside for our revenue. Although we negotiate the amounts of the per-play minimums, . . . with each streaming service, our ultimate goal in these negotiations is to ensure that WMG and its recording artists are fairly compensated for providing the one essential element without which an audio streaming service simply could not function—the music. Another important component of negotiated deals is the non-refundable advance payments that WMG typically receives. Even when these advance payments are recoupable against future royalty payments, they essentially serve as minimum revenue guarantees, which can be significantly higher than the minimum payment requirements under the statutory rate and the WSA settlements." Testimony of W. Tucker McCrady before the CRB, Associate Counsel, Digital Legal Affairs, Warner Music Group, 2009 (p. 113), http://www.loc.gov/crb/proceedings/2009-1/statements/wds-sx.pdf.

134. Merlin is the global rights agency for the independent music label sector, representing over 20,000 labels from 39 countries. Merlin focuses purely on the interests of the global independent music sector and has deals with many digital services, including Spotify, on behalf of some of some of the world's largest independent labels. These music labels use services such as AudioSalad, Consolidated Independent, finetunes, FUGA, NueMeta, etc. to deliver their metadata to Merlin and use Merlin to avoid a distribution fee. Similar to a SoundExchange, Merlin is a not-for-profit that just allocates its overhead, which is currently just 2.5 percent for trade organization members (http://www.merlinnetwork.org/whowelicense).

135. Testimony of Darius Van Arman, Cofounder of Secretly Group, Committee on the Judiciary: Subcommittee on Courts, Intellectual Property, and the Internet, June 25, 2014, http://judiciary.house.gov/_cache/files/f6f6cd17-fe27-4a67-8d7e-c7c6b92f0c09/062514-music-license-pt-2-testimony-a2im.pdf.

136. Id. Van Arman also made the point that there would be no royalties flowing to indie labels that used the majors to distribute to the digital services unless they had enough bargaining power to make special deals as well.

137. In "It's Not Just David Byrne and Radiohead: Spotify, Pandora and How Streaming Music Kills Jazz and Classical" by Scott Timberg, *Salon*, July 20, 2014, http://www.salon.com/2014/07/20/its_not_just_david_byrne_and_radiohead_spotify_pandora_and_how_streaming_music_kills_jazz_and_classical/?utm_source=hootsuite&utm_campaign=hootsuite.

138. "The Major Labels Are Trying to Sell Spotify for $10 Billion, Sources Say" by Paul Resnikoff, *Digital Music News*, June 11, 2014, http://www.digitalmusicnews.com/permalink/2014/06/11/major-labels-trying-sell-spotify-10-billion-sources-say.

139. "Vivendi Sells Its 13 Percent Beats Stake to Apple for $404 Million" by Kristen Schweizer, *Bloomberg*, August 1, 2014, http://www.bloomberg.com/news/2014-08-01/vivendi-sells-its-13-beats-stake-to-apple-for-404-million.html.

140. http://www.youtubelicenseoffer.com/faq#Q4.

141. http://www.nmpa.org/media/showrelease.asp?id=151.

142. The result of $800,000 is the lesser of the two different calculations in 1(b). But, for the sake of completeness, let's calculate the other 1(b) calculation. Currently there are no "pass-through" services, that is, interactive services that pay the label exclusively, and the label is obligated to pay publishers. So we will use the non "pass-through" rate (i.e., the rate that applies to services that pay the publishers directly) of 21 percent multiplied by the monies payable to the labels. Usually the labels receive at least 50 percent. So the calculation would be 21 percent x (50 percent x $10 million dollars) = $2.1 million. Since $800,000 is less than $2.1 million we used the former amount.

143. The source for this fact is a senior executive at one of the PROs. The actual deals with Spotify and other services are confidential. Six percent is a little better than what the PROs receive from noninteractive services such as Pandora. See Chapter 7 for how the publishers are trying to increase the rates for both interactive and particularly noninteractive streaming by trying to amend the consent decrees under which ASCAP and BMI operate or by withdrawing from the PROs.

Chapter 6

144. A 2009 federal appeals court decision illustrates the meaning of "noninteractive." In 2001, a group of major record companies sued LAUNCHcast, one of the earliest music webcasters. Eight years later, the Second Circuit handed down a decision in *Arista Records, LLC, et al. v. Launch Media, Inc.* 578 F.3d 148 (2d Cir. N.Y. 2009). The issue was whether a webcasting service that provides users with individualized Internet radio stations—the content of which can be affected by users' ratings of songs, artists, and albums—is an interactive service within the meaning of the DMCA. The court noted that a service would be interactive "if a user can either (1) request—and have played—a particular sound recording, or (2) receive a transmission of a program "specially created for the user." In holding that the LAUNCHcast service did not allow users sufficient control over the playlist to qualify as "interactive," the court determined that LAUNCHcast was not required to pay individually negotiated license fees to rights holders. LAUNCHCast was eventually purchased by Yahoo! and then discontinued in 2013. But the decision assures that services such as Pandora, which is famous for allowing users to create their own channels using complicated algorithms generated by the service, will avoid legal attack for not being interactive.
145. 17 U.S. Code § 114.
146. However, SoundExchange cannot pay everyone, because not everyone has registered with them. So SoundExchange holds those funds until the copyright owners come forward. The major record companies have all registered on behalf of themselves and their artists, as have the leading indies.
147. In the first half of 2014, SoundExchange paid out $323.6 million to artists and labels, an increase of almost 22 percent over 2013. According to *Billboard*, if SoundExchange simply pays an equal amount in the second half of the year, annual distributions will rise 9.6 percent to $647 million: "SoundExchange Royalty Payouts Rise Again, Is Poised for Another Record Year" by Glenn Peoples, *Billboard Biz*, August 21, 2014, http://www.billboard.com/biz/articles/news/digital-and-mobile/6228946/soundexchange-royalty-payouts-rise-again-is-poised-for.
148. http://www.soundexchange.com/wp-content/uploads/2014/06/2013-SoundExchange-Fiscal-Report.pdf.
149. Id.
150. http://www.soundexchange.com/?s=administration+fee.
151. http://www.digitalmusicnews.com/permalink/2012/04/14/soundexchangerevenues. The blog quotes copyright attorney Angus MacDonald that Pandora and Sirius XM Radio now account for roughly 90 percent of SoundExchange's total annual revenues in 2012. Since that time iHeart Radio, another stand-alone Internet radio station owned by Clear Channel, has emerged as a serious player.
152. http://investor.pandora.com/phoenix.zhtml?c=227956&p=irol-govBio&ID=212488.
153. http://www.pandora.com/about.
154. http://expandedramblings.com/index.php/pandora-statistics/#.VAVIEPldU4I.
155. In Re Petition of Pandora Media. Related to *U.S. v. ASCAP* (S.D.N.Y.) 2014, http://c.ymcdn.com/sites/www.csusa.org/resource/resmgr/NY_Chapter_April2414/Pandora_SDNY.pdf at p. 23.
156. Id. at p. 23.
157. http://expandedramblings.com/index.php/pandora-statistics/#.VAVIEPldU4I.
158. http://www.forbes.com/sites/greatspeculations/2014/02/07/pandora-turns-profitable-but-stock-falls-on-slightly-weak-outlook/.
159. http://www.forbes.com/sites/greatspeculations/2014/04/23/pandora-earnings-preview-profitability-will-continue-to-improve/.
160. http://rainnews.com/pandora-is-now-over-50-soundexchanges-royalty-collections-implications-for-webcasting-iv/.
161. http://www.nytimes.com/2014/03/21/business/media/pandora-wins-a-battle-but-the-war-over-royalties-continues.html?_r=0.
162. http://www.forbes.com/sites/greatspeculations/2014/07/31/sirius-xm-beats-estimates-as-subscriber-growth-picks-up/.

163. Id.
164. http://www.Sirius XM.com/whatisSirius XM.
165. http://www.forbes.com/sites/greatspeculations/2013/04/12/can-sirius-xm-tune-in-big-subscriber-growth-this-year/.
166. http://www.marketwatch.com/investing/stock/siri/financials.
167. However, see the end of this chapter for the reasons that SoundExchange and the record industry believe that the satellite service has been illegally withholding a portion of its revenues.
168. http://www.soundexchange.com/about/general-faq/.
169. Id.
170. Id.
171. http://www.soundexchange.com/wp-content/uploads/2014/06/2013-SoundExchange-Fiscal-Report.pdf.
172. Id.
173. The tortured history of rate setting for noninteractive digital audio services is laid out in law revenue articles such as "Copyright Arbitration Royalty Panels and the Webcasting Controversy: The Antithesis of Good Alternative Dispute Resolution" by Jeremy Delibero, *Pepperdine Dispute Resolution Law Journal*, December 1, 2004, http://digitalcommons.pepperdine.edu/cgi/viewcontent.cgi?article=1112&context=drlj.
174. These rates would apply to other "stand-alone," that is, Internet-only webcasting services such as iHeart Radio (owned by Clear Channel) and Songza (now owned by Google).
175. In fact, streams on Pandora's premium service are subject to an even higher rate, that is, $0.0023 per stream.
176. "Pandora and SoundExchange Spar over Royalty Fees," by Austin Carr, *Fast Company*, January 2012, http://www.fastcompany.com/1806776/pandora-and-soundexchange-spar-over-royalty-fees.
177. Id.
178. Check www.futureofthemusicbusiness.com for updates.
179. Sound Recordings Act, Pub. L. No. 140, 85 Stat. 39 (1971).
180. "SoundExchange Launches Campaign for Royalties on Pre-1972 Recordings" by Glenn Peoples, *Billboard*, May 29, 2014.
181. *Capitol Records, LLC et al., v. Sirius XM Radio*, No. BC520981 (Cal. Supp. Ct. Sept. 11, 2013). The plaintiffs included Capitol Records LLC, Sony Music Entertainment, UMG Recordings Inc., and Warner Music Group Corporation as well as ABKCO Music & Records, Inc.
182. *Capitol Records et al., LLC v. Pandora Media, Inc.*, No. 651195 (Sup. Ct. N.Y. April 17, 2014). This lawsuit included the same plaintiffs as the case against Sirius.
183. Cal. Civ. Code § 980(a)(2).
184. *Flo & Eddie, Inc. v. Sirius XM Radio, Inc., et al.*, No. 2:13-cv-05693 (C.D. Cal. Sept. 22, 2014).
185. *Flo & Eddie, Inc. v. Sirius XM Radio, Inc., et al., No.* 13 Civ. 5784 (S.D.N.Y. Nov. 14, 2014).
186. H.R.4772—RESPECT Act, 113th Congress (2013–2014).

Chapter 7

187. Most commercially successful publishers in the US are members of all three PROs. This is because they have writers who are members of each of the three PROs. All three PROs require, in regard to any particular song, that both the writer and the publisher be members of that society. So if a writer is with BMI and registers songs there, the publisher must be registered with BMI also. Writers, however, cannot be members of more than one society at the same time.
188. Sony/ATV's direct license to digital music service DMX, discussed below.
189. "Pandora Suit May Upend Century-Old Royalty Plan" by Ben Sisario, *The New York Times*, February 13, 2014. Note that ASCAP received 1.85 percent and BMI received 1.75 percent. It is not public

information what SESAC receives, although their standard Internet license requires 0.6 percent, so they probably receive a similar amount from Pandora if not the same.

190. In Re Petition of Pandora Media, Inc. Related to *U.S. v. ASCAP* (S.D.N.Y. 2013), http://www.digitalmusicnews.com/wpcontent/uploads/2013/11/pandoravascap1.pdf?b56280 at p 2.

191. In Re Petition of Pandora Media, Inc. Related to *U.S. v. ASCAP* (S.D.N.Y. 2014), http://c.ymcdn.com/sites/www.csusa.org/resource/resmgr/NY_Chapter_April2414/Pandora_SDNY.pdf.

192. *BMI v. Pandora Media, Inc.* (S.D.N.Y. 2013I), http://c.ymcdn.com/sites/www.csusa.org/resource/resmgr/mw14_pre72_mats/stanton.pdf.

193. In addition to efforts to amend the consent decrees, the three PROs and the National Music Publishers' Association (which, among other things, manages the legislative and legal agendas for most US music publishers and operates the Harry Fox Agency) are supporting a piece of legislation entitled the "Songwriter Equity Act" (HR 4079). Introduced by Congressman Doug Collins (R-GA), the bill would allow the rate court to consider other royalty rates, specifically, what the record companies are receiving, as evidence when establishing digital performance rates for songwriters and composers. Currently Section 114(i) of the Copyright Act forbids the federal rate courts from considering sound recording royalty rates as a relevant benchmark when setting rates between ASCAP, BMI, and their licensees. As discussed previously, the PROs are currently receiving only approximately 4 percent of gross revenues (subscriptions and advertising) from Pandora and approximately 6–7 percent of gross revenues from interactive digital services such as Spotify. The record companies and artists, on the other hand, are receiving approximately 50 percent from Pandora and the interactive services. The publishers consider this unfair, although the labels do spend a great deal more than publishers for the production, marketing, promotion, advertising, and distribution of the music. In any event, the bill would amend 114(i) to allow ASCAP and BMI to present evidence to the courts of how much the labels are getting.

    The bill would also amend the standard by which the Copyright Royalty Board determines the statutory rate for the mechanical royalties. The bill would amend Section 115 of Copyright Act to allow the CRB to consider the "fair market value" of songs. The initial rate set by Congress in 1909 was 2 cents per song. Today, the rate is 9.1 cents per song. This is considered too small by the publishing community (http://www.ascap.com/~/media/files/pdf/advocacy-legislation/sea-one-pager.pdf).

194. *Digital Music News*, April 6, 2014.

Chapter 8

195. http://www.ifpi.org/downloads/Digital-Music-Report-2014.pdf ("IFPI Report").

196. The IFPI reports emphasizes that overall global revenues in 2013 would have decreased only .01 percent except for a dramatic 16.7 percent decrease of revenues from recorded music in Japan, the second biggest market in the world after the US. The report does not provide a reason for this decline. See note 5 for a possible explanation.

197. Id. at pp. 6–7.

198. Id. at p. 7.

199. However, see "Japan Hits a Sour Note on Music Sales" by Hannah Karp and Miho Inada, *Wall Street Journal* March 18 2014, for an article that suggests that the introduction of YouTube in Japan may have led to its 16.7 percent decline in revenues. Ad revenues from YouTube apparently did not compensate for lost income from declining CD sales. The article quotes Tatsuyoshi Kimura, a 22-year-old college student, who used to spend 3,000 to 4,000 yen a month on CDs but rarely spends money on music any more. "There are many sites like YouTube where I can listen to music free," he said. "That was not possible five years ago."

200. Amanda has for over 20 years been operating a discreet IP consultancy for a wide range of high-profile international clients across all sectors of the creative industries in Europe and North America. She began her English legal career by conducting a global audit into author and performer collecting society revenue for Irish writer/performers U2—an inquiry widely considered as responsible for beginning the overhaul of collective administration. With some exceptions, Harcourt's consultancy works almost exclusively for authors, performers, collecting societies, and small independent companies. The consultancy provides

advice in relation to contracts, licensing, rights and revenue, international royalty restructuring, forensics and audit support, as well as domestic and international policy across the entire spectrum of the creative industries: music, film and television, theater, fine art, photography, literature, and design. However, she also has excellent legal and commercial experience at a senior level in a number of global companies and has contributed to government policy both the United Kingdom and internationally.

201. Many of my questions were based on discussions with Jeff Liebenson, a former senior vice president of international business affairs at BMG. Jeff is now an attorney in private practice at Liebenson Law in New York City and president of the International Association of Entertainment Law (IAEL). He also was a former partner at the law firm of Rosenman & Colin LLP.

Chapter 9

202. One such firm is Universal Media Inc., with whom I work on a number of projects.
203. Labels usually do not require cue sheets, because, as we discussed in Chapter 1, there is no public-performance right for sound recordings except for digital transmissions.

Chapter 10

204. Note that outside the US rates for home video rates are generally set by foreign collection societies. For instance, in England the rate is set by the collection society (PRS for Music Limited, formerly the MCPS-PRS Alliance Limited), and is 6.25 percent of the "Published Dealer Price" (i.e., wholesale price). This amount covers all the music in the program and is usually paid out by the society to the copyright owners on a pro-rata basis depending on the number of music copyrights in the program or by duration of use. The foreign home video distributor is usually responsible for paying these fees.
205. This issue also comes up occasionally in clearing old TV shows containing performances. Most of the performances on the old *Soul Train* show, for instance, were performed to track. See "Lip Syncs" in Chapter 9.
206. Nike paid $500,000 for the right to use the song for one year, split between recording owner Capitol-EMI and song publisher ATV Music Publishing (at that time owned by Michael Jackson). "Nike & the Beatles, 1987–1989" by Jack Doyle, September 27, 2008, http://www.pophistorydig.com/?tag=the-beatles-vs-nike.
207. The actual figure was probably less, but not less than several million. See "What Microsoft Paid the Stones to Help Launch Windows 9" by Paul McNama, June 29, 2011, *Network World*, http://www.networkworld.com/article/2220097/data-center/what-microsoft-paid-the-stones-to-help-launch-windows-95.html.
208. *Bette Midler v. Ford Motor Company,* 849 F.2d 460 (9th Cir. 1988).
209. *Waits v. Frito-Lay* 978 F. 2d 1093 (9th Cir. 1992).
210. In fact, the Content ID system works a lot better if the original track was used, because it's easier for the software recognition program to identify watermarked tracks, à la Shazam, then underlying musical compositions.
211. How well the Content ID system works in practice depends on whom you ask. To my knowledge, the bigger publishers and labels have specially assigned staff to work with the Content ID program.

Chapter 11

212. Of course, if the song is in the public domain (PD), as most of the classical repertoire is, you will not need permission at all. However, new arrangements of PD songs may be protected by copyright, and in that case a license and payment are required.
213. Section 115(a)(2).
214. The procedures required under the compulsory-license provisions in the Copyright Act are burdensome, such as those calling for monthly rather than quarterly accounting and notice conforming to strict regulation.

215. As we noted in Chapter 10 in the section on special event videos, the Content ID system works a lot better if the original track was used, because it's easier for the software recognition to identify watermarked tracks, à la Shazam, then underlying musical compositions.

216. https://secure.harryfox.com/songfile/faq.jsp.

217. *Grand Upright Music, Ltd. v. Grand Upright Music Limited v. Warner Bros. Records Inc., WEA International Inc., Marcel Hall, professionally known as Biz Markie* 780 F. Supp. 182 (S.D.N.Y. 1991).

218. The client would probably have had to pay a label the same amount had he used the original master.

219. *Newton v. Diamond,* 204 F. Supp. 2d 1244 (C.D.Cal.2002).

220. Id. at 1259.

221. In fact, the district court found that the recording contained "highly developed performance techniques."

222. *VMG Salsoul, LLC v. Madonna Louise Ciccone, et al.* CV 12-05967 (C.D.Cal.2013), http://www.scribd.com/doc/185237664/VMG-Salsoul-v-Madonna.

Chapter 12

223. If a theatrical producer did use a copyrighted master recording, she might need a master-use license because, although owners of sound recordings do not enjoy public-performance rights except via digital transmissions, use of a master in connection with a theatrical production would probably constitute a "derivative work." Section 101 of the Copyright Act defines "derivative work" as a work based upon one or more preexisting works, such as a "dramatization . . . or any other form in which a work may be recast, transformed, or adapted." Under Section 102 of the Act, the owner of copyright, including a sound recording, has the exclusive right "to prepare derivative works based upon the copyrighted work."

224. Unlike a theatrical play, a fashion show that used a master recording would probably not be a derivative work (see immediately previous note) because fashion shows generally do not use music to tell a story or as part of a story or plot.

225. ASCAP also has a special license for IMG, the major talent/modeling agency, which produces a lot of shows during Fashion Week in New York, but the rates are confidential.

226. Shows such as *Saturday Night Live* would need longer terms to cover reruns.

Chapter 13

227. See http://copyright.gov/title17/92chap1.pdf.

228. For quantities over 10,000 streams, licenses for interactive streaming can be obtained through another compulsory license mandated by the Copyright Royalty Tribunal. The rates for that license are set forth in Chapter 6.

229. "Google Shuts Down Music Blogs without Warning" by Sean Michaels, theguardian.com, February 11, 2010. The article reported in relevant part:

> Despite the de facto alliance between labels and blogs, not all of the record companies' legal teams have received the message. In a complaint posted to Google Support, Bill Lipold, the owner of I Rock Cleveland, cited four cases in the past year when he had received copyright violation notices for songs he was legally entitled to post. Tracks by Jay Reatard, Nadja, BLK JKS, and Spindrift all attracted complaints under the USA's Digital Millennium Copyright Act, even when the respective MP3s were official promo tracks.

230. http://en.wikipedia.org/wiki/Childrens_Hospital.

231. For instance, in February 2014, Facebook purchased WhatsApp, a texting service, for the amazing price of 19 billion dollars. "Inside the Facebook-WhatsApp Megadeal" by Parmy Olson, *Forbes* March 4, 2014, http://www.forbes.com/sites/parmyolson/2014/03/04/inside-the-facebook-whatsapp-megadeal-the-courtship-the-secret-meetings-the-19-billion-poker-game/.

232. "How Many Apps Are in the iPhone App Store" by Sam Costello, About.com, http://ipod.about.com/od/iphonesoftwareterms/qt/apps-in-app-store.htm.

233. App Brain, June 15, 2014, http://www.appbrain.com/stats/number-of-android-apps.
234. Gartner press release, September 19, 2013, http://www.gartner.com/newsroom/id/2592315.
235. However, it is important to note that most mobile applications are not generating profits and that mobile apps are not designed to generate revenue, but rather are used to build brand recognition and product awareness or are just for fun. "Gartner Says Less than 0.01 Percent of Consumer Mobile Apps Will Be Considered a Financial Success by Their Developers through 2018," January 13, 2014, http://www.gartner.com/newsroom/id/2648515.
236. Gartner press release, September 19, 2013, http://www.gartner.com/newsroom/id/2592315.
237. "iTunes App Store Now Has 1.2 Million Apps, Has Seen 75 Billion Downloads to Date" by Sarah Perez, TechCrunch, June 2, 2013, http://techcrunch.com/2014/06/02/itunes-app-store-now-has-1-2-million-apps-has-seen-75-billion-downloads-to-date/.
238. Both offers limited the territory to the US, so the app would have to negotiate with the labels' foreign affiliates and potentially pay additional advances and guarantees.
239. "Minimum guarantee" means that if the app does not pay royalties at least equal to the guarantee, then the app must pay the balance to the label so that the label will receive at least $250,000.
240. This is similar to iTunes' deal with labels. iTunes pays labels 70 percent of the retail selling price of each download, but the labels are responsible for payments to publishers. However, iTunes does not pay advances to labels or commit to minimum guarantees. See Chapter 4.
241. After receiving these offers the client asked me to stop following up with the third major.
242. "NMPA Targets Unlicensed Lyric Sites, Rap Genius among 50 Sent Takedown Notices" by Alex Pham, November 11, 2013, *Billboard Biz*, http://www.billboard.com/biz/articles/news/legal-and-management/5785701/nmpa-targets-unlicensed-lyric-sites-rap-genius-among.
243. http://www.nmpa.org/media/showwhatsnew.asp?id=94.
244. "What's New" at www.nmpa.org/media/showwhatsnew.asp?id=94.
245. "NMPA Sues Two Lyric Websites" by Chris Cooke, May 22, 2014, http://www.completemusicupdate.com/article/nmpa-sues-two-lyric-websites/.
246. "Publisher's Association Says Rap Genius Is 'Blatantly Illegal'" by Chris Martins, *Spin*, November 11, 2013, http://www.spin.com/articles/rap-genius-takedown-lyrics-site-lawsuit-nmpa-illegal/.
247. "Rap Genius Pays Sony for Lyrics in Bid for Legitimacy" by Chris Martins, *Spin*, November 14, 2013, http://www.spin.com/articles/rap-genius-lyrics-licensing-deal-sony-illegal-site/.
248. "Rap Genius, Universal Music Publishing Group Strike Licensing Deal" by Alex Pham, *Billboard Biz*, January 22, 2014, http://www.billboard.com/biz/articles/news/digital-and-mobile/5877856/rap-genius-universal-music-publishing-group-strike.
249. "Rap Genius and Sony/ATV Reveal Licensing Deal" by Glenn Peoples, *Billboard Biz*, November 14, 2013, http://www.billboard.com/biz/articles/news/digital-and-mobile/5793024/rap-genius-and-sonyatv-reveal-licensing-deal-exclusive.
250. E-mail dated April 28, 2014.
251. Ringtones are songs that play aloud when a phone receives an incoming call, usually a 30-second clip. Ringbacks, on the other hand, are the music that you hear when you call someone until they pick up or your call goes to voicemail.
252. "Ring My Bell: The Expensive Pleasures of the Ringtone" by Sasha Frere-Jones, *The New Yorker*, March 7, 2005, http://www.newyorker.com/archive/2005/03/07/050307crmu_music?printable=true.
253. IFPI *Digital Music Report 2014*, http://www.ifpi.org/downloads/Digital-Music-Report-2014.pdf.
254. NMPA press release dated October 2, 2008, "NMPA Hails Copyright Board's Rate Decision," http://www.nmpa.org/media/showrelease.asp?id=153.
255. That section states in relevant part: ". . . the following are not infringements of copyright: . . . (4) performance of a nondramatic literary or musical work otherwise than in a transmission to the public, without any purpose of direct or indirect commercial advantage and without payment of any fee or other compensation for the performance to any of its performers, promoters, or organizers . . ."

256. http://www.gartner.com/newsroom/id/2614915.

257. "Farewell (for Now) to Guitar Hero" by Seth Schiesel, *The New York Times*, February 10, 2011. The article reads in relevant part:

> Wednesday may be remembered as the day the music died in the video game business. While announcing its latest financial results, the big game publisher Activision Blizzard revealed that it would not release a *Guitar Hero* or *DJ Hero* game this year and that it was disbanding its Guitar Hero publishing division.
>
> When the original *Guitar Hero* was released in 2005, the innovative game rocked the video game business like a hurricane. . . . Here, for the first time, was a game that let players, if not actually make music, at least feign the experience of jamming out in their living room. Soon after came the *Rock Band* games, which went beyond *Guitar Hero* by allowing multiple people to evoke music together with representations of various instruments, and the DJ Hero series, which focused on hip-hop and electronic music instead of more traditional guitar rock.
>
> But even as music games have remained popular with players, the business has struggled mightily. The problem for the publishers is that once someone has invested several hundred dollars in electronic "guitars," drum kits, keyboards, microphones and other peripherals, they certainly don't want to buy any more of them, and they have no need to. And yet the publishers continued to need to subsidize the manufacturing of these complex and relatively expensive physical controllers in the hope of drawing in new players.
>
> Meanwhile, it appears that once players had acquired a library of perhaps a few hundred *Guitar Hero* or *Rock Band* songs, many felt little desire to buy new games. And so sales of music games have tailed off sharply in recent years, even while recent games like *Rock Band 3* and *DJ Hero 2* have been hailed by critics as the best music games yet.

http://artsbeat.blogs.nytimes.com/2011/02/10/farewell-for-now-to-guitar-hero/?_php=true&_type=blogs&_r=0.

258 "Celluloid Heroes: Music Documentary Filmmakers Deserve a Break on Licensing Fees" by Steve Gordon, *Billboard*, November 7, 2009.

Chapter 15

259. .Random House Audio Voices; abridged edition (March 2, 2004).

260. Since Apple Records has denied permission, you still can't hear any Beatles' record on Spotify, Pandora, and most other authorized services, except iTunes.

261. *A&M Records, Inc. v. Napster*, 239 F.3d 1004 (9th Cir. 2001).

262. *MGM Studios, Inc. v. Grokster, Ltd.*, 545 U.S. 913 (2005).

263. "Requiem for Napster" by Michael Gowan, *Pcworld.com*, May 18, 2002, http://www.pcworld.idg.com.au/article/22380/requiem_napster/.

264. The court also rejected Napster's "safe harbor" defense under the Digital Millennium Copyright Act of 1998 (see Chapter 3) finding: "Plaintiffs have raised and continue to raise significant questions under this statute, including: (1) whether Napster is an Internet service provider as defined by 17 U.S.C. § 512(d); (2) whether copyright owners must give a service provider "official" notice of infringing activity in order for it to have knowledge or awareness of infringing activity on its system; and (3) whether Napster complies with § 512(i), which requires a service provider to timely establish a detailed copyright compliance policy." 239 F.3d 1004 at 1025.

265. 2001 US Dist. LEXIS 2186 (N.D. Cal. Mar. 5, 2001), aff'd, 284 F. 3d 1091 (9th Cir. 2002).

266. With regard to Kazaa, the industry first tried pursuing the company in the US in the same lawsuit that it started against Grokster and Morpheus, but since its servers were off shore, Kazaa was able to evade US jurisdiction. The industry caught up with Kazaa in Australia, however. In *Universal Music Australia Pty Ltd v. Sharman License Holdings Ltd.*, Federal Court of Australia, September 5, 2005, the Federal Court of Australia ruled that Kazaa, though not itself guilty of copyright infringement, had "authorized" its users to illegally swap copyrighted songs. The company was ordered to modify the software within two months. Kazaa tried to continue as a paid service but died soon after.

267. *MGM Studios, Inc. v. Grokster, Ltd.*, 259 F. Supp. 2d 1029 (C.D. Cal. 2003).
268. *MGM Studios, Inc. v. Grokster, Ltd.*, 380 F.3d 1154 (9th Cir. 2004).
269. *MGM Studios, Inc. v. Grokster, Ltd.*, 545 U.S. 913 (2005). The Supreme Court of the US unanimously held that defendant peer-to-peer file-sharing companies Grokster and Streamcast (maker of Morpheus) could be sued for inducing copyright infringement for acts taken in the course of marketing file-sharing software.
270. The Napster system employed a proprietary centralized indexing software architecture in which acollective index of available songs was maintained on servers it owned and operated. In contrast, Grokster and Morpheus did not maintain such a central index. Under a decentralized index peer-to-peer file-sharing model, which both Grokster and Morpheus used, each user maintains an index of only those files that he or she wishes to make available to other network users. Under this model, the software broadcasts a search request to all the computers on the network and a search of the individual index files is conducted, with the collective results routed back to the requesting computer.
271. *Sony Corp. ofAmerica v. Universal City Studios, Inc.*, 464 U.S. 417 (1984), also known as the "Betamax case."
272. The first page of the Ninth Circuit's decision stated: "This appeal presents the question of whether distributors of peer-to-peer file-sharing networking software may be held contributorily or vicariously liable for copyright infringements by users. Under the circumstances presented by this case, we conclude that the defendants are not liable for contributory and vicarious copyright infringement and affirm the district court's partial grant of summary judgment." *MGM Studios, Inc. v. Grokster, Ltd.*, 380 F.3d 1154 (9th Cir. 2004).
273. *MGM Studios, Inc. v. Grokster, Ltd.*, 545 U.S. 913 at 923-924 (2005).
274. Id. at 937.
275. Id. at 939.
276. BitTorrent software is now as popular as any of the old pirates. However, because it is an easily shared software protocol and not its own company, it is almost impossible to shut down.
277. http://cs.stanford.edu/people/eroberts/cs201/projects/1999-00/dmca-2k/sdmi.html.
278. "The Truth about Sony's Rootkit Disaster: Two Years after It Happened, Lawyers Rake Over the Embers" by Rob Mead, TechRadar, December 17, 2007, http://www.techradar.com/news/software/applications/audio/hi-fi-radio/the-truth-about-sony-s-rootkit-disaster-164615.
279. H.R.3261—Stop Online Piracy Act; House Judiciary Committee; October 26, 2011.
280. The US Stop Online Piracy Act: A Primer, by Grant Gross, *PCWorld*, November 16, 2011, http://www.pcworld.com/article/244011/the_us_stop_online_piracy_act_a_primer.html.
281. Id.
282. "SOPA Explained: What It Is and Why It Matters" by Julianne Pepitone, @CNNMoneyTech, January 20, 2012, http://money.cnn.com/2012/01/17/technology/sopa_explained/.
283. "Critics of Online-Piracy Bills Release Their Own Draft Legislation" by Juliana Gruenwald, *National Journal*, August 12, 2011.
284. "SOPA/PIPA Internet Protests Go Viral, Hit Home" by qubit, Techpowerup, January 18, 2012, http://www.techpowerup.com/158971/sopa-pipa-internet-protests-go-viral-hit-home.html.
285. "Internet Strikes Back: Anonymous' Operation Megaupload Explained," RT, January 20, 2012.
286. "After an Online Firestorm, Congress Shelves Antipiracy Bills" by Jonathan Weisman, *The New York Times,* January 20, 2012.

Chapter 16

287. http://www.bbc.com/news/technology-23510065.
288. In a related story, Sony, Universal, and Warner Music have each filed a case accusing the Russian social network VKontakte (VK)—dubbed the "Facebook of Russia" —of "large-scale" copyright infringement. The action has been coordinated by the International Federation of the Phonographic

Industry (IFPI), which represents record labels worldwide. The labels have accused VK, which is the second-biggest social network in Europe, of creating a "huge library" of music it does not have the rights for and offering it as a service within its site. The labels are seeking a court order in Russia to make VK to remove a number of files from its service.

289. Copyright holders can go to a Russian agency called Roskomnadzor and flag websites that either host pirated content or simply provide links to sites that do. Once the agency has notified the site's owner, the offending website has 72 hours to remove content and links—or risk having its entire domain blocked, pending a formal court ruling.

290. According to written testimony to Congress submitted in March 2014 by Cary Sherman, chairman of the RIAA, a "new generation of pirate sites and services has emerged to provide links directly to . . . illegal copies. Pirate sites like mp3skull provide instantaneous access to innumerable copies of recordings for download." Statement for the Record of Cary Sherman, Chairman and CEO, Recording Industry Association of America, on "Section 512 of Title 17," March 13, 2014, http://76.74.24.142/5185C0A1-9775-6988-0FE7-BC2A76C3F940.pdf.

291. See e.g., Digital Citizens Alliance, "Good Money Gone Bad: Digital Thieves and the Hijacking of the Online Ad Business; A Report on the Profitability of Ad-Supported Content Theft," February 19, 2014, available at https://media.gractions.com/314A5A5A9ABBBBC5E3BD824CF47C46EF4B9D3A76/4af7db7f-03e7-49cb-aeb8-ad0671a4e1c7.pdf. (The 30 largest pirate sites studied, which were supported by ads, average $4.4 million annually; even small sites can make more than $100,000 a year from advertising.) See also "Profiting from Filesharing Services: A Measurement Study of Economic Incentives in Cyberlockers" by Zubin Jelveh et al., P2P '12 IEEE International Conference on Peer-to-Peer Computing, September 2012, available at http://cis.poly.edu/~ross/papers/Cyberlockers.pdf.

292. See testimony of Cary Sherman.

293. Some emerging artists may make their music available for free using BitTorrent to expand their audience.

294. BitTorrent is a method of file sharing whereby the file is simultaneously uploaded for other users when you download the file. When multiple people download the file at the same time, the file is simultaneously uploaded in pieces to everyone in the group. For example, if a person has 94 percent of the file downloaded, that person is directed to the people with the remaining 6 percent needed.

295. "BitTorrent to Try a Paywall and Crowdfunding" by Michael Cieply, *The New York Times*, July 13, 2014: "BitTorrent has failed in the past to make entertainment buyers of those who use its wares to share content. In 2008, the company shut down a short-lived operation, called BitTorrent Entertainment Network, that had joined Hollywood companies in offering a menu of movie and television downloads for a price" (http://www.nytimes.com/2014/07/14/business/media/bittorrent-to-try-a-paywall-and-crowdfunding.html?_r=0).

296. "Bruno Mars, Rihanna Top List of Most-Pirated Artists in 2013" by Glenn Peoples, *Billboard*, December 31, 2013.

297. "Most Illegally Downloaded Music of 2013 Revealed" by Michael Baggs, Gigwise, January 2, 2014, http://www.gigwise.com/features/87243/the-most-illegally-downloaded-music-artists-of-2013-revealed/.

298. The Pirate Bay was launched by the Swedish anti-copyright organization Piratbyrån (The Piracy Bureau) within a few months after a few activists established Piratbyrån in 2003. Piratbyrån had many purposes, but could be described as a pro-piracy lobbying organization. It was founded in response to Antipiratbyrån, the local antipiracy outfit in Sweden. The goal was to start a debate on copyright issues and how they affect society. Piratbyrån decided to launch the first Scandinavian BitTorrent community, using the then relatively new BitTorrent protocol (*TorrentFreak,* June 23, 2010, https://torrentfreak.com/pirate-bays-founding-group-piratbyran-disbands-100623/).

299. On April 17, 2009, Peter Sunde, Fredrik Neij, Gottfrid Svartholm, and Carl Lundström were found guilty of assistance to copyright infringement and sentenced to one year in prison and payment of a fine of 30 million Swedish kronor (app. $4,200,000 US). The defendants appealed the verdict and accused the judge of giving in to political pressure. On November 26, 2010, a Swedish appeals court upheld the verdict, decreasing the original prison terms but increasing the fine to 46 million kronor. On May 17,

2010, because of an injunction against their bandwidth provider, the site was taken off-line. Access to the website was later restored with a message making fun of the injunction on their front page ("The Pirate Bay," Wikipedia).

300. "The Pirate Bay Has a Plan to Avoid Blockades" by Nick Bilton, *The New York Times*, January 1, 2014.

301. ". . . this new mobile-conscious design provides the same legally dubious amenities, just in a more appealing package. No longer do you have to zoom in just to read the normal Pirate Bay site jammed into your handset. The iconic pirate ship logo is still there, front and center, only now sections are optimized for touching instead of clicking" ("The Pirate Bay Is Now Mobile-Optimized, If That's Something You Want" by Darren Orf, *Gizmodo*, July 26, 2014, http://gizmodo.com/the-pirate-bay-is-now-mobile-optimized-if-thats-someth-1611425968). Also see section below, "Piracy Goes Mobile."

302. Isohunt.to.

303. "Isohunt BitTorrent Site Rises from the Dead as Isohunt.to" by Dara Kerr, CNET, October 30, 2013.

304. "Global Internet Phenomena Report," November 8, 2013, p. 6, https://www.sandvine.com/downloads/general/global-internet-phenomena/2013/2h-2013-global-internet-phenomena-report.pdf.

305. Id.

306. "Decline in US BitTorrent Traffic, Says Study," BBC News, November 12, 2013.

307. Id.

308. The Sandvine report should be viewed with a pinch of skepticism as Sandvine is the company that provided Comcast tools to limit the number of sessions of Internet traffic generated by BitTorrent several years ago. However, there does seem to be a consensus that peer-to-peer is less popular as more authorized services have made content available, especially YouTube, which, like P2P, is free. See my interview with Glen Peoples of *Billboard* in Chapter 18.

309. "Global Internet Phenomena Report" at p. 6.

310. "Internet Pirates Will Always Win" by Nick Bilton, *The New York Times*, August 4, 2012.

311. "Cyberlockers Take Over File-Sharing Lead from BitTorrent Sites" by Ernesto, *TorrentFreak*, January 11, 2011, http://torrentfreak.com/cyberlockers-take-over-file-sharing-lead-from-bittorrent-sites-110111/.

312. "Cyberlocker: What Is a Cyberlocker? Why Are They Considered Music Pirate Tools?" by Paul Gil, 2014, http://netforbeginners.about.com/od/internet101/f/What-Is-A-Cyberlocker.htm.

313. "Kim Dotcom, Pirate King" by Bryan Gruley, David Fickling, and Cornelius Rahn, *Businessweek*, February 15, 2012, http://www.businessweek.com/articles/2012-02-15/kim-dotcom-pirate-king.

314. "Kim Dotcom Extradition Hearing Delayed Again," BBC News, July 14, 2014, http://www.bbc.com/news/technology-28193718. Dotcom is, as of the submission of this manuscript in summer 2014, out of jail pending extradition proceedings scheduled for February 2015. However, a New Zealand court has already found that seizure of evidence during the raid was illegal and Dotcom has launched another cyberlocker called "Mega."

315. "Kim Dotcom, Pirate King" by Bryan Gruley, David Fickling, and Cornelius Rahn, *Businessweek*, February 15, 2012, http://www.businessweek.com/articles/2012-02-15/kim-dotcom-pirate-king.

316. Id.

317. "Cyberlockers Take Over File-Sharing Lead from BitTorrent Sites" by Ernesto, *TorrentFreak*, January 11, 2011, https://torrentfreak.com/cyberlockers-take-over-file-sharing-lead-from-bittorrent-sites-110111/.

318. "RIAA Joins Congressional Caucus in Unveiling First-Ever List of Notorious Illegal Sites," May 19, 2010, http://www.riaa.com/newsitem.php?id=58185AFD-5525-19D4-FFD2-4233518393AD.

319. "Piracy Websites Attract Billions of Visits," BBC News, January 11, 2011, http://www.bbc.com/news/technology-12163161.

320. OLG Dusseldorf, Judgement of 22.03.2010, Az I-20 U 166/09 dated March 22, 2010.

321. Roettgers, Janko (2010-05-03). "RapidShare Wins in Court," http://gigaom.com/2010/05/03/rapidshare-wins-in-court/.

322. From the *Atari v. RapidShare* ruling: "entspricht einem Generalverdacht gegen Sharehoster-Dienste und ihre Nutzer, der so nicht zu rechtfertigen ist" (*corresponds to a general suspicion against shared hosting services and their users, which is not to justify such*).

323. OLG Dusseldorf, Judgement of 22.03.2010, Az I-20 U 166/09 dated March 22, 2010.

324. "RIAA: Online Music Piracy Pales in Comparison to Off-line Swapping" by Ernesto, *Torrent Freak*, July 26, 2012, http://torrentfreak.com/riaa-online-music-piracy-pales-in-comparison-to-off-line-swapping-120726/; "Proof the Major Record Labels Are Lying to You" by Al Newstead, Tone Deaf, August 3, 2012, http://www.tonedeaf.com.au/186107/proof-record-labels-lying.htm.

325. http://riaa.com/physicalpiracy.php?content_selector=What-is-Online-Piracy.

326. See footnote 324.

327. *Sony Corp. of America v. Universal City Studios, Inc.*, 464 U.S. 417 (1984), also known as the "Betamax case."

328. "Music Piracy Goes Mobile" by Dawn Chmielewski, Re/code, March 24, 2014, http://recode.net/2014/03/24/music-piracy-goes-mobile/.

329. Id.

330. Id.

331. "The Pirate Bay Launches a Mobile Website for Torrenting from Your Smartphone," by Sarah Perez, TechCrunch, July 25, 2014, http://techcrunch.com/2014/07/25/the-pirate-bay-launches-a-mobile-website-for-torrenting-from-your-smartphone/.

332. "The Pirate Bay Goes Mobile with New Site," by Nick Bilton, *New York Times*, July 24, 2014, http://bits.blogs.nytimes.com/2014/07/24/the-pirate-bay-goes-mobile-with-new-site/.

333. "Technological Advances Have Led to a Market Breakdown," by Steve Gordon, *Billboard*, August 2, 2003.

334. http://www.ifpi.org/downloads/Digital-Music-Report-2014.pdf.

335. http://www.similarweb.com/website/mp3skull.com.

336. In regard to the US, according to Cary Sherman, chairman of the RIAA, "Google places limitations on the tools we can use and limits us to delivering notices for a relatively minor number of infringing files on a site compared with the total number of potential infringing files. It then states that since the number of notices it receives is small related to the total number of files, there isn't much of a problem. You can imagine the frustration. Google has no duty under the DMCA to monitor sites for infringing files. We have that responsibility. But they don't allow us the tools to bear that duty, either." Statement for the Record of Cary Sherman, Chairman and CEO, Recording Industry Association of America, on "Section 512 of Title 17," March 13, 2014, http://76.74.24.142/5185C0A1-9775-6988-0FE7-BC2A76C3F940.pdf.

337. "Music Piracy Goes Mobile" by Dawn Chmielewski, Re/code, March 24, 2014, http://recode.net/2014/03/24/music-piracy-goes-mobile/.

338. Statement for the Record of Cary Sherman, Chairman and CEO, Recording Industry Association of America on "Section 512 of Title 17," March 13, 2014, http://76.74.24.142/5185C0A1-9775-6988-0FE7-BC2A76C3F940.pdf.

339. Id. footnote 2.

340. Id.

Chapter 17

341. Although they officially never admitted doing it, it was well documented that Comcast slowed speeds (also referred to "throttling") for BitTorrent traffic on their network in 2007. Some commentators saw this violation of net neutrality as actually helping the record business by slowing bandwidth speeds of those who use the BitTorrent protocol to avoid paying for permanent copies of recorded music as well as movies and TV shows. See the commentary of attorney Chris Castle in "Intelligentsia Round-Up—Net Neutrality," *Creative Intelligentsia*, January 27, 2014, http://musicintelligentsia.com/intelli-

gentsia-round-up-net-neutrality/. But others point out that if Comcast could start tampering with traffic of one kind of stream, they could do it with any others they didn't like for any reason, such as those with whom they were not doing business.

342. "Intelligentsia Round-Up—Net Neutrality," *Creative Intelligentsia*, January 27, 2014, http://musicintelligentsia.com/intelligentsia-round-up-net-neutrality/.
343. Id.
344. Statement of Chairman Julius Genachowski, Re: Preserving the Open Internet, GN Docket No. 09-191, Broadband Industry Practices, WC Docket No. 07-52, https://apps.fcc.gov/edocs_public/attachmatch/FCC-10-201A2.pdf.
345. "T-Mobile's 'Music Freedom' Is a Great Feature—and a Huge Problem" by Chris Ziegler, *The Verge*, June 18, 2014, http://www.theverge.com/2014/6/18/5822996/t-mobile-music-freedom-net-neutrality.
346. Id.

Chapter 19

347. http://www.ifpi.org/downloads/Digital-Music-Report-2014.pdf at p. 36.
348. "China Launches Copyright Monitor System for Music and Video" by Ailun Zhang, *MusicDish*, June 30, 2013, http://www.musicdish.com/mag/index.php3?id=13422.
349. "Online Chinese Portals Take Joint Action against Baidu and QVOD for Online Video Piracy" by Eric de Fontenay, *MusicDish*, November 16, 2013, http://www.musicdish.com/mag/index.php3?id=13489.
350. "Is Baidu Ting a Genuine First Step towards Legality?" by Xingyue Peng, *MusicDish*, June 14, 2011, http://www.musicdish.com/mag/index.php3?id=12942.
351. "Guangdong Telecom to Launch Exclusive Data Package with QQ Music" by Ailun Zhang, *MusicDish*, August 12, 2013, http://www.musicdish.com/mag/index.php3?id=13457.

Chapter 23

352. "YouTube's Parity Problem, or Why a Billion Isn't That Impressive," by Jon Maples, *Billboard*, March 4, 2014, http://www.billboard.com/biz/articles/news/digital-and-mobile/5923137/youtubes-parity-problem-or-why-a-billion-isnt-that.

Chapter 24

353. "Facebook to Expand Video Ads to Seven Countries Outside U.S." by Alexei Oreskovic, Reuters, May 20, 2014.
354. www.youtube.com/yt/press/statistics.html.
355. www.statista.com/statistics/282087/number-of-monthly-active-twitter-users/.
356. "There Will Never Be Another Myspace" by Ari Herstand, *Digital Music News*, March 2014.

Chapter 26

357. "Here's Why Google Bought Songza," by Gail Sullivan, *The Washington Post*, November 23, 2014.
358. http://pando.com/2012/08/15/songzas-founders-realized-they-werent-thinking-radically-enough-heres-how-they-changed-that/.

Chapter 28

359. www.hollywoodreporter.com/news/top-hollywood-music-schools-hollywood-651336.

INDEX

INDEX